Cases in International Relations

Cases in International Relations

PORTRAITS OF THE FUTURE
Third Edition

Donald M. Snow
University of South Carolina, Beaufort

PEARSON
Longman

New York San Francisco Boston
London Toronto Sydney Tokyo Singapore Madrid
Mexico City Munich Paris Cape Town Hong Kong Montreal

Acquisitions Editor: Vikram Mukhija
Executive Marketing Manager: Ann Stypuloski
Production Manager: Ellen MacElree
Project Coordination, Text Design,
    and Electronic Page Makeup: TexTech Inc.
Cover Designer/Manager: Wendy Ann Fredericks
Senior Manufacturing Buyer: Roy Pickering
Printer and Binder: Courier, Stoughton
Cover Printer: Courier, Stoughton

Library of Congress Cataloging-in-Publication Data

Snow, Donald M., 1943–
    Cases in international relations : portraits of the future/Donald M.
Snow. —3rd ed.
        p.   cm.
    Includes bibliographical references and index.
    ISBN 13: 978-0-205-53908-6
    ISBN 10:   0-205-53908-4
    1. International relations.   I. Title.
JZ1242.S658 2008
327—dc22

                                                    2007010981

Please visit us at http://www.ablongman.com

ISBN 13: 978-0-205-53908-6
ISBN 10:   0-205-53908-4

1 2 3 4 5 6 7 8 9 10—CRS—10 09 08 07

Brief Contents

Detailed Contents

Preface
Portraits of the Future

The twenty-first century is now over a half-decade old. Some of the newness of the new millennium has faded, but it is natural to want to know how the new century compares with the last century and how it will likely look in the future. How will the relations between states and other entities change or remain the same? What forces are likely to emerge to promote and resist change? Where will the world's most serious troubles be? Will there be positive signs of hope and improvement in the human condition? For that matter, how has the future changed since the first two editions of this book were released in 2002 and 2005?

The environment in which international relations (IR) is played out is dynamic and rapidly changing. The world system has been convulsed fundamentally twice since the end of the 1980s (in less than twenty years!). The collapse of operational communism in the earliest days of the 1990s scrambled the power map of the world and set in motion or accentuated forces like American international ascendancy, globalization, and democratization, trends that continue (albeit in altered form) today. On September 11, 2001, international terrorism pushed its way violently onto the international center stage, unleashing new, unsettling sources of violence and instability into the mix with the trends of the 1990s and holdover forces from the Cold War. The nearly photographic clarity of the present and the seeming ability to draw clear images of the future that distinguished the 1980s and before has given way to a much more blurred present and future from which to compose a portrait.

Depending on one's perspective, we are privileged or doomed to live in exciting times (to paraphrase an old saying), and this third edition attempts to capture some of the changing elements that are part of the portrait of the future. The system is changing, and so are the contents of this book. To that end, four new chapters have been added to this edition. Chapter 1, "Popular Terror and the Democratic Peace," examines the process of democratization in light of electoral challenges by Palestinian voters and others, principally in the Middle East. Globalization, another trend of the 1990s, has changed, and those changes are highlighted in Chapter 8, "Debating Globalization," and Chapter 9, "Evaluating Globalization." The former case contrasts how India and Venezuela have reacted to globalization, whereas the latter measures the performance of globalization through the NAFTA experience. Another aspect of change has been the danger of the spread of weapons of mass destruction, and the result is a new Chapter 11, "The Perils of Proliferation." In addition, two chapters have received major revisions. Chapter 6 now deals more explicitly with the Israeli-Palestinian conflict as an instance of irresolvable conflict, and Chapter 14 hones in more specifically on the dual resource conflicts of oil and water. Other chapters have been updated as events warrant.

The dynamics of international change also contribute to an opacity that makes drawing a clear portrait of the future more difficult. Because political science is not a precise science like physics or chemistry, the quality of theory possessed by the hard sciences is unavailable to aid explanation or predictive ability. With imprecise theoretical lenses, one can only guess—draw general portraits of the present and extrapolate them into an uncertain future unknowable in photographic detail.

A word about what this book is—and is not—is appropriate at this point. It is a case book, presenting a series of individual instances of problems and trends within the international arena in the early 2000s. The effort is neither inclusive nor encyclopedic; it covers topics that are currently important, not the universe of international concerns. All cases provide the reader with the opportunity to apply IR concepts to real-world situations, with the hope that in doing so he or she will come to better understand current and enduring problems facing the international system. As such, this book is not a systematic overview of the system or its history, which is the province of core textbooks in the field. Many of the most interesting historical cases have been written, and their rewriting would not be terribly helpful. At the same time, the book is not a systematic exposition of various political science theories explaining international phenomena, which I view as more appropriate for advanced students than for the undergraduate students whom I assume will be the primary readers of this book.

A word about pedagogy may help at this point. Each of the cases begins by identifying a particular problem or dynamic in the international system. The case study that uses Israel and Palestine as its example, for instance, begins with the observation that there are some international disputes that are so intractable as to be essentially irresolvable. The troubling Israeli-Palestinian situation is examined as an instance of this irreconcilability. The case concludes by looking at some options and why they have failed and ends with study/discussion questions and references for future reading and research, including a sample of relevant Web sites.

What distinguished this effort from other supplementary texts is that all the essays included are original papers written by the author specifically for this volume. The reason was to allow more timely coverage of situations that are ongoing than is possible with the lag time involved in publication in scholarly journals and the like, and also to allow the cases to be cast within a more standard format than is possible with preexisting materials written for other purposes. In addition, writing original articles means that it is possible to update and modify materials as events and dynamics change and, hopefully, to facilitate both the freshness and accuracy of the material that appears in these pages. Certainly, doing these things has been a major intent and concentration of this edition.

The rationale for choosing the cases flows from the book's subtitle, "Portraits of the Future." Clearly, it is not possible to include as much breadth in a casebook as in a core text without either making the casebook encyclopedic and massively long or making the cases so brief as not to be particularly helpful. Rather, a casebook is by its nature a sample of examples presented in sufficient depth to highlight and explain principles, events, and the like in more detail than a conventional text. The trick is in picking the right cases to meet the reader's needs.

Why were these particular cases chosen? Beyond their amenability to case treatment, five criteria were employed in choosing the subjects included in this volume. The first was that the subject was important and represented an enduring issue or problem. Cases such as continuing terrorism, the democratic peace hypothesis given the election of Hamas as the government of Palestine, the direction of China, and AIDS in Africa meet this criterion. Second, the cases attempt to look at problems that are fresh, timely, but not covered extensively in other places. The study of asymmetrical warfare as the military problem of the future fits this criterion, as does the problem of resource scarcity and the success of one of the pillars of globalization, NAFTA.

Third, the subjects represent real-world problems with which the international system will have to come to grips and about which students need to know in order to be informed citizens. Nuclear and other exotic weapons proliferation as an international problem clearly fits this criterion, as does the problem of the future of war crimes. Fourth, the subjects are future oriented and likely will endure for a period of time. The precedential value of how the world deals with the AIDS pandemic in Africa meets this criterion, as does the question of how countries and groups deal with globalization and how the process of democratization evolves. Fifth, the subjects were inherently interesting, so that the reader would approach and consume them with some enthusiasm that, hopefully, will translate into a broader interest in international relations. At a practical level, the intractability of the Kashmir and Israeli-Palestinian questions and the debate over global warming fall into this category. At a more abstract level, the question of the future of sovereignty and the future of war meet this criterion.

Individual cases were chosen with these criteria in mind, and the book was then divided into five parts. Within each part, the intention was to select substantive topics that both illustrate important principles operating within the international system and that exemplify important concerns in the contemporary environment. In doing so, there were visible themes that the author felt needed to be included. Four general topics were chosen—new forces and evolutionary change in the post–Cold War world (which comprise the first two parts of the text); globalization; national and international security; and transnational issues—and then cases were selected that would provide illustrations of these dynamics. In picking these cases, the author tried to invoke the five criteria cited above—importance, freshness and timeliness, real-world importance, endurance, and interest.

Each case meets these criteria. For the problem of new forces (Part I), three cases were chosen that are not unique to the post–Cold War world, but have attracted increasing attention since the fall of the Soviet empire. The first case examines the notion of democratic peace that was so prominent in the 1990s and that underlies the democracy-promotion emphasis of the Bush administration and assesses that notion in light of the election of Hamas as the majority party in the Palestinian legislature. Nongovernmental organizations (NGOs) are not a new phenomenon, but they have become more prominent and even intrusive actors in diverse situations, such as peacekeeping. *Médicins sans Frontières* (MSF or "Doctors without Borders") is a prime example. The case in Chapter 2 looks at the MSF experience, particularly as it has been affected by Afghanistan and Iraq. The case on China (Chapter 3) reflects both the growing economic and political importance of China and provides some criteria by which people look at how China may evolve in the future—either as a looming threat or as a strategic partner (or both).

The dynamics of change are addressed in Part II. The roots of the problem of war crimes and how to deal with them emerged originally after World War II, but have been reenergized by atrocities in diverse parts of the developing world, including the Balkans and Iraq. It is an evolving problem that has yet to be resolved and to which the United States has been a major barrier because of its refusal to ratify the International Criminal Court statute. The assault on national sovereignty is an important theme that will continue to reverberate through the 2000s and beyond, prominently within the context of the debate over American foreign policy. Finally, the issue of Israeli-Palestinian conflict, which seemed near resolution in 2000 but which continues to derail the international relations of the Middle East, illustrates dramatically the phenomenon of irresolvable conflicts: situations so intractable that resolution may be impossible.

The other concerns in the book are more discrete, although I have attempted to choose "portraits" from parts of the subject matter that are outside normal textbook treatment. Part III deals with globalization and how it affects those to whom globalization is being sold as the vehicle to their success. Much of the controversy surrounds questions of free trade, the history and issues surrounding which are the subject of the first case in Part III. The second case deals with diverse reactions to globalization, highlighting the very different responses in two prominent countries, India and Venezuela. Whether globalization succeeds or not (and what constitutes success) is highly controversial and partisan, and Chapter 9 examines the progress of the North American Free Trade Agreement after more than a decade and focuses on and reinforces the contentiousness of that debate.

Part IV deals with security in the international environment. Although there is general agreement that the environment has changed fundamentally since September 11, 2001, there is much less agreement on exactly how it has changed, which is the focus of the cases in this part. The section begins with an assessment of what future war will be like, with particular emphasis on the rise of increasingly asymmetrical challenges to American (and other Western) conventional warfare prowess, drawing examples from places like Afghanistan and Iraq. The question of the spread of weapons of mass destruction, and especially nuclear weapons, to countries that do not currently have them—proliferation—is the subject of the second case in the part, with special emphasis on Iran and North Korea. To demonstrate the endurance and intractability of some problems, the problem of Kashmir forms the third case, which, along with the Israeli-Palestinian confrontation, has been one of the most difficult world problems to solve.

Part V deals with transnational issues, and it attempts to follow the criteria of the rest of the volume by bringing fresh looks at how some transnational issues can be viewed in a new light and how some other problems can usefully be examined through the lens of transnational issues. It begins with the familiar problem of global warming and the Kyoto Protocol, because this is clearly an ongoing problem that is not going to go away. If the Kyoto Protocol itself may be seriously or mortally wounded, what will we do about the underlying problem, which remains? Conflicts over scarce resources, especially water and petroleum, represent a second global problem that can be viewed as a transnational issue. Similarly, there has been a great deal of rhetorical concern and promises of action given to the problem of AIDS in Africa, but not much attention to thinking of it as a transnational issue and the precedent that will be set for dealing with outbreaks of AIDS elsewhere or other diseases like SARS and avian flu. Finally, international terrorism is the overriding concern of our day, and one that can only be surmounted by concerted international efforts as terrorism has evolved in the post–September 11, 2001, environment.

The result is a stack of portraits of the future that hopefully the reader will find both broad and enriching. I have dedicated this edition of the book, like the original, to my longtime friend, the late D. Eugene Brown. Gene and I met in 1989 and shared an office at the U.S. Army War College for two years before he returned to Lebanon Valley College and I to the University of Alabama. Our time together led to a collaboration that produced several book projects brought to fruition. In most cases, Gene was the ideational force who suggested new projects that were then completed by collaborative effort.

Cases in International Relations was to be a continuation, even culmination, of our joint efforts. The idea of a casebook of original essays was Gene's; unfortunately, he was unable to complete the task we had set for ourselves, and I had the burden of completing the work after Gene left us over the Thanksgiving holiday, 2000. I hope Gene would have been pleased with how our final collaboration has evolved.

I would like to thanks the reviewers who made useful comments on the manuscript. They are: Douglas Blum, Providence College; J. Barron Boyd, LeMoyne College; John Calhoun, Palm Beach Atlantic University; Dan Cox, University of Nebraska-Kearney; Ruth Ediger, Lee University; Larry Elowiz, Georgia College and State University; Gregory Hall, St. Mary's College of Maryland; Linda Petrou, High Point University; Brian Potter, Tulane University; Michael A. Preda, Midwestern State University; Abdoulaye Saine, Miami University of Ohio; Michael E. Smith, Georgia State University; Lawrence LeBlanc, Marquette University; and Michael Clancy, University of Hartford.

DONALD M. SNOW
Hilton Head Island, South Carolina

Cases in International Relations

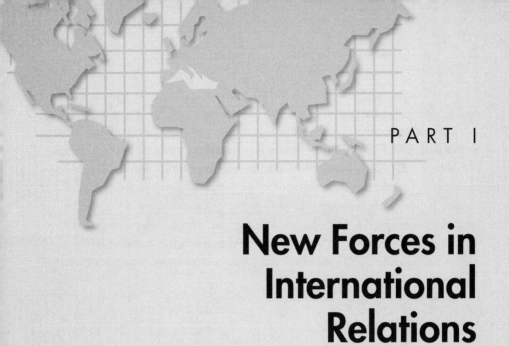

New Forces in International Relations

A common theme in the post–Cold War international environment is change, the extent to which that environment is somehow different than it was before and the implications of those changes for the operation of international relations.

Part I identifies three ways in which the system appears to have changed. There is nothing systematic or inclusive about the changes that are included in the three cases; rather, they seek to illustrate the ways in which change has occurred. The three themes that are developed are the changing nature of power by states in the system, the emergence of significant new actors in the process, and a new dynamic in the politics within and between states.

Chapter 1, "Popular Terror and the Democratic Peace," examines a well-regarded explanation of international relations (democratic peace) in light of a contemporary phenomenon, the free election of terrorist-supporting organizations (popular terror), focusing on the election of Hamas to a majority of seats in the Palestinian Legislative Council in January 2006. After laying out the basic democratic peace construct, the case examines the apparent repudiation of parts of this construct by the Palestinians and others, and how this may suggest changes in the democratic peace thesis.

Chapter 2, "The Growing Significance of NGOs," looks at a form of actor, the nongovernmental organization (NGO), that has become an increasingly prominent part of international interactions. The focus of the case is how these international organizations make a difference. To study this phenomenon, the case looks at one particularly active

NGO, *Medicins sans Frontieres* (MSF, which translates as "Doctors without Borders") and its role in an important post–Cold War phenomenon, participation in violent conflicts and especially its recently concluded role in Afghanistan and Iraq; and what the withdrawal of MSF from these conflicts may portend for the future.

Chapter 3, "China Rising," looks at the emergence of the People's Republic as a major player in the system, a so-called rising power. In the past decade, China has become a major manufacturing center and economic force in the world, as its economy becomes more capitalist. At the same time, China has engaged in a program of military expansion and diplomatic initiative. The question raised by the case study is how much difference that makes: Will a more powerful China be a disruptive or a supportive part of the evolving international system?

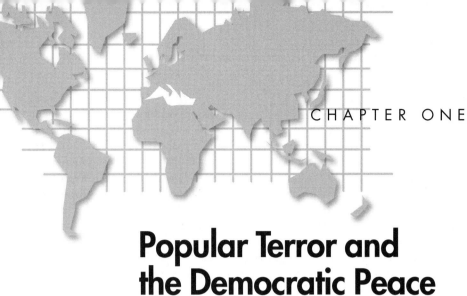

CHAPTER ONE

Popular Terror and the Democratic Peace
THEORY VERSUS PRACTICE

PRÉCIS

The 1990s was an expansive period for the growth of political democratization around the world. With the collapse of the ideological opposition to
Western-style political democracy and market economics accompanying the
collapse of operational communism, a wave of democracy swept the globe.
Expansive claims were made about what was widely called a "democratic
peace" by theoreticians and practitioners based on the assumption and statistical evidence that democratic states are more responsible and peaceful
than nondemocratic states. The fact that the end of the Cold War was accompanied by a decline in war generally supported that this trend toward democratic peace would lead to a more tranquil, orderly international system.

Events of the middle 2000s, especially but not exclusively in the Middle
East, have raised questions about both the theoretical underpinnings and the
practical outcomes of democratic peace. The challenge stems from the rise of
democratically elected governments and groups that reject the model of
moderate democracy. The most notable example of this trend has been the
Palestinian election of Hamas, an openly terrorist organization, to a majority
in its parliament, although the trend is apparent elsewhere as well. This case
study examines the democratic peace theory, how it holds up under the challenge of apparent exceptions to its expectations, and how contemporary situations suggest or demand changes in the theory.

In his letter of transmittal of the 2006 *National Security Strategy of the United States* to the Congress on March 16, 2006, President George W. Bush stated a belief about international relations widely held by both international relations scholars and foreign policy elites in the United States and elsewhere in the Western world. "The first pillar (of strategy) is promoting freedom, justice, and human dignity. . . . Free governments are accountable to their people, govern their territory effectively, and pursue economic and political policies that benefit their citizens. Free governments do not oppress their people *or attack other free nations. Peace and international stability are most reliably built on a foundation of freedom.*" (Emphasis added.) This statement captures the essence of the two strands, one implicit and one explicit, of the democratic peace theory: that democratic political systems are moderate, stable, and peaceful; and that an international system composed of these democratically elected governments will be much more peaceful than any alternative, because free people (democratic states) do not choose to fight other free people (other democratic states). Further, this formulation equates freedom and democracy, assuming free people will choose a moderate democratic political system. This perception formed the basis of the foreign policy of "engagement and enlargement" of the Clinton administration during the latter 1990s, and the virtue of democracy has been a basic tenet of the so-called neoconservatives who have underpinned policy under President Bush.

The January 2006 election of a majority of members of Hamas to the Palestinian Legislative Council (Palestine's parliament) sent shivers through an international community wedded to the democratic peace idea. During the 1990s, an academic consensus had emerged around the idea of democratic peace. The most basic tenet of the academic democratic peace theory is, according to political scientist Jack Levy, "the absence of war between democratic states," and this notion had been elevated to "as close as anything we have to an empirical law in international relations." This optimistic, and thoroughly Western, idea has spread widely through both academic and policy circles.

The electoral victory of Hamas, a political organization with an openly terrorist past that is dedicated to and refuses to renounce its intention to destroy Israel, raises at least indirect questions about the democratic peace idea. Its assault is, at least as of this writing, not yet direct on the basic democratic peace assertion: Hamas has not yet openly attacked any other democratically elected state, although it has arguably engaged in warlike acts against Israel. The democratic peace thesis is at least implicitly built on the idea that democratic states are more moderate than their nondemocratic counterparts; therefore, the unwillingness of Hamas to renounce its terrorist past or to preclude the possibility of a terrorist future raises at minimum an indirect challenge to the thesis. Moreover, if democratically elected regimes are, as Bush says, "accountable to their people" and Palestinian voters freely chose a political movement that openly associates itself with terror, this also seems to fly in the face of the moderating influence of democratic processes.

The Hamas case is not unique either in the Middle East or elsewhere in the world. In 2005, for instance, voters in Lebanon demonstrated significant support for another political movement with a terrorist past, Hizbollah, by electing Hizbollah members to its parliament. Iraqi voters have repudiated the secular political parties that are the mainstay of Western-style, liberal democracy in elections there. In Egypt, the political strength of the Muslim Brotherhood, in many ways the conceptual inspiration of radical (including terrorist) movements elsewhere in the region, reached such proportions that the American government acceded to the suggestion of the Egyptian government of Hosni Mubarak that new elections be postponed for fear of a repeat of the Palestinian result. In the Western Hemisphere, the December 2006 reelection of Venezuela's Hugo Chavez is further evidence that democratization alone may not be the cure-all for international violence and instability that some optimists of the 1990s suggested.

The democratic peace, and the assault on it in the form of "popular terror" represented by Hamas, Hizbollah, and other similar phenomena, forms the basis of this case study. It is a study both of theory and practice. At a theoretical level, we will examine the substance of the democratic peace theory: What does it maintain, what does it project about the phenomenon of spreading democratization for international peacefulness, and what modifications has it made in the face of challenges to it? Although democratic peace is advertised, as Professor Jack Levy points out, as an "empirical" (i.e., scientific, not value-laden) approach, we will note that the theory is heavily Western in content and influence. Many of its adherents trace its lineage back to the work of German philosopher Emmanuel Kant and forward through Woodrow Wilson to the present. This historical lineage makes the implicit, and explicit, assumption of the attraction and superiority of Western liberal democracy that makes the adherents of the scientific study of the subject more than mere observers some of the time.

The rise of Hamas and other groups that have adopted democratic methods to pursue nonliberal democratic positions represents the practical reality of the current challenge. Some writers have suggested that employing the methods of the liberal democrats to solutions that are not compatible with that theory's expectations has historical precedents in the rise of movements such as the National Socialists in Germany in the 1930s, or that movements like Hamas do not represent so much a repudiation of the democratic peace as a need to qualify more precisely in what circumstances its tenets do and do not hold. Based on an examination of the contemporary challenge, we will look at possible modifications to the democratic peace idea in the conclusions.

THE DEMOCRATIC PEACE IDEA

In a 1993 speech, President William Clinton stated clearly and succinctly the underlying premise of the democratic peace theory: "[D]emocracies rarely wage war on one another." In a world emerging from the grim reality of a Cold War between the generally democratic West and the communist East, the vanquishing of communism appeared to create what neoconservative Francis Fukuyama described as the "end of history," by which he meant that for the time being, there was no effective alternative nor intellectual opponent to the idea of liberal democracy. With the opposition removed, democracy would (and has) spread widely around the world, and because it was empirically obvious that few if any political democracies engage in wars against one another, then the expansion of political democracies should also mean a more tranquil international system less interrupted by war and violence. That observation, in turn, also represented a cherished value of many who formulated the "theory" of democratic peace: Researchers both thought *and* hoped it was true.

In the context of the 1990s, democratization became entangled with economic expansion that had both domestic and international facets. Domestically, developed economies had been stimulated both by the burgeoning impact of the telecommunications revolution that was greatly changing both production and commerce and by a wave of governmental acts emanating from Great Britain and the United States that were changing the environment in which business took place. Deregulation of private enterprise by states and privatization of enterprises formerly controlled by governments were creating a model of economic activity that could be exported to other countries and that appeared to thrive particularly well in conditions of political democracy (there were, of course, apparent exceptions to this latter generalization, such as China). Internationally, the 1990s saw the widespread adoption of the value of free trade (see Chapter 7 for a discussion) as the norm for international economics. Free trade among those states that accepted the Western model of economic organization suggested that economics in the form of globalization (trade partners do not fight one another) could add to the peace created by like-minded political democracies.

The notion of democratic peace needs to be disaggregated into two levels as a phenomenon to be understood and placed in the context of the current challenge. One aspect of that phenomenon is the process of democratization within a broader number of states than had previously been democratic. This process is reflected in Samuel P. Huntington's thesis of the "third wave" of democratization of the twentieth century arising at the end of the Cold War (previous waves occurred after the world wars). At the policy level, it was reflected in the movement toward the Clinton administration's desire to expand the "circle of market democracies" (which the Bush administration renamed the "circle of development"), thereby conjoining democratization and globalization. The second aspect is the result set of relations between the states that have adopted democratic norms and that, as a result, are contributors of the democratic peace.

It is important to break the two phenomena apart. On one hand, they are clearly sequential. It is necessary to develop democratic national societies domestically before one can develop a peaceful system based on the interactions of those states. Because democratic societies are accountable to the citizens who must fight wars, they presumably will calculate more carefully the consequences of war than will nondemocratic societies in which such accountability is absent. The result is that democracies presumably will be less likely to go to war—except in self-defense—than nondemocracies. Iraq, of course, challenges this hypothesis.

Much of the democratic peace theory has emphasized the second part of the equation—the resulting democratic peace—without giving adequate attention to the first step in the process. Indeed, some modifications of the democratic peace hypothesis—that democratic peace holds best between mature, established democracies but not necessarily among less mature, evolving democracies—offers testimony to this point. Emphasis on the second step tends implicitly to assume that the process of democratization will produce the kinds of moderate states that form the basis of the democratic peace. It is that premise of the rise of what democratic peace theorists deride as "illiberal" states—those that use democratic methods to gain power but do not conform to our ideas of democratic practices—that is basic to the challenge represented by Hamas and other democratically elected states that oppose the international order we advocate (but which democratic peace theory suggests they *should* embrace).

The Domestic Basis of Democratic Peace: Peaceful Democracies

If the interactions *between* states are to be peaceful, then it follows that states that interact must desire to avoid fighting one another. If, on the other hand, states themselves are warlike, then it is likely that their interactions will be more conflictual and violent than if they were peaceful. Thus, a peaceful international system would seem logically to presuppose peaceful members of that system. The democratic peace theory acknowledges this assumption by noting that while democratic states do not fight one another, they do fight nondemocratic states (generally, but not exclusively, because they are forced to by the actions of nondemocratic states), and nondemocratic states clearly fight one another. Indeed, most democratic peace studies indicate that democratic and nondemocratic states are about equally warlike in their relations with one another; it is only democratic states acting toward one another that are noticeably more peaceful. This observation, of course, forms part of the rationale for advocating democratization (and globalization) because expanding the number of democratic states reduces the number of pairs of states that are likely to go to war with one another.

Why are democratic states more peaceful than nondemocratic states? More to the point, what characteristics of democratic states make them less prone to provoke or become involved in violent conflict with one another than are nondemocratic states or the interactions of democratic and nondemocratic states? Distilling the arguments that are made in defense of peaceful democracies, one can distinguish four separate threads: shared political values, institutional restraints, economic self-interest, and openness in communications.

The most basic characteristic of democratic societies is their inherent freedom, and it is asserted that free people do not freely choose to fight other free people. At the most basic level, there are two reasons for this. One is that free people are politically similar: They both possess and cherish the freedom that democracy provides. Even if they are evangelical in their advocacy of this condition, they have no reason to proselytize people in other democracies by word or the sword because they all share the same conditions. Communists may seek to impose communism on democracies or vice versa, but democracies have no reason to impose their own identical ideas on other democracies. Thus, the impact of political ideology, which was such a common feature in the causation of warfare in the twentieth and twenty-first centuries, is essentially altogether absent in the relations among democracies. Democracies, in a phrase, do not have anything important enough to fight each other about.

This argument is most clearly true when speaking of the well-established Western democracies, all of which come from a common set of civilization-based values, and from other states (Japan, for instance), which come from a different cultural and political legacy but have accepted Western values. Two of the most important underlying values that are shared by these states are political tolerance of opposing ideas and secularism (the separation of religious and political values in government); the two values are joined in that one of the most basic items requiring tolerance is acceptance of the religious values of others and the nonimposition of those values on others. Collectively, those values largely define "liberal" democracy, and some democratic peace advocates argue that states that are democratic in their means of selecting political officials, but not in terms of tolerance and secularism, are not truly democratic. This distinction, of course, is important in assessing the impact of free elections in places like Palestine.

The problem is that the desire for freedom *and* democracy are not necessarily the same thing. Ralph Peters argues that Americans "imagine that all other humans desire both freedom and democracy" and that "the freedom and democracy desired by others are bound to reflect our own." This may be false. Freedom may instead be the removal of constraints to act in decidedly undemocratic ways, such as newly empowered groups suppressing their adversaries.

The second reason that democratic states foster peacefulness is because of the institutional features and restraints inherent in democratic societies. Arguments supporting this notion usually claim that democratic institutions promote peace in two different ways. One is that the institutional structure in place in most established democracies places legal and constitutional restraints on the ability of political actors, notably the political executive who typically commands the instruments of political power. This idea, of course, is basic to the rationale for the separation of powers found in the U.S. Constitution that arose from the founding fathers' fear that a strong political executive might accrue so much power as to usurp the constitutional order. Constitutional restraints, including the right to free speech, ensures a more open and extensive debate within the populace at large and the political system whenever the use of violence is contemplated. Because free people theoretically have little animosity toward other free people, such debate dampens the propensity to resort to war among free peoples. As the relative absence of negative prewar debate should indicate, these same processes do not provide a definitive barrier to democratic states going to war—even preemptively—against nondemocratic states and, in the Iraqi case, it can even be argued that democratic forces can be convinced of the virtue of a warlike policy.

A second variant of this argument is that the desire of democratic elites to be reelected serves as a further inhibition to going to war, since those who might be involved in proposing war may fear that the failure of a warlike policy might result in voter retaliation against them in future elections (as apparently occurred in the United States in 2006). This assertion, of course, can be questioned if policy elites believe that the decision to engage in force will create a positive, "rally around the flag" effect in public support for them—a proposition that is by no means universally accepted.

A third basis of support for the peaceful democracies argument arises from the economic similarities between stable democratic states. Max Singer and Aaron Wildawsky pointed out in their 1996 *The Real World Order* that the advanced democracies possess similar commitments to political freedom and its economic equivalent in terms of capitalism, and the result is "quality economies" made up of politically and economically free entrepreneurs who share common values across national boundaries. In the resulting system of economic globalization that was the hallmark of the 1990s, those countries that become members are or are on their way to becoming democratic and have a commitment and incentive to act democratically and nonviolently. Thus, the gradual spread of the system of economic globalization contributes to an increasingly pacific international order.

Finally, the openness of democratic societies also affects the clarity of their warlike intentions. Because the determination to use force must be publicly debated in democratic societies, potential adversaries have far less reason to misread the resolve of democratic societies—notably, to assume they are bluffing when they are not—than is the case when national decision processes are less open and transparent.

These arguments suggest that democratic societies are more peaceful than their nondemocratic alternatives, and that their democratization contributes to the quality of the relations between them: Peaceful democracies result in a democratic peace (at least among themselves). We will look at this proposition in the next section. Before turning to it, however, it is worthwhile to examine two caveats that are raised by advocates of the democratic peace proposition and its opponents that we will see are parallel to objections about the democratic peace between states.

The first objection, raised as a limitation by some democratic peace theorists but rejected by the majority of them, is that the peaceful democracies' designation only clearly applies to well-established, mature democracies. In part, this is a matter of the length and duration of their democratic experience. When people are suddenly given their freedom, for instance, their first reaction may be to express pent-up frustrations and anger, which may include the desire to attack the sources of that frustration. Such a reaction can, for instance, certainly be suspected in the Palestinian vote in 2006. At the same time, the political elites in newer democracies by definition are less experienced with and possibly less committed to the restraints inherent in established political democracies and may not act with the same restraint in their international relations. The result may be "immature," even "illiberal" democracies that are more war-prone than nondemocratic states. At least in the early stages of transition, freedom may *not* equal democracy. In some extreme cases (Germany in the 1930s, for instance), democratic processes may even be used to *reverse* decisions to be democratic.

A second question about peaceful democracies concerns what stage in the process of democratization different countries occupy. The basic democratic peace argument suggests, if implicitly, that democracy (at least its mature manifestations) will lead to moderation in policy and thus peace (democracy, then peace). But what if the order is actually reversed? Mark Pietrzyk, for instance, argued in a 2002 book that moderation comes first: economic prosperity, similar worldviews, secure borders and the like create a moderation in national politics in which political democracy can flourish (moderation, then democracy *and* peace). Which sequence is correct is important both theoretically and practically and has been the subject of considerable scrutiny. If democratization is the key to peacefulness, then it should be promoted as a first step toward a more pacific world. If, on the other hand, democracy requires a more stable social and economic foundation to be successful and thus to contribute to peace, then that suggests a different approach to producing a stable order.

The International Effect: Democratic Peace

The real theoretical and normative concern of proponents of the democratic peace is its effect on the international order. Concern about the domestic aspects of the process are largely instrumental in the sense of suggesting why peaceful democracies act peacefully in international relations. While the evidence is strong that the democratic peace hypothesis is true regarding the relations among well-developed, stable democratic states, there have been enough exceptions to create the need to qualify the original idea. We have mentioned two of the most prominent of these limitations: The pacific nature of relations among democratic states clearly does not extend to the relations between democratic and nondemocratic states; and states in the process of becoming democratic may actually be less peaceful than their nondemocratic (and their stable democratic) counterparts.

If the normative value underpinning the democratic peace idea is the promotion of a more democratic order (and it certainly is for at least some advocates), these are serious limitations that must be addressed. There clearly are nondemocratic states in the world; therefore, the interactions between democratic and nondemocratic states will be marked by violence (the absence of peace). There is certainly nothing unusual about this situation: Democratic states have rarely attacked one another over the past hundred years, and certainly not during the Cold War (which was a confrontation between democratic and nondemocratic states); and political (ideological) disagreements have historically been a reason countries fight (as mentioned earlier). Stated so simply, the solution is greater democratization, with two caveats. One is that democratic and nondemocratic states fight (although democratic states do not *usually* initiate the violence), meaning the spread of democracy must continue toward universality to reach the desired end. The other is the popular terror phenomenon, which raises this question particularly starkly.

The simplicity of the democratic peace thesis—that "democracies do not go to war with one another" (Clinton's words) and that the extension of this principle universally could be a "perpetual peace"—may reflect that, as stated, it is an oversimplification. It is certainly born of an optimistic view of the nature of human interactions that was stated originally by the idea's intellectual forefather, Emmanuel Kant: "As culture grows and men gradually move toward greater agreement over their principles, they lead to mutual understanding and peace." This notion was based in Kant's assertion that people would choose peace when they recognized it was in their self-interest to do so.

Perhaps, but perhaps not. It may also be (and both the evidence and interpretations of the evidence by supporters of the democratic peace idea seem to suggest it is) that both key terms in the thesis—democracy and peace—need to be qualified. Peaceful democracies appear to be those that share the common characteristics of being long-standing and associated with mature political systems and advanced, prosperous economic systems—the countries of the so-called first world of market democracies or what Singer and Wildawsky call the "zone of peace" (North America, western Europe, northeast Asia, the Antipodes). Among these countries, there is indeed peace, and quantitative studies basically do little more than to confirm what common sense (these similar countries have little to fight over) and simple observation (none of them have fought one another since World War II) would suggest.

The problem, of course, is that not all democracies are stable and long-standing, particularly in a turbulent world where globalization creates and frustrates countries seeking to join the democratic prosperity of the most advanced democracies. Democratic peace supporters have been faced with two problems they have had to reconcile within the democratic peace hypothesis. One, which requires modifiers and qualifications of the term *democratic,* is the need to differentiate between those states that are democratic but warlike from those that are democratic and peaceful. This requires two distinctions.

The first distinction deals with defining democracies. During the 1990s, the trend toward democratization was generally acknowledged when countries carried out free elections and those elected then took office. It was argued that stable democracies required that this process be repeated at least once and that a succession occurs in accord with the results to demonstrate the viability of democratic practices. The problem has been that these early-generation manifestations of democratic forms do not always result in the moderate politics that democracy is supposed to enjoy (acting peacefully is, of course, one form of that moderation). Because not all democracies have acted the way proponents of democratic peace predicted, one response may be to add qualifications to widely accepted definitions of what constitutes a democracy—toleration of political opposition, for instance. When such qualifications are added to the definition, it then becomes possible to maintain that freely elected governments do not act the way democracies are supposed to because they are not *really* democracies. This qualification is helpful in explaining why a phenomenon like the Palestinian election is not an exception to the democratic peace hypothesis.

The second distinction flows from the first and has to do with differentiating kinds of democracies based on the definition used. If not all freely elected governments are peaceful democracies, what kinds of exceptions are there? One exception is that countries in the process of becoming democratic may be more warlike than stable democracies and *even* may be more bellicose than when they were not democratic. One frequent argument surrounding these *emerging* or *transitional* democracies is that the attainment of freedom simply allows people with old, repressed animosities to express these (often for the first time) and that the result may be political violence.

The other exception is so-called *illiberal* democracies. The countries that are clearly part of the democratic peace all share a commitment to the values of Western civilization, which include political moderation and tolerance, *liberal* characteristics that tend to make their conduct of politics more measured and less warlike. When states that do not have that same tradition (the Middle East is the obvious example) attain political freedom, the result may be that they use democratic mechanisms to serve values other than those of peace and liberal democracies. To achieve stable, peaceful democracy, it is argued that such states must also adopt the values of liberal democracy before they can function within the circle of states defined by the democratic peace.

When democracies do not act the way we want and expect them to act, we tend to view their heresy as a pathology that must be corrected before they qualify as true democracies. Thus, the term *democratic* within the concept of democratic peace has to be modified and qualified to establish the full value of the proposition. A similar qualification may also be necessary with regard to the second concept, peace.

The question here is what peacefulness means. The democratic peace idea originally was intended to suggest that because democracies do not fight one another, then perhaps they do not fight as much generally. Much of the underlying basis of this idea flows from the notions already discussed under the heading of peaceful democracies—institutions and values, for instance, moderate the warlike behavior of democracies toward other democracies.

Research on the democratic peace suggests that such an unqualified extension simply is not true. In fact, democratic states go to war about as often as nondemocratic states even if they are less likely to start those wars than are nondemocratic states. Admittedly, essentially all wars in which democratic states engage are with nondemocratic states whose political and other ideas are sufficiently different to make the need for war plausible, but the fact that they do occur removes some of the piety from those who want to believe (as most of us do) that democratic states are less warlike than societies based on other political values.

Two other qualifications should be added to the democratic peace thesis. One has to do with the relationship between economic globalization and democratic peace: Does globalization promote the emergence of democratic systems that in turn promote peace? Or does globalization create transitional and illiberal democracies that make peace less likely? The other has to do with the causal sequence of what creates that peace: Does the emergence of stable democracies allow a system of democratic peace to exist? Or does a condition of peace and stability permit the rise of democratic states that can afford to exist peacefully?

The connection between the democratic peace and globalization was one of the prominent mantras of the 1990s. It was widely believed and trumpeted that there was a close conjunction between the two. Globalization is supposed to suffuse its membership with the values of Western liberal democracy and to create financial incentives to avoid war with other globalizing states. Globalization contributes to prosperity for members of included societies, and this in turn contributes to the adoption of liberal democratic political norms. Countries that join the globalization system contribute to the spread of the democratic peace in two ways. First, they become liberal democracies and thus join the ranks of those liberal democracies that do not fight one another. Second, the fact of economic interdependence rising from globalization ties member countries together in ways that make it difficult to fight one another: It would be too economically costly to go to war with countries with which one has close economic ties (the Chinese–American relationship, discussed in Chapter 3, is a prime example often cited). The conjunction of similar economic and political values further reduces the reasons countries might want to fight one another.

This rationale has also come under increasing scrutiny. It is no longer so obviously true that the benefits of globalization are uniform within and across member states. Globalization may, for instance, actually exacerbate rather than moderate economic inequalities within countries, thereby contributing to political turbulence rather than moderation arising within negatively impacted groups. At the same time, not all states uniformly benefit, and there are societies (notably in the Middle East) that resist globalization because they reject the underlying values that globalization promotes. This problem is discussed in some detail in Chapter 9.

The same question of causal direction raised about peaceful democracies also applies to the international phenomenon of democratic peace. Advocates of the democratic peace posit that the emergence of peaceful democracies causes the democratic peace, but some observers disagree. Pietrzyk, for instance, proposes just the opposite, arguing that it is the stable international order of the so-called long peace (the Cold War period in which no major wars involving major powers fighting one another occurred) created the atmosphere in which liberal democracies could emerge and flourish, so that peaceful democracies (which are not predisposed to fight one another) were the result of the peace among states, not the cause.

THE CHALLENGES: HAMAS AND OTHERS

The January 25, 2006, election of Hamas by the Palestinian people to majority status in the Palestinian Legislative Council was a dramatic red flag for those who believed that political democratization was the automatic answer to global instability and violence. Hamas won a majority in elections that were monitored by international observers, who judged them to be adequately fair and honest, and that actually followed results from the previous year in local elections on the West Bank and in Gaza that had not received widespread attention. The background of Hamas is anything but peaceful, and yet it achieved electoral success. How could this be?

The election of Hamas drew the international spotlight to other places where the outcome of democratically prescribed electoral processes had not produced the results suggested by the democratic peace. In Lebanon, for instance, the Iranian-sponsored Hizbollah became the largest opposition party in the parliament in 2005 elections, and in Iraq, voters rejected the secular parties that most closely incorporate Western values of liberal democracy, turning instead to religious, fundamentalist alternatives akin to Hamas and Hizbollah. In March 2006, the United States acceded in the postponement of general elections in Egypt because of fear that those elections could produce substantial success for the Muslim Brotherhood, the spiritual forefather of many of the Islamist movements elsewhere in the region. The continuing anti-Americanism of Hugo Chavez in Venezuela and other emerging Latin American leaders suggested the phenomenon is not geographically isolated.

What we are witnessing is the emergence, through democratic processes, of electoral outcomes that do not conform to the expectations of Western advocates of democratic peace. In the Middle East in particular, voters given the liberty to voice their emotions at the ballot box are not choosing liberal democratic alternatives, but are instead making judgments more compatible with transitional and especially illiberal democracy. Thus, at one level the popular terror is a more direct assault on the propositions of unqualified peaceful democracy than anything else; it suggests that when conditions are not ripe for the emergence of peaceful democracy, people choose something else. If they freely choose alternatives that are not peaceful (popularly supported terror, for instance), the result likely will be an international system not universally marked by democratic peace.

The question this raises is whether the democratic peace idea is wrong, or whether it is correct only when it is qualified in ways that reduce its universality. Democratic peace may hold among peaceful democracies (if not in their relations to others), but if the qualifications for peaceful democracy are not met, is democratic peace not the result? To look at this possibility, we will examine what happened in Palestine and is happening elsewhere. The question we will ask is why people chose not to accept the path to peaceful democracy and democratic peace. The answer may help us suggest qualifications for the democratic peace idea and its broader utility as a guiding principle of international relations.

Hamas and the Palestinian Election

Hamas burst on the international scene in January 2006, when it participated for the first time in parliamentary elections (the Palestinian National Council). It scored a stunning success, winning 74 out of 132 seats in the parliament, compared to 45 for Fatah (the political wing of the Palestinian Liberation Organization), and 13 seats for other parties. Polls prior to the election (and exit polls when the voting occurred) did not predict or anticipate this result—most assumed support for Hamas would be no more than about thirty percent of the electorate and that Palestinian voters would return the Western-backed Fatah. Because Hamas has a well-documented and admitted background as a terrorist organization, the outcome seemed anomalous to Western observers and especially democratic peace theorists: The vote for Hamas was decidedly not the kind of endorsement of Western, secular democracy that the democratic peace predicts. Something clearly went wrong.

At least two shortcomings seemed to affect the predictions. In December 2004 Hamas had made a strong showing in local municipal elections on the West Bank, winning 75 seats to 135 for Fatah. A month later in Gaza (where Hamas has its headquarters), it won 77 of 118 seats in 10 council elections (figures are provided by the Council on Foreign Relations [CFR]). Thus, Hamas had already demonstrated some political appeal. The second fault was that a comparison was not drawn between the impending Palestinian elections and results in Iraq in 2005. In Iraq, secular parties (of the kind predicted in the democratic peace) akin to Fatah had suffered significant defeats against sectarian parties with apocalyptical visions like those attributed to Hamas.

What happened? The initial reaction—that Palestine had somehow been kidnapped by terrorist extremists who had to be isolated in the international realm—seems overwrought. Clearly, the elections do not support the unqualified democratic peace thesis, but that can partly be attributed to the fact that Palestine is also not a mature, moderate democracy (peaceful democracy) but is rather at best a transitional, and possibly illiberal, democracy. In either case, the notion that the workings of democratic processes (an election) would reinforce the democratic peace notion are a stretch at best. Moreover, the idea that Palestinian voters may have cast their ballots as an act of popular terror may also oversimplify reality. As a consequence, the dual conclusions that the Palestinians have somehow violated the "law" of democratic peace and that they must be punished somehow for their transgression requires some examination that begins by looking at Hamas itself.

Hamas came into formal existence in 1987. Its predecessor, the Islamic Center, was formed as a Palestinian extension of the Muslim Brotherhood in 1973 to coordinate

Muslim Brotherhood activities in the occupied territories under the leadership of Sheikh Ahmed Yassin. Throughout its existence, it has had two purposes. One is to provide social and other services including, according to CFR's background on the organization, funding schools, orphanages, mosques, health care centers, soup kitchens, and sports leagues. CFR quotes Israeli scholar Reuven Paz, who says of Hamas, "Approximately 90 percent of its work is in social, welfare, cultural, and educational activities." It receives funding for these activities from a number of sources, notably Palestinian expatriates, and private benefactors from Saudi Arabia and other Islamic states, according to the U.S. Department of State. Hamas is respected for its honesty and lack of corruption in carrying out these functions, in stark contrast to the notoriously corrupt Fatah. In this role, Hamas can be thought of as a reasonably orthodox political actor.

It is Hamas's other role that has received the most attention and notoriety. Hamas is also a Palestinian nationalist organization committed to the creation of an independent Palestinian state. The name *Hamas* is an acronym for Harakat al-Muqawamah al-Islamiyyah, which translates as the "Islamic Resistance Movement," and the acronym Hamas is also the Arabic word for "zeal." Its most strident expression of its purposes is found in its 1988 Charter, which calls upon Muslims to "obliterate" Israel and asserts "[t]here is no solution for the Palestinian question except through Jihad." Among the methods that Hamas has commissioned are acts of terror, including suicide/martyr terror against Israel conducted by or under the auspices of its so-called military wing, the Izzedine al-Qassam Brigades. It is this face of Hamas, and the refusal of its leaders to renounce these goals and methods, that has led to the near universal international condemnation of the election results and the resulting Hamas cabinet headed by Ismail Haniyeh.

What went wrong here? Did the Palestinian voters somehow pervert the democratic process by not voting for the kind of moderate candidates that democracy is supposed to produce? There are two mitigating factors to such a judgment. Palestinians clearly did not meet the expectations of a mature democracy in how they voted, but that can largely be explained by qualifying the kind of democracy they have. Had they been a mature, peaceful democracy and voted the way they did, that would have been a repudiation of the peaceful democracy hypothesis. *But they were not.* This was a vote of fledgling, transitional democrats who have long lived under repression and could be expected to vote against those who frustrated them. Second, their vote was not a clear referendum of terrorists versus democrats. As noted, Hamas is both a terrorist organization and the administrator of public services. For what were voters voting? We do not know. Moreover, in choosing Hamas over Fatah, they were also repudiating neither democracy nor good government, given the record of Fatah in administering the Palestinian Authority. Were the Palestinians voting for good government that happened to be administered by terrorists? Or did they vote for terrorism carried out by leaders who also coincidentally produced good government services?

International reaction has been strident, even arguably hysterical. Alleging that Hamas had somehow "hijacked" Palestinian democracy, the initial international response was to refuse to recognize the new government and to withdraw and withhold international assistance (on which the Palestinian Authority is highly dependent) until Hamas renounced both terrorism and its jihad against Israel. The Haniyeh regime has refused to buckle under to such demands, presumably because part of its electoral appeal is its militancy against Israel and its tactics against the Israelis. In Hamas's view, which is apparently supported by many Palestinians, it is up to the Israelis to initiate peace talks. In a March 2006 interview with *Newsweek,* Haniyeh threw down the gauntlet to the Israelis: "[L]et Israel say they will recognize a Palestinian state along the 1967 border, release the prisoners and recognize the rights of the refugees to return to Israel." These preconditions, as we will see in Chapter 6, are absolutely unacceptable to Israel. Haniyeh, in an obvious attempt to appear more moderate, offers hope if they are accepted: "We do not have any feelings of animosity toward Jews. We do not wish to throw them into the sea. All we seek is to be given our land back, not to harm anybody."

Whether the Hamas declarations can be accepted at face value is open to debate and disagreement. In the interim, this freely elected government that refuses to conform to expected norms of democratic peace remains a pariah, isolated and unsupported by the international community amid wild speculation about what it will do. Jennifer Windsor, for instance, argues it is too early to judge: "[I]t is simply too soon to tell whether Hamas, whose membership is diverse, will work to strengthen or dismantle democratic institutions and processes in Palestine." The Lebanon-centered violence in summer 2006 clouds the horizon. International forces argue they will not restore assistance to Palestine until Hamas conforms to international expectations. This isolation in turn has forced Hamas to turn to other "rogue" states for assistance: On April 16, 2006, it was reported that Iran had agreed to provide $50 million in aid to Hamas with the promise of more to follow. Who wins in this situation?

Other Challenges

Hamas's rise to prominence is not an isolated phenomenon. As already noted, there have been other examples in Middle Eastern countries, which we will describe briefly below. This rise is part of a more general phenomenon in the region, described by Marina Ottaway in an online article for the Carnegie Endowment for International Peace ("Promoting Democracy after Hamas' Victory") on April 13, 2006: "Islamist movements are today the major opposition political force in most Arab countries. No amount of U.S. or European support for liberal and secular politicians will change the reality for the foreseeable future." In noting this reality, she adds that most of these movements maintain military wings and that one reason for their success lies with secular political movements "that have largely ignored the imperative of political organizing." These challenges, and others like Chavez in Venezuela, pose problems both for the democratic peace and the peaceful world system its champions propound.

The most mature and organized challenges parallel to Hamas currently come from Egypt and Lebanon, both considered among the more Westernized Middle Eastern states. In Egypt, the challenge comes from the Muslim Brotherhood, founded in 1928. The Brotherhood has become the leading regional advocate of Islamist activity, spreading its influence abroad through organizations like Hamas. The Brotherhood became active politically in Egypt in the 1970s, becoming powerful enough by the early 1990s that it was suppressed by the Mubarak regime. Aligning itself with the pro-democratic Kifaya movement in 2005, it emerged as a major electoral force in the 2005 parliamentary elections. Although the Brotherhood is technically banned in Egypt, its candidates ran as independents and won 88 seats (20 percent of the total), as opposed to legal opposition parties, which won only 14 seats. The fear that the Brotherhood might be swept into power at the ballot box has caused the Mubarak government to postpone presidential elections slated for 2006 until 2009, with American blessing. Hizbollah (the "Party of God"), an outgrowth of the Iranian Revolutionary Guards campaign in Lebanon in 1982, has emerged as a powerful political force in that country as well, and its continuing anti-Israeli stance and actions have been a powerful ingredient in the violence that engulfed Lebanon in July 2006.

CONCLUSION

In the midst of the generally optimistic post–Cold War climate of the 1990s, the democratic peace hypothesis emerged as a powerful academic explanation of the evolving international system and as a goal toward which policymakers in the United States (notably the Clinton and Bush administrations) guided foreign policy as a way to produce a more pacific world system. Because so much of the dynamic of international relations surrounded the emergence of formerly communist states from authoritarian to democratic rule (which turned out to be much easier than skeptics predicted) and the spread of economic globalization and attendant democratic forms to much of East Asia, it was easy and natural to extrapolate the democratizing movement in its unqualified sense: Democracies do not fight one another.

The early twenty-first century has caused some pause in this process and observation. The beneficial outcomes of globalization economically have not been as great as some assumed and have had political backlashes in places like Latin America (discussed in Chapter 9). More dramatically, democracy has proved far less inexorable in areas like the Middle East, where the process of democratization has been far less certain and its impact has not been so obviously the emergence of the kind of stable, liberal democracies that the democratic peace projected. The victory of Hamas has been the most dramatic exception to the democratic peace idea crafted in the 1990s; there have been other challenges in the Middle East and elsewhere.

What does this case examination of democratic peace in the middle-2000s mean for the democratic peace idea and the resulting growing political tranquillity it hopes to engender? Does it mean the democratic peace is simply false? The answer is probably not, because there are instances when its dynamics clearly apply (the First World of advanced market democracies). Is the problem that it has been overly generalized and needs to be qualified in light of recent experience? Do the exceptions, following scientific procedure, disconfirm the hypothesis, or do they call for recrafting it?

The preliminary conclusion is that the democratic peace hypothesis needs to be qualified. It most clearly holds where mature, stable democracies exist (in peaceful democracies, as we have used the term). The crux of the beneficial effect that democratic emergence is supposed to create is the moderation of politics within and between democratic states (those that are both peaceful democracies and which practice democratic peace). The experience of the early 2000s in countries that have emerging, transitional democracies is that they may, at least for a time, produce an illiberal radicalization of politics (which may be distinctively nonpeaceful) rather than the liberal moderation the thesis suggests. That does not mean the democratic peace hypothesis is incorrect. Rather, it means it is correct with qualifications: When the preconditions necessary for democratic peace to hold are present, it does; when they are not present, it is not so clear whether or how it holds.

This modification and qualification, of course, has implications for the foreign policies of countries promoting a more tranquil international system. It suggests that democracy is not the universal, instant panacea to all countries' ills or to the shortcomings of the international system. This, in turn, suggests that a part of the concern of those promoting the democratic peace must now turn in greater earnest to how the conditions that allow for the emergence of peaceful democracies (the apparent precondition to democratic peace) can be nurtured and achieved.

STUDY/DISCUSSION QUESTIONS

1. State the major thesis of the democratic peace. What are the major components of the idea? How do they represent both the observation and aspiration of those who promote the idea?

2. Discuss the idea of peaceful democracy. What are its characteristics? Why does it appear to be a necessary prerequisite for democratic peace?

3. What are the major alternatives to peaceful democracy? Where they exist, how do they pose a threat to democratic peace?

4. How have economic globalization and the democratic peace been linked? Can one reject one notion and accept the other in practice?

5. Is the basic thesis of democratic peace too simply put and unqualified, or must it be subjected to qualifying "adjectives" to be true? Discuss.

6. Describe the rise of Hamas as a form of popular terror. Is Hamas simply a terrorist organization, or is it more? If it is more, how does this complicate explaining it as a rejection of democratic peace?

7. What kind of "democracy" is Palestine? Why do you think the Palestinians elected Hamas? What does that mean for the democratic peace hypothesis?

8. Is Hamas an isolated case? If not, what other evidence is there of exceptions to the democratic peace? What do these mean for the democratic peace and policies deriving from that hypothesis?

READING/RESEARCH MATERIAL

Carothers, Thomas. "Think Again: Democracy." *Foreign Policy* 107, Summer 1997, 11–18.

Encarnacion, Omar G. "The Follies of Democratic Imperialism." *World Policy Journal* 22, 1 (Summer 2005), 47–60.

Freedom House. *Freedom in the World, 2004–2005*. New York: Freedom House, 2004. Available online at http://freedomhouse.org/.

Friedman, Thomas L. *The Lexus and the Olive Branch: Understanding Globalization*. New York: Farrar, Straus and Giroux, 1999.

Fukuyama, Francis. *The End of History and the Last Man Mar*. New York: Free Press, 1992.

Huntington, Samuel P. *The Third Wave: Democratization in the Late Twentieth Century*. Norman: University of Oklahoma Press, 1991.

Kant, Immanuel. *Kant's Political Writings*. (Hans Reiss, ed., H. B. Nisbet, trans.). Cambridge, UK: Cambridge University Press, 1970.

Levy, Jack S. "The Causes of War: A Review of Theories and Evidence." In Philip E. Tetlock, Jo L. Husbands, Robert Jervis, Paul C. Stern, and Charles Tilly (eds.), *Behavior, Society and Nuclear War* (vol. 1). New York: Oxford University Press, 1989.

Mead, Walter Russell. "America's Sticky Power." *Foreign Policy* 141, March/April 2004, 46–53.

Oneal, John R. and Bruce M. Russett. "The Classical Liberals Were Right: Democracy, Interdependence, and Conflict, 1950–1985." *International Studies Quarterly* 41, 2 (June 1997), 267–294.

Ottoway, Marina S. "Promoting Democracy after Hamas' Victory." Washington, DC: Carnegie Endowment for International Peace, April 13, 2006.

Peters Ralph. *New Glory: Expanding America's Global Supremacy*. New York: Sentinel, 2005.

Pietrzyk, Mark E. *International Order and Individual Liberty: Effects of War and Peace on the Development of Governments*. Lanham, MD: University Press of America, 2002.

Pina, Aaron D. "Fatah and Hamas: The New Palestinian Factional Reality." *CRS Report for Congress*. Washington, DC: Congressional Research Service, March 3, 2006 (Order Code RS22395).

Singer, Max, and the Estate of Aaron Wildavsky. *The Real World Order: Zones of Peace, Zones of Turmoil*. Chatham, NJ: Chatham House, 1996.

Windsor, Jennifer. "Advancing the Freedom Agenda: Time for Recalibration?" *Washington Quarterly* 29, 3 (Summer 2006), 21–34.

WEB SITES

Information on groups promoting global democracy

Democracy Resource Center at http://www.ned.org/research/research/html

Freedom House at http://freedomhouse.org

Center for the Study of Democracy at http://www.demo.uci.edu/democ

Information on Hamas and Other Middle Eastern Groups

British Broadcast Company at
http://news.bbc.co.uk/1/hi/world/middle_east/987626.stm

Council on Foreign Relations at http://www.cfr.org/publication/8968/

Palestine Facts at http://www.palestinefacts.org

CHAPTER TWO

The Growing Significance of NGOs
MÉDECINS SANS FRONTIÈRES,
MILITARY CONFLICTS, AND
BEYOND

PRÉCIS

The phenomenon of international activity being conducted by international organizations whose members are not governments of state—referred to as nongovernmental organizations or NGOs—is not a unique but is an increasingly prominent attribute of the contemporary period. NGOs, in a number of guises, have been in operation for over a century, and some, such as the International Red Cross, have been prominent actors on the international scene.

In the contemporary world, NGOs have become more obvious actors in at least two distinct ways. First, they have become increasingly activist in the pursuit of their interests, and this is especially true in the area of peace-keeping and other military operations. Second, at least some of the more activist NGOs pose an open challenge to the principle of state jurisdiction and sovereignty. The *Medicins sans Frontieres*, the NGO that is the subject of this case, is especially open in its disdain for trappings of sovereignty like national frontiers, particularly when great physical suffering is occurring. The two factors combine to help form the thrust of this aspect of NGO activity in the contemporary environment, including problematical places such as Iraq and Afghanistan.

Nongovernmental organizations (NGOs) are playing an increasingly important and in some cases controversial role in the international relations of the post–Cold War world. Much of this controversy arises from their independence from the controls of national governments, which frees them to engage in activities unconstrained from governmental concerns. One area in which they are playing a significant but controversial role is in their participation alongside governments in a variety of humanitarian efforts in ongoing and recently pacified war zones. French-based *Medecins sans Frontieres* (MSF), whose title in English is "Doctors without Borders," is one of the most prominent examples of this phenomenon and one of the best examples of NGOs not only ignoring but virtually flaunting their independence from national control.

International organizations (IOs) are generally divided into two groups for analytical purposes. The most prominent kind are *intergovernmental organizations (IGOs)*. The defining characteristic of an IGO is that its members are the governments of states. The most obvious examples of IGOs are the United Nations and its specialized agencies such as the International Monetary Fund or the World Bank.

The other kind of international organization is the nongovernmental organization. The NGOs are also international in their membership, but unlike IGOs, their members are private individuals or groups from different countries rather than governments. NGOs are far more numerous than IGOs, and their numbers have swelled markedly in an Internet age in which communications across borders is both easy and cheap. For instance, there were around 200 NGOs in 1909, according to Stephen Krasner. Today, there are over 17,000. Most NGOs are narrow in their focus and operate well outside the public eye. Some, however, have very ambitious agendas and play a role in the most public areas of international relations. MSF is one of those prominent organizations.

One of the venues in which MSF and other high-profile, activist NGOs have been active is war zones and areas where wars have recently been concluded. The origin of the resulting operations, often operated with at least a mandate from the United Nations (UN) and often under UN authority, goes back to the Cold War. In that environment, such operations were often described as peacekeeping missions and generally were mounted to separate physically two formerly warring states and to oversee implementation of some form of peace agreement. More minimally, they would prevent formerly warring parties from resuming hostilities by providing a physical barricade of blue-helmeted soldiers to any potential attacker that he would have to penetrate before reaching his foe. The prototype of this kind of operation was the United Nations Emergency Force (UNEF), which separated Israel and Egypt from the end of the Suez War in 1956 until the outbreak of the Six Days' War in 1967. (The UNEF was asked to leave Egypt, where it was stationed, prior to the war.)

The nature and thrust of these efforts changed radically with the end of the Cold War. During the Cold War, most civil conflicts were fought between a recognizable government and an armed and organized insurgent movement. The clear purpose of the two sides was to gain (or maintain) control of the political system over the country in question. Although civilians were sometimes the victims of terrorist or other forms of suppression by one side or the other, the major form of combat was between armed units of the government and the insurgency. In most cases, the Soviets supported one side (usually the insurgents until the Reagan Doctrine championed U.S. support of anticommunist insurgents in places like Nicaragua and Afghanistan) and the United States supported the beleaguered government.

Among the effects of sponsorship was the ability to place some restraints on how the client group conducted hostilities.

The post–Cold War pattern, which I have called *new internal war* (NIW) in *UnCivil Wars* and *When America Fights,* has become a distinctive form of violence in the post–Cold War world. The list of places where these conflicts have occurred is familiar—Somalia, Bosnia, East Timor, Sierra Leone, Kosovo—and so is the aura of tragedy and savagery that has been a major characteristic of these conflicts. The countries where NIW have occurred generally have had governments in tatters (where they existed at all) and the armed insurgents have been little more than armed thugs who roam the countryside, terrorizing, uprooting, or murdering innocent, unarmed civilians, usually for criminal or other non-exemplary purposes. With the retreat of the former Cold War competitors from much of the developing world, there is little to restrain the participants in their reigns of terror.

The results of these "wars" were familiar during the 1990s: the starving children of Somalia with their distended bellies and pencil-thin extremities, the emaciated prisoners of war in Bosnian detention camps, the homeless natives of East Timor sitting outside their burned-down homes, the Sierra Leoneans with their multiple amputations, and the displaced Kosovars attempting to return home after the ethnic cleansing ceased. The common thread has been the extreme human suffering endured by the victim populations and the obviously compelling need for someone to take action to alleviate the human tragedies being endured.

Not all violence in the international system follows this pattern. Wars in places like Afghanistan and Iraq are not NIWs: Afghanistan was a civil war decisively swayed by U.S. intervention, and Iraq was the direct result of an American invasion. The humanitarian toll and need for outside assistance, however, is similar to the outcomes of NIWs.

Part of the short-term problem is how to stem the worst of the immediate effects of war or an imperfect peace; in the longer run, there is also the question of making the target societies whole and stable once again (if they ever were). MSF is a major part of the answer to the short-term question; increasingly, it is also part of the longer-term solution as well.

The current case study thus has two related focuses. The major focus is on MSF as an example of a highly activist, dedicated, and visible NGO. Because it is a medical organization, there is a natural bridge to the second focus on civil and post–September 11, 2001, conflicts, as the kinds of human medical suffering that MSF is dedicated to relieving is nowhere more obvious than in these conflicts.

MÉDECINS SANS FRONTIÈRES

Although it had been active for nearly 28 years, MSF did not attract the broad public eye until 1999. Between its formation in December 1971 and its emergence in the public spotlight with the receipt of the Nobel Peace Prize in 1999, its relative anonymity was, to a large degree, a matter of choice; its mission is to provide relief to those suffering through natural and man-made disasters, and its methods are often highly unorthodox (some would argue occasionally controversial and even illegal). The doctors who work for MSF prefer to operate in the shadows of the international stage. These shadows were illuminated when the organization was awarded the Nobel Prize for peace, thereby making its low profile less possible to maintain.

Background and Evolution of MSF

MSF is largely the result of the experiences of a handful of young doctors attempting to relieve the hardships of the civilian population during the Nigerian-Biafran civil war of 1967–1970. The "French doctors," as they are known, worked under the auspices of the International Red Cross, a highly respected but very conservative NGO, during that conflict. The Red Cross has a tradition of strict neutrality and deference to political and legal authorities that makes it respected and trusted by governments in matters such as the conformance of prisoner-of-war camps to international conventions on the treatment of military prisoners. In the eyes of the young, idealistic doctors who formed MSF, this conservatism came at the expense of providing maximum relief and succor to those civilians suffering the kinds of indignities associated with modern internal wars. The French doctors were frustrated by the impact of the International Red Cross's conservative approach and practices on their efforts in Biafra; MSF was their answer.

The Biafran experience convinced a small group of participating doctors who had attempted to alleviate the worst civilian suffering inflicted by Nigerian soldiers against Ibo tribesmen in Biafra that the approach practiced by the Red Cross had worsened the suffering there (for instance, the Red Cross would not go into certain areas the government forbade it to enter). They thus set out to form a more aggressive, interventionist, and independent organization. The result was MSF, whose first activity was to provide medical care for victims of flooding in Pakistan and gradually enlarged its activities to encompass both man-made and natural disasters that have carried them around the world to locations as diverse as Ethiopia, Honduras, El Salvador, Peru, Yemen, Mozambique, Liberia, and Sudan. MSF's goal is to find those suffering medical problems and to alleviate those problems; overt political and other concerns are excluded from its motivations.

The organization has grown dramatically. There were originally six founding members of MSF, the most prominent of whom was Dr. Bernard Kouchner, who later became the French Health Minister and who served as the Special Representative of the Secretary-General (SRSG) of the UN effort in Kosovo. Kouchner was the operational leader of peacekeeping and state-building efforts in that bitterly torn land, the first time someone with a primary background in an NGO had ever occupied that kind of position. In 1999, MSF had 23 offices in various countries (the American chapter of MSF uses the English translation "Doctors without Borders" to designate itself). MSF has over 2,000 medical volunteers at work in 80 countries. Underlying its operation is a budget of over $167 million, almost four-fifths of which comes from private donations worldwide. Such an extensive operation with such a modest budget is possible because most of the medical personnel, including physicians and nurses, participate voluntarily and do not receive remuneration beyond living and travel expenses.

Most of MSF's medical activities are carried out far from the public eye. In 1980, for instance, MSF sent medical teams into Afghanistan to care for the wounded that resulted from the Soviet invasion and occupation of that country. In the process, they gained a reputation as a human rights monitor because MSF doctors witnessed and reported violations. In 1984, it instituted a nutrition program in Ethiopia, and ended up denouncing the misuse of humanitarian assistance to that country. In 1988, MSF had the only medical team to reach the Kurdish town of Halabja in Iraq after Saddam Hussein's forces attacked the Kurdish stronghold with chemical weapons. When the Persian Gulf War broke out, it set up camps in the no-man's-land between Iraq and Jordan to provide aid to refugees. When the Kurds fled Iraq at the end of the war to avoid Hussein's vengeance, MSF was the first to arrive on the Turkish mountainsides to provide relief to the 70,000 refugees clinging to the most tenuous existence until global publicity, much of it created by MSF itself, resulted in the United States government intervening under the banner of Operation Provide Comfort (later renamed Northern Watch).

MSF has grown to be the world's largest nonprofit medical relief agency. In addition to its willingness to involve itself in man-made emergencies, it has also been very active in other, less controversial activities such as programs of innoculation against deadly diseases and its Access to Essential Medicines Campaign that seeks to raise awareness about and to bring relief to poor peoples who are routinely denied access to medical treatment.

But it is MSF's willingness to insert itself into highly political situations—notably war zones where civilians are subjected to grossly inhumane treatment—that has become its international claim to fame. No one argues that its basic mission, the alleviation of human suffering from whatever source, is not noble or praiseworthy. But MSF is also the subject of criticism, much of which follows from its origin. MSF was, after all, born out of a fairly scornful rejection of the means of international medical caregiving by the most establishment of caregiving organizations, the International Red Cross. MSF began as something of a maverick, and it is a reputation in which it takes satisfaction, even pride. And that does not always sit well with the organizations with which it must interact in providing its services.

Controversies Surrounding MSF

In some ways, MSF resembles another highly activist organization, Greenpeace. Although Greenpeace has a different substantive mission, the organizations share the characteristic of being reasonably scornful "of governments and journalists," according to *The Economist*. MSF and Greenpeace share a level of devotion to their mission that some argue borders on zealotry. It also leads to a set of controversies about what MSF does and how it carries out its mission that has an impact on its ability to work effectively within the framework of violent situations. Five interrelated sources of controversy are worth mentioning.

The first controversy surrounds the very core of the reason for MSF's existence, the notion of being "without borders." The idea that political boundaries cannot and should not be a barrier to the provision of medical attention is the basic reason MSF was created in the first place. As cofounder Rony Brauman explained in an interview in *Time International* in 1999, "International relief agencies were too respectful of notions of non-interference and sovereignty. When we saw people dying on the other side of the frontiers, we asked ourselves, 'What is this border? It doesn't mean anything to us.' "

This statement summarizes a major source of irritation between MSF and other help-ing agencies and also governments in the countries where MSF operates. The organization Brauman accuses of being "too respectful" was, of course, the International Red Cross, suggesting a less-than-cordial relationship with that NGO. MSF regularly ignores the sover-eignty of states where it operates; when officially denied permission to enter countries to provide medical relief, the response by MSF has been simply to sneak across borders, in effect illegally infiltrating the sovereign territory of states in an act of overt defiance of inter-national norms. Aside from a firm belief in the righteousness of what they are doing, MSF understands that the nature of their mission and their willingness to publicize unfortunate conditions means governments are reluctant to arrest and deport MSF personnel (although this occasionally does happen), making them less-than-welcome guests some of the time.

This leads to the second controversy surrounding MSF, which is its explicitly polit-ical character and nature. Generally speaking, it is a hallmark of international organiza-tions that they must remain fundamentally politically neutral in order to be effective. Certainly this is true of most IGOs, and in most cases, it is also true of NGOs as well. The constraints on NGOs in this regard are less than IGOs, because they are not accountable to the national governments of their origin or where they do business.

MSF has never denied that it is political, at least in the impact it has on situations in which it acts. As cofounder Kouchner (who split with MSF in 1980 to form a competi-tior, *Medecins du Monde*) puts it, "The movement was political from the start. The tradi-tion was medical, the action was medical, but we had to convince people that borders should not protect disgraceful conduct and suffering." This frank admission, of course, puts MSF at direct odds with governments that are the source of suffering in their coun-tries; their virtually monomaniacal devotion to their mission also puts them at odds with peacekeepers and occupying powers on occasion.

The role MSF has taken upon itself leads to a third controversial characteristic, its tendency to view itself and to be viewed as a loner. The doctors who work for the organi-zation have a mission, "a 'duty to interfere' in troubled areas and to speak out about what they saw," in the words of the *Time International* article. This notion of special mission sets MSF apart as something different from others around it. MSF volunteers are proud of the fact that they are often the first caregivers on the scene (e.g., ministering to the Kurds in the wake of the Persian Gulf War) and that when all the others have left, they will still be there. Being aloof is, indeed, part of MSF's effectiveness, as its Nobel citation observes: "By maintaining a high degree of independence, the organization has suc-ceeded in living up to its ideals." It does so, of course, at the expense of being thought of as something less than a team player.

The tendency to be viewed as a loner reinforces the fourth characteristic, MSF's penchant for honesty and integrity, some would argue to a fault. The agency's single-minded concern (some would argue obsession) not only with treating but with publiciz-ing the human causes of suffering clearly does not endear it with those organizations (which are often national governments) against whom it levels charges. The leaders of MSF are medical personnel, not diplomats, and whereas this may endow them with a refreshing degree of candor not usually present in complex international situations, it may also compromise their effectiveness in dealing with others.

Finally, MSF has particular disdain for peacekeeping operations (PKOs). This feeling arises from the MSF's perception that these missions simply get in the way of their performance of their duties and that the peacekeepers rapidly adopt self-protection as their basic mission rather than the promotion of the well-being of the target population that MSF seeks to protect. A variation of this theme has led MSF to conclude missions in Afghanistan and Iraq.

The attitude of MSF toward traditional peacekeepers was made explicit in a 1993 report dealing with the UN effort in Somalia and titled "Life, Death, and Aid." The report begins by criticizing governments for their selectivity in terms of which humanitarian disasters they deal with and which they ignore—mounting a major effort in Somalia but turning a blind eye toward the equally horrendous slaughter in nearby Sudan. Turning to the actual operation in Somalia, MSF argues additional points. On one hand, MSF maintains that UN PKOs often have imprecise mandates that tie their hands in providing needed assistance to those suffering the effects of war. Instead, the peacekeepers come to define their mission as self-protection rather than the promotion of agendas such as MSF's. Moreover, in their efforts to be fair and impartial, the peacekeepers may actually make it more difficult to conduct operations than it was before their arrival. In Somalia, for instance, the report alleges that UN efforts to provide protection to food supplies being convoyed to remote locations disrupted an informal arrangement MSF had with various warlords, whereby the warlords would be allowed to plunder a share of humanitarian relief supplies in return for allowing the rest to get through. When the peacekeepers arrived and restored an open transportation system, this informal arrangement was interrupted; the clans then began attacking the supply caravans, with the effect that delivery became more, rather than less, difficult than it had been under the clan–MSF arrangement.

PEACEKEEPING AND OTHER OPERATIONS

International involvement in the internal violence in the Third World has become an increasingly prominent component of contemporary international affairs. The frequently gory nature of these conflicts makes them difficult to ignore, especially if television's roving eye happens to capture the gross human suffering that accompanies them. A few places, such as Sudan, avoided scrutiny for years by terrorizing journalists to keep them out of the country—Sudan's situation went largely unreported until refugees flowed into Chad and told their horrific stories. In any case, there will be a great temptation to intercede to right the situation.

In the contemporary world, breached peaces that must be restored are of two types. The 1990s produced the NIWs, chaotic civil wars with massive civilian suffering and disruption. The 2000s have seen the resurgence of more traditional forms of conflict, such as outside intervention in traditional civil wars (Afghanistan) and traditional interstate wars with overtones of civil war (Iraq). What the two variants share is residual suffering that requires attenuation.

Nature of the Problem

In internal wars of the 1990s variant, the potential target situation is either an active war zone or a former war zone where some form of ceasefire (probably not very durable) is in place. In all likelihood, the violence has largely been perpetrated against civilian groups within the country by other indigenous groups, leaving a strong residue of bitterness, hatred, and suspicion among the warring parties. Outsiders will normally enter with an initial mandate to restore order and to stop the killing. As the report by MSF cited in the last section indicates, they may have little direction beyond that.

The initial conditions frame the sequential tasks that the outsiders may undertake. Their first duty, unless a peace of sorts is in place, is to stop the fighting, what I call *peace imposition* (PI). This is a combat job and requires well-equipped combat soldiers. Once peace has been imposed, the task moves to making sure the situation does not revert to fighting once again, or what I call *peace enforcement* (PE). This task requires combat soldiers to convince or intimidate the former fighters into remaining peaceful, but it also involves providing conditions conducive to a return to normalcy, such as reinstating some form of physical order and civil justice (police and courts) or instituting such structures if they did not preexist the violence. Providing health care and basic services such as power and water also fall unto this category. Military forces may provide the necessary safety—or shield—to undertake these tasks, but the actual tasks are more clearly civil in nature. If peace enforcement produces an atmosphere in which animosities are overcome to the point that the former warring parties prefer continuing peace to the resumption of war, then the task can move to simply maintaining the peace, or *peacekeeping* (PK). Once peacekeeping has reached the point that peace will likely be maintained in the absence of the peacekeepers, then the mission is accomplished and can be terminated.

Afghanistan and Iraq-like situations share some of these stages, although the forces that must try to move the situation from war to peace may be the same forces that caused the breach of the peace in the first place (e.g., the United States in Iraq).

If leaving behind a stable peace is the goal (which it almost always is), then any mission must successfully complete all three stages of the PI-PE-PK sequence. If the situation in a country has deteriorated to the point that war has raged, there must have been underlying reasons that must be addressed if there is to be a reasonable chance for a stable postmission peace. The same is true when a government has been overthrown by rebels or outsiders with no obvious successor. In all likelihood, political institutions and processes are dysfunctional or nonexistent; economic conditions are either so wretched or so skewed toward a minority that most people have little stake in the ongoing system; and social, cultural, ethnic, or religious differences are so deep as to leave a thoroughly noncohesive social structure. When one adds the animosities generated by the war itself, it is clear that a simple cooling-off period is not going to be sufficient to heal the wounds and scars that war has produced. Something more must be done.

In order to reach stable peace, the system must be built (or rebuilt) so that the population prefers the peaceful situation to war, the task of *state building*. (The term *nation building* is sometimes used as a synonym, but that is technically incorrect, as the actions are aimed at changing the nature of the political unit, the state.) Only by creating political, economic, social, and psychological conditions that the population prefers to war can a stable postmission peace be established where war is unlikely to recur.

The task of state building is very complex, given the very large and varied number of tasks that must be performed and the variety of actors that must be involved in the enterprise. Moreover, there is no agreement on how these tasks can be completed or who should undertake them, but human suffering requiring medical intervention is a constant factor. Among the actors who have a part in any operation are NGOs; for the medical needs that are always one of the major by-products of these wars, that means MSF.

The Structure of State Building

Outsiders entering a former war zone face one of two major political problems. They may enter a country that at one time was reasonably well-ordered, although in all likelihood any form of political organization was authoritarian in one way or another (Iraq or Afghanistan, for instance). In these circumstances, the war has likely disrupted whatever organization there was (indeed, the political structure may well have been the major target of fighting), leaving behind a dysfunctional, disrupted set of institutions that can only be rebuilt with some effort and care to avoid replicating whatever it was about the old order that precipitated violence in the first place. In addition, it is very likely that the economic and social systems, whatever their prior condition, have suffered similar disruptions.

The other possibility is virtual chaos, where either there never was a viable political and economic system, or where whatever system may have preexisted has been so thoroughly destroyed that no semblance of order and authority can be identified. Most of the countries where this condition holds are deeply divided along ethnic, religious, or some other (e.g., clan) lines and cannot agree on a single form of organization that is acceptable to all groups. Iraq is a prime example.

In either case, the situation is bleak, and its alleviation is difficult, if not impossible. Once the fighting is stopped, which is often the easier of the tasks, outsiders are faced with a solid wall of problems, many of them life-threatening. The scourges of war have left many victims as refugees, living in squalid conditions without adequate shelter, sanitary conditions, medical help, or food. Others have had their homes destroyed and huddle in the ruins. Electrical power has long since gone out, as has water, garbage pickup, and other services. Employment has ceased for many as factories have been destroyed and crops torched. Many suspect neighbors of being the sources of their suffering, which may include the violent loss of loved ones that leaves physical and psychological wounds that need to be tended. And there is either no political authority to turn to, or available officials are viewed as part of the problem.

The human needs fall into several categories. One is the simple restoration of order and safety, a task that intervening troops can perform for a time but must eventually be provided indigenously. A second is basic survival needs, including an adequate supply of food, potable water, shelter against the physical elements, cooking facilities, medical care for those who need it, inoculations against diseases (the occurrence of which may increase because of the wretchedness of conditions), and more. A third is rebuilding whatever structures have been destroyed, beginning with basic services and infrastructure. Finally, there is the need to begin to expand the preexisting structures to improve conditions so that there will be no incentives for a recurrence of the violence in the future.

Enter the NGOs

The list of tasks is obviously extensive, and it all cannot be performed simultaneously. Disasters attract those organizations and individuals who want to provide assistance in the specific areas of their expertise: The soldiers arrive to restore the order, the Red Cross to coordinate aid and to provide things like warm clothing and blankets. CARE and other food providers are likely to be close behind. And, of course, MSF will be among the first to arrive.

The problem is coordination of the overall effort in a way that allows each element and thus the whole effort to succeed. A welter of governmental and nongovernmental agencies will almost certainly descend on the scene, each with a specific agenda but with no coordinated plan for the comprehensive provision of services across the board. In fact, each aid giver is likely to view its own mission as supreme and to treat other priorities and providers whose missions conflict with theirs as detrimental or less important. Those who would help thus can become part of the problem as well as the solution.

Here is where the case of MSF, specifically in terms of its relations with military forces on the scene, becomes illustrative. MSF is likely to be one of the first international agencies on the scene when disaster befalls a particular location. In fact, they are often present before the problem reaches the level of suffering and atrocity that creates international awareness and the impetus necessary to authorize some form of international action. MSF, for instance, was continuously active in Afghanistan between 1980 and 2004, when it withdrew for reasons discussed below.

Part of the problem is perspective. For MSF, the central problem is medical, and alleviating the immediate medical suffering of the target population is by far the most important task it believes needs to be undertaken. Anything that other agencies do to make the provision of medical assistance easier is valued; anything that does not contribute to that end, and especially if it makes medical caregiving more difficult, is to be opposed.

Military forces entering a new internal war are likely to have a different perspective on the problem. Certainly they are aware of medical problems and want them dealt with. But the military also realizes that medical attention is only one of a number of priorities within the general mandate of restoring normalcy in the countries where they operate. Securing areas from military violence and restoring physical order are likely to be their highest priorities, followed closely by providing reasonable security for the peacekeepers themselves.

Beyond purely mechanical security concerns (protecting MSF doctors may put soldiers at risk), Afghanistan revealed a more fundamental incompatibility of missions. In that case, MSF alleges the U.S. military "contributed to the blurring of identities," according to MSF Secretary-General Marine Buissonniere, by using "humanitarian assistance to be a support for its military and political ambitions." Specifically, eligibility for MSF relief was tied to support for American forces; the result was that the opponents of the Afghan regime came to consider MSF workers hostile combatants and thus legitimate targets. In 2004, an MSF team of caregivers traveling in an unsecured part of the countryside (an area not controlled by the Afghan army or NATO forces) was attacked by Afghan tribesmen, and all five members of the team were killed.

This type of instability was also apparent in Somalia in the early 1990s. MSF doctors were in the country dispensing medical aid and assisting in the distribution of food in those areas where it was most needed before the United Nations arrived to help alleviate the starvation. In order to carry out its function, MSF was forced to compromise with the clan warlords who controlled various parts of Somali territory. As noted, MSF worked out an arrangement in which the clans were allowed to commandeer enough grain to feed their followers in return for allowing the rest of the supplies to go forward, a practice the UN peacekeepers ended. At the same time, MSF doctors working in war zones sometimes allowed themselves to be put into service to run military hospitals that treat wounded soldiers.

The UN mission would not accept these compromises. The first and major mission of UNISOM (United Nations in Somalia) I was to reestablish the integrity of the food distribution system, which required securing the country's road network and convoying food supplies. Doing so prevented the warlords from skimming their previous shares, thereby interrupting their bargain with the MSF. To the UN forces, this was simply a matter of restoring order and integrity to the country; to MSF, it amounted to the disruption of a functional—if extralegal—means to ensure that people got the medical services they required.

MSF also believes that peacekeepers are likely to get in the way of solving problems the longer they stay. Partly, this is the case because, as the "Life, Death and Aid" report maintains, "humanitarian aid permits intervention by armed forces yet gives them no precise political programme." In some sense, this charge is true, but it may be misleading as well. The purely military aspect of the missions is peace imposition and peace enforcement. During peace enforcement it has an ongoing role in maintaining the absence of a return to violence, but it has little other intrinsic role to play. The role a group like MSF seeks to play is not antithetical to that of the peacekeeping outsiders, but it goes beyond their mandate.

The problems go beyond conflicts of mission definition, reflecting very different institutional and organizational cultures. MSF is, quite openly and proudly, antiestablishment and iconoclastic. It was, after all, born because the traditional, establishment providers of medical assistance were, in its view, dysfunctionally hamstrung by conventions (in this case, honoring sovereign borders) from performing necessary medical tasks. In some ways, Doctors without Borders is Doctors *against* Borders, a way of thinking hardly likely to endear them to political authorities and their agents, notably the military. One result is that each group, and its members, tends to treat the other with suspicion, even disdain. From a military viewpoint, MSF personnel are likely to be seen as impractical dreamers who obstruct orderly operations and who make demands that can put military forces in unnecessary danger. From an MSF viewpoint, the military is likely to be seen as a reactionary barrier to mission accomplishment, a force to be avoided and circumvented, not a partner in a broader enterprise to build states and leave behind conditions of stable peace.

MSF in Afghanistan and Iraq

MSF's experience in Afghanistan and Iraq offers a new permutation in the NGO–state relationship. In both countries, MSF essentially became a pawn in the ongoing conflict and attempt to establish peace. The result was unsatisfactory from the MSF viewpoint and caused the organization to withdraw from both countries in 2004, actions it publicly lamented given its long history of staying the course in these kinds of physical tragedies.

MSF involvement in the region goes back to 1980, when MSF teams entered Afghanistan—illegally crossing the border to get there, of course—to aid medical victims of the Soviet invasion of 1979. They remained active within the country throughout that war and into the early 1990s, when their emphasis shifted toward favorite MSF projects such as inoculation of children and the provision of basic medical care in a country whose primitive health care system had been essentially destroyed by years of war (a not unusual circumstance in war-torn Third World countries). MSF returned in force after the Afghan Taliban government was overthrown by the indigenous Northern Alliance, with the help of the United States, to lend their expertise and experience to state building in the medical arena. In 2002, they launched a parallel effort in Iraq, which was expanded after the United States overthrew the Saddam Hussein regime and occupied the country, in 2003.

In both countries, MSF's self-designated role was to relieve the very real medical suffering resulting from nearly a quarter century of war in Afghanistan and the aftermath of the American invasion of Iraq. In both countries, resistance to an unstable peace enforced largely by the United States meant substantial parts of each country were not pacified, and it was in these areas that MSF assistance was most needed. The familiar problem for MSF was finding a way to operate successfully but safely in an undeclared war zone that the occupying powers would not admit was still a war zone. For different reasons in the two countries, it was unable to accomplish this task, and the result was its reluctant withdrawal.

The problem in Afghanistan was the inability or, in the minds of some MSF officials and supporters, the unwillingness of the Afghan government to protect them from hostile clansmen seeking to overthrow the government in Kabul. Part of the problem was that MSF put itself in harm's way by operating in hostile, unsecured areas (not unusually) where the fact that most of its personnel was ethnically European made them stand out suspiciously in the population. Their penchant for candid, non-politically correct reporting on the conditions they encountered also did not endear them with Afghan authorities. The relationship came to a head on June 2, 2004, when five MSF personnel were shot and killed by Taliban forces while on a mission in the countryside. The Taliban later stated "that organizations like MSF work for U.S. interests and are therefore targets for future attacks," according to MSF. MSF insisted that the Afghan government bring the perpetrators to justice, which the government failed to do. This incident, and its aftermath, and similar attacks on other organizations like CARE precipitated MSF's withdrawal from the country in August 2004. In explaining why MSF was leaving, MSF's director of Afghan operations stated, "The lack of respect for the safety of aid workers is seen in the government's unwillingness or inability to produce a credible investigation of this atrocity and to provide sufficient follow-up in terms of arrest and prosecution of those who are guilty."

The theme of perceived involvement of MSF in American operations recurred in Iraq and left the organization in a similarly untenable position. In this case, the provision of humanitarian assistance in postinvasion Iraq became tied to cooperation with occupation forces (an allegation the U.S. government denies). The result was a situation in which, in MSF's own words, "humanitarian aid workers began to be viewed by some as a component of the Western military effort." As such, these NGOs became targets of the Iraqi resistance, with increasingly unacceptable casualties. MSF had thus become an unwitting and unwilling partisan in the civil conflict, and the intolerability of this situation was reflected in its withdrawal notification on November 4, 2004. "It has become shockingly clear that the work of humanitarian organizations is not being respected by certain insurgent groups, and that humanitarian agency staff are by no means immune to kidnappings and brutality. . . . The level of risk for humanitarian aid workers is now simply unacceptable. It would be irresponsible for us to ask any of our staff to continue working in these conditions." After the fact of MSF withdrawal from the country, *The Iraq Study Group Report* acknowledges this problem: "participation of the international intergovernmental organizations is constrained by the lack of security."

CONCLUSION

This case study is only a microcosm of the growing roles of NGOs in important international situations, in this case the provision of services in circumstances in which breaches of the peace are involved. The experience of MSF and other NGOs in the 1990s offered one model, and MSF's aggressive ignoring of political barriers to the relief of misery in war-torn lands became a model of sorts. The sober experience of MSF and others in Afghanistan and Iraq may call the continuing validity of that model into question.

What this very narrow case (narrow in the sense of the mandate and goal of MSF) seeks to illustrate is how difficult it is to coordinate the relations among emerging international actors in a new and largely uncharted environment. The MSF–peacekeeper relationship is no more than the tip of the iceberg in suggesting the multiple difficulties and opportunities that interaction may produce.

What can we draw from this experience? The question is worth exploring, both because traditional peacekeeping opportunities and situations similar to Iraq and Afghanistan are likely to continue, possibly even proliferate, in the international relations of the upcoming years; and because nongovernmental organizations like MSF will probably be asked to play an increasing part in the system in general and in violent situations in particular. The problem, in other words, is both prominent and difficult.

There is little agreement on what evolving relationship NGOs like MSF and governmentally based international state-building missions will have in the future. One reason is the lack of consensus on exactly what state building is and how to organize and accomplish its goals. The evolving situations in Afghanistan and Iraq, where the efforts, begun as a virtual afterthought, arguably have been half-hearted, have done little to create the "guidebook" for future operations. Part of the reason is also institutional and perspectival. MSF is not only a *non*governmental organization, it is also, in many cases, an *anti*govermental organization. Its disdain for politics means it shies away from entering the kinds of authority relations on which governments are based. A quick reference to the MSF Web page quickly reveals the scorn MSF has for government; in some ways, the relationship is reciprocal. At the same time, both sides in fact need one another for maximum effectiveness: State building will always have a medical component, and MSF is there to provide it. It is not clear who would take its place if MSF were to withdraw or cease to exist.

What makes these situations controversial? Partly, it is the intractability of the circumstances in which the relief of humanitarian disasters and state building are contemplated. By and large, these are very difficult, bitter situations: It is often unclear of how much assistance outsiders can be beyond stopping (or interrupting) the violence and tending to the immediate suffering of populations. Long-term solutions have remained elusive, at least in part because we have no reliable methods for moving situations toward positive outcomes. A good bit of our uncertainty in this regard is the absence of anything like a plan to integrate and coordinate the activities of a large number of individual organizations with differing and sometimes contradictory missions they seek to accomplish. Some of these actors will be NGOs like MSF, and some of them will be contentious and even contemptuous of other authorities, as MSF often proudly is. NGOs like MSF must be viewed as neutral and beneficial by all parties to be accepted in these situations. They must also cooperate with local authorities when some of those whom they seek to help will view them as partisan enemies. How do they achieve a balance between the need to be seen as humanitarian helpers and parts of a political solution in war-ravaged situations?

The highly politicized situations in Afghanistan and Iraq, where the power and prestige of great powers like the United States is added to the humanitarian mission of relieving suffering, complicated matters and presents MSF and other NGOs with new problems for which the solutions are currently not apparent. Should, for instance, the United States modify its occupation policies in a country like Iraq to accommodate the humanitarian efforts of organizations like MSF, even if doing so may compromise efforts against recalcitrant opponents? Should occupiers be allowed in effect to preempt the efforts of the aid givers to further their own goals, as apparently has been perceived in Afghanistan and Iraq? An apparent main difference between the operations of MSF in the 1900s and the 2000s has been the intrusion of major power politics in the 2000s, a problem largely not encountered in the 1990s. How that changes the environment is a question with which the aid givers must grapple. It will not be easy. As MSF reluctantly announced it was leaving Iraq, Marc Joolen, the MSF coordinator for that country, framed the dilemma: "It's become increasingly difficult to operate as an international NGO in a situation ruled by the 'war on terror.' "

STUDY/DISCUSSION QUESTIONS

1. What is a nongovernmental organization (NGO)? Contrast NGOs with inter-governmental organizations (IGOs).

2. Compare and contrast the pattern of internal wars in the Third World during the Cold War and post–Cold War periods.

3. How and why did *Medicins sans Frontieres* (MSF) come into being? What are its major self-proclaimed missions and purposes?

4. Why is MSF a controversial organization?

5. Discuss the nature of contemporary efforts to restore peace in war-torn societies, including the sequential military problems they have and the goals for which they may be commissioned and their interactions with humanitarian aid givers.

6. What is state building? Why is it a controversial goal? Where do organizations like MSF fit into state-building operations?

7. How is the MSF experience in Afghanistan and Iraq a variation on previous experiences? Compare and contrast the two experiences from the vantage point of MSF.

8. What have been the outcomes of MSF missions in Afghanistan and Iraq? What problems do these raise for future operations?

9. Should the operations of organizations like MSF remain entirely independent of the operations of partisans in conflict areas, including the United States, or should they become part of the broader American effort? What are the consequences on those operations?

READING/RESEARCH MATERIAL

Baker, James A. III, and Lee H. Hamilton(co-chairs). *The Iraq Study Group Report: The Way Forward-A New Approach* (authorized edition). New York: Vintage Books, 2006.

Dorozynski, Alexander. "*Medicins sans Frontieres:* 20 Years Old." *British Medical Journal* 303, 6817 (December 21, 1991), 591.

Krasner, Stephen D. "Sovereignty." *Foreign Policy* (January/February 2001), 20–30.

Nolan, Hanna. "Learning to Express Dissent: *Medicins sans Frontieres.*" *British Medical Journal* 319, 7207 (August 14, 1999), 446.

"No Thanks: Armed Protection for Aid." *The Economist (U.S.)* 329, 7839 (November 27, 1993), 43.

Sancton, Thomas. "Distinguished Service: *Medicins sans Frontieres* Receives the Nobel Prize." *Time International,* October 25, 1999, 68.

Snow, Donald M. *UnCivil Wars: International Security and the New Internal Conflicts.* Boulder, CO: Lynne Rienner, 1996.

———. *When America Fights: The Uses of U.S. Military Force.* Washington, DC: CQ Press, 2000.

Spencer, Miranda. "The World Is Their Emergency Room: *Doctors* Without *Borders.*" *Biography* **4,** 6 (June 2000), 55–58.

WEB SITES

Database on intergovernmental and nongovernmental international organizations

Geneva International at
http://geneva-international.org/GVA/Directory/Welcome.E.html

Home page for Doctors without Borders

Doctors without Borders at http://www.doctorswithoutborders.org

Worldwide organizations promoting human rights

Amnesty International at www.amnesty.org

Global Impact at http://www/charity.org

Human Rights Watch at www.hrw.org

Alphabetical listing of NGOs affiliated with the United Nations

NGO Global Network at http://www.ngo.org

CHAPTER THREE

China Rising
LOOMING THREAT OR GLOBAL PARTNER?

PRÉCIS

One of the ways in which the international system changes is in the emergence of new major powers, called "rising powers." China appears to be poised to assume that role in the contemporary world. China was a consequential country during the Cold War, but its significance was overshadowed by its relative position within the communist world. With the demise of the Soviet Union and its adoption of different policies, especially in the economic realm, China has become a much more important factor in the international politics of the new century.

The question is how this rising power will fit into the international politics of the twenty-first century. With its growing economy and increased military might, will China be a force for stability and peace, or for disruption? Will China challenge American world leadership or become a productive part of the globalizing international scene? While the phenomenon of rising powers may be a general occurrence, the difference particular new powers makes varies. The question is, what kind of impact China will have?

One of the most certain things one can say about the dominant powers of any period of international history is that eventually their dominance will be eclipsed by the emergence of some different country or countries. While the United States has been *a* dominant power since World War II and *the* dominant power since the end of the Cold War, this observation is undoubtedly true for the United States as well.

Whether the changing nature of power relationships are necessarily upsetting for those whose dominance is threatened is uncertain, and the process need not be traumatic, depending on two factors. One is what country(s) will challenge existing dominance. The other is the kind of challenge the rising power poses. Most observers see China as the rising power of the twenty-first century; there is less agreement on the kind of challenge China poses. The heart of this case study will be to examine the alternatives: What kind of rising power will China be?

What does it mean to be a "rising power"? In the most general sense, a rising power refers to a country that, by virtue of increased military, economic, or other power, is or has the potential to play a more prominent role in the international system than it has heretofore played. The United States was such a rising power in the late nineteenth and early twentieth centuries, as was the Soviet Union during the middle of the twentieth century. Now, it would appear to be China's turn.

The impact of rising powers is important. At the level of the international system, rising powers change the relative power balance between the major powers, with ripple effects throughout the system, often in ways that are controversial and difficult to predict. Will, for instance, a rising China eventually challenge American international predominance and lead to a transformation from an essentially unipolar to a bipolar or multipolar balance? Would such a transformation be stabilizing or destabilizing?

The impact of rising states also creates foreign policy questions for countries affected by the rising power. The basic question is whether the impact will help or hinder the realization of interests of the affected power. Will the rising power be, to borrow from this chapter's subtitle, a looming threat to those interests or a global partner assisting in their accomplishment? Or will it be both? Like the systemic impacts, these changes are never entirely clear in advance, leading to speculation and disagreement. Europe worried about the impact of an industrially gigantic United States, and the United States worried about the impact of a militarily powerful Soviet Union. The United States ended up a strategic partner of Europe, and the Soviets emerged primarily as a threat. Where does China fit?

The world's oldest continuous civilization, with a history rich in both creativity and tragedy, China stood largely outside the quantum leaps in wealth and power made possible by Western-centered advances in modern science, technology, and industrialization since the eighteenth century. From the mid-nineteenth to the mid-twentieth centuries China endured its "century of humiliation," as the once grand but then defenseless country fell under the domination and exploitation of the West and of newly industrialized Japan.

Today, however, China is again on the rise economically, politically, and militarily. Though still much less economically advanced than nearby Japan or South Korea, for example, China's sheer mass—it accounts for fully one-fifth of the earth's population—means that already no Asian state can contemplate its own strategic requirements without taking China into account. Should its ascent continue, China will become a leading power of global, not merely regional, status.

China already possesses some of the trappings of superpower status: It has nuclear weapons and is one of the five permanent members of the United Nations Security Council. If its economy continues the robust growth of the past two decades, then China may truly arrive as a state capable of wielding power on a large scale. China's growth raises two questions about its future growth: Will China continue to grow to the point that it *can* upset the power balance? And will a newly robust China (if it emerges) accommodate itself to the existing international system or instead act in ways that defy international norms and threaten international stability and security? In other words, will China pose a threat to the emerging international order, or will it become another major, but orthodox, member of the international system?

The purposes and structure of the case study follow from this introduction. The first purpose is to describe how China has risen from the status of a semicolonized state in the early twentieth century to its current position as a rising power. To this end, we will look briefly at that evolution, culminating in the 1979 promulgation of the Four Modernizations and their applications to raising Chinese economic, military, and political power. There is, of course, disagreement on each of these dimensions. The second purpose is to apply these descriptions of China's rise to whether China will be a looming threat or global partner, a question prominently imbedded in the American foreign policy debate about China. The overall purpose, of course, is to show how uncertainties affect the assessment of the impact of rising powers more generally.

THE SETTING: FROM HUMILIATION, CHAOS, AND POVERTY TO MODERNIZATION

China's "century of humiliation" reduced it to a semicolony. The situation resulted from the loss of creativity; corruption and resistance to reform within the imperial court; the obsolescence of its emperor-based political system that relied on a corps of bureaucrats chosen for their mastery of Confucian classics rather than their command of modern ideas; and the numerous unequal treaties imposed on it by foreign powers since its defeat in the Opium War with Great Britain in the 1840s. Westerners roamed throughout China. Merchants, adventurers, diplomats, and missionaries all enjoyed special privileges placing them beyond Chinese authority, a situation that was humiliating to all Chinese. Those privileges included foreign spheres of influence and foreign concessions, foreign troops and police, foreign post offices and telegraph agencies, and consular jurisdiction that kept foreigners beyond the reach of Chinese justice.

Layered atop all of China's other discontents was a split between two centers of political and military power, each of which was determined to unify, govern, and strengthen China. The Guomindang—or Nationalist—forces led by Chiang Kai-shek were generally supported by the United States. But beginning in the 1920s, an initially small upstart group of communists led by Mao Zedong articulated its own vision of mobilizing mass support to overthrow China's antiquated social order and to restore unity to the nation.

As the two forces began their titanic struggle in earnest, China endured yet another devastating blow, this time from Japan's exceptionally brutal aggression, first in its invasion of Manchuria in 1931 and then throughout its bloody drive through China proper from 1937 to 1945. The defeat of Japanese forces by the United States in 1945 renewed the violent conclusive phase of the internal battle to control China between Chiang Kai-shek's

Nationalist forces and Mao Zedong's communist followers. By the autumn of 1949, China's communists emerged victorious and drove Chiang's forces to the island refuge of Taiwan.

In October 1949 Mao could boast to the assembled mass in Beijing's Tiananmen Square that "China has stood up." China was at long last unified under a strong central authority and foreign intervention in its internal affairs would no longer be tolerated. Beyond unification and the reclamation of China's sovereignty, it was Mao's abiding passion to create within China a radical, egalitarian society. In so doing, China remained largely outside the international community, terribly repressive within, and its people mired in poverty throughout his rule from 1949 to 1976.

Mao's death created a scramble for power among China's ruling elites. Within a year, Deng Xiaoping had effectively consolidated governing authority within his own hands. Purged three times during Mao's reign and standing less than five feet tall, Deng seemed at first glance to be an unlikely ruler of the world's most populous state. Deng soon implemented his famous "Four Modernizations" campaign. Undaunted by the giant shadow cast by Mao, Deng announced an audacious series of reforms designed to advance China beyond the revolutionary dogma of Maoism and to create instead a stronger, more modern country by loosening the reins of state authority; more fully embracing economic globalization in search of foreign markets, technology, and investment; and accepting income differentials in a society that had so recently been singularly animated by radical egalitarianism.

The Four Modernizations—agriculture, science and technology, industry, and -military—began in the countryside, home to three-fourths of all Chinese. Gradually, socialist-style communal farming was phased out, and explicitly, peasants were now allowed to lease land individually from the state. Without quite admitting it, Deng's regime injected market—that is, *capitalist*—incentives by allowing peasants whose production surpassed their obligatory quotas to the state at fixed prices to sell any surplus that they could produce for as much money as they could get for it. A system of rural markets and distribution systems sprang up to buy farm produce and sell it to independent urban vendors. As longer land leases gave peasants new incentives to undertake capital improvements, food production soared. With it, rural incomes rose sharply, with the most successful peasant families reaping the greatest rewards.

The older norm of imposed egalitarianism was quietly shelved. What the regime today calls "Socialism with Chinese Characteristics" took its place. With the passage of time this slogan has simply become a euphemism for capitalism with state supervision, but with less direct central control. Gradually, the limited market system begun in the countryside spread to the cities. Individuals were allowed to open restaurants, shops, and factories. Workers could be hired and fired, something that had been utterly unthinkable under Mao's "people's" regime. The wheels of a more market-driven economy were thus set into motion.

The second and third modernizations—industry plus science and technology—inherently required China's leaders to turn outward to the most advanced industrial countries for investment capital, markets for Chinese goods, scientific know-how, and the most modern production technology and management skills. Four Special Economic

Zones (SEZs) were established in southeastern China in which foreign corporations were allowed to form joint ventures with Chinese partners and thus transfer their leading-edge technological, manufacturing process, and managerial expertise to initially quite limited enclaves of capitalist experimentation.

As local laboratories of industrial modernity, the SEZs were intended to, among other things, create a new leadership cohort of technologically sophisticated managers whose expertise, it was hoped, would in time fan out from the SEZs themselves and help jump-start China's obsolescent and inefficient state-owned enterprises (SOEs). During Mao's era, "redness"—that is, communist ideological purity—was more highly prized than substantive expertise in filling leadership ranks. But Deng was much more of a pragmatist. In his famous aphorism, he said, "It doesn't matter if a cat is white or black, as long as it catches mice." Results, then, would be the new measure of the country's rising managers and leaders, not their ritual incantation of Marxist-Maoist dogma. The Deng program provided the launching pad for China's ascent into the realm of world powers, including the fourth modernization, military power. How far will it ascend? How will China use its new status? To answer these questions, we will assess China on three dimensions: economic growth, military strength, and diplomacy.

ECONOMIC GROWTH, BUT QUESTIONS

China's economic results have been the most dramatic. Riding a boom powered by foreign capital inflows and an aggressive export strategy, China's economy grew at an average annual rate of around 10 percent from the 1980s into the 2000s. Not all China specialists accept these astounding government-promulgated growth statistics at face value. Regardless of the figures one accepts, there is no denying the fact that China's economy has grown dramatically during the past quarter century. It is today the world's third-largest economy, ranking only behind the United States and Japan. In critical consumer sectors such as clothing, shoes, toys and other low-technology products, China dominates world markets.

China's recent leaders—Deng Xiaoping and Jiang Zemin—have realized that for their country to develop and modernize economically, they would have to thoroughly repudiate Mao's policies of economic self-sufficiency and instead fully embrace economic globalization. The international trend toward reducing barriers to the free movement of goods and capital has very much worked to China's advantage. In recognition of this fact, China made a major initiative to gain membership in the World Trade Organization (WTO), a goal it achieved late in 2000. As a precursor to its accession to the WTO, China negotiated a complex commercial agreement with the United States that contains a number of key concessions on China's part. Especially notable among them are market-opening measures that place many of its state-owned industries at a competitive disadvantage, thus risking a substantial loss of jobs for Chinese workers. This process has produced both WTO membership and permanent trade relations for China with the United States, but at the cost of forcing China to accept international norms that tie the country more fully to the international community and limit its ability to act outside systemic rules.

China's dramatic economic ascent is also conditioned by a litany of domestic woes that, taken together, raise the alarming possibility of widespread unrest. Its internal preoccupations include a mounting political crisis of regime legitimacy in what Minxin Pei describes as the "Chinese neo-Leninist state," severe environmental degradation, immense population pressures, official corruption, a growing gap in urban versus rural incomes, high unemployment, a steady loss of arable land, a diminished social safety net for the poor and displaced, scarcity of resources like water and petroleum, and secessionist movements in Tibet and in the westernmost province of Zinjiang.

China's rise as an economic power is thus paradoxical. China has made great strides as an industrial power, but it has done so within the confines of a political and social system that places serious constraints on the ability of China to expand, especially into a world power, if that is its desire. Thus, individually and collectively, what do these trends and problems mean, and how do they affect our assessment of China as a rising power?

Assessing China's Economic Rise

Does China's economic and technological rise pose a threat to the world power balance? The sheer potential size of an economy energized by one-fifth of mankind raises concern: If China were to become competitive structurally with the world's most advanced economies, would that size not pose a danger of simply overwhelming the global economy and establishing itself as the "800-pound gorilla" that everyone else would have to treat with care and deference? As an illustration of this possibility, China's announced intent to increase automobile production to up to 15 million vehicles per year to service its domestic market has created palpitations in the petroleum market worldwide, as such a move could greatly increase China's presence in the petroleum-buying market, and increase demand worldwide and drive up energy prices.

Opinions vary on this subject, based on differing assessments of the nature of the Chinese economy and the impact on the Chinese political system. Analysts critical of the notion China poses a threat tend to point to factors in Chinese development that limit the threats China could pose. In a recent *Foreign Affairs* article, for instance, David and Lyric Hughes Hale point to three of what they call the "dragon's ailments." The first is demographic and points to the extremely uneven character of Chinese development. There are, they point out, "great disparities between the integrated, largely urban coastal areas in the eastern part of the country and the fragmented, rural economies in the western part." In addition, there is a considerable unemployment problem, especially in western China that results in considerable migration to the industrialized areas. China also faces the need "to find a way to support its rapidly aging population," a dilemma shared by many industrialized countries.

That is not all. As already noted, much of the prosperity associated with the SEZs is the result of foreign collaboration and investment that limit future independence for the Chinese economy, and thus potentially threatens further development. In the July/August 2004 *Foreign Affairs*, Gilboy accentuates how this attenuates the threat posed by Chinese growth. "First, China's high-tech and industrial exports are dominated by foreign, not Chinese, firms. Second, Chinese industrial firms are deeply dependent on designs, critical components, and manufacturing equipment they import from the United States. . . . Third, Chinese firms are taking few effective steps to absorb the technology they are importing." Huang and Khanna, writing in *Foreign Policy*, agree, pointing out that "[f]ew of these products are made by indigenous Chinese companies. In fact, you would be hard-pressed to find a single homegrown Chinese firm that operates on a global scale and markets its own products abroad. The Chinese economy has taken off, but few local firms have followed." In fact, most of the collaboration is between foreigners and the notoriously inefficient SOEs. Minxin Pei adds that the private sector is no more than 30 percent of the overall Chinese economy.

Most observers also agree that the emergence of a technologically competitive China requires political reform. As Orville Schell argues in the July/August 2004 *Foreign Affairs*, "Whether the PRC will be able to continue straddling the widening divide between the economic system and its anachronistic political system is the most critical question China faces." The situation is ironic, because of the likely effect political reform would have on China's role as a world power. As George Gilboy puts it, "The paradox of China's technological and economic power is that China must implement structural political reforms before it can unlock its potential as a global competitor. But if it were to undertake such reforms, it would likely discover even greater common interests with the United States and other industrialized democracies." In this view, China can be antagonistic and not very threatening or competitive, vibrant, and friendly.

China's economic rise since 1979 has been spectacular, especially in the area of industrial production of lower-end goods like textiles and toys, but the growth of other Asian states like Japan, South Korea, and Taiwan has been as great or greater. Martin Wolf, for instance, suggests the Chinese "miracle" should be taken in context. As he puts it, "Given where the country started in 1978, the country should have grown even faster."

THE "FOURTH MODERNIZATION": MILITARY ENHANCEMENT

In recent years, China's leaders have introduced major changes in the nature, missions, and size of the Chinese military, and especially the People's Liberation Army (PLA). Originally designed to wage defensive "people's wars" on the ground, the PLA traditionally stressed massive numbers of light infantry and sought to compensate for China's low industrial and technological base with an overwhelming mass of ground forces.

That emphasis has changed. In recent years, China has moved to modernize its military force and to create a more technologically sophisticated defense mechanism that is more reflective of and competitive with the force of other states.

Three factors have influenced this change, two of which were based in observations about the past. The first was China's disastrous intrusion into Vietnam in 1979 to chasten the Vietnamese for their activities in Cambodia but which ended in a major embarrassment for Chinese forces. The second was the enormous success of highly technological U.S. forces in the Persian Gulf in 1991. The Gulf War created in China a heightened awareness of its own backwardness in weapons technology, unit coordination, and force mobility.

Third, China's strategic priority has shifted somewhat away from defending against receding threats of ground invasion of its core home territory. Today, its political-military strategy is more focused on (1) defending its new industrial centers concentrated along its Pacific coast, (2) preventing the Chinese-claimed Taiwan from making a formal bid for independence, and (3) securing China's claim of sovereignty over all of the Spratly Islands in the South China Sea, a potentially oil-rich assortment of islets also claimed in whole or in part by Taiwan, Brunei, Malaysia, and the Philippines. With the end of the Cold War, China's potential military confrontation with traditional rivals like Russia, Japan, India,

Map 3.1 Map of China and surrounding areas, including Spratly Islands

and even the United States have unquestionably receded, but the new environment is more fluid and unpredictable. As an example, David Zwieg and B. Jainhai point out that increased Chinese dependence on Persian Gulf oil means that "whoever controls the Straits of Malacca and Indian Ocean could block China's oil transport route."

Elements of Modernization

China has clearly invested heavily in updating its military forces. Two measures of this commitment are changes in the size of the military and in the amount of military spending.

In terms of *size,* China's forces had recently shrunk from a three million to a two-and-a-quarter million–man force in 2003, and additional uniformed slots are currently being phased out. Prevailing doctrine has it that a leaner, better trained, and more technologically equipped force is better suited to meet the country's security requirements in light of the extraordinary advances made by other states, particularly the United States. As measured by *spending,* China has clearly made military modernization a leading priority. In 2000, for example, official on-the-books defense spending rose by 12.7 percent in an economy that grew by only 7 percent. In 2004, Chinese defense spending was $67.5 billion, compared to over $400 billion by the United States. Although these figures are not directly comparable (the Chinese pay their soldiers far less than their American counterparts, for instance), the gap is in orders of magnitude.

What has increased spending bought? China's recent *weapons acquisition* program has proceeded along two tracks: (1) indigenous development and (2) foreign purchases. As noted earlier, Beijing's strategic focus has shifted toward potential clashes over disputed islands in the South China Sea, with Taiwan should it make a formal attempt at independence, and against any threat to its new industrial centers near the Pacific Ocean. Each emphasis requires modernization efforts in China's air and naval forces.

China's fleet of fighter aircraft is outmoded by today's standards. Its domestically produced F-8II (one of which crashed after colliding with an American "spy" plane off the Chinese coast in April 2001) is broadly comparable to a U.S. F-4, a 1960s aircraft. The J-10, a more advanced fighter, is now under development. Based in part on Israeli technology, the J-10 will enhance China's jet fighter capabilities, but a substantial amount of time is required to develop, test, manufacture, and deploy complex modern aircraft.

As to warships, China's "blue water" fleet—that is, its oceangoing ships as opposed to its "gray water" coastal vessels—is relatively small and not terribly advanced by contemporary standards. Its navy has equipped some of its fleet with radar-guided surface-to-surface missiles. In some ways, this represents a substantial enhancement of its naval might, but it must be noted that the missiles deployed—the old-fashioned HY-2—are liquid-fueled and inherently volatile, and thus could be quite dangerous to China's navy itself. Also, they can be reloaded only while the ships are in port. To date, China has been unable to acquire the one naval asset that represents true long-distance power-projection capability—a fleet of aircraft carriers. Attempts to negotiate foreign purchases have thus far been unsuccessful. And indigenous development seems quite unlikely for the near future given the extraordinary cost involved; the specialized, highly advanced engineering skills required for carrier construction; and the logistical capacity necessary to manage the substantial flotilla of supply ships necessary to support a carrier's operations. Moreover, there is growing agreement that carriers are increasingly vulnerable to missile attacks that will make them obsolescent in the future, making development questionable.

Assessing China's Military Strength

Defense analysts agree that China possesses the military manpower and equipment needed to fend off any foreseeable land-based assault on its core homeland. The sheer size of both the country and of the PLA make a "defense in depth" strategy both feasible for China and daunting to any would-be invader. Any currently imaginable scenario in which an aggressor sought to quash the Beijing regime through invasion would require it to penetrate deep into the country's heartland. Chinese defense planners also believe that the probability that the country will be attacked by nuclear weapons is rather low. Absent an extraordinary escalation of a regional conflict, the states that currently possess both proven warhead and missile delivery capability—the United States, Russia, Britain, France, India, and Pakistan—lack a rational incentive to launch a doomsday nuclear assault on China. Zbigniew Brzezinski points to China's inattention to the nuclear question: "Forty years after acquiring nuclear-weapons technology, China has just 24 ballistic missiles capable of hitting the United States."

What, then, of China's power projection capabilities, that is, what is its ability to impose its will outside of its borders? What, in other words, is China's ability to challenge the current balance of power and stability within the crucial East Asian region? This issue is best divided into two distinct questions: its strategic position vis-à-vis nearby states within continental Asia, and its ability to project its power beyond its territory into the more distant continental and maritime states of East Asia. The possibility that China will assert itself regionally most concerns those who see China as a future threat.

As to its potential to coerce its continental neighbors, it is necessary to stress that China's *latent* strategic dominance of both the Korean peninsula in Northeast Asia and of Indochina (Laos, Cambodia, and Vietnam) in Southeast Asia is a widely accepted reality. The likelihood of it actually employing its coercive capabilities in either location may not be great, but its capacity to wield power in both theaters is simply a reality.

In order to be able to alter significantly the existing balance of power in the broader East Asian region, however, China would have to achieve the ability to project power beyond the mainland. Doing so would require attaining sufficient aerial and naval power-projection capability both to operate in distant locales and to do so with capabilities that surpass those of other states in the region.

As Robert Ross has shown in his insightful article, "Beijing as a Conservative Power," China must contemplate the requirements of acting in three distinct maritime theaters in East Asia: (1) the East China Sea, (2) the northern portion of the South China Sea, and (3) the southern reaches of the South China Sea.

China would have to establish its clear dominance over the first—the East China Sea—in order to seize Taiwan or to reassert its historical primacy over Japan and South Korea. Acquiring and sustaining that primacy would require superior air power in support of naval operations against an adversary. In this theater, China could take advantage of its geographic proximity to utilize its land-based aircraft. But, as noted earlier, China's air force is technologically primitive and severely limited in range. Its outdated inventory of aircraft would fare poorly against Japan's much more sophisticated F2 fighter jet. Also, Japan's aerial defenses are greatly enhanced by its possession of modern AWACS (airborne warning and control system) aircraft, and its fighters are being equipped with much more advanced air-to-air missiles than are China's.

Much the same could be said of Taiwan. More economically advanced than mainland China, Taiwan possesses the wealth, the technology base, and the manufacturing capability to maintain a sophisticated defense against a potential armed takeover by Beijing. Equipped with both an advanced navy and a highly sophisticated air force that includes U.S.-built F-16s, Taiwan can most likely repulse a military assault from the mainland. The important caveat for Taiwan, however, is China's current drive to acquire a growing arsenal of quite accurate cruise and ballistic missiles, virtually all of which are deployed in coastal southeast China and targeted at Taiwan. The warning time for launch of these modern missiles is brief, and in any case Taiwan is unable fully to defend itself against a missile barrage. This is the instrument of choice for Beijing to prevent Taiwan from carrying out a policy of formal independence from the mainland during the next decade or two while China lacks a credible air, sea, and land capability to hold the island against formal secession. Such a barrage could virtually destroy Taiwan, but the results would be a Pyrrhic victory, wiping out one of the largest sources of foreign investment in China. China can destroy Taiwan if it chooses, but what would be the point?

Similarly, China is currently incapable of effectively projecting a great deal of armed might into the southern portion of the South China Sea, the Straits of Malacca, or the Indian Ocean, a region that includes Indonesia, the Philippines, Singapore, and Malaysia. Absent either aircraft carriers or difficult-to-master aerial refueling, the sheer distances involved buffer this region against any potential threat from China's land-based aircraft. Singapore, Malaysia, and Indonesia all have fleets of sophisticated American and British fighters capable of repulsing hostile intrusion by China's navy.

It is in the third regional theater—the northern portion of the South China Sea—where China's land-based aircraft could provide aerial support for both ground operations in Indochina and for operations in the waters near the Paracel Islands east of Vietnam and in the northernmost disputed Spratly Islands. Rightful ownership of the Paracels—which China seized from Vietnam in 1974—is a matter of dispute among Taiwan, Vietnam, and China.

On current evidence, then, fears of a militarily predatory China both bent on, and capable of, imposing its will across East Asia would appear to be minimal. It is true, of course, that China's Fourth Modernization is an evolving phenomenon, and that with the passage of time the country's power-projection capabilities will become more potent than they are today. Whether those forces evolve in a menacing way that poses a threat to its neighbors and to American interests in Asia is the major foreign policy question discussed in the next section.

NONCOERCIVE INFLUENCE: CHINA'S NEW DIPLOMACY

Well aware of its military backwardness and of its economy's growing dependence on trade, China has in recent years adopted what for it is a new style of diplomacy. Until quite recently, the characteristic style of Beijing's envoys abroad was one of secrecy, aloofness, inaccessibility to host media and public organizations, and a pronounced rigidity in repeating abroad the "line" laid down by the Chinese government. Today, however, there is a growing awareness that the old-style diplomacy was an ineffective instrument of advancing China's interests abroad.

Increasingly, Chinese diplomacy reflects a growing sophistication about how best to get the country's message out, an appearance—at least—of sensitivity to the other states' apprehensions, and the appearance in prominent posts of a new generation of diplomats more skilled at the arts of gentle persuasion rather than the dogmatic assertion of unilateral pronouncements. This change represent what Yong Deng and Thomas Moore call "a new foreign policy choice (that) highlights the potential role of globalization in transforming great-power politics from an unmitigated struggle for supremacy . . . to a more cooperative form of interstate competition that increases prospects for China's peaceful rise."

Beyond mere style, Chinese diplomacy has recently focused on (1) joining literally hundreds of international organizations from which it was previously aloof and (2) mending fences with its Asian neighbors. In Southeast Asia, for example, China has adroitly cultivated bilateral ties (its preferred method in international dealings) in order to dilute the political will of the region's states to adopt a common stance in opposing China's claims in the South China Sea. In initiatives as diverse as resolving its longstanding border dispute with Vietnam in 1999 or agreeing to import more of Thailand's goods in exchange for Thai diplomatic efforts on China's behalf in 1997, China's concerted drive to improve its bilateral ties throughout Asia are beginning to pay off.

Diplomacy has become an important foreign policy instrument for a developing China whose coercive and economic instruments of influence remain quite constrained. Thus, its emphasis has shifted to a more cooperative tone. As Chinese official Zheng Biajin puts it, "China advocates a new international political and economic order. China's development depends on world peace—a peace that its development will in turn reinforce."

POLICY ALTERNATIVES: CONTAINMENT OR ENGAGEMENT?

In June 2004, the Organization of Economic Cooperation and Development announced that, for the first time, foreign direct investment to China exceeded that to the United States, knocking the United States from its perpetual position as the number-one recipient of global investment. This reversal was partly the result both of declines in investment in the United States (foreign direct investment to this country went from $167 billion in 2001 to $127 billion in 2002 to $40 billion in 2003) with steady levels of investment in China ($55 billion in 2002 and $53 billion in 2003). Generally, such fluctuations reflect the judgment of investors about the strength of recipient economies. By this measure, at least, China's rise is concrete and undeniable.

But what does China's rise mean for America and the world? Should we worry about it, or embrace it?

Answers to these questions vary considerably and sharply along lines developed throughout this case study. The basis of difference is largely the interpretation of the implications of China's rise. One argument, largely associated with the neoconservatives prominent in the George W. Bush administration, sees China's rise in largely negative, geopolitical terms and concludes that American policy should be to curb or contain China's rise and to use American influence to force China to change into a less threatening place. The opposite position is that the way China is evolving is evidence of the policy of engagement and enlargement of the Clinton years and that, as a result, the United States should continue to emphasize cooperation with an increasingly close global partner. Doing so, they argue, will encourage continued evolution of China to a position as a peaceful member of the international system.

These contrasts are at the heart of this purpose of this study. There are two aspects of the analysis on which the sides agree. First, they agree on the basic data describing China's rise on both the economic and military levels: China rising is not a point of disagreement. Second, they agree on the desired outcome of China's rise: Both the containers and the engagers desire a liberalized, democratic, and capitalist China that is a responsible, "normal" member of the international system. In its 2006 *National Security Strategy*, the Bush administration straddled the issue, arguing the United States "seeks to encourage China to make the right strategic choices for its people, while we hedge against other possibilities."

Containing the Looming Threat

Those concerned with the trajectory of China's rise begin from the premise that China presents a serious geopolitical threat to the United States. As a close advisor to Vice President Richard Cheney argues, "Virtually every serious strategic thinker in the United States agrees that China, if current trends continue, represents a greater potential threat in the long run than any other nation in the world." Robert Kagan and William Kristol, writing in *Present Dangers* (a kind of neoconservative bible), put it: "The past decade also saw the rise of an increasingly hostile and belligerent China." The bases of these assessments include greater Chinese spending on defense coupled with the conviction that the Chinese will divert their growing economic resources to geopolitical ends, including establishing China as the major power in Asia. As Aaron Friedberg argues, "The bottom line is simple: one way or another, China's economic growth will provide it with an increasing array of instruments with which to try to exert influence on other countries and, if it chooses, to carry forward a strategic competition with the United States."

Those who see China primarily as a threat favor a policy of containment of China. In Kagan's words, "A successful containment strategy will require increasing, not decreasing, overall defense capabilities. . . . Containment would seek to compel Beijing to choose political liberalization as the best way to safeguard their economic gains and win acceptance in the international community." Kagan dismisses the idea that China will move toward political liberalization on its own as "Marxian foolishness" and concludes that "as long as China maintains its present form of government, it cannot be peacefully integrated into the international community." The *National Security Strategy* concurs, encouraging "China to continue down the road of reform and openness." According to Friedberg, the alternative to accepting this analysis of China's intention is strategic competition: "[T]he first order of business is to see the situation plain—namely, that in several important respects a U.S.–PRC strategic competition is already underway, and there is a good chance that it is only going to become more intense and open. In recognizing these realities, the Chinese are well ahead of the United States."

Engaging the Global Partner

Not everyone accepts the neoconservative facts as true or their realities as real. Looking at the same set of conditions and trends, Gilboy, for instance, finds those conclusions overblown but potentially dangerous: "[O]verestimates of China's achievements and potential are fueling fears that the country will inevitably tilt global trade and technology in its favor, ultimately becoming a military threat to the United States." In addition, these fears are based, according to Segal, "on the fear that the United States provides China both with money and particularly advanced technologies."

This latter point clearly demonstrates conflicting interpretations of trends. As noted earlier, the Chinese indeed import American technology, mostly from American firms operating in China. But does this create a problem, and for whom? One interpretation can be that such importation increases China's technological base, which can be applied to military prowess. Another interpretation is that importing technology simply makes China more dependent on the United States. Or it may be a bit of both.

Those who interpret China's rise positively contradict the assertion of increased Chinese hostility. Evan Medeiros and M. T. Fravel, for instance, suggest that "in recent years, China has begun to take a less confrontational, more sophisticated, more confident, and, at times, more constructive approach toward regional and global affairs." Moreover, Deng and Moore maintain the Chinese have basically accepted their role in the evolving order: "In the minds of most Chinese observers, the persistence (and even strengthening) of U.S. primacy after the Cold War has rendered balancing a relatively impractical alternative." Medeiros and Fravel concur: "Chinese analysts now acknowledge that their country cannot (and will not) challenge U.S. global dominance anytime soon." China, in other words, will become a responsible global citizen because it has little choice.

CONCLUSION

China is, as pointed out at the beginning, unquestionably a rising power, and like rising powers in the past, the consequences of its ascent are uncertain and subject to varying, even diametrically opposed, interpretation. No one can reliably look into the future and know for certain how it will be: whether China will be an increasingly looming threat or a global partner. The facts are not terribly at odds with one another, but what they mean differs greatly, depending on one's perspectives.

Of course, there is a third alternative: China could evolve as *both* a rival and as a partner. Or, it may be that the kinds of policies that evolve for dealing with China may influence the trajectory of that development. In this latter regard, Walter Mead makes a case for using American economic power—what he calls sticky power (institutions and policies that attract others toward U.S. policies and then traps them in it)—to influence China's rise. "As China develops economically, it should gain wealth that could support a military rivaling that of the United States; China is also gaining political influence in the world. Sticky power offers a way out. China benefits from participating in the U.S. economy and integrating itself into the global economy."

How China evolves as a power depends partly on how Chinese politics evolve. Minxin Pei, for instance, argues, "It is premature to dismiss the inherent instability of China's authoritarian politics," which "rests on fragile political institutions, little rule of law, and corrupt governance." On the other hand, Kishore Mahhubani admits ongoing corruption, but maintains "China is run by the best governing class in generations . . . including many young mayors who have been trained at U.S. universities."

In the end, what kind of a rising power will China be? And how does the world deal with China? In terms of accommodating the new power, Zwieg, and Jianhai maintain the old power must adapt or face the consequences: "The United States, as the world's hegemon, must somehow make room for the rising giant, otherwise, war will become a serious possibility." In less negative terms, Wang Jisi suggests "China and the United States cannot hope to establish truly friendly relations. Yet, the countries should be able to build friendly ties." And yet, the outcome remains uncertain. In Minxin Pei's words, "China may be rising, but no one knows whether it can fly."

STUDY/DISCUSSION QUESTIONS

1. What is a rising power? Why is the concept important in understanding the nature of international politics and changes in the balance of power? As suggested in the introduction, rising powers arise periodically. To get some flavor of the process and why it is confusing and controversial, put yourself in the position of being a European in the late nineteenth century trying to assess the impact the United States would eventually have. Would you view the United States as a looming threat or a global partner? Why?

2. A primary source of China's rise is economic. Although China's economy has indeed expanded greatly, there is disagreement about the nature of that growth and what it means. Try to construct two arguments, one that points to the emergence of China as a major competitor and rival, and one that suggests Chinese economic development is less ominous. Compare the two arguments. Where do they agree and disagree?

3. China has also been engaged in military development. Describe the nature and outcomes of that development and the military problems to which they are aimed. Based on your reading, do these developments provide basic threats to the United States and its interests? Why or why not?

4. What are the commonly accepted facts about China's rise on which analysts on both sides of the question agree? How do they reach diametrically opposed conclusions based on these facts?

5. Describe and assess the arguments that a rising China is primarily a looming threat and that it is moving toward being a global partner. Based on your understanding of the facts and arguments, which do you find more compelling? Why?

READING/RESEARCH MATERIAL

Biajan, Zheng. "China's 'Peaceful Rise' to Great-Power Status." *Foreign Affairs* 84, 5 (September/October 2005), 18–24.

Brzezinski, Zbigniew. "Make Money, Not War." *Foreign Policy,* January/February 2005, 46–47.

Deng, Yong, and Thomas G. Moore. "China Views Globalization: Toward a New Great Power Politics?" *Washington Quarterly* 27, 3 (Summer 2004), 117–136.

Friedberg, Aaron L. "The Struggle for Mastery in Asia." *Commentary,* November 2000.

Frisbie, John, and Michael Overmayer, "U.S.-China Economic Relations: The Next Stage." *Current History* 105, 692 (September 2006), 243–249.

Gilboy, George J. "The Myth Behind China's Miracle." *Foreign Affairs* 83, 4 (July/August 2004), 33–48.

Hale, David, and Lyric Hughes Hale. "China Takes Off." *Foreign Affairs* 82, 6 (November/December 2003), 36–53.

Huang, Yasheng, and Tarun Khanna. "Can India Overtake China?" *Foreign Policy,* July/August 2003, 74–81.

Jisi, Wang. "China's Search for Stability with America." *Foreign Affairs* 84, 5 (September/October 2005), 39–48.

Kagan, Robert. "What China Knows That We Don't: The Case for a New Strategy of Containment." *The Weekly Standard,* January 20, 1997.

———, and William Kristol (eds.). *Present Dangers: Crisis and Opportunity in American Foreign and Defense Policy.* San Francisco, CA: Encounter Books.

Lampton, David M. "The Faces of Chinese Power." *Foreign Affairs* 86, 1 (January/February 2007), 115–127.

Mahhabuni, Kishore. "Understanding China." *Foreign Affairs* 84, 5 (September/October 2005), 49–60.

Mead, Walter Russell. "America's Sticky Power." *Foreign Policy,* March/April 2004, 46–53.

Medeiros, Evan S. and M. Taylor Fravel. "China's New Diplomacy." *Foreign Affairs* 82, 6 (November/December 2003), 22–35.

The National Security Strategy of the United States of America. Washington, DC: The White House, March 2006.

Pei, Minxin. "Dangerous Denials." *Foreign Policy,* January/February 2005, 54–56.

———. "The Dark Side of China's Rise." *Foreign Policy,* March/April 2006, 32–40.

Ross, Robert S. "Beijing as a Conservative Power." *Foreign Affairs* 76; 2 (March/April 1997), 33–44.

Schell, Orville. "China's Hidden Democratic Legacy." *Foreign Affairs* 83, 4 (July/August 2004), 116–124.

Segal, Adam. "Practical Engagement: Drawing a Fine Line for U.S.-China Trade." *Washington Quarterly* 27, 3 (Summer 2004), 157–173.

Starr, John Bryan. *Understanding China: A Guide to China's Economy, History, and Political Structure.* Hill and Wang, 1997.

Swaine, Michael D., and Ashley J. Tellis. *Interpreting China's Grand Strategy: Past, Present, and Future.* Sonta Montea, CA: RAND, 2000.

Wolf, Martin. "Why Is China Growing So Slowly?" *Foreign Policy,* January/February 2005, 49–52.

Zwieg, David, and Bi Jianhai. "China's Global Hunt for Energy." *Foreign Affairs* 84, 5 (September/October 2005), 25–36.

WEB SITES

A general overview of China at www.insidechina.com

Comprehensive overview of the Taiwan question at http://taiwansecurity.org

A compendium of online sources about Chinese military policy and capabilities

Chinese Military Power at http://www.comw.org/cmp

Index of Web-based information relating to Chinese foreign relations

Chinese Foreign Policy Net at http://www.Stanford.edu/-fravel/chinafp.htm

A compendium of Chinese foreign affairs position papers

State Council Information Office at www.china.org.cn

Ministry of Foreign Affairs at www.fmprc.gov.cn

Systematic overview prepared by Federal Research Division of Library of Congress

China, a Country Study at http://memory.loc.gov/frd/cs/cntoc.html

PART II

Evolving Dynamics of International Relations

The cases in this part of the book deal, directly or indirectly, with the question of sovereignty within the international system, a major area of concern both to practitioners and students of international relations. Two of the studies deal with areas that represent direct challenges to the total supremacy of the territorial state in specific areas of state practice; the third deals with adjustments of sovereign boundaries within one of the traditionally most volatile parts of the world, the Middle East.

Challenges to sovereignty certainly are not a unique characteristic of the post–Cold War world. The concept has evolved over time from a justification for the ruling monarchs of Europe to hold total sway over their kingdoms (and to treat their citizens however they wanted) to a more restrained version of what constitutes sovereign authority and how it can be exercised consistent with international norms. Many of the challenges have their genesis in the Cold War period and have continued with the breakdown of the Cold War competition. The two direct challenges in this part are of that general nature.

Chapter 4, "War Crimes," examines the evolution of international consideration of criminal actions taken during wartime. The case traces the emergence of the idea of "crimes against humanity," which is used more or less synonymously with war crimes in contemporary usage, from the war crimes trials against the Axis powers at the end of World War II through the ad hoc tribunals set up in the 1990s in places like Bosnia and Rwanda to the present. The case culminates with the controversy over the creation of a permanent war crimes tribunal, the International Criminal Court, as a tool of international justice, examining the court's utility in cases like those involving the late Slobadan Milosevic and Saddam Hussein.

Chapter 5, "International Permission Slips," is connected to the war crimes' chapter in two ways. First, many of the war crimes occur in contemporary internal wars, and it is the atrocities that are committed that cause members of the international system to consider intrusion. Second, the assertion that there is an international right to intervene is a direct assault on the territorial sovereignty of states where it is invoked. The consequences for sovereignty and international norms come in direct conflict in these cases. Iraq serves as an example of these difficult problems.

The third chapter, "Irresolvable Conflicts: The Israeli-Palestinian Conflict," examines the attempts of the parties and outsiders like the United States to negotiate a peace settlement between Israel and the Palestinians. The case is illustrative of important dynamics in international relations in two ways. First, the issues dividing the parties may be so fundamental that they cannot be resolved to the satisfaction of both parties, despite the concerted efforts of outside mediators (notably the United States) over a long period. Second, the case also reflects the enduring importance of sovereignty, since the most basic cause of intractability centers on the question of sovereign control and access over the disputed territories.

CHAPTER FOUR

War Crimes

THE PAST IN THE PRESENT
IN THE FUTURE

PRÉCIS

Although events in the 1990s in places like Bosnia and Rwanda made the idea of war crimes and their prosecution a widely recognized part of international relations, the notion is relatively recent in its derivation. There have always been more or less well-accepted and enforced rules for conducting war, the violation of which was deemed criminal, but the ideas of crimes against peace and, especially, crimes against humanity are largely the result of the prosecution of German and Japanese officials after World War II. The 1990s revived this interest, which had receded during the Cold War.

Major aspects of the war crimes issue are highlighted in this case. Following an introduction that lays out basic history and concepts, the case concentrates on three related aspects, all of which have placed the U.S. government in a controversial situation in the international community. One aspect is the International Criminal Court (ICC), a permanent tribunal with jurisdiction over alleged war crimes. The second aspect is the assault on sovereignty implicit in the ICC statute; by granting jurisdiction to the court over war crimes, the sovereign control of a country over its citizens who may be accused of war crimes is compromised, a possibility that has led the United States and a handful of other states to reject the ICC's jurisdiction. Finally, the case will examine the viability of the ICC concept through the hypothetical use of the court in the trials against the late Slobadan Milosevic and Saddam Hussein.

In the middle of the 1986 Vietnam War movie *Platoon,* the group of American soldiers who are the subject of the story are on patrol and discover one of their fellows killed, presumably by the Viet Cong (VC), for whom the patrol is searching. The incident occurs near a small Vietnamese village, raising suspicions that it was VC from the village who perpetrated the killing, although members of the patrol have no direct evidence linking the village to the death of their comrade.

The patrol enters the village, apparently populated by innocent civilians, mostly older men and women, children, and one obviously severely retarded young man. The patrol discovers food supplies clearly excessive to the needs of the villagers and concludes this is a VC food stash, providing "evidence" of VC presence. Members of the patrol attempt to coerce admissions from village residents that they are VC. When the villagers refuse to confess, the soldiers become physically abusive: an old woman is executed with a pistol, the young retarded man is beaten to death with a rifle butt, a young girl is raped, and ultimately the village is set on fire as the remaining villagers flee in a panic.

Did the platoon engage in war crimes for which they might—or should—have been punished? At the time the film was released, the major purpose of the scene was to demonstrate the brutality of the Vietnam War, including the outrageous acts committed by both sides, in this case by American soldiers, and the psychological effects committing these acts had on them and the war.

Although the scene draws on the factual My Lai incident, almost no one at the time raised the question of whether the scene depicted war crimes; had the movie been released in 2007, that would have been one of the first questions asked. More recently, revelations of criminal behavior against prisoners in Abu Ghraib prison in Baghdad and at Guantanamo Bay in Cuba have reenergized our concern. What had changed in the interim?

The answer is that an important phenomenon to reenter the international dialogue during the 1990s was the subject of war crimes. The immediate precipitant had been a rash of so-called humanitarian disasters, in which intolerable acts against groups within states, often grouped under the name "ethnic cleansing," occurred during the decade. The worst of these occurred in Bosnia during the early 1990s and in Rwanda in 1994. A somewhat more limited case occurred in Kosovo in 1998–1999. The result, according to one source, is a paradox: "Humanitarian law and international human rights has never been more developed, yet never before have human rights been violated more frequently. This state of affairs will not improve absent a mechanism to enforce those laws and the norms they embody." The engoing tragedy in Darfur, Sudan accentuates these concerns.

This quote suggests that the contemporary concern with war crimes stems from two parallel developments. One is the assertion that there are universal human rights to which people and groups are entitled and that, when they are violated, are subject to penalty. The second is an interest in some form of *international* mechanism for dealing with violators of these norms.

While the ideas of defining criminal behavior and enforcement of laws in international, universal terms may not seem extraordinary, both are in fact of recent origin in international affairs. The idea of universal human rights transcending state boundaries is really a phenomenon of the post–World War II period; the primary crime that has been identified in war crimes, genocide, was not identified until the word was coined by Richard Lemkin in 1944, and the United Nations Convention on Genocide, which bans the commission of genocide, was not passed until 1948. Similarly, the term *war crimes,* which now refers to a broad range of activities associated with war, was basically associated with violations of the so-called laws of war (actions permissible and impermissible during wartime) until war crimes trials were convened in Nuremburg and Tokyo to prosecute accused Nazi and Japanese violators after World War II. Following those trials, the subject remained fallow until it was revived in the 1990s.

The subject of war crimes is unlikely to disappear from international discourse any time soon, for at least three reasons. First, acts now defined as war crimes continue to be committed in many places. Exclusionary nationalism (when national groups persecute nonmembers) in some developing-world states may actually increase the number of savage acts that are now considered war crimes. Second, the war crimes trials involving Bosnia and Rwanda that were empanelled in the early 1990s have only begun their work, and the international legal community fully recognizes that the outcomes of those trials will influence the subject in the future. Third, definitions are rapidly evolving. Rape, for instance, has only recently been added to the list of punishable crimes against humanity. Terrorist mass murders almost certainly qualify as well. The trial of Saddam Hussein gave wide publicity to these phenomena. Fourth, one outcome of the concern for war crimes has been the establishment of a permanent International Criminal Court with mandatory jurisdiction over war crimes.

This statement of the problem suggests the direction this case study will take. We will begin with a brief historical overview of war crimes, emphasizing the major point that whereas the idea of crimes of war has long been part of international concerns, war crimes as we now think of them are of recent vintage. We will then look at the various categories of war crimes that arose from the experience of the war crimes trials at the end of World War II. Since concern for war crimes was dormant during the Cold War, the discussion will move forward to the contemporary period, when the existence of well-documented atrocities in places like Bosnia and Rwanda rekindled interest in the subject. The Bosnian and Rwandan cases sparked interest in a permanent war crimes tribunal, the International Criminal Court (ICC). The major opponent of the ICC as proposed at the Rome Conference of 1998 has been the United States, for a variety of reasons. The case concludes with an assessment of the problem of war crimes and the barriers to creating a permanent tribunal, the key elements of which revolve around the concept of sovereignty. The trials of Milosevic and Hussein provide examples of points raised.

BACKGROUND OF THE PROBLEM

The idea of war crimes is both very old and very new. Throughout most of history, the term has been associated with conformity to the so-called laws of war. This usage can be traced back as far as 200 B.C., when a code of the permissible behavior in war was formulated in the Hindu Code of Manu. Enumeration of codes of warfare were part of Roman law and practiced throughout Europe. These rules began to be codified into international law following the Thirty Years' War (1618–1648), when most of Europe was swept up in very brutal religiously based warfare. The first definitive international law text, Hugo Grotius's *Concerning the Law of War and Peace,* was published in 1625 and included the admonition that "war ought not to be undertaken except for the enforcement of rights; when once undertaken, it should be carried on only within the bounds of law and good faith." Definitions of the laws of war, and hence violations of those laws, developed gradually during the eighteenth and nineteenth centuries, culminating in the Geneva and Hague Conventions of 1899 and 1907.

The concerns expressed in the laws of war continue to be an important part of international law, but the idea of war crimes has been expanded to cover other areas of conduct in war in the twentieth century. The precipitant for this expansion was World War II and wartime atrocities committed by the Axis powers (notably Germany and Japan). Some of the crimes fit traditional definitions of war crimes—the mistreatment of American and other prisoners of war (POWs) by the Japanese during the infamous Bataan death march, for instance. Many actions, however, went well beyond the conduct of war per se, as in the systematic extermination of Jews, Gypsies, and other groups in the Holocaust by Germany and the so-called Rape of Nanking, in which Japanese soldiers went on a rampage and reportedly slaughtered nearly 300,000 citizens of that Chinese city (some Japanese sources dispute the numbers) on the pretext that some of them were soldiers hiding among the civilians.

The laws of war as they had evolved before World War II were inadequate to deal with this expansion in the use of military force to systematically brutalize civilian populations. There had been discussion about limitations on fighting and the treatment of noncombatants prior to World War I, but there were no real enforcement mechanisms to deal with transgressions, a recurring problem in enforcing war crimes violations that the ICC seeks to rectify.

The Impact of World War II

World War II provided the impetus for change. It was a truly global and brutal war, and one of its major "innovations" was to extend what the American general William Tecumseh Sherman called the "hard hand of war" during the Civil War to civilian populations. The Allies discussed the problem throughout the war. The first formal statement on the subject was the Moscow declaration of 1943, which stated that Nazi officials guilty of "atrocities, massacres, and executions" would be sent to the countries in which they committed their crimes for trial and appropriate punishment.

The document that defined modern war crimes precedent was the London Agreement of August 8, 1945. It did two major things. First, it established the International Military Tribunal as the court that would try alleged war crimes and thereby set the precedent for a formal, permanent body later on. At the time, it specifically set the groundwork for the Nuremberg and Tokyo tribunals. Second, the agreement established the boundaries of its jurisdiction, which have become the standard means for defining war crimes.

The London Agreement defines three kinds of war crimes. The first is *crimes against peace,* "namely, planning, preparation, initiation, or waging of a war of aggression, or a war in violation of international treaties, agreements or assurances, or participation in a common plan or conspiracy for the accomplishment of any of the foregoing." This admonition was reinforced by the United Nations Charter that same year, in which the signatories relinquished the "right" to initiate war. Under this definition, the North Korean invasion of South Korea in 1950, or the invasion and conquest of Kuwait by Saddam Hussein's Iraq in 1990 both qualify as crimes against peace. What should be clearly noted is that this definition applies most obviously and directly to wars between independent states because of its emphasis on territorial aggression. The U.S. invasion of Iraq arguably also qualifies as a crime against peace.

The second category reiterates the traditional usage of the concept. *War crimes* are defined as "violations of the laws or customs of war. Such violations shall include, but not be limited to, murder, ill-treatment or deportation to slave labor or for any other purpose of civilian population of or in occupied territory, murder or ill-treatment of prisoners of war or persons on the seas, killing of hostages, plunder of public or private property, wanton destruction of cities, towns or villages, or devastation not justified by military necessity." This enumeration, of course, was a virtual laundry list of accusations against the Germans and the Japanese (although the Allies arguably committed some of the same acts). Although acts against civilians are mentioned in the listing, the crimes enumerated are limited to mistreatment of general civilian populations rather than their systematic extension to individuals and segments of the population.

The third category was the most innovative and controversial. It is also the type of war crimes with which the concept is most closely associated in the current debate. *Crimes against humanity* are defined as "murder, extermination, enslavement, deportation, and other inhumane acts committed against any civilian population, before or during the war; or persecutions on political, racial or religious grounds in execution of or in connection with any crime . . . whether or not in violation of the domestic law where perpetuated." The statute goes further, establishing the basis of responsibility and thus vulnerability to prosecution. "Leaders, organizers, instigators, or accomplices participating in the formulation or execution of a common plan or conspiracy to commit any of the foregoing crimes are responsible for all acts performed by any persons in execution of such plan." This latter enumeration of responsibility justified the indictment of former Yugoslav president Slobadan Milosevic, who was never accused of carrying out acts qualifying as war crimes, and also against Saddam Hussein.

To someone whose experience is limited to the latter part of the twentieth century, this notion of crimes against humanity may not seem radical, or possibly even unusual. At the time, however, they clearly were, for several reasons. First, they criminalized actions by states (or groups within states) that, while not exactly common in human history, were certainly not unknown but previously not thought of as criminal. Imagine, for instance, Genghis Khan and the leaders of the Golden Horde being placed in the docket. Or the Ottoman Turk executors of the genocidal campaign against the Armenians early in the twentieth century. Or, for that matter, the post–Civil War campaigns by the U.S. government against the Western Indian tribes (e.g., Wounded Knee).

The second radical idea contained in the definition is that of jurisdiction. By stating that crimes against humanity are enforceable "whether or not in violation of the domestic law" of the places they occur, the definition creates a universality to its delineation which, among other things, seems to transcend the sovereign rights of states to order events as they choose within their territory. That assertion remains at the base of controversy about the institutionalization of war crimes, because it entwines war criminal behavior (the reprehensibility of which is agreed upon) with the controversy over sovereignty (about which there is considerable disagreement). Third, the statute seeks to remove the defense that crimes against humanity can be justified on the basis they were committed on orders from a superior (a matter of some interest in the Abu Ghraib case). Thus, anyone with any part in crimes against humanity is equally vulnerable under the law, and this provision allows the tribunal to delve as deeply as it wishes into the offenders' hierarchy.

The statute does not address one element about war crimes prosecution that is almost always raised. It is the problem of so-called victor's law: the charge that war crimes are always defined by the winning side in a war, and those tried are always those from the losing side. The Nuremberg and Tokyo tribunals labored hard and long to make the proceedings as judicially fair as they could; it is nonetheless true that it was Germans and Japanese in the dock, not Americans or Britons. It is possible, but not very likely, that no one on the Allied side ever committed a war crime or a crime against humanity during World War II. It is arguable, however, that the officials who ordered and carried out the firebombing of Tokyo or the leveling of Dresden, in which many innocent civilians were killed, were guilty of crimes against humanity. None of these officials came before the war crimes tribunal. The recognition of the potential charge that any trial applies victor's law has been an ongoing concern in the further development of the concept of war crimes, and is reflected in the jurisdiction of the International Criminal Court.

Post–World War II Efforts

This concern carried over into the postwar world. In 1948, the General Assembly of the United Nations passed the International Convention on the Prevention and Punishment of the Crime of Genocide, known more compactly as the Convention on Genocide. Building on the assertion of crimes against humanity, the Convention on Genocide provided clarification and codification of what constituted acts of genocide. According to the convention, any of the following actions, when committed with the intent of eliminating a particular national, ethnic, racial, or religious group, constitute genocide: (1) killing members of the group; (2) causing serious bodily or mental harm to members of the group; (3) deliberately inflicting on the group conditions of life calculated to kill; (4) imposing measures intended to prevent births within a group; and (5) forcibly transferring children out of a group.

In important ways, enunciating the Convention on Genocide (and the parallel UN Declaration on Human Rights) was a form of international atonement for Axis excesses, and especially for the Holocaust. Most countries signed and ratified the Convention, which took force—without, one might quickly add, any real form of enforcement. A few countries, notably the United States, refused to ratify the document for reasons based in infringement of sovereignty discussed later.

EVOLUTION OF THE PROBLEM

With the completion of the war crimes tribunals after World War II and the flurry of activity that produced the Convention on Genocide, the subject of war crimes dropped from the public eye, not to reemerge publicly until the 1990s. Well beneath the surface of public concern, attempts were made to create some sort of enforcement mechanism for dealing with these issues, but they never received much public attention, nor did they generate enough political support to gain serious international consideration.

Why was this the case? It is not because crimes against humanity became less unacceptable, although those acts and traditional war crimes certainly continued to occur, at least on a smaller scale than had happened during World War II. Rather, the more likely explanation is that the subject matter became a victim of the Cold War, as did other phenomena such as the aggressive promotion of human rights.

It is almost certainly not a coincidence that the emergence of a broad international interest in war crimes emerged at a time of U.S.-Soviet cooperation right after World War II, that concern and progress ground to an effective halt during the ideological and geopolitical confrontation between them, and that the subject has resurfaced and been revitalized since the cessation of that competition.

Why would the Cold War competition hamstring progress on a subject that would, on the face of it, seem noncontroversial? No one, after all, officially condones acts that we have described as war crimes, and yet, in the Cold War context, neither was their clarification and codification aggressively pursued internationally.

The problem was similar to, and had the same roots as, the advocacy of human rights, which also lay fallow on the international agenda through most of the Cold War period. In a sense, war crimes are a flip side of human rights: The crimes against humanity clearly violate the most basic of human rights, and traditional war crimes violate those rights in times of combat.

In the Cold War context, issues like human rights tended to get caught up in the propaganda war between the superpowers. The Soviets would assume that American advocacy of certain principles (for instance, free speech) was championed to embarrass the Soviet Union, where such rights were certainly not inviolate, an assumption with at least some validity. Had the Soviets decided to push for greater progress on war crimes during the American participation in the Vietnam War between 1965 and 1973, the United States would, with some justification, have assumed the purpose was to embarrass American servicemen and discredit the American military effort. The incident depicted in *Platoon* and the reality of My Lai illustrate the extension of this dynamic to war crimes. Innocent civilians were slaughtered at My Lai in what was a clear crime against humanity, but dispassionate consideration was drowned out by wartime propaganda duels over Cold War issues. In such circumstances, little if any progress could be expected on issues with a Cold War veneer; by and large, there was little attempt to pursue agreements in areas where one side or the other might impose a formal veto in the United Nations Security Council or an informal veto by convincing its friends and allies not to take part.

There was a second problem with extending the idea of war crimes, and especially the codification of the idea into some enforcement regime, that has been a particular sticking point for the United States government: the issue of sovereignty. Among the major states in the international system, the United States (as well as nondemocratic states like China) has been among the staunchest supporters of the doctrine of state sovereignty, the idea that supreme authority to act (in other words, sovereignty) resides exclusively with states and that any dilution of that status is unacceptable and thus actively to be opposed.

Because the Convention on Genocide is universally applicable to all states that have signed and ratified the convention and thus have acceded to its provisions, it can be viewed, and was by powerful political elements in the United States, as an infringement of the authority of the United States government to regulate its own affairs. This argument may seem strained in the area of genocide: One way of looking at the objection is that it preserves the right of the United States to commit genocide without breaking agreements of which it is part. Nonetheless, the argument against diluting American national sovereignty was sufficient politically to prevent the United States Senate from ratifying the convention until 1993, when it was submitted to the Senate by President Clinton and approved by the necessary two-thirds majority. This same objection has caused the United States to be one of a handful of countries, and the only prominent democracy, to refuse to sign or ratify the statute of the International Criminal Court.

BOSNIA AND RWANDA: THE PROBLEM REVIVED

The problem of war crimes remained a moot point until the 1990s. There undoubtedly were instances in which questions of war crimes, and especially crimes against humanity, could have been raised previously but, because of their Cold War entanglement, were not. The extermination of well over a million citizens by the Khmer Rouge in Cambodia between 1976 and 1979 is a good example. The struggle in Cambodia was between rival communist forces, one supported by the Soviets and the Khmer Rouge supported by the People's Republic of China, so it was viewed as an intramural struggle in which the West had little direct interest. China's Great Cultural Revolution between 1966 and 1976 probably qualifies as well.

Two other things had changed between the 1970s and the revived concern about crimes against humanity in the 1990s that help explain international indifference in the 1970s and international activism in the 1990s. The first change was the emergence of much more aggressive global electronic media with the physical capability to expose and publicize apparent violations. In 1976, there was no such thing as global television; Cable News Network (CNN), with which we tend to associate the globalization of world news, was not launched until 1980 and did not become a prominent force for some time thereafter. Moreover, media tools such as handheld camcorders and satellite uplinks were theoretical ideas, not the everyday equipment of reporters. As a result, there was much less coverage of the slaughter in Cambodia than there typically is today of similar events. There were lots of rumors and verbal accounts by escaping refugees and reporters (the gist of the 1980s movie *The Killing Fields*) but little graphic visual accounting of the tragedy. The stacks of the victims' skulls that are our lasting memory of what happened are products of the latter 1980s and early 1990s, well after the fighting and killing were over. Moreover, the death of Pol Pot, the leader of the Khmer Rouge, in 1999 has removed much of the focus on the event.

The other change has been the growing *de facto* (in practice) if not *de jure* (in law) acceptance of the permissibility of international intervention in the internal affairs of states when they (or factions within states) grossly abuse other people or groups—in other words, commit crimes against humanity and especially genocide. Without an elaborate statement of the principle of *humanitarian intervention,* this is what the United Nations authorized when it sent UN forces into Somalia in 1992. This action was widely touted by then UN Secretary-General Boutros Boutros-Ghali as a precedent-setting exercise for the future—the establishment of international enforcement of universal codes of behavior.

Thus, by the early 1990s, three dynamics affecting international politics had changed sufficiently to raise the prospects of dealing with war crimes onto the international agenda. The end of the Cold War meant atrocities would not be hidden or accusations about them suppressed on ideological or propaganda grounds. A more aggressive and technologically empowered electronic media with global reach was available to report and publicize atrocities wherever they could reach. At the same time, the UN operation in Somalia had established something like a precedent about the notion of humanitarian intervention. The only unresolved issue was the question of the implications of all this for state sovereignty, a problem that remained latent until the formal call for a permanent war crimes tribunal was issued by the Rome Conference of 1998.

THE BOSNIAN "ETHNIC CLEANSING"

The first test of this new environment came in Bosnia and Herzegovina (hereafter Bosnia). As part of the general dismemberment of communist Yugoslavia in 1991 and 1992 at the end of the Cold War, the multiethnic state of Bosnia joined several other former Yugoslav states like Croatia and Slovenia and declared its independence from Yugoslavia in 1991. Because of its ethnic composition (with sizable Serb, Croat, and Muslim minorities) and its geographical location (bordering both Serbia and Croatia), the result was the bloodiest civil fighting anywhere within the old Yugoslav boundaries. Part of this fighting involved the displacement of ethnic minorities by groups with claims to different parts of Bosnian territory, a process that became known as ethnic cleansing. One outgrowth of ethnic cleansing was the allegation of atrocities against different ethnic groups—crimes against humanity, or war crimes.

This is not the place for a detailed description of the Bosnian war, but it was (and in some ways still is) a triangular affair. The three principal antagonists were: Bosnian Serbs, who wished either for a Bosnian state they controlled or reunion with Serb-controlled Yugoslavia (effectively reduced to Serbia—including Kosovo—and Montenegro until 2006); Bosnian Croats, who wanted either an independent state or, in most cases, union with Croatia; and the Bosnian Muslims, who desired full independence and who had declared the Bosnian state.

The war, such as it was, was primarily a land grab, in which one of the three sides would seek to occupy territory in which the other ethnic groups resided, thereby creating a claim to territorial possession when partition inevitably occurred. Although there

Map 4.1 Map of Yugoslavia after breakup (featuring Bosnia)

was some traditional combat in places like the Krajina region between Croatia and Serbia, a great deal of the "action" consisted of "militia" units attacking basically defenseless members of the other groups to force them from territory the attackers desired. In some cases, large numbers of civilians were killed and interred in mass graves, forming one of the strongest bases for later war crimes indictments. All three groups participated in this action at one time and to one extent or another. The Bosnian Serbs, backed physically and politically by the Yugoslav government in Belgrade, were the best armed and most brutal and successful, and their efforts thus attracted the most—negative—attention.

The nature of this decidedly unmilitary conflict inevitably raised the likelihood that its conduct could be described in terms of war crimes defined nearly a half century earlier. The fact that much of the "fighting" involved attacks on civilians meant traditional war crimes probably occurred, and that crimes against humanity were committed too. This constellation of dynamics had occurred before, and no one had cried "war crimes." Why was this case different?

Two factors stood out. The first was the role of the media, which, accurately or not, portrayed the slaughter largely in terms of Serb responsibility but, more important, in ways that raised the worst memories of World War II war crimes. The most vivid depiction was the publication of still photographs and television footage of Bosnian Muslim prisoners of war in Serb detention camps. The images were explosive: gaunt, sunken-eyed prisoners staring through the wire fences who looked eerily like pictures of Jewish prisoners in the Nazi death camps a half century earlier. The analogy was impossible to ignore, whether it was accurate or not (a matter of some controversy); the implication that something had to be done to rectify the situation was equally difficulty to resist.

The second factor was the physical presence of the United Nations on the scene. During a lull in the fighting between Croatia and Serbia over contested territory in 1992, a UN peacekeeping mission, the UN Protection Force or UNPROFOR, was put in place to monitor the cease-fire. While the cease-fire quickly (and predictably) broke down and UNPROFOR was incapable of reinstating it, the UN presence had two impacts that helped frame the situation in war crimes terms. First, UN inspectors associated with UNPROFOR investigated allegations of atrocities against civilians and unearthed evidence (in some cases literally) that could not be dismissed by the contestants as mere propaganda: crimes against humanity in forms like the mass graves in which the bodies of executed civilians had been unceremoniously dumped.

Second, these revelations meant that the parent organization, the UN itself, was involved; in 1993, the UN Security Council passed a resolution setting up a temporary, ad hoc war crimes tribunal. The location would be at the International Court of Justice (ICJ), which is itself affiliated with the UN. On November 29, 1996, the tribunal handed down its first sentence against Serb leader Drazen Erdemovic. It was the first conviction of an individual for war crimes since Nuremberg and Tokyo. The Bosnian tribunal remains in session; the prosecution of its most famous defendant, Slobodan Milosevic, was conducted until his death. Its greatest problem has been the ability to capture indicted violators who remain in Yugoslavia, where the government refuses to extradite them.

The Rwandan Rampage

War crimes in Bosnia were soon followed by even more spectacular, gruesome events in Rwanda, a small east African country. On May 8, 1994, members of the Hutu majority (encouraged by Hutu politicians) began a systematic, countrywide campaign of genocide against their fellow countrymen, the Tutsi. By the time the slaughter was finally halted, over a half million people had been brutally slaughtered.

The rampage in Rwanda was a crime against humanity on a scale that dwarfed events in the Balkans. Ethnic cleansing in Bosnia had largely had the purpose of displacing, not systematically eliminating, rival groups. Crimes against humanity undoubtedly occurred; systematic genocide to extinguish part of the population generally did not.

The campaign in Rwanda was a clear case of genocide. The purpose of the "fighting" was to kill all Tutsi who could be identified, often hacking them to death with machetes. Given the scale of the slaughter and the number of people who took part in the atrocities (and one must recall that the London Agreement standards stipulate that there are no limits about how low in the decision process one can go to prosecute offenders), the potential task of sorting out and prosecuting the war criminals was daunting.

Rwanda raised a quandary for the international community. Who should investigate and administer war crimes trials? The UN system offered the best hope for legitimacy and fairness, but it clearly lacked the resources to conduct a comprehensive investigation and trial, given the number of Rwandan Hutu undoubtedly vulnerable to prosecution (the UN initially assigned 12 investigators to the task). The Rwandans themselves (notably the surviving Tutsi who took control of the government) promised swift and comprehensive justice, but that alternative was fraught with the chance that justice would turn into retribution—victor's law at its worst. Ultimately, an ad hoc war crimes tribunal was created at The Hague on the model of the Bosnian panel. Like that panel, it remains in session, with little prospect of an early disbanding.

The precedent of the Bosnian and Rwandan special war crimes tribunals inevitably created momentum for a permanent court. There was very little objection in principle to the idea of a war crimes court to deal with these two instances. Moreover, it was increasingly clear from atrocities being committed in other countries that there would be no shortage of situations in which allegations of crimes against humanity would emerge. Internal conflicts in places as widely separated as Sierra Leone in Africa, Kosovo nearby on the Bosnian border, and East Timor on the Indonesian archipelago provided evidence of both geographic diversity and numerous opportunities to enforce sanctions against a new breed of war criminals, who perpetrate gross crimes against humanity—their fellow citizens. Beyond the anticipated amount of demand there would be for a permanent structure was the hope that the existence of such a court and the knowledge that it could bring criminals to justice might deter some future crimes against humanity. But, how should the international community react?

PROPOSALS FOR A PERMANENT WAR CRIMES TRIBUNAL

Advocacy of a permanent court to adjudicate war crimes accompanied the flurry of activity surrounding Nuremberg and Tokyo and the adoption of the Convention on Genocide. In 1948, the UN General Assembly commissioned the International Law Commission (a private body) to study the possibility of establishing an International Criminal Court (ICC). The commission examined this problem until 1954 and produced a draft statute for the ICC. Unfortunately, it appeared during the darkest days of the Cold War; there were objections from both sides of the Iron Curtain, and the UN dropped the proposal.

The idea of an ICC lay dormant until 1989, when the tiny island country of Trinidad and Tobago revived the proposal within the UN. Their motive, oddly enough, was to provide an instrument in their struggle against drug traffickers from South America. Nonetheless, the events in Bosnia and Rwanda revived broader interest that produced ad hoc tribunals to deal with the situations in those countries. Those ad hoc efforts suggested the wisdom of a permanent body to provide a more effective, timely response to war crimes.

The proposal has been controversial, especially surrounding the matter of jurisdiction. Champions contend that the court must have mandatory jurisdiction over all accused instances of war crimes and that its jurisdiction must supercede national sovereignty to be effective. Opponents object that this infringement on national sovereignty is unwarranted and could form the basis for future abuses of sovereignty. The ICC statute contains provisions for mandatory jurisdiction.

The Case for the ICC

The idea of an ICC has several advantages over impaneling ad hoc tribunals. First, it would avoid having to start essentially from scratch each time suspected war crimes are uncovered. A permanent ICC would have, among other things, a permanent staff of investigators and prosecutors, and its staff would have the authority and jurisdiction to ascertain when crimes against humanity have indeed occurred.

Second, and related to the first point, a permanent ICC could be much more responsive to the occurrence—or even possibly the likelihood—that war crimes had occurred or were about to occur. Not only would a permanent staff have or develop the expertise for efficient intervention in war crimes situations, they could be rapidly mobilized and applied to the problem.

Third, it was hoped that a permanent ICC would act as a deterrent to future potential war criminals. Would, for instance, the Bosnian Serb leaders who have been indicted (mostly in absentia) for authorizing ethnic cleansing in Bosnia have been dissuaded from doing so if they knew there was an international criminal authority that could bring them to justice for their deeds? What influence would a permanent ICC have had on the planners and implementers of the slaughter in Rwanda? Although no one can know the answers to these questions, the existence of the ICC might have made a difference.

Pressure to negotiate a treaty to create an ICC grew during the 1990s. As early as 1995, the Clinton administration became an activist in the movement in support of the idea. The movement culminated with the Rome Conference of 1998 (technically the United Nations Diplomatic Conference on the Establishment of a Permanent International Criminal Court). The conference produced a draft treaty to establish the ICC as a permanent court for trying individuals accused of committing genocide, war crimes, or crimes against humanity, and gave the court jurisdiction over individuals accused of these crimes. When the draft came to a vote, it passed by a vote of 120 states in favor, 7 opposed, and 21 abstentions. In order for the treaty to come into force, at least 60 states must ratify the treaty. It reached that level in 2002 and came into official existence on July 1, 2002.

The United States government was one of the seven states to vote against the treaty in Rome and has neither signed nor ratified the document, despite the Clinton administration's involvement in promoting and drafting its statute. In one of his final acts in office, President Clinton signed the statute in December 2000. In February 2001, Secretary of State Colin S. Powell announced that President George W. Bush had no intention of submitting it to the Senate for ratification; the Bush administration subsequently announced it was "unsigning" the treaty, an ambiguous international legal act punctuating its high level of opposition.

Objections to the ICC

While the United States advocating and then opposing the ICC statute may seem anomalous, it is not entirely unusual. The apparent schizophrenia represents different views of America's place in the world, the American attitude toward the world, and especially the question of sovereignty. The Clinton administration saw the ICC statute as a way both to demonstrate responsible U.S. leadership and to improve the quality of the international environment, and thus became a champion of a war crimes court with "teeth." Other powerful political forces, however, summoned the specter of the loss of sovereignty that joining the treaty might entail. The problem came to focus on the potential loss of control of the U.S. government over its own forces in the field.

David Sheffer, head of the American delegation, delivered the heart of the United States' objection at the end of the Rome Conference. He began by pointing out that the ICC would have jurisdiction only in countries that were parties to the treaty, and he noted that a number of the countries that were producing accusations of war crimes could and would evade prosecution by simply not joining the treaty. Iraq was an example. The qualifying point of this objection was that a UN Security Council Resolution (UNSCR) can extend that jurisdiction in a given case. Helena Cobban argues this extension of jurisdiction is itself objectionable, since it extends authority over countries to which the court has only "an indirect line of accountability."

The heart of the objection was that the treaty forces countries to relinquish their sovereign jurisdiction over their forces and leaves those forces vulnerable to international prosecution with no U.S. ability to come to their aid when the United States participates in UN-sponsored peacekeeping operations, such as those in Bosnia and Kosovo. As Sheffer put it, "Thus, the treaty purports to establish an arrangement whereby U.S. armed forces operating overseas could be conceivably prosecuted by the international court even if the U.S. has not agreed to be bound by the treaty. Not only is this contrary to the most fundamental principles of treaty law, it could inhibit the ability of the U.S. to use its military to meet alliance obligations and participate in multinational operations, including humanitarian interventions to save civilian lives." The sovereign control of American forces potentially accused of war crimes thus stands at the base of the United States' refusal to sign off on the ICC statute.

In order to get around the problem of sovereignty forfeiture, the United States has dredged up a tactic it used after World War II to ensure Senate ratification of the statute of the International Court of Justice (ICJ or World Court), to which the ICC is affiliated.

In the case of the ICJ, the United States insisted that the statute state the court would only have jurisdiction in individual cases if *both* (or all) parties granted jurisdiction for that action only. In other words, countries, including the United States, can only be sued and have judgments made against them in situations in which they have given their permission: Sovereign control is only abrogated by explicit consent. This so-called Connally Amendment (named after the Texas Senator who proposed it) has been used on numerous occasions by the U.S. government (for instance, in 1986, when Nicaragua tried to sue the United States for mining the harbor at Managua, the United States simply refused the jurisdiction).

The same argument is incorporated in the American approach to the question of the jurisdiction of the ICC. The proposed "supplement" to the Rome Treaty reads: The United Nations and the International Criminal Court agree that the Court may seek the surrender or accept custody of a national who acts within the overall direction of a U.N. Member State, and such directing State has so acknowledged *only in the event (a) the directing State is a State Party to the Statute or the Court obtains the consent of the directing State, or (b) measures have been authorized pursuant to Chapter VII of the U.N. Charter against the directing State in relation to the situation or actions giving rise to alleged crime or crimes.* (Emphasis added.) Parties to the statute have consistently rejected this American position.

Is the American position realistic? The U.S. government, and especially the military, argue the United States, as the remaining superpower, is uniquely vulnerable to international harassment in the absence of this kind of protection. More specifically, there are usually American forces involved in major peacekeeping missions globally, where accusations of war crimes are commonplace. The military fears that unfounded accusations against Americans can become a means of harassment of the United States against which they should guard and which the American amendment seeks to protect.

The concern is neither abstract nor academic. During the early stages of American participation in the Kosovo Force (KFOR) peacekeeping mission, American Army Staff Sergeant Frank J. Ronghi was arrested for sodomizing and murdering an 11-year-old Albanian Kosovar girl, whose body was found on January 13, 2000. Under terms of the ICC (the provisions of which were not yet in force), Ronghi could have been arrested and tried by the international body for crimes against humanity. He was tried by an American military tribunal in Germany, before which he pleaded guilty and received a life sentence without parole on August 2, 2000. He will serve his sentence in a U.S. military prison. The swift prosecution of Ronghi and a sentence as severe as the ICC could have handed down (it has no provision for the death penalty) muted international criticism of the U.S. action in this case.

What must the international community, which, by and large, rejects the American objection, do to gain acceptance—including American—of the ICC? Clearly, it must acknowledge that the absence of the world's most powerful state from the regime greatly undercuts its legitimacy and physical clout. As the Clinton administration's secretary of state, Madeleine Albright, put it, the ICC without the United States is "dead upon arrival." Thus, some way must be found to overcome the objections of the Americans and others who find fault with the statute as written. But how?

The ICC in Prospect

There are two contemporary high-profile situations in which recourse to the ICC might have been a useful option but was not because the crimes being tried occurred before the Statute of the ICC came into force, thereby precluding its jurisdiction. One involves the trial of the late Slobadan Milosevic of Serbia, and the other is the recently concluded trial and execution of Saddam Hussein in Iraq. Because there will likely be leaders accused of forms of war crimes in the future, it is worthwhile to speculate whether these situations would have been handled differently—better?—had they been submitted to the ICC.

Milosevic, the former president of Yugoslavia, was on trial before the International Criminal Tribunal for the former Yugoslavia (ICTY) for crimes he allegedly authorized during the Yugoslav civil war during the 1990s (notably, actions in Bosnia and Kosovo). In the absence of a permanent court, the ICTY was convened as an ad hoc tribunal at The Hague (Netherlands), and along with a parallel tribunal to deal with the 1994 events in Rwanda, became part of the rationale for a permanent ICC to deal with future situations. The trial began in February 2002 and was still ongoing when he died of an apparent heart attack on March 11, 2006, while still in custody. According to *Wikipedia,* there were "just fifty hours of testimony left before the conclusion of the trial" at the time of his death.

The precedent set by the removal of Milosevic from Yugoslavia (who was surren-dered to international officials by the Yugoslav government on March 31, 2001) has been controversial. The rationale for creating an international court was based on trying to defuse a highly emotional situation had he been tried in Yugoslavia itself, or worse, had he not been tried at all by local officials. Much of the emotion was indeed removed from the proceedings by having Milosevic physically distant from the site of his alleged crimes, but the sheer length of the trial (Milosevic's health, for instance, resulted in numerous delays in proceedings) have been greatly criticized. In retrospect, removing him from Yugoslavia may have been useful in defusing the situation and minimizing potential accusations of victor's law by his opponents, but the convoluted proceedings suggest the need for some reform in the future.

The Iraqi case is somewhat different. It has centered on the highly publicized trial of Saddam Hussein in Baghdad by a special court appointed for that purpose. Although formally concluded with Hussein's conviction, the trial was controversial, both substan-tively and procedurally. Substantively, controversy has swirled regarding the nature of the charges against Hussein and the fairness both of the proceedings and the impartiality of Iraqi judges selected (and replaced) to judge the trial. Its location in Baghdad has helped focus local public attention on the proceedings and thus undoubtedly helped inflame public passions about it. Global Policy Forum, in a November 2005 article by Robert Verkaik, alleges other irregularities, including the lengthy detention of Hussein by U.S. officials before his trial, court impartiality, and the possible death penalty that could be exacted against Hussein. The question is whether the problems that swirl around the trial of Saddam Hussein could have been reduced had it been possible to move the trial to a neutral site such as The Hague, and tried it before a presumably less partisan group of jurors such as the justices of the ICC. The execution by hanging of Hussein on December 30, 2006 closed the issue.

There is, however, another aspect of the Iraqi situation that has received less international attention: the prosecution of those Americans accused of crimes against humanity for their actions at the Abu Ghraib prison in Baghdad. The alleged crimes took place in 2004, at which point the ICC was in operation, so that its jurisdiction could apply. The United States, as part of its general disdain for the ICC, denies any ICC jurisdiction, preferring to try alleged perpetrators within the American military justice system. This preference, it must be added, effectively shields superior officers and officials in the U.S. chain of command from prosecution in a situation in which international standards would expose the entire chain of command to potential cupidity.

The Abu Ghraib situation is mixed. United States control over those accused salves American concerns that American personnel will turn into scapegoats subject to unfair harassment simply because they are American, and although the United States can cite the much-less-complicated Ronghi case as precedent, there will undoubtedly be international concern about a cover-up. Turning the case over to the ICC would largely mute those kinds of criticisms through a thorough and fair trial but would run the risk of reversing the direction of the statute's concerns about levels of responsibility. Any U.S. effort to shield those higher up in the decision chain would be more difficult in an atmosphere in which anyone with knowledge or a role in the authorization process is fair game for prosecution.

CONCLUSION

Now that it has been raised and publicly entered the international agenda, the question of war crimes is not likely to go away. In a gradually democratizing world in which authoritarianism is still practiced but rarely extolled, there is no longer any organized, principled objection to the notion that there are limits on the conduct of war and the limits on how individuals and groups can be treated. Although the development of something like a consensus on this matter is really quite recent in historical terms (particularly the idea of crimes against peace and humanity), it nonetheless seems well on its way to being established as an international norm.

The major remaining question is institutionalization of war crimes enforcement. As noted in a quote at the beginning of this study, the emergence of a consensus has coincided with a spate of war crimes, principally in the bloody, brutal internal wars in a number of developing-world states. Darfur is the current symbol of man's inhumanity to his fellow man. The practical implication of this situation is that there are almost certainly going to be places where war crimes tribunals will need to be formed if there is not a permanent court.

Is the ICC the answer? Clearly, it would solve some problems and have some advantages, as already noted. It would certainly be more responsive when problems arise; it would maximize whatever deterrent value a potential violator would experience knowing the court was waiting for him or her; and it would insulate the system from accusations of victor's law in future cases. Moreover, it would contribute to the general promotion of lawfulness in the international system, and in specific cases, may help defuse public passions by removing trials from the places in which alleged crimes took place. To its proponents, these are powerful and compelling justifications for the ICC.

Then there is the American position. The U.S. objection to the ICC is not a defense of war crimes or an explicit defense of international disorder. Rather, it stems from a long-standing American fixation with state sovereignty and the need for the American government to have sole jurisdiction over its citizens. In practice, this policy puts the United States at cross-purposes with most of the international community, including most of its closest allies, and on the same side as some rogue states on this and similar issues. Within the United States, there is division on the position we should take: The Clinton administration did, after all, both champion and subsequently back down into opposition about the ICC, and the Bush administration has redoubled that opposition. Given the American status as the remaining superpower, the American decision on ratifying the ICC statute or an amended version is probably critical. If the United States remains opposed, Secretary Albright could well be correct in her assessment about the ICC.

In the end, the international debate pitting the United States against most of the rest of the world (and especially its principal allies) is not about war crimes or the establishment of a court. No one is *for* war crimes or *against* a tribunal to prosecute offenders. The debate is over the nature of the court's jurisdiction. Should that jurisdiction be mandatory, automatic, and supreme? Or should that jurisdiction be tempered by a filter by which states can maintain primary control over their own citizens accused of war crimes? Ultimately, the issue all boils down to the question of sovereignty.

STUDY/DISCUSSION QUESTIONS

1. Assuming that the definitions of war crimes arising from the post–World War II experience are acceptable, should their application be retroactive, either before the standards were adopted or in cases in which violations may have occurred since 1947 but prosecution did not occur at the time? If so, what criteria can you think of to choose among instances?

2. Why do you suppose that war crimes tribunals were authorized for Bosnia and Rwanda but not for Chechnya? Does this suggest a double standard in which the weak are vulnerable but the powerful are not? Since the United States is clearly a powerful country, should we also be exempt?

3. Are the arguments in favor of the International Criminal Court compelling? How much of the American objection to the question of automatic, overriding jurisdiction should be accommodated?

4. Is the participation of the United States necessary for the success of the permanent war crimes tribunal? Assess the American objection. Is it reasonable, arrogant, or possibly both? If you were the representative of another government, how would you feel about the American position?

5. The trial of Sgt. Ronghi by an American military court avoids the precedent of American acquiescence to the ICC statute, and his sentence is as severe as it could have been under ICC jurisdiction. Is such an outcome an adequate and justifiable alternative to full U.S. participation in the ICC?

6. Would it have been helpful if ICC jurisdiction could have been extended to Slobodan Milosevic and Saddam Hussein? If there are future similar cases, would the ICC "option" be valuable? Should the United States be part of such cases?

7. Most situations in which allegations of war crimes are likely to occur are internal wars in the developing world; how does this affect the value of having a permanent court rather than ad hoc tribunals, as we have done up to now? Would a permanent ICC be more effective in deterring or investigating and bringing to justice violators?

8. Should some measure of national sovereignty be surrendered to make the ICC effective? Which value is more important: national control over a country's citizens, or justice for the victims and perpetrators of war crimes when those two values come into conflict?

READING/RESEARCH MATERIAL

Cobban, Helena. "Think Again: International Courts." *Foreign Policy,* March/April 2006, 22–28.

Dempsey, Gary. *Reasonable Doubt: The Case Against the Proposed International Criminal Court.* Cato Policy Analysis No. 311. Washington, DC: Cato Institute, 1998.

Gutman, Roy, and David Rieff (eds.). *Crimes of War.* New York: W. W. Norton, 1999.

Kahn, Leo. *Nuremberg Trials.* New York: Ballantine Books, 1972.

Neier, Aryeh. *War Crimes: Brutality, Genocide, Terror, and the Struggle for Justice.* New York: Random House, 1998.

Tusa, Ann, and John Tusa. *The Nuremberg Trial.* New York: Atheneum, 1983.

Verkaik, Robert. "Saddam on Trial: Ten Reasons Justice May Not Be Served." *Global Policy Forum,* November 25, 2005 (http://www.globalpolicy.org/intljustice/tribunals/iraq/2005/1129ten.htm).

WEB SITES

Collaboration of journalists, lawyers, and scholars on laws of war and war crimes
   Crimes of War Project at http://www.crimesofwar.org

Overview of documents and events leading to Rome Statute
   Rome Statute at http://www.un.org/law/icc/index.html

Arguments about ICC and U.S. security interests
   The United States and the ICC at http://ww/amacad.org/projects/icc.htm

"A Summary of United Nations Agreements on Human Rights."
   http://www.hrweb.org/legal/undocs.html

"Sheffer on Why U.S. Opposed International Criminal Court."
   http://www.usembassy.org/uk/

Update on Status of ICC Ratification. http://www.iccnow.org/html/us2000.html

Human Rights Watch: http://www.hrw./Org/English/docs/2003,12/19/ira_6770.htm and http://hrw.org.europe/083104milo.htm

CHAPTER FIVE

International Permission Slips

SOVEREIGNTY AND THE RIGHT OF INTERVENTION

PRÉCIS

The principle of sovereignty, or supreme authority, has been the bedrock principle of operation of the international system since the end of the Thirty Years' War in 1648, a process known as the Peace of Westphalia. Over time, sovereignty has come to reside in the governments of states, where it is generally conceded to exist today. Because war is a primary result of the international system that has evolved around the principle of sovereignty, it has never been without critics who would prefer a more peaceful order. The effort to internationalize war crimes, the topic of the last chapter, is one aspect of that criticism.

This case study looks at the assault on sovereignty through a prominent and very important problem of contemporary international relations—the bloody internal wars raging in the poorest countries of the world and instances of outside invasion. The frustration associated with these situations has called for intervention in a number of cases by outside groups to end the fighting or to restore some international order. Such missions, usually undertaken under the auspices of the United Nations, represent direct violations of the sovereignty on the countries in which they occur. The American invasion of Iraq is a blatant example. Assessing the effects on eroding the overall quality of sovereignty in the system is a major purpose of the case.

In his 2004 State of the Union Address, President George W. Bush offered a one-sentence justification for the American invasion of Iraq and a possible harbinger for the future.

He declared that the United States would not ask for an international "permission slip" before it intervened in foreign countries in pursuit of American interests. The line was a virtual throwaway hardly noticed or commented on at the time. The statement, however, represented a fundamental challenge to the most basic principle of the international system, state sovereignty.

For more than 350 years, the bedrock principle of international relations has been the evolving concept of sovereignty, and more specifically, the idea of state sovereignty. Although its philosophical roots extend back farther, this concept was first formulated formally in a book written in the sixteenth century as the philosophical underpinning for the consolidation of power by Europe's monarchs, and in particular, the authority of the king of France. With the settlement of the extraordinarily brutal, religiously based Thirty Years' War in 1648, the triumphant secular monarchs of northern Europe adopted the concept as part of asserting their independence from papal authority.

State sovereignty, the idea that state governments have supreme authority in the international system and that there can be no authority superior to the state, has been around ever since as a first principle by which international relations is organized. The primacy of sovereignty has never lacked its critics, either in terms of the concept's validity or its philosophical and practical implications. Nevertheless, the principle has endured, and governments cling tenaciously to their possession of sovereignty.

Sovereignty has always done more than provide the philosophical underpinning of international relations. The idea—even the necessity—of possessing and protecting sovereignty has formed the basis of much state action, and particularly the geopolitical task of protecting the state from its enemies. The idea of a "national security state" that was a popular depiction during the Cold War was based in the need to protect the state's supreme authority over its territory from predators that threatened that authority. Among the defenders of this notion, the United States has stood out for its staunch defense of the sanctity of state sovereignty.

The sacrosanct status of unfettered sovereignty is being increasingly questioned. Part of the assault has come from the traditional critics of sovereignty; for instance, opponents of war who argue that armed conflict is an integral, inevitable, and regrettable consequence of a world in which sovereignty reigns. From this view, dismantling sovereignty is the necessary prerequisite for world peace. At the same time, the rise of other concerns such as human rights creates collision points with state sovereignty. Why? Because a major historical justification for mistreatment of individuals and groups within states is that sovereign states possess absolute authority over their citizens, and how states act within their sovereign jurisdiction is their own business, not the concern of the international order. This is roughly the position that the Russian government has taken with regard to its treatment of Chechnya during the attempted Chechen secession during the 1990s and into the 2000s. More indirectly, but no less fundamentally, the Bush doctrine's assertion of an American "right" to attack foes preemptively, as in Iraq, represents a de facto denial of the sovereignty it seeks to preserve.

One area in which state sovereignty collides most directly with the realities of the post–Cold War world is internal war in the developing world, and that violence is often chaotic, brutal, and bloody. Often, gross violations of human rights occur and instances of war crimes (see Chapter 4) abound. When these kinds of tragedies occurred in the past, the vast majority of the world simply averted its gaze from, for instance, the slaughter of Cambodians by their countrymen, the extermination of Armenians by the Ottoman Turks, or even the Holocaust against European Jews, Gypsies, and others. The reason for ignoring these events was that they were acts of sovereign governments toward their own citizens, over whom they had total authority. No matter how badly a government treated its citizens within its own boundaries, that was its own problem and prerogative, not the business of outsiders.

This indifference may seem incredible in contemporary terms, but it is an idea that was virtually unchallenged as little as a half century ago. Take a real example. When the war crimes trials at Nuremberg were being organized, there were questions about what crimes the Nazi defendants could be charged for committing. The leading U.S. jurist at the trials, a member of the U.S. Supreme Court, offered the official view that the Nazis could be charged with killing non-German citizens on German soil, but not with exterminating German Jews, because, as German citizens, they could treat them any way they saw fit. The position was not particularly controversial at the time (partly because as a practical matter, there were plenty of war crimes with which to charge them).

The bloody internal conflicts in places like the Balkans and parts of Africa have challenged the idea that state sovereignty provides an unfettered license for governments to do as they please to their citizens or, where governments are incapable or nonexistent, not to protect portions of their populations from ravage. Using the United Nations as a vehicle to justify actions, the international system has, on numerous occasions that will almost certainly continue into the future, intruded itself into these situations in order to prevent further abuse and to protect citizens. The Bush doctrine assertion that the United States does not need an "international permission slip" to intervene in other states in violation of their sovereignty carries the effect a step forward.

The collision of traditional conceptualizations of sovereignty with the evolution of the post–Cold War world generally is thus a major question in international relations, a question of whether the world and its values are changing so much that the principle of sovereignty must be modified or abandoned to adjust to a new reality. One aspect of that reality is the collision between sovereignty and the assertion of an international right or need to intervene in civil wars within states or, more recently, to pursue international terrorists. The outcome of that collision will help answer the broader question of the role of sovereignty in the twenty-first century and is thus the focus of this case study.

Does the international system or do individual states have a right to violate the sovereignty of states when the state is at war with itself—with hideous consequences for its population? In order to examine the problem, we will begin with a brief overview of the content and evolution of the concept of sovereignty, and some major criticisms of the concept and its implications for international relations. We will then look at the problem of internal wars and the justifications that are used when interventions are contemplated and implemented, as well as the assertions of the Bush doctrine. We will conclude by examining the consequences of accumulated interventions on the underpinning of sovereignty in the system.

THE CONCEPT OF SOVEREIGNTY

The basic concept of sovereignty has three distinct elements, which collectively define what it means to possess sovereignty. The first element is legitimate authority. Authority is simply the ability to enforce an order; the qualifier "legitimate" means that authority is invested with some legal, consensual basis. Put another way, sovereignty is more than the exercise of pure force.

The second element of sovereignty is that it is supreme. What this means is that there is no superior authority to the possessor of sovereignty; the sovereign is the highest possible authority wherever the sovereign holds sway. The third and related element is that of territory; sovereignty is supreme authority within a defined physical territory. Since the Peace of Westphalia, the political state came to embody the territorial definition of sovereignty. Thus states (or countries) have supreme authority over what occurs within their territorial boundaries, and no other source of authority can claim superior jurisdiction to the sovereign.

Before looking at why sovereignty has developed the way it has as a concept, it is worthwhile briefly to look at the consequences of these characteristics politically. In the *internal* workings of states, sovereignty is the basis of the political authority of state governments; the idea of supreme authority provides the state with the power to order its own affairs and the government to create and enforce that order. When the concept of sovereignty was first developed, this internal application was the emphasis. *Externally,* in the relations between states, this same sovereignty creates disorder, because there can be no superior authority to the sovereign within the defined territory of states. The result is *anarchy,* or the absence of government (political authority) in the relations among states. Thus, sovereignty has the schizophrenic effect of creating order and disorder, depending on the venue in which it is applied.

Early Origins and Evolution

This consequence was not so clear when Jean Bodin formally enunciated the concept of sovereignty in his 1576 book *De Republica*. Bodin, who was French, decried the inability of the French monarchy to establish its authority throughout the country, since lower feudal lords instead claimed what amounted to sovereignty over their realms—especially through charging taxes (tolls) to cross their realms. Bodin countered with the idea of sovereignty, which he defined as "supreme authority over citizens and subjects, *unrestrained by law*." (Emphasis added.) The added and italicized element, Bodin felt, was necessary to avoid the unifying monarch being hamstrung by parochial laws in his quest to establish the power of the French monarchy. This part of the definition has fallen from common conceptions of sovereignty, but its implications remain and are part of the ongoing controversy central to this case: If the sovereign is above the law, then nothing he or she does can possibly be illegal, at least when committed within the sovereign jurisdiction over which the sovereign reigns.

When Bodin enunciated his principle of sovereignty, he was unconcerned about it as a maxim for international relations. This is not surprising in that the period of its gestation was a period when monarchs were consolidating their holds on what became the modern states of Europe and the modern state system. Given that all these states were absolute monarchies, it is further not terribly surprising the presumption quickly evolved (aided by philosophical publicists like Thomas Hobbes) that sovereignty resided with the monarch (which, among other things, helps explain why monarchs are sometimes referred to as sovereigns).

The concept of sovereignty was extended to international relations as the state system evolved and the structure of the modern state emerge and solidifed. Hugo Grotius, the Dutch scholar generally acknowledged as the father of international law, first proclaimed state sovereignty as a fundamental principle of international relations in his 1625 book *On the Law of War and Peace*. By the eighteenth century, the principle was well on its way to being in place, and by the nineteenth it was an accepted part of international relations.

By the nineteenth century, the content of sovereignty had evolved from its context. Because virtually all countries were still ruled by more or less absolute monarchies (the fledgling, and not very important, United States, revolutionary France, and slightly democratizing Great Britain being the exceptions), the idea of absolute state sovereignty was the rule, and this principle governed both domestic and international relations. From the view of the international system, a prevailing way to describe international politics was in terms of something called the *billiard ball* theory. The idea, never to be taken entirely literally, was that state authority resembled an impermeable billiard ball, and that international relations consisted of these impermeable objects bouncing against one another, causing them to change course in their international behavior from time to time. Important to the theory, however, was that the balls were also impermeable, which meant that nothing in international interactions could affect what went on within the balls, as, for instance, how states treated their citizens. Under this principle, it was simply impermissible for states to interfere in the internal affairs of other states, no matter how distasteful or disgusting domestic practices might be.

Even during its heyday, this conceptualization was not universally accepted. In fact, conceptual challenges tended to be grouped around two related questions that continue to be important in the contemporary debate. How much authority does the sovereign have in the territorial realm over which it is exercised? Within whom, or what body, does sovereignty reside? Different answers have decidedly different implications for what sovereignty means in the relations among states.

As sovereignty was originally formulated and implemented, the answer to the first question was that sovereignty is absolute, that the possessor has total authority over his or her realm. This interpretation flows from, among other sources, the idea that the sovereign is "unrestrained by law," to repeat Bodin's term. The contrary view emerged during the eighteenth and nineteenth centuries and reflected the growing notion of political rights asserted in the American and French Revolutions, each of which claimed the sovereign's powers were limited and could be abridged. Among the primary publicists of this view was the English political philosopher John Locke and his French counterpart, Jean-Jacques Rousseau.

The assertion that there are limits on sovereignty reflects the second question: Where does sovereignty reside? It was a question about the basis on which that authority is legitimately claimed by those who sought to wield power within their political jurisdictions. The traditional view was that sovereignty resides in the state. In the sixteenth and seventeenth centuries when sovereignty was taking hold as an organizational principle, this meant the king or queen had sovereignty, because the monarch was the unchallenged head of government. It was what we would now call a "top down" concept; the government exercised sovereignty over the population, whose duty it was to submit to that authority.

Beyond the philosophical positions taken by Locke and Rousseau, the contrary argument had its base in, among other places, the American Revolution. A major theme of the American complaint against the British monarch was his denial that the colonists had *rights* in addition to obligations. From that assertion, it was a reasonably short intellectual odyssey to the assertion that the *people,* not the state (or monarch) were the possessors of sovereignty. Under the notion of what became known as *popular sovereignty,* the idea was that the people, as possessors of sovereignty, ceded some of that authority to the state in order to provide the basic legitimacy for the social and political order. Ultimately, however, sovereignty resides with individual citizens, who can grant, withhold, or even, in some interpretations, rescind the bestowing of authority to the state.

These distinctions are more than abstract, academic constructs. Their practical meanings and implications become particularly clear if one combines the two ideas in matrix form.

Sources and Extent of Sovereignty

		Extent of Sovereignty	
		Absolute	*Limited*
	State	(Cell 1)	(Cell 3)
Source	Individuals	(Cell 2)	(Cell 4)

The idea that sovereignty is absolute can be associated with authoritarian governance of one sort or the other. Traditional authoritarian regimes derive their claim to authority on the combination of absolute sovereignty and the state locus of authority (Cell 1). The populist/fascist regimes in Italy and Germany that arose between the world wars combine absolutism with some popular, individual base, Cell 2 (both regimes originally came to power popularly). On the other side of the ledger, the idea that sovereignty is limited is associated with democratic regimes. The idea of state sovereignty derived from the people is the backbone of traditional western democracy (Cell 3). When the conferral of sovereignty to the state is denied and maintained by subnational individuals or groups, the result can be the kinds of instability one associates with many of the unstable regimes in the developing world (Cell 4). Much of the debate about intervention in the internal affairs of states derives from the situation depicted in Cell 4. If one accepts the notion that sovereignty resides with individuals, then the possibility of legitimate interference on behalf of those sovereign individuals can be argued to override the sovereignty of the state.

Objections to Sovereignty

The idea and consequences of sovereignty have come under increasing assault as the twentieth century evolved toward the twenty-first century. Two broad categories of criticism, however, relate directly to the question of international intervention in the internal affairs of states and thus have direct relevance to our task of examining the impact of intervention on sovereignty. Both are attacks on the operationalization of the concept.

The first critique is aimed at absolutist conceptions of sovereignty. Critics of this argument maintain that sovereignty in application has never been as absolute as sovereignty in theory. The myth of the impenetrability of states by outside forces, including other states, is no more than a fiction to buttress the principle. States have always interfered in the internal affairs of other states in one way or another. The billiard ball theory is not, in the scientific sense, a theory at all, but instead a false hypothesis.

According to this argument, sovereignty not only has never been as absolute as its champions would assert, but it is becoming increasingly less so. A major reason for this dilution derives from the scientific revolution in telecommunications, which is making national borders entirely more penetrable from the outside, a trend anticipated more than a half century ago by Sir Anthony Eden in a speech before the British House of Commons on November 22, 1954: "Every succeeding scientific discovery makes greater nonsense of old-time conceptions of sovereignty."

Those "old-time" conceptualizations refer, of course, to state-centered, absolutist interpretations of sovereignty. Forces such as the spread of the Internet, economic globalization, the emergence of a homogenized commercial and popular culture around the world, and the desire to embrace the globalized world system all make the factual content of total sovereign control by governments over territory increasingly suspect. From our vantage point, however, we must ask whether this factual dilution of sovereign control extends to the "right" of the international system to infringe on the sovereign ability of the state to treat its citizens in ways that the international community disapproves? Is the spread of popular global culture, for instance, any kind of precedent to assert the rightfulness of forceful interposition by foreign troops into civil strife or to effect domestic change?

The other objection to absolute sovereignty has to do directly with the consequences of a system based in state sovereignty. Once again, a number of assertions are made about the pernicious effects of this form of organization on the operation of the international system. Two will be explored here.

The first, and most commonly asserted, objection to state sovereignty is its legitimization and, in some constructs, even glorification of war as a means to settle disputes between states. In a system of sovereign states, after all, there is no authority to enforce international norms on states or to adjudicate or enforce judgments resolving the disputes that arise between then, except to the extent states voluntarily agree to be bound by international norms or, ironically, can be forced to accept international judgments. If states cannot agree amicably on how to settle their differences, then they must rely on their own ability to solve favorably those disagreements they have.

The principle involved is known as *self-help,* the ability to bring about favorable outcomes to differences, often at the expense of the other state. This resolution becomes an exercise in *power* (the ability to get someone to do what he would not otherwise do), and one form of power available to states is military force. In situations that states deem to be of sufficient importance to settle with armed force, then war may be the conflict resolution means of choice. In a system of self-help, there is thus no alternative to possessing, and in some instances using, armed force to get your way.

Despite the fact that all member states of the United Nations have renounced the waging of war as a means to resolve conflict (we simply do not call them *wars* anymore), the resort to force is understood and accepted in international practice (with some reservations). A fairly large number of analysts, including many scholars and practitioners of international relations, however, decry this situation, because they abhor war and would like to see it end. Because sovereignty and the legitimate recourse to war are closely related, therefore, they welcome its dilution and replacement as an international principle.

The other, more contemporary, objection to the consequences of sovereignty is the power it gives governments over their people. In an international sense, governments still are, after all, legally "unrestrained" by international norms in dealing with their own populations, except, once again, to the extent that states have voluntarily limited their rights by signing international agreements. Historically, the notion that governments could do horrible things to their citizens was abhorred by many in the international community, but the right to such behavior was unchallenged on the basis of sovereignty. The phrase "Patriotism is the last refuge of a scoundrel," first uttered by the English author Samuel Johnson in 1775, could easily be paraphrased as, in international terms, "sovereignty is the last refuge of a scoundrel."

Whether this is good or bad is debatable. Governments strongly support sovereignty because it preserves the ability to conduct affairs without undue interference from outside. Unfortunately, the greater the protection of internal actions, the greater is the potential for abuse. In those cases in which abuse results in atrocity and human suffering, the calls for outside intervention arise as a challenge to that sovereign authority.

The sanctity of this concept of sovereignty began to erode with the global reaction to the reality of the Holocaust that surfaced after World War II. The active revival of this objection came at the end of the Cold War. Scoundrel-like behavior did not, of course, go into hibernation during the Cold War (Pol Pot and the Khmer Rouge guaranteed that), but condemnation—and especially proposing action to combat it—tended to get entangled in Cold War politics. Could, for instance, the United Nations have proposed a peacekeeping mission to Cambodia in 1975 (when the Khmer Rouge seized power and began their slaughter), when the fighting and killing involved two communist factions, each aligned with a different communist superpower (China and the Soviet Union), each of which had a veto in the Security Council? Of course not!

The Assault on Sovereignty Through the UN

To borrow a term from military tactics, the attack on sovereignty emanating from actions from the United Nations during the 1990s was not a "frontal assault." None of the actions authorized by the UN Security Council directly challenged the concept of state sovereignty or aligned itself explicitly with a particular interpretation of the concept, such as limited sovereignty residing in individuals. Rather, they have been justified under Chapter VII of the UN Charter, which gives the council the authority to determine threats to or breaches of the peace and to authorize responses, including the use of military force.

The assault on sovereignty has thus been conducted indirectly and inductively. It began when the Security Council authorized a peacekeeping force (UNOSOM I) to go to Somalia on December 3, 1992. The official reason for the mission was to alleviate human suffering (the threat of massive starvation) due to a five-year-long drought and a civil war, one consequence of which was that international relief efforts to get food to the afflicted were being interrupted by the combating factions. The motivation for the mission was hence humanitarian, to alleviate suffering in what would subsequently be referred to as a major humanitarian disaster.

The UN action was a major precedent in at least two ways that were influenced by the unique circumstances in Somalia at the time. First and possibly most important, it was a mission authorized and implemented without any consultation with the government of the country to which it was dispatched. The idea that the UN would in effect invade a member state presumably for its own good was a major change of policy for the international community working through the world body.

Circumstances on the ground in Somalia made this an easy course to take. The government of Somalia was not consulted before the intervention because *there was no legal government to consult*. Since the overthrow of Siad Barre the previous year, Somalia had been in a state of anarchy, and the overall objective of the civil war was to install one clan leader or another to form a new government capable of rule. The United Nations could not negotiate with any leader, because intervention in a civil war at the invitation of any party is illegal under international law. The UN in effect skirted the issue by invoking Chapter VII of its charter and using its provisions to determine a breach of the peace had occurred and to take appropriate action to restore the peace. One could argue, although no one did publicly at the time, that the absence of a government meant there was no sovereign territory involved; the issue was officially ignored.

The second precedent was that this was the first occasion when the Security Council interpreted its jurisdiction to include purely humanitarian crises. Without going into the legislative history of the charter, it is clear that the framers meant for Chapter VII to be invoked primarily in the case of cross-border invasions by states (interstate wars). The Persian Gulf War effort of 1990–1991 was the prototype the framers had in mind. Although the UN had (rather unhappily) intervened in a civil war in the former Belgian Congo (later Zaire, now the Democratic Republic of Congo), the decision to engage in humanitarian intervention in a civil war in a country for which the term *failed state* was later coined represented a major change of direction. The involvement raised the question of what it meant to the overall nature of the international system if the world body could simply ignore the sovereignty of its members. It did so by deed, not by explicit acknowledgement that this was its intent or its effect. It was the beginning of an inductive process, because the 1990s witnessed more situations with similar sources and arguably similar precedents.

The Assault on Sovereignty Outside the UN: The Iraq Precedent

The American invasion of Iraq has become controversial on a number of grounds largely concerned with whether it was necessary or whether it did, or eventually will, accomplish its purposes. Lurking behind these questions is a more fundamental systemic concern: Did the invasion represent an illegal, precedent-setting assault on the very principle of sovereignty of which the United States has been the most ardent defender?

The Bush administration has argued the invasion was not illegal, and thus indirectly against any negative precedent, on two debatable grounds. One is the principle of preemption, which says that a state can legally attack another whenever it faces an imminent threat that can be thwarted by preemptive action. The other is the authorization to use force under Article VII of the UN Charter. Alleged Iraqi possession and intention to use weapons of mass destruction in support of terrorism has formed the justification for preemption. UN Security Council Resolution 1444, which demanded Iraqi compliance with weapons inspections and warned of unspecified consequences (that did not specifically include force) were used to justify Chapter VII. A large portion of the international community denies both claims. Why?

One reason is factual: a rejection of the claim of an imminent threat and a denial the use of force was authorized. More fundamental, however, is the principle of sovereignty as elaborated in the UN Charter and UN Resolutions. Members of the UN renounce the right to commit aggression (defined by UN General Assembly Resolution 3314 in 1974 as "the use of armed force by a state"). The underlying rationale, according to Pascal Boniface in a 2003 *Washington Quarterly* article, is the sovereignty-based principle of noninterference in the internal affairs of states, a main purpose of which is "to protect weak states against intervention from strong states."

The Bush doctrine argues that the protection of U.S. national interests overrides these rejoinders and that, as a result, the United States does not have to seek "international permission slips" to protect those interests. As the world's most powerful country, there is, as a practical matter, little the international community can do to prevent actions based on these assertions. If, however, the United States does not have to get a permission slip, why should anyone else? Or is noninterference only null and void for the most powerful country in the world? Is sovereignty universally undermined, or only for the relatively weak and defenseless? Or is the United States inadvertently undermining the principle of sovereignty to which it has been slavishly devoted?

INTERNATIONAL INTERVENTION

The Somali case was not the last instance in the 1990s in which a chaotic, bloody civil war would break out in a developing-world country that the citizens of that country would prove incapable of resolving and in which there would be gross instances of individual and collective human rights abuses. The list of places where these situations have occurred has become familiar and a litany of the world's trouble spots: Bosnia, Haiti, Rwanda, Liberia, Kosovo, Sierra Leone, and East Timor, to name the most obvious. All are fragile states, where full sovereign control by governments is tenuous and where breakdowns of control almost invite interference from outside parties on humanitarian bases. Not all have evoked the same kind of international responses, but each raised the same kinds of questions about international rights and obligations in situations in which humanitarian violations occur and the degree to which traditional views of sovereignty are applicable or require amending. In addition to involvement in these new internal wars, the invasions of Afghanistan and Iraq pose other questions about the impact on sovereignty.

New Internal Wars

The existence of organized armed violence within countries for the purpose of displacing a government and replacing it with some alternative is certainly not a unique characteristic of the period since the end of the Cold War. Largely connected to the unraveling of the European colonial empires that began shortly after the end of World War II, internal—or civil—war has been the dominant form of political violence for a half century.

This pattern has continued since the end of the Cold War, although with some changes. During the Cold War, civil conflicts generally took on a Cold War ideological flavor, with one side (usually the insurgents) "sponsored" by the major communist states and the other (usually the government under siege) aligned with the West. This provided a surrogate battleground for the superpowers, and it also meant that the sponsoring states could (and usually did) impose some constraints on how their proxies conducted themselves. Moreover, these wars clearly were fought for the purpose of gaining or maintaining political control in order to govern the state.

The new internal wars of the post–Cold War international environment are often not like this traditional pattern. The end of the Cold War was accompanied by the retreat first of the dying Soviet Union and then the United States from active participation in much of the developing world. The restraint they imposed on their clients left with them, and the result was a new breed of war.

These wars have tended to be especially brutal and chaotic, accompanied by large-scale accusations and evidence of atrocities that have, among other things, resuscitated interest in war crimes. Part of the bestial, bloody conduct of these conflicts (for instance, the systematic amputation of hands and feet by Sierra Leone's Revolutionary United Front and the genocide in Rwanda) reflects the absence of outsider influence on the "rebels." At the same time, many participants, rather than being trained and disciplined soldiers, are instead untrained "fighters" who are only nominally under anyone's control. Especially in African variants of new internal war, the forces are often little more than children (the 10- to 12-year-old "child soldiers" of the Liberian civil war, for instance). Moreover, beyond pure criminality (much of the war in Sierra Leone was about who would control the diamond-rich area of the country), it is often difficult to discern the purposes of the wars.

These wars generally occur in the poorest, most destitute parts of the world. Somalia was, as mentioned, the prototype of the so-called failed state (countries that have historically shown an inability to govern themselves in a stable manner), and a number of other conflicts have been in similar countries (Haiti and East Timor, for instance). The failed states also tend to be very poor, meaning there is little materially to fight over but also meaning that ending them and restoring a stable order is difficult, because there is little material base on which to build. Moreover, most countries and regions where these wars occur are clearly outside the areas of important interests of the major powers (the Balkans are an arguable exception); as a result, it is difficult to argue that any outcome would much discomfort major countries like the United States and thus to generate great enthusiasm for moderating involvement. In a growing number of instances, the internal parties seem totally incapable of resolving their differences, either militarily or through negotiations.

Ignoring the problem is made difficult by the very public nature of the conflicts. Modern electronic media are able to penetrate, cover, and report on the tragedy in a Rwanda in a manner that would have been quite impossible two decades earlier in Cambodia. The world knew of the rampage by the Khmer Rouge as they decimated their own population, but the accounts were in the print media, not on television, as the slaughter was in Rwanda. The steady flow of wretched refugees in Kosovo was a daily CNN story that could only be avoided by not watching the news. The result is to activate a desire to alleviate the problem. The question is, what kind of effort?

Afghanistan and Iraq

These two neighboring countries offered distinct but connected challenges. The distinction came in the form of the preintervention situation in each. In Afghanistan, there was an ongoing civil war being contested inconclusively, but more important, the Taliban government was openly providing sanctuary for the renegade Al Qaeda terrorists and refused to rescind that refuge and turn them in, a decision that flew in the face of virtually global demand. In Iraq, by contrast, there was no civil uprising, and though Saddam Hussein had drug his heels on the issue of weapons inspections, he had basically complied by the time the invasion occurred. The alleged connection between the two was the global war on terrorism (GWOT), but given the contrasting situations, there was great international sentiment to act in Afghanistan but not in Iraq.

The Intervention Response

In an international environment that has embraced human rights as a primary value, the new internal wars have been the system's black eye, its not-so-well-kept dirty little secret, as have Iraq-style wars. We are embarrassed at the slaughter of the innocents wherever the carnage occurs, although we feel more impelled to act in some cases than in others.

The pattern of international response to intervention questions has not been uniform. The international community, and especially the major powers, has been willing to act forcefully in places like the Balkans, but not in Africa, for instance, where we have sought regional solutions. Similarly, the major powers heaved a sigh of relief when nearby Australia agreed to provide the bulk of the resources for the International Force in East Timor (INTERFET) in 1999. American intervention was supported in Afghanistan but was far short of universal in Iraq.

When some sort of response is deemed unavoidable, the common mechanism for authorizing an international response has been to take it to the Security Council of the UN for a United Nations Security Council Resolution (UNSCR) under Chapter VII. The precedent for this route was Somalia, which in turn was the outgrowth of the successful use of UNSCRs in the Persian Gulf War. The effect, on an ad hoc basis, was to legitimize violations of states' sovereignty. But how?

First, because most of the world's countries are members of the world body, passing a resolution serves as a kind of statement of world opinion, a legitimating action that says an action has the support of the international community. The second, and more controversial, purpose of the use of UNSCRs is to create a kind of legal basis for intervention in civil wars. Intervention in civil wars violates international law and, especially when done without invitation, is clearly a violation of the sovereignty of the country where the intervention occurs.

The UN Charter, however, does authorize the UN to act in the name of peace. Articles 39 and 42 (both part of Chapter VII) create the authority. Article 39 states, "The Security Council shall determine the existence of any threat to the peace, breach of the peace, or act of aggression and shall make recommendations or decide what measures shall be taken . . . to maintain or restore international peace or security." Article 42 makes the military option explicit: "[T]he Security Council . . . may take such action by air, sea or land forces as may be necessary to maintain or restore international peace and security." These provisions appear to refer to *international* rather than internal disputes. Earlier in the Charter, Article 2 (7) makes an ambivalent statement to that effect: "Nothing contained in the present Charter shall authorize the United Nations to intervene in matters which are essentially within the domestic jurisdiction of any state or shall require the members to submit such matters to settlement under the present Charter; but this principle shall not prejudice the application of enforcement measures under Chapter VII." One can use this language to justify intervening in a country's civil strife under two apparent circumstances: if there is a question about whether there is a domestic institution with jurisdiction; or if one determines that whatever is happening within a given country constitutes a threat to or breach of "international peace and security." The latter would appear to be the justification for Afghanistan and Iraq. The Taliban protection of Al Qaeda justified an Article 42 action; Iraq did not in any obvious way.

Why would the members of the UN go to all this trouble to justify interfering in internal matters? At least part of the answer has to be that it is a way to avoid the direct assault on national sovereignty that such actions involve. The UN Charter is quite explicit in its defense of the "territorial integrity or political independence of any state" (Article 2 (4)), or in other words, its sovereignty. The organization cannot directly admit that it is violating sovereignty without violating its own constitution, and its members, by signing the charter, have also agreed to the sanctity of sovereignty. And yet violating sovereignty is exactly what the members do when they pass UNSCRs favoring intervention in internal wars and then dispatch their troops to foreign shores to enforce those decrees. Manipulating the charter effectively finesses the underlying issue of the violation of sovereignty.

How long can the sovereignty issue effectively be skirted? The answer would appear to be not indefinitely. The reason for this assertion is the length of the missions and the conflicts they produce with native populations, who over time decreasingly may see the UN peacekeeping missions as helpful rather than as an unwelcome intrusion. The same is certainly true in situations like the American occupation of Iraq.

What more than a decade's experience has shown is that interventions are more complicated and their success more difficult to attain than was believed when American and other UN forces waded ashore in Somalia. We have learned that it is relatively easy to end the violence by inserting well-armed peacekeepers into situations such as Bosnia, Kosovo, and East Timor (as well as Afghanistan and Iraq) and to keep the peace as long as the peacekeepers remain (Iraq is an exception to this point). We have also learned, however, that the presence of an intervening force in and of itself does not cause the formerly warring parties to settle their differences, so that the intervening forces can pack their bags and leave behind a tranquillity that will result in continuing peace.

The effect is to create open-ended commitments in which foreign troops are in place for a long time and eventually may be viewed as occupiers, even neocolonialists, rather than saviors or protectors. In extreme situations like Kosovo, the UN operation (including the deputized NATO military force) is dedicated to an outcome—Kosovo returning to the status of an autonomous region within the Yugoslav federation—that the vast majority of Albanian Kosovars oppose. When (or if) the hosts come publicly to oppose the continued presence of the outsiders, then it will become increasingly difficult to maintain the fiction that the intervening forces are not directly violating the sovereignty of their hosts.

CONCLUSION

The question of outside intervention in the affairs of countries has come into question most dramatically over Iraq. In the United States, the primary reasons for questioning have been political and practical. The issue has two facets. In the 2000 presidential election campaign, Republican George W. Bush came out strongly against the use of American forces in peacekeeping operations. The reason was practical: These deployments had arguably placed a strain on declining manpower and financial resources that could be devoted to more traditional military priorities. The implication was clear: Such interventions should be strictly limited or avoided in the future. Yet, the new president had been in office for less than nine months before the terrorist attacks of September 11, 2001, opened the window for new interventions—possibly protracted—in Afghanistan and later in Iraq. President Bush even embraced state building in postwar Afghanistan, an idea he had previously rejected for other places like Kosovo.

The position had changed. Questions of Afghan sovereignty were not raised in the deliberations over that intervention, although the administration made a point of "restoring" Iraqi sovereignty in June 2004. The sovereignty question has never been raised very publicly in discussions of American intervention in Iraq. Does this mean there is a reluctance to open a Pandora's box of problems if the relationship is addressed directly? Are we afraid to raise a position that is at odds with the more politically correct notion of humanitarian rights or other issues? Or is the question simply unimportant?

Whether we admit it openly or not, international intrusion into the domestic politics of states, no matter how objectionable or horrific the behavior of states may be, reflects a far different conceptualization of sovereignty than the one that reigned for the first 300 years of the modern state system. Had one asked in 1946 whether it was permissible to mount Operation Restore Hope in Somalia without the permission of the Somali government, the answer would have been overwhelmingly negative. The explanation would have been that such a mission would have been a direct violation of Somalia's sovereignty.

The conception of sovereignty reflected in that argument, of course, would have been the traditional definition based in state sovereignty as an absolute and exclusive possession.

The situation has clearly changed in the interim. What we have witnessed is a de facto, indirect assault on the idea of absolute state sovereignty as a consequence of the rise in legitimacy of the idea of human rights and arguably in combating terrorism. As noted in Chapter 4, the idea that all human beings have certain inalienable rights simply because of their humanity is a surprisingly recent development, as is the idea of interventions to thwart violations of those rights or to punish terrorist "evil doers" in the more recent debate over intervention.

The unintended effect of recent interventions has been to move the rationale for outside interference into alignment with the conceptualization of sovereignty based in the individual and the limited grant of individual sovereignty to the state. In terms of the meaning of sovereignty, there can be no other rationale for violating state sovereignty other than saying that state sovereignty *is no longer an inviolable principle of international relations*. To make that assertion, in turn, it is necessary to locate sovereignty somewhere else, as in individuals and groups whose rights are being violated and to whose rescue international efforts are directed to support higher international values like the eradication of terror.

No state makes the justification of their participation in UN or other peacekeeping activities or for Iraq-style interventions in these terms. Why not? The answer is simple and straightforward: No state is willing to admit to the dilution of the concept of state sovereignty because to do so concedes its own sovereignty is potentially diminished in the process; sovereignty is too much a bedrock of national jurisdiction to make such an admission. And no state will admit that its ability to control absolutely what occurs within its territory may not be entirely its own but may be subject to internationally imposed limits. Nowhere is that sentiment held more fiercely than in the United States.

The idea that no outside force should have the ability to interfere in internal American affairs can be dated back certainly to the Revolutionary period and the very negative view of governmental power held by most supporters of the American Revolution, and it remains an untouchable first principle that, if suggestions of its possible breach are raised, brings howls of protest. The result is schizophrenic but long-standing. The United States asserts the absolute nature of American national sovereignty, but has for a long time been willing in effect to ignore the sovereignty of others when it served American purposes. The numerous U.S. interventions in Central America and the Caribbean in the nineteenth and early twentieth centuries were nothing more than gross violations of the sovereignty of countries like Nicaragua, Panama, and Haiti. In some ways, the United States was simply acting as a large power in its "domain," the Western Hemisphere. Its profession of principles about sovereignty and its actions were, however, hardly consistent with one another.

The United States, of course, is not alone in this hypocrisy. The Russians (as Soviets), after all, invaded and occupied Afghanistan during the 1980s, a clear violation of Afghan sovereignty, and then turned around during the 1990s and used the absolutist rationale for sovereignty to argue that it was nobody's business but their own how they dealt with the uprising in Chechnya while simultaneously concurring in UNSCRs that violated the sovereignty of several other countries.

Afghanistan and especially Iraq bring life to this issue. Regardless of whether the U.S. invasion of either country was justifiable on policy grounds, both represented clear violations of the sovereignty of those countries. The United States simply ignored that it was ignoring a principle that it holds dear when applied to interfering with the United States. Doing this is not unique to the United States. Power trumps principle in these situations: The powerful do what they can, and the weak endure what they must, to paraphrase the old saw. The United States forced Iraq to endure what it could not avoid.

The United States may decide to forego future interventions on pragmatic bases such as interests or costs, thereby making the erosive effect of such actions on sovereignty a moot point. The general international trend toward asserting the legitimacy of human rights and the need to punish terrorists and others who threaten American interests and the international order (by no means always the same thing), however, makes abstinence on these grounds unlikely. The alternate justification for abstinence is based in its effects on sovereignty. If international interference in the often chaotic affairs of states occurs, eventually the question of the impact on sovereignty will have to be confronted directly and decisions made by the international community as to how much of the principle of state sovereignty it is willing to jettison in the name of humanity. The outcome is yet to be determined.

STUDY/DISCUSSION QUESTIONS

1. Is the idea of outside intervention in the civil wars of countries a viable, justifiable action by the UN or the international community more generally? Can you think of a circumstance in which such interference is or is not wise?

2. With which conception of sovereignty do you agree? Are, in other words, the rights of state more important that the rights of individuals and groups within states? How would the international system be different without the supremacy of state sovereignty?

3. Does American participation in military operations in countries torn by civil war or allegedly involved in terrorism violate American principles, such as our position on sovereignty? Or should the question of our participation be made on pragmatic grounds rather than on principles? If you were in a position to do so, how would you advise President Bush when the next intervention is proposed at the UN or elsewhere?

4. What would be worse for the relations among countries, a situation in which sovereignty is overridden in cases of large-scale abuse of human rights, or a situation in which such abuses are ignored and the sovereign rights of states upheld?

5. The American intervention in Afghanistan in 2001 represents a direct violation of Afghan sovereignty, tempered by virtual global approval of the action. Do the circumstances justify this violation of sovereignty? Do we have to add terrorism to the list of permissible violations of state sovereignty? Apply the same analysis to the American invasion and occupation of Iraq.

6. Iran and North Korea are often cited as the next "candidates" for American military activity because of their nuclear programs. In the debate over what to do in these situations, how important should the potential violations of the sovereignty of those countries be? Or should American national interests in preventing those states from becoming nuclear powers override the possible negative impact on the international system because of the potential dilution of sovereignty?

READING/RESEARCH MATERIAL

Boniface, Pascal. "What Justifies Regime Change?" *Washington Quarterly* 26, 3 (Summer 2003), 61–71.

Cusimano, Mary Ann (ed.). *Beyond Sovereignty.* Boston, MA: Bedford St. Martins, 1999.

Hashmi, Sohail H. (ed.). *State Sovereignty: Change and Persistence in International Relations.* University Park: Pennsylvania State University Press, 1997.

Kantor, Arnold, and Linton F. Brooks (eds.). *U.S. Intervention Policy for the Post–Cold War World.* New York: The American Assembly, 1994.

Lyons, Gene M., and Michael Mastanduno (eds.). *Beyond Westphalia: State Sovereignty and International Intervention.* Baltimore, MD: Johns Hopkins University Press, 1995.

Mills, Kurt. *Human Rights in the Emerging Global Order: A New Sovereignty?* New York: St. Martin's Press, 1998.

Snow, Donald M. *UnCivil Wars: International Security and the New Internal Conflicts.* Boulder, CO: Lynne Reinner, 1996.

———. *When America Fights: The Uses of American Force.* Washington, DC: CQ Press, 2001.

———, and Eugene Brown. *International Relations: The Changing Contours of Power.* New York: Longman, 2000.

WEB SITES

Organization promoting comprehensive debate on intervention and sovereignty
   International Commission on Intervention and State Sovereignty at
      http://www.icis.gc.ca

Comprehensive collection of views on moral dilemmas of humanitarian intervention
   Human Rights Initiative at http://www.cceia.org/themes/hrdwinter2001.html

Report of Stanley Foundation on humanitarian intervention
   "Any Means Necessary" at http://reports.stanletfdn.org/UNND01.pdf

Reports on international security, sovereignty, and intervention
   Pugwash Regional Conflict and Global Security Studies at
      http://www.pugwash.org/reports/rc/reclist.htm

CHAPTER SIX

Resolving the Irresolvable

THE ISRAELI-PALESTINIAN CONFLICT

PRÉCIS

A difficult problem facing the international system that largely arises from sovereignty is the existence of irresolvable conflicts, disputes so difficult that they defy successful attempts at resolution. The most extreme example of such conflicts in the contemporary international system is the conflict between the Israelis and the Palestinians, which is the subject of this case study.

The case will begin with a description of irresolvable conflicts, including their common characteristics and the basic methods that are available to try to resolve them. With that framework established, the dynamics of irresolvable conflicts will be applied to the conflict between Israel and the Palestinians arising from the partition of the "holy lands" that began in 1948 and has evolved since. Following a brief description of the issues involved, we will look at the American-brokered peace process that has been ongoing for over a quarter century, both in terms of its successes and ultimate failures. We will then look at the difficult and intractable differences between the two sides (and collateral examples like Lebanon) and will conclude with the prospects of moving this conflict to resolution—resolving the irresolvable.

In a world composed of sovereign states and marked by a scarcity of resources pursued by those states, conflict is an unavoidable, ubiquitous aspect of international relations. In most cases, the conflicts that divide states are not so basic and fundamental that the states cannot find means to resolve those differences. Ideally, processes of diplomacy yield outcomes that are mutually acceptable and thus satisfactorily resolve the differences in ways with which both sides can live. In other cases, differences cannot so easily be resolved and, at least some of the time, armed force becomes the way in which attempts are made—not always successfully—to resolve these differences. Between peaceful and warlike resolution, there is a continuum of means available that produce results more or less satisfactory to the contending sides.

IRRESOLVABLE CONFLICTS

There is another, thoroughly vexing category of conflicts, those presenting irreconcilable, unresolvable conflicts. In these kinds of conflicts, the issues that divide the two (or more) sides are so deep and fundamental that they cannot be resolved peaceably through diplomatic methods, either because the positions are so far apart or the animosities between the parties so great (or both) that the parties cannot find a basis to reach accord. Moreover, in these situations a military resolution wherein one side imposes its will on the other is either impossible or is unacceptable to the international community as a whole—or some part of it that influences the parties involved—so that a coerced solution cannot be implemented.

These kinds of situations, fortunately enough, are comparatively infrequent, but they do occur and are particularly intractable and difficult for the system to deal with. Within the contemporary international system, the ongoing differences between Taiwan and mainland China about the status of the island Republic of China (touched on in Chapter 3) and the Indo-Pakistani conflict over Kashmir (the subject of Chapter 12) stand out, but the most difficult example is the division between Israel and the Palestinian people over the political future of the piece of real estate known as Israel or Palestine, depending on the person to whom one is talking. The Israeli-Palestinian conflict is such a textbook example of irresolvable conflict that it is the subject of this chapter.

Irresolvable conflicts share at least six common characteristics. The first, which flows from the introductory discussion, is that the scarce resource normally involved is territory, the scarceness of which arises from the fact that there are multiples claimants to sovereign control over a piece of territory over which only one side can exercise sovereignty. In the case of China and Taiwan, for instance, both sides agree that Taiwan is rightly a part of China (some native Taiwanese disagree), and the question is over which political groups should exercise that sovereignty. The Kashmir question similarly revolves around whether India or Pakistan should exercise sovereignty over the mountainous formerly princely state of Jammu and Kashmir. The centerpiece of the Israeli-Palestinian feud is over whether the Palestinians or Israelis should rule all or different parts of the pre-partition territory once known as Palestine and now known variously as Israel or Palestine.

The second characteristic is that these territorial conflicts tend to be extremely emotional, deep, and fundamental. The emotion and depth arises from the fact that the territory is generally viewed as the rightful homeland of one or both sides, or the claims are rooted in some deep and fundamental division such as religion or ethnicity. Often (in the case of Palestine, for instance) individual plots of land in the disputed territories are viewed as the rightful home sites of individuals on both sides of the conflict, making their emotional attachment all the deeper than it might be otherwise. This emotional element can be—and often is—politically manipulated by those either seeking to avoid resolution of the conflict or wanting to subvert outcomes that do not work to their advantage. The fundamental source of division also makes compromise solutions extremely difficult to discover: It is, for instance, daunting to try to figure out how to divide a single dwelling between two hostile families that claim it.

Third, this emotional, fundamental base creates positions on the issue that become mutually exclusive and that consequently require mutually exclusive outcomes. Irresolvable conflicts tend to be viewed by both or all parties as strictly zero-sum exercises, in which one side's success is the other side's loss; there is little effort made or point in trying to find an accommodation in which both sides can benefit (a positive-sum exercise) or in which losses are equitably and acceptably apportioned (negative-sum games). In irresolvable conflicts, both sides will only accept outcomes in which they triumph and the other side loses.

Fourth, this intractability resonates throughout the populations affected in such a way as to reinforce the unwillingness and unacceptability of compromise. The position of both sides often becomes viewed as "righteous" by the antagonists to the point that the simple idea of compromise becomes virtually a sacrilege and those who promote compromise become suspect. Such depth of emotion may be limited to the extremists on both sides of the conflict, but their influence may be disproportionate to their numbers. One way this can occur is by the extremists succeeding in establishing the rhetorical high ground and thus being able to relegate the compromisers to the status of infidels or traitors. Another way is to resort to violence to pump up the emotions of followers against any movement toward resolution by peaceful means. Both these methods have been prominently evident in the Israeli-Palestinian conflict.

A fifth shared characteristic is often the failure of outside mediation to move the dispute toward resolution. When disputes become heated to the point of combustibility, as irresolvable conflicts often do, it is only natural for outsiders with interests on one or both sides of the conflict to want to help a process that will help defuse the situation, either by resolving it or by at least reducing its intensity so that it loses the ability or likelihood of bubbling over and disturbing international tranquility.

In some sense, the degree to which the particular conflict could endanger the situation affects the degree to which outsiders become interested. Conflicts between the government of Indonesia and East Timorese seeking independence did not attract much attention until reports of large-scale killings focused attention on the island of Timor; the isolation of the region from the global system meant that intervention was effectively regionalized with the lead involvement of Australia (which was mostly motivated by the fear of a stream of East Timorese refugees crossing the 600-mile straits to its shores). Similarly, the conflict over Kashmir attracted little outside interest until both India and Pakistan tested nuclear weapons in 1998. The more volatile Middle East, on the other hand, has ensured a high level of interest by the outside world in making sure their conflict does not spread to a general conflagration.

The sixth and final characteristic is the inability of the parties to find acceptable outcomes to the conflict, thereby guaranteeing its continuation. Conflicts over exclusive possession of scarce territorial resources are, of course, inherently difficult to resolve in an amicable manner, meaning that normal methods of conflict resolution have generally failed (that failure is what defines irresolvable conflicts). In this case, the only way to reach a conclusion may be through the imposition of a settlement favoring one side at the expense of the other, which may be impossible for one of two reasons.

One reason may be that neither side has the resources available to force a settlement on the other, at least within acceptable bounds of resource expenditure. The reason Kashmir remains in a state of uncertain sovereignty is that neither India nor Pakistan has the required military might to impose a settlement on the entire territory. The only way either could conceivably do so would be to escalate the conflict to the point that it might become nuclear, an alternative the international community would find unacceptable (as would the affected populations, presumably). The failure of Israel to eliminate Hiz'ballah in Lebanon in 2006 suggests the possibility that there is no military solution to the Israeli-Palestinian problem as well.

In other cases, the imposition of force may be physically possible but geopolitically unacceptable. Israel, after all, has maintained authority over a good bit of land jointly claimed by it and the Palestinians since at least 1967, and militarily it is certainly conceivable-although more questionable since the Lebanon invasion-that Israel could reassert its sway over all the contested territories. Doing so, however, would likely broaden the conflict within the region, with uncertain outcomes—the worst of which could be catastrophic; and doing so would strain Israeli resources and relations with the rest of the world. As a result, any instincts the Israelis may have toward an imposed solution are effectively stifled by the consequences such an imposition might bring.

The nature of irresolvable conflicts makes them entirely more difficult to resolve than lesser conflicts and narrows the possible outcomes that can occur. Unlike less intense and fundamental disagreements, irresolvable conflicts (as the name implies) may be *impossible* to resolve to the acceptable satisfaction of all parties, and if the imposition of solutions in which one side or the other decisively prevails, they may become problems that are not solved but are simply "worked" (kept under control). In this case, the only "resolution" may be a status quo that is basically unacceptable to all parties but is less unacceptable to one or the other than an outcome in which one side decisively loses. In that case, the only real possibility of a breakthrough must involve some shift in the perceptions of what is and is not acceptable by one or both sides.

THE ISRAELI-PALESTINIAN CONFLICT

The ongoing conflict between Israel and Palestine meets all the criteria for an irresolvable conflict. It is quintessentially about sovereign control of territory that is coveted with great passion by both sides. The positions that both the Israelis and the Palestinians take toward their claims to the land are fundamental, deep, and emotional, deeply shrouded in historical tenure and even religious claims and bases. Because "God" has empowered both sides in their own minds, the claims each has are deeply held by their supporting populations and make it essentially impossible for leaders on either side to propose major concessions or compromises, which can be (and are) viewed as heresy by those at the extremes on both sides. The positions are thus intractable, and outside attempts to mediate (in this case led mostly by the United States) have not succeeded in reducing the issues dividing the sides, despite strong and concerted efforts at trying to act as the midwife of settlement. Moreover, no imposed settlement in which one side is forced to accept great sacrifices is acceptable to that side, and even if it could physically be imposed by one side on the other, such a settlement would be internationally unacceptable, particularly in a region as volatile and important as the Middle East.

In these circumstances, the actors remain at loggerheads, with no immediate prospect of breakthroughs that can attain settlement. Progress has been made in periodic efforts to resolve the problem, but they always are dashed on the hard facts of basic and irresolvable differences. Until something happens to change the basic views of the two sides toward one another and the issues, the Israeli-Palestinian conflict will remain a disagreement to be worked, not to be solved.

In order to understand this conflict as irresolvable, we need to examine it and how it has evolved. We will thus begin by looking at the structure of the problem, how it has evolved, and what the basic unresolved obstacles to resolution are. One factor that distinguishes this conflict from other irresolvable conflicts is the extraordinary efforts and prestige a major power—the United States—has ultimately unsuccessfully invested in trying to overcome the conflict, and thus we will review the record of attempted solutions, beginning with the efforts of Jimmy Carter at Camp David in 1978 and going forward through George W. Bush's "road map" for peace. This background will form the backdrop for examining the contemporary conflict and its current most vexing manifestations—the security fence being constructed by Israel to separate it from the Palestinian territories, the Palestinian election of a majority of members of Hamas to the Palestinian Legislative Council in January 2006, and the Israeli attack on Lebanon in 2006. The study will conclude with an assessment of what, if any, prospects exist for resolving the irresolvable.

The Israeli-Palestinian Problem

The heart and soul of the disagreement between Israel and the Palestinians is a real estate dispute over the rightful ownership and sovereign control of the territory known historically as Palestine and now largely controlled by Israel. The contemporary basis of this dispute has its roots in the late 1800s, when the Zionist movement in Europe resulted in the migration of increasing numbers of Jews to Palestine to avoid religious persecution and to fulfill a biblical admonition to return to the "promised land." The movement gained momentum after World War II and the Holocaust stimulated a surge of Jewish immigration to what they called Israel. It crested and became a problem with the establishment of the state of Israel in 1948.

The piece of territory over which the conflict alternately simmers and rages has been the subject of contention and violence for far longer than is reflected in the current impasse, which is in some ways just the most recent chapter in the saga over the "holy land." The roots of this disagreement, which date back to biblical times, have been the subject of innumerable treatises and arguments regarding rightful ownership over centuries and millennia that need not be repeated here, other than to note both that these claims exist and that they form underlying arguments to which both (or all) sides make reference to buttress their claims. For present purposes, suffice it say that all parties have impressive, if contradictory, historical and scriptural arguments that buttress the cases they wish to make.

The current dispute has its roots in the immediate post–World War II period, although the movement to return much of the Jewish population (largely European) to the area goes back to the nineteenth-century Zionist movement calling for a return of the disapora after a thousand-year absence. This movement was essentially peaceful and was absorbed by the Muslim Palestinians before World War II, and the two peoples, Israeli and Palestinian, essentially lived side-by-side in peace. Only when the post–World War II flood of Holocaust survivors found its way to Israel did the question of land become critical.

ISRAELI INDEPENDENCE, WAR, AND DISPLACEMENT

The movement of a large number of Jews into Palestine (at the time a part of Transjordan) stimulated the desire for the creation of a Jewish state of Israel that had been central to the Zionist appeal and that many Jews believed had been promised them by God. This movement obviously disquieted many of the Muslim Palestinians, who found this possibility inimical to their centuries-long possession of the territory (which had, until the end of World War I, been part of the Ottoman Empire). When the Israelis declared their independence in 1948, a declaration supported by the major powers (including the United States and the Soviet Union) in the United Nations and Israel's statehood was proclaimed, the result was violence.

There were two basic reactions to Israel's declaration as a sovereign state. One was the exodus of a large part of the Palestinian Muslim population, which feared retribution and repression under the new Israeli government. (There had been numerous instances of inter-communal violence on both sides in the months and years leading to the creation of the new state, thereby enlivening the fears of the Palestinians.) Most Palestinians who fled left with little more than the shirts on their backs and a few possessions, so that they became an instant refugee problem in the territories—especially the West Bank of the Jordan River—to which they went. The second reaction was for most of the surrounding Muslim states to declare war on the new Israeli state and to launch attacks designed to destroy Israel. These attacks were ineptly carried out and absolutely uncoordinated, so that military and para-military forces within the new Jewish state (which had been part of the resistance to post-war British administration of the area) easily repulsed the attacks. In the process, the original territorial boundaries of the Israeli state were actually enlarged by the outcome.

The 1948 war established the basic conditions that continue until today, although the details have changed over time. There were two major effects. The first, most profound, and most relevant was the effect on the Palestinian Muslims. Most of the Palestinian population fled their homes in Israel and became refugees, and collectively the Palestinians constituted a *stateless nation* (a distinct people with no home state that they could claim). Such statelessness had been part of the burden of the Jewish population for nearly a millennium; the status was now transferred to the Palestinians. Because the surrounding territories into which the Palestinians fled were generally poor and incapable of absorbing the new residents, the status of most refugees was wretched and powerless, and as time went by, increasingly hopeless. This set of circumstances forms the basic rationale for a demand for the creation of an independent Palestinian state. Such a state could be of two natures, which divides the current debate. One possibility is that the Palestinian state could be carved out of part of the original Palestine (leaving both an Israeli and a Palestinian state as the outcome—an arrangement that was part of the original Zionist plan for the area). The other possibility is to return Palestinian domain over the entirety of the area, thereby eliminating Israel. As we shall see, the nature of the resulting Palestinian state remains the most basic division between the two sides, the resolution of which is necessary if the conflict is to be resolved. A particularly vexing part of the territorial puzzle is the final disposition of Jerusalem, and especially the Old City, the site of religious symbols basic to Islam, Judaism, and Christianity.

The other outcome was to endow the new state of Israel with a kind of special status. On the surface, the Israelis were severely disadvantaged when they were attacked by forces from the surrounding states, including Egypt, Jordan, Syria, Iraq, and Saudi Arabia. Post-conflict analysis has shown that the forces arrayed against the Israelis were nowhere near as formidable as a cursory examination would suggest and that the Israelis actually had their attackers significantly outgunned and were better organized militarily than their assailants. Nonetheless, the Israelis emerged from the conflict as the heroes of a David-and-Goliath struggle in which they had prevailed. That aura would gradually fade, but it was a worthwhile adjunct for a period of time.

Israel and its neighbors fought three subsequent wars, each with different impacts on the ongoing conflict. In terms of its direct impact on the current situation, the first of these conflicts, the 1956 Suez War, was the least consequential. In that conflict, a coalition of Britain, France, and Israel attacked Egypt, with the purpose of seizing control of the Suez Canal, which had been nationalized by Egyptian president Gamal Abdul Nasser in 1955. The canal had been jointly owned by the British and French (a combination of private and public ownership), and the nationalization threatened their investments. Israel joined the effort to occupy and potentially to annex the Sinai Peninsula. While the military operation succeeded easily, negative international reaction—led jointly by the Soviet Union and the United States—demanded, and succeeded in obtaining, a reversal of the results. The major impact on the region was that it began the final withdrawal of Great Britain from the region, thereby creating the opportunity for other outside influences, a role eventually adopted by the United States. (The French, who felt betrayed by American opposition to their operation, also began the process of loosening ties with the United States as a result.)

The other two wars were of greater consequence, if in different ways, one rewriting the map of the region and the other creating the geopolitical incentive to move concertedly toward resolution of the difficulties between Israel and its Muslim opponents. Each is thus important to view at least briefly.

The Six Day's War of 1967

Slightly less than eleven years after the Suez conflict, war broke out again between Israel and its neighbors. The precipitant of the fighting was the removal of a United Nations force (the United Nations Emergency Force, or UNEF) from the Egyptian-Israeli border, where it had acted as a tripwire to prevent either country from attacking the other. When it left, Egypt launched an attack on Israel and was joined by the armies of Jordan and Syria. The result was an utter disaster for the Muslim states. The Israelis managed to decimate their opponents in the remarkably short period of six days, changing fundamentally the power balance in the region and setting the groundwork for the current conflict.

When the dust had settled at the end of the war, Israel not only had defeated the armed forces of each of its opponents, it had also occupied significant territories belonging to each. From Egypt, the Israelis gained the Sinai Peninsula and the Gaza Strip, a small appendix of Sinai along the Mediterranean coast adjacent to Israel, as shown in Figure 6.1.

This territorial exchange greatly enhanced the physical security of Israel, because any future Egyptian attack against them would first have to fight its way across Sinai, which the Israelis fortified against such an incursion. At the same time, Egypt was badly embarrassed by having such a large part of its territory taken from it, and the occupation also meant that the east bank of the Suez Canal was now in Israeli hands (although the canal was closed for a time because of ships sunk in its waters during the war). The Israelis seized the West Bank of the Jordan River from Jordan, thereby further increasing its physical security by making it much more difficult for a future enemy to dash across the narrowest parts of Israel and effectively cut the country in two. Jordan, however, lost its most economically productive region. The Israelis completed the occupation by seizing the Golan Heights, a mountainous region bordering northern Israel that the Syrians had used to launch artillery attacks against Israeli *kibbutzes* before the war. As we shall see in Chapter 14, the Israelis also gained control of the water supply for the Jordan River in the process.

These outcomes both altered the geopolitical balance in the region and created the physical basis for the peace process that would follow. Egyptian humiliation at the loss of Sinai and Gaza and the consequent desire to regain those lost territories helped form the basis for negotiations with Israel a decade later that would begin the peace process at Camp David. At the same time, Jordan's loss of the West Bank changed greatly the Palestinian situation. Part of the change was that many Palestinian refugees had settled on the West Bank after 1948, and they were again displaced by the events of 1967, as more fled into Jordan and also Lebanon, where they added to political problems in those countries. Many Palestinians, however, remained in the occupied West Bank, where they were subjected to Israeli rule over what they considered part of their own historic lands. Some of the fuel for the *intifadas* (uprisings) in the 1990s and 2000s was sown in this change of control. At the same time, the seizure effectively ended the Jordanian claim on the West Bank and allowed negotiators to think of a solution to the Palestinian real estate dispute in terms encompassing both Israel and the occupied West Bank and Gaza. This transformation is especially important in so-called two-states proposals (proposals to create a Palestinian states alongside Israel). The exact manner for dividing those territories among sovereign jurisdictions remains one of the major issues dividing the sides.

Yom Kippur War of 1973

The Six Days' War created the conditions with which the peace process would have to deal, and the Yom Kippur War created the perceived necessity and impetus to begin that process. The reasons had to do with the conduct and outcome of the war, and more important, what almost—but did not—occur during its conduct.

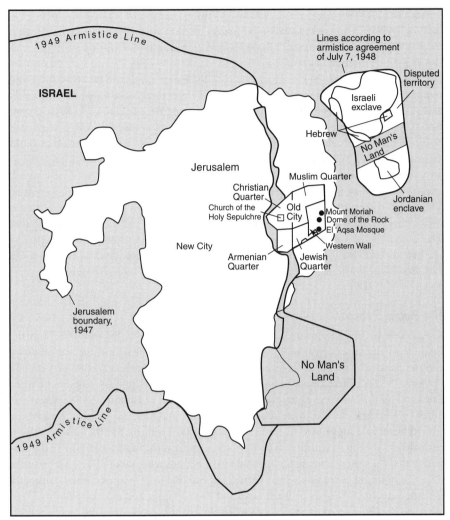

Map 6.1 Map of Jerusalem

Two things stand out about the 1973 war. The first is that it was the first time the Israelis suffered significant military defeats against their Muslim rivals. As a result, at the darkest hours early in the conflict, the Israelis were reported to have authorized the arming of their clandestine nuclear arsenal for possible use against neighboring capitals to reverse their fortunes on the battlefield (the Israelis neither confirm nor deny that they either possess such weapons or that they activated them). This twist of fate greatly increased the likelihood that a Middle East conflict might escalate into a superpower nuclear confrontation, as the United States backed Israel and the Soviet Union backed the Islamic states in the conflict. Second, after the Israelis reversed the tide of military events and routed their opponents, the Soviets threatened to airlift troops to the front to save an Egyptian army from possible extinction, thereby further increasing the possibility of a superpower showdown. Like the nuclear arming by Israel, this possibility was also averted by diplomatic means.

The outcome changed the calculation of Middle East conflict in two ways. First and most fundamentally, the very real prospect that the war could have somehow reluctantly drawn the United States into a confrontation that could have led to World War III convinced both sides, but especially the United States, that such a possibility had to be avoided in the future: The Arab-Israeli conflict was simply not worth a nuclear war that could destroy the United States. This recognition created the determination that finding a peaceful settlement (or at least averting future war, an important distinction to which we will return) was absolutely necessary. The second change made this outcome possible to pursue. The Soviets did not resupply their allies in the war—notably the Egyptians—as fast or as well as they would have liked, and as a result, Egypt broke its ties with the Soviet Union. The United States leaped into the power vacuum created by the Soviets forced departure and quickly established leverage with the Egyptians, in addition to its previous relationship with Israel. The possibility of a peace process was thus added to its perceived necessity.

The Peace Process

The process of attempting to end the territorial imbroglio over Palestine was both the result of an outside determination by the United States that such an effort was necessary and an initiative by the parties involved. In fact, some outside pressure was almost certainly necessary, because there had been no formal—or significant informal—relations between Israel and the surrounding Islamic states since the creation of Israel in 1948. Thus, it was necessary for some outsider to create a forum in which to pursue a settlement. Because the United States had supplanted Great Britain as the major influence in the area (a position enhanced by the forced withdrawal of the Soviets) and saw the necessity of ending the possibility that the region could ignite a global war, it became a logical candidate for that role.

The resulting peace process has been going on for over a quarter century, without a decisive outcome. The wars between Israel and its neighbors, and especially the Six Days' War, had created a set of territorial issues that the Islamic states of the region felt needed resolving, and that perceived need created leverage for the Israelis to engage their enemies. The Israelis had territory the status of which they could negotiate; the states that had lost territory wanted that territory back, and thus had to be willing to talk to Israel about issues the Israelis valued; notably, their right to exist.

The process began with the convening of Egypt and Israel for peace negotiations in the United States by U.S. president Jimmy Carter in 1978 at the presidential retreat at Camp David, and President William J. Clinton reprised that process in 2000. Between those events, Israel and Jordan independently negotiated an agreement, leaving only Syria and the Palestinians with unsettled differences with Israel. George W. Bush reactivated outside assistance in the process in 2003 when he presented his "road map" for solving the differences between the two.

The result of this process has been some progress toward a peace settlement, but the ultimate achievement of a comprehensive settlement of this intractable conflict remains elusive. As is normally the case in complex negotiations, the parties negotiated and settled what in retrospect appeared to have been the easier differences first, and as they peeled away the onion skin of differences, what has remained are the most difficult issues. At the very core of these intractable issues is the irresolvable conflict between Israel and Palestine. An examination of the steps both shows what progress has been made and why this irresolvable conflict remains unresolved.

Camp David I

That there even was a first meeting at Camp David is one of the miracles of twentieth-century diplomacy. Prior to the dynamics that led to the meeting, Israel had never held officials meetings of any kind with its neighbors (or the Palestinians), and all the Muslim states in the region were committed, to one degree or another, not only to denying the legitimate existence of Israel but also to destroying the Israeli state and hence to restoring Palestine to Muslim rule. In fact, this shared hatred for Israel was the major component of what little sense of "Arab unity" there was in the Middle East.

The process leading to Camp David begins with the Yom Kippur War, as noted. When Jimmy Carter came to the White House in 1977, a peace in the region was at the top of his list of foreign policy priorities, and one of his first acts was to issue his plan for peace. The governments on both sides rejected the plan Carter proposed, but it became at least a beginning point for future discussions.

Egyptian president Anwar Sadat jump-started the process. In 1977, Sadat flew to Jerusalem, where he pointedly visited the Dome of the Rock and Al Aqsa mosque (the second-holiest sites in Islam, Muslim access to which had been denied since 1967) and met with Israeli prime minister Menachem Begin. The move was extremely bold because going to Jerusalem implicitly recognized the existence of Israel and thus broke ranks with his Islamic brethren in the region. Egypt and Sadat were roundly condemned in the region because of this contact, and after the Camp David accords, were diplomatically and economically isolated. Begin was also taking a chance because there was considerable Israeli opposition to the potential return of Sinai and Gaza to the Egyptians, a prospect that contacts between the two states raised.

Sadat's visit to Jerusalem proved the stepping-stone for the meeting convened by Carter between the two leaders at Camp David in 1978. As just noted, there were considerable negative influences on the process, and the very idea of accommodation between Israel and its enemies seemed a long shot at best. Part of the reason the meetings succeeded was that Begin and Sadat showed extraordinary leadership in the face of tremendous opposition to the enterprise. At the same time, they both needed something that only the negotiations could provide, and each side had something it could give to achieve those goals. At the same time, what they could agree on was less than the entirety of the issues dividing Israel from the other states and from the Palestinians; on those issues that could not be resolved, the result was to defer the matter to future efforts.

There were three basic issues between the two negotiators. The first was Israel's desire to be recognized by its neighbors, including an admission of Israel's right to exist. Movement on this issue was sufficiently important to Begin that he was willing to compromise on other issues to realize the desired outcome. Egypt represented the second and third interests. Egypt felt enormously humiliated by the forced cessation of Sinai and Gaza and badly wanted both back as a matter of national prestige and pride. At the same time, Egypt hoped that opposition to its discussions with the hated Israelis would be moderated in the Muslim world if it also managed to get the Israelis to move toward a Palestinian state.

Two of the three issues could be and were included in a quid pro quo, while the third was too difficult to settle in detail and was deferred for future consideration. As a result, the Camp David Accord (as it was known) consisted of three agreements:

1. The withdrawal of Israel from the Sinai Peninsula;
2. A peace treaty between Israel and Egypt that included recognition of Israel;
3. A promise to resolve the Palestinian question in the form of autonomy for the West Bank and Gaza Strip, which were to become the basis for a Palestinian state.

The first two provisions were implemented routinely. The Israelis withdrew from Sinai in two steps in 1979 and 1982, returning control (including control of an oil-producing capability developed by Israel during its occupation) to the Egyptians. The peace treaty between the two countries was signed in 1979, beginning the process leading to normal relations between them. Egypt got back the territory it wanted, and Israel got the recognition it desired.

The agreement foundered on the Palestinian question. The fate of the Palestinian state was a much more complex and contentious matter than the other two issues, and thus it was deferred. The disposition of Jerusalem, a question that was and remains contentious, symbolic of this dispute. The problem is that both sides claimed (and continue to claim) the Old City (East) Jerusalem as their capitals, and there are numerous religious shrines that neither religious group is willing to entrust control over to the other side. The issue was thus intractable and effectively too difficult to resolve, so it was left unresolved for future negotiators. Carter explained the situation in a *New York Times* op-ed piece shortly after the conclusion of the negotiations: "We knew that Israel had declared sovereignty over the entire city but that the international community considered East Jerusalem to be legally part of the occupied West Bank. We realized that no Israeli leader could renounce Israel's position, and that it would be politically suicidal for Sadat or any other Arab leader to surrender any of their people's claims regarding the Islamic and Christian holy places." The fate of Jerusalem has remained a major sticking point in the process. At Camp David I, it was effectively deferred for the future.

Camp David II

Between 1978 and Clinton's convening of a second Camp David summit in 2000, the peace process had evolved. In the interim, there had been progress on some aspects of the relationship between Israel and her neighbors, but reaching a mutually satisfactory understanding and progress on the question of the Palestinians remained elusive.

The first Camp David accord had promised a movement toward Palestinian "autonomy," but there was disagreement about exactly what autonomy implied. In the eyes of most of the Muslim world and among Palestinians themselves, autonomy over specific parts of the occupied territory was part of a process leading to full Palestinian control and sovereignty over the West Bank and Gaza and, eventually, to the establishment of a Palestinian state. To many in Israel, autonomy certainly meant turning over various local governmental functions to the Palestinian Authority, but not necessarily total authority and not necessarily entailing a commitment to a sovereign Palestinian state. Most Muslim states saw this Israeli interpretation of Camp David I as simply further evidence of Israeli duplicity and intransigence.

A major breakthrough appeared to occur in 1993, when representatives of Palestine and Israel met secretly in Oslo, Norway, at the invitation of the Norwegian government. At those meetings, the parties agreed to what became known as the Oslo framework as a way to move talks forward. The Palestinian Liberation Organization (PLO) represented the Palestinians and agreed to end its call for the destruction of Israel and to renounce terrorism. In return, the Israelis agreed to withdraw their authority from Gaza and the West Bank city of Jericho and turn that authority over to the Palestinians. A deadline was also set for a final agreement to all issues by September 12, 2000.

With the Oslo framework in hand, Israel and Jordan managed to reach agreement on a peace accord in 1994 that removed Jordanian resistance to Israeli existence and created a territorial settlement allowing the creation of a Palestinian state on the West Bank, which had formerly been part of Jordan. This agreement left only Syria as a contiguous opposition state to Israel with which it had not achieved peace (there was no peace agreement with Lebanon, but the Lebanese had also never taken part in the wars against Israel). Thus, the focus of the peace process had shifted to direct negotiations between the Israelis and the Palestinians.

Like Camp David I, progress toward fulfilling the promises of the Oslo accord lagged as well. Violence continued on both sides, in the form of the first *intifada* by Palestinians and isolated acts such as the assassination of Israeli prime minister Yitzhak Rabin by an Israeli extremist in 1995 and an attack against a Jerusalem mosque that left over 25 dead. At the same time, both sides accused the other of not living up to its side of the Oslo accords. The Israelis accused the PLO of failing to renounce violence and terrorism and used Palestinian suicide terrorist attacks as evidence. The Palestinians countered that the Israelis were not living up the agreements they had made for turning over jurisdiction to the Palestinian Authority.

Camp David II

With the September 2000 deadline looming and the end of his second term impending, American president William J. Clinton sought to revive the peace process in July 2000 by inviting Yasir Arafat, head of the Palestinian Authority, and Israeli prime minister Ehud Barak for a reprise of the 1978 meeting at Camp David. His hope was to achieve a comprehensive peace agreement that would simultaneously end the world's most intractable conflict and provide a pinnacle to his own term in office. Because of what proved to be irresolvable differences, the process ultimately failed.

By the time Clinton convened the parties at Camp David II, there were four major outstanding issues facing the conferees. They are presented in reverse order of the difficulty of their settlement.

The largest and most public issue was the pace and extent of transfer of the West Bank and Gaza from Israel to the Palestinian Authority (PA). Both sides had their own, very different timetables and formulas; as might be guessed, the Palestinians consistently insisted that more territory be transferred more quickly than Israel proposed. Israeli settlements in both Gaza and the West Bank exacerbated the problem. These housing areas had been built after the 1967 occupation to accommodate the immigration of more settlers to Israel and were permanent enough in appearance to suggest that Israel would not turn them back to the Palestinians, although they were on land claimed as part of Palestine. Moreover, the Israelis placed the settlements on prime territory (for instance, where there was access to water, a scarce commodity), and the settlers stubbornly insisted that these settlements were permanent. These settlers, who feared being abandoned by Israel to what they assumed would be the not-so-tender care of the PA, became a highly emotional, vocal factor in Israeli politics; to many Israelis, abandoning the settlements and the settlers became equated with capitulating to the Palestinians.

This question of timetables was the most negotiable and tractable of the issues dividing the two sides. Despite the emotions surrounding the settlements on both sides, it was possible to find enough areas on the West Bank and Gaza that could be ceded without inflaming the Israelis while assuaging the Palestinians, at least for a while. When the discussion moved to the "final solution" of the territorial problem, these compromises were not enough.

The second issue was the timing of the declaration of Palestinian sovereignty and total independence. The issue was, of course, related to land transfer by the question of sovereignty over what. This issue thus could be divided into two questions, on neither of which was there agreement: (1) *when* the transfer of authority would take place, and (2) the *physical extent* of the territory that would be ceded.

To Arafat, the answer to the first question was the deadline set under the Oslo accords, and he proposed that the declaration of the Palestinian state should occur on September 12, 2000, as set at Oslo, and he threatened to do so unilaterally if the conference at Camp David failed to reach an agreement. Barak, reflecting Israeli popular sentiment, believed the date should be deferred, when the PA had clearly put an end to terrorism against Israel by Palestinians (a position supported by Israelis who opposed any Palestinian independence).

The other question was the physical extent of the Palestinian state that would be created. At the time of Camp David II, the PA administered about 40 percent of the West Bank, and the question was, how much more territory (in addition to Gaza) would be added. As one would expect, the two sides were also divided on this issue, with Israel proposing less expansion than the Palestinians, who wanted the whole West Bank (the entire occupied territory). Such a division would deprive the Israelis of all the settlements they had built and was thus politically unacceptable in Israel. In the end, the two sides agreed that 95 percent of the West Bank would be ceded to Palestine, leaving the Israelis in control only of a few settlements basically contiguous to Israeli territory. Arafat eventually rejected this concession as part of rejecting the entire peace settlement.

Something like a compromise was possible on the first two issues, but the same was not true of the third and fourth issues. The third was the question of East Jerusalem. As Jimmy Carter had noted over two decades earlier, the problem of who would control

Jerusalem (or specific parts of it) had been a deal stopper that had been simply shelved in 1978, and no progress toward accommodation had ensued in the interim. The only difference now was that the eventual status of Jerusalem became an open matter of contention, and without a resolution to its status, an overall peace settlement could not be reached in 2000.

The issue itself had not changed. Both Israel and Palestine claim the city as their own, and Israel claims all of the city as its capital, whereas the Palestinians claim the Old City (East Jerusalem) as their capital. The positions are mutually exclusive, which means an agreement can only be reached if one or both sides agrees to compromise.

Compromise, of course, is made all the more difficult because of the religious significance of Jerusalem to adherents of both Judaism and Islam (as well as Christianity). Access to the holiest sites (the Wailing Wall and the Little Wall to Jews, the Temple Mount to Muslims) is a *sine qua non* to both, but the physical contiguity of the sites makes the division of jurisdiction difficult or impossible. Because both Muslims and Jews have been denied access when the area has been controlled by the other, there is an understandable reluctance to cede control in any manner. How can this impasse be overcome?

At Camp David I, the parties had agreed to the general principle that the city is holy to all three religions and that members of all three religions should have free access to their holy sites. These sites, in turn, should be controlled by followers of the relevant religion. The conferees in 1978 could not, however, agree on a mutually satisfactory resolution to who should exercise sovereignty over the city as a whole, and thus access to the religious sites.

Camp David II unsuccessfully attempted to redraw sovereign authority to the satisfaction of all involved. The United States proposed splitting sovereignty over different parts of the Old City, with Palestinian control over the Islamic and Christian Quarters and Israeli control over the Jewish and Armenian Quarters. This division was not satisfactory to the parties, and so a second proposal was drafted that included giving the Palestinians sovereign control over several neighborhoods surrounding the Old City and administrative autonomy within the walls of the Old City. This proposal was unacceptable to Israel.

The status of Jerusalem could not be resolved, because the positions of each side is absolute (both sides claim sovereignty) and a history of animosity and treachery does not allow them to reach compromise solutions in which trust must inevitably play a part. This intractability is also built into the fourth and most irresolvable issue, repatriation.

The issue underlying repatriation (or what Palestinians call the "right to return") is conceptually simple, if extremely difficult to resolve. Palestinians who fled their homes in what is now Israel or were otherwise displaced from such home sites have never given up their belief that they are entitled to return and reclaim those pieces of real estate. Thus, they cling tenaciously to their supposed right to return to their homes. Israelis, who have since resettled and developed the land claimed by the Palestinians, equally believe they now hold clear legal title and that the Palestinian "right" to repatriation is not a right at all.

The issue is both geopolitical and political. The number of Palestinian expatriates who claim territory in Israel, when combined with the million or so Palestinian Muslims who reside in Israel, would exceed the Jewish population of the country if all were to return. Thus, allowing the immigration of the Palestinians back to Israel/Palestine would effectively mean Israel would no longer be a Jewish state. Even though there are many Israelis who oppose the idea of a sectarian Jewish state, very few believe Jews should not be the majority in Israel. Additionally, the return of the Palestinians would essentially double the population of the country, and it is not clear how such an influx could be physically accommodated.

These geopolitical facts frame the political dilemma: The question of repatriation is fundamental, absolute, and nonnegotiable on both sides. No Israeli government could even consider repatriation because of the effects on the Jewish state and on individual Israelis who would suddenly find themselves in legal battles over their homes from former Palestinian occupants. Equally, no Palestinian politician can possibly renounce or negotiate away the right of the Palestinian refugees to return to what they view as their homes. The immediate prospects of return may be exceedingly dim, but the long-term goal is so strongly held as to be nonnegotiable.

The inability to find solutions to the third and fourth basic issues meant the comprehensive peace settlement that the Clinton administration favored could not be realized, regardless of whether agreement on timetables and the eventual shape of the Palestinian state (not including Israel) could have been resolved. As long as positions on Jerusalem and the right of return remain as far apart and irreconcilable as they are, the prospects of resolution remain elusive.

Beyond Camp David: The Road Map

After the Camp David II talks collapsed without a final resolution, Palestinian violence returned in late 2000 in the form of the second *intifada* that has included Palestinian suicide/martyr bombings and reprisals by the Israeli Defense Forces (IDF). In February 2001, the Israelis elected a government that made Ariel Sharon prime minister, and he quickly visited the Wailing Wall, sparking predictable violence by the Palestinians. In addition, his government renounced the Camp David proposals, a spokesman declaring "everything in Camp David is null and void unless it was signed, and nothing was signed." The government also took a hard line on remaining issues. Sharon backed away from Barak's offer of a Palestinian state composed of 95 percent of the West Bank, saying such a state would be based on the 42 percent of the territory administered at the time by the Palestinian Authority. On Jerusalem, Sharon declared the Old City is "the united and indivisible capital of Israel—with the Temple Mount as its center—for all eternity." On repatriation, he announced the renewal of the Zionist goal of Jewish immigration to Israel, which physically precludes the return of the Palestinians. None of these positions, of course, is acceptable to the Palestinians.

The Bush administration made its contribution to the peace process in 2003, when it announced its "road map" for achieving peace, a set of guidelines to measure progress toward settlement. The road map proposed three sequential steps toward peace. In step one (2003), the Palestinians were to put an end to terrorism by Palestinians operating from Palestinian soil, and the Israelis were to suspend the building of new settlements on the West Bank and Gaza. In step two (2004), a provisional Palestinian government was to be established. In step three (2005), all "remaining differences" were to be settled and a Palestinian state was to be established.

THE CURRENT IMPASSE

The road map failed to move the parties on any of the major issues. Between 2000 and 2004 there were no major changes in the conflict, but four sequential factors have coalesced more recently that could influence the future. The first was the beginning of the erection of a fence dividing Israel from the West Bank, which began in 2004 and continues to the present. When completed, it could seal off the West Bank from pre-1967 Israel. Second, in 2005, the government of Ariel Sharon agreed to and carried out the end of the occupation of Gaza, thereby moving the territorial possibilities forward. In 2006, the dynamics changed as governments changed on both sides. Most dramatically in January, the Palestinians elected a majority of members of Hamas to the Palestinian Legislative Council. When Ariel Sharon was forced to resign his prime ministership after a massive stroke left him incapable of remaining in office, new Israeli elections in April resulted in the election of Ehud Olmert as his successor. Fourth, the outcome of the Israeli invasion of Lebanon in summer 2006 clouds the military balance in the region. Do these changes make a difference?

"The Fence," as it is known simply in the region, is a physical barrier gradually separating all of the West Bank from Israel proper. The Israelis erected a similar fence between its territory and Gaza in 1994. As David Makovsky explains, "since early 2001, not a single Palestinian suicide bomber has infiltrated Israel from Gaza." The Gaza fence thus serves as a precedent for building the similar structure dividing the West Bank from Israel proper. Moreover, Makovsky adds, the fence serves the Israeli interests "to reduce terrorism and to find a way out of the settlement morass that lets Israel keep a Jewish majority within its borders."

The fence has been loudly, and occasionally violently, opposed by the Palestinians on grounds as diverse as cutting through Palestinian territory to preventing (or making exceedingly difficult) Palestinian commuting to jobs in Israel. At the same time, an effective fence is bound to assuage Israeli fears of continued terrorism and thus relieve that barrier to creating a Palestinian state. By now, the fact of the fence is well enough established that its existence is not so much the issue as *where* it is placed, as it will form a boundary between Israel and a Palestinian state. If the fence minimizes Israeli settlements and thus maximizes the territory available to Palestine, it may turn into a blessing rather than a curse in the peace process. In an interview published in the April 17, 2006, edition of *Newsweek,* Olmert suggested that the final shape of the fence will reflect adjusted realities, saying, "The fence will have to be adjusted to the makeup of these blocs of settlements," which include the consolidation and elimination of some existing settlements.

An independent Gaza physically walled off from Israel has been established, and the same may be occurring on the West Bank, although whether it happens a matter of future negotiations. Since the latter part of 2005, when Sharon suffered his stroke, the political leadership that will have to conduct negotiations has also changed, and these changes will undoubtedly also affect the outcome.

The most fundamental change has occurred in Palestine, where the January 2006 elections swept Arafat's Fatah party from control of the Palestinian Legislative Council, replacing it with a militant government led by Hamas. As discussed in Chapter 1, Hamas has a dual image as both a scrupulously honest political movement (in contrast to the notoriously corrupt Fatah) as well as a continuing commitment to violence (including terrorism) and the destruction of the Israeli state. Its election resulted in international isolation (especially from outside assistance) for Palestine as a means to try to force Hamas to moderate its stance, especially on terrorism and the future existence of Israel. Its earliest statements have not spoken directly to either of these points (which Israel considers "deal breakers" on future progress), instead arguing that the initiative on future peace discussions lies with Israel. The ascension of Hamas does, however, create "a momentous experiment—the results of which will have a major impact on the future of Palestine, Israel, and the Middle East at large," according to Michael Hertzog (the son of Israeli military hero Chaim Hertzog).

The impact of Israel's failed attempt to destroy Hiz'ballah in Lebanon is related. It changes the military factor in two ways. First, as Salem argues, it punctures "the area of invinciblity long projected by the Israeli defence forces." Second, it makes the prospect of a forced resolution less plausible. As Djerejian argues, the "confrontation has further proved what should have been painfully clear to all: there is no viable military solution to the Arab-Israeli conflicts."

The Israeli situation has changed as well. Before his second stroke, Sharon orchestrated the turnover of Gaza (the stronghold of Hamas) to the Palestinians, despite enormous resistance from settlers and their supporters in Israel. The emergence of the Kadima Party (which Sharon created) as the leader of a new coalition after his stroke accentuates the winds of change. New prime minister Olmert has taken the bold position of favoring removing most Israeli settlements from the West Bank under a policy he calls "convergence." This policy means "most of the settlements that would have to be removed . . . will be converged into the blocs of settlements that will remain under Israeli control," he said in his *Newsweek* interview. Although details have not been specified at this writing (January 2007), the result could resemble the 2000 borders negotiated at Camp David II reinforced by the fence.

CONCLUSION

The Israeli-Palestinian dispute has remained irresolvable despite nearly 30 years of negotiations in which the United States has taken an active lead. Some progress has been made along the way, including the narrowing of the dispute to its current status as an Israeli-Palestinian conflict and the narrowing of the unresolved—and to this point unresolvable—issues to the troika of the size and shape of Palestine; Jerusalem; and the right of return. The recent elections in Palestine and Israel may reactivate the negotiations by inserting new players. The most notable prospect for progress is the territorial issue of Palestinian statehood. A negotiation of the location of the fence may produce a Palestinian state on the West Bank and Gaza on which both sides can agree. Such an agreement will not, however, alter the intractability of the remaining issues, Jerusalem and repatriation.

The problem with both the Jerusalem and repatriation issues is that they are either/or propositions with little leeway for compromise. Both meet the criteria for irresolvable conflicts: They are territorial; they are based on mutually exclusive perceptions of outcomes; they are deeply held and emotional; the positions held on both sides do not facilitate compromise; outside efforts at mediation have failed to remove the issues; and unilateral solutions are unacceptable internationally.

Of the two issues, Jerusalem is—at least in principle—resolvable. A formula for dividing physical sovereignty over parts of Jerusalem is conceptually possible, if both sides find ways to lower the emotional trappings of devotion to their religious shrines and the question of what parts of the city might be the capital of each state. Achieving an agreement on these matters will clearly not be easy, but it is at least conceivable.

Repatriation, the right of return, is another matter. Palestinians either have or do not have a right to return to their former homes, and Israelis either do or do not have a legal or moral imperative to accommodate the Palestinians. The only possible forms of compromise are possible to state, but not to implement. One solution is deferment of the problem, which is the de facto current nonsolution. Under this arrangement, neither side must compromise, but the implementation of the outcome is put off to a future time. This solution lacks closure for either side and simply puts off the problem. The other solution is to allow *some,* but not all, Palestinians to return. Such a solution eliminates the outcome of a non-Jewish state of Israel, but leaves for future resolution *who* gets to return and *which* Israelis have to forfeit their property. It is hard to imagine how that can be done, but until it is, the Israeli-Palestinian conflict remains a classic example of an irresolvable conflict.

STUDY/DISCUSSION QUESTIONS

1. What is an irresolvable conflict? What distinguishes such a conflict from differences that can be resolved?

2. What are the characteristics of an irresolvable conflict? How do they build on and reinforce one another?

3. In terms of the six characteristics of an irresolvable conflict, assess the Israeli-Palestinian conflict.

4. Discuss the basic dynamics of the Israeli-Palestinian conflict. How did it come about? How did it evolve between 1948 and the beginning of the peace process in 1978? Why are the Six Days' and Yom Kippur Wars so important in that evolution?

5. What have been the steps in the peace process between the Israelis and Palestinians? Discuss each step in terms of accomplishments and failures.

6. What basic issues continue to divide the two parties? Rate and discuss each in terms of intractability and thus its contribution to the inability to resolve the conflict.

7. What is the current status of the conflict? What recent events have occurred that might affect the dynamics? Will they?

8. Is there realistic hope for a resolution of the Israeli-Palestinian conflict? Why or why not?

READING/RESEARCH MATERIAL

Carter, Jimmy. "A Jerusalem Settlement Everyone Can Live With." *New York Times* (electronic edition), August 6, 2000.

————. *Keeping Faith: The Memoirs of a President.* Fayetteville: University of Arkansas Press, 1995.

Djerejian, Edward P. "From Conflict Management to Conflict Resolution." *Foreign Affairs* 85, 6 (November/December 2006), 41–48.

Hedges, Chris. "The New Palestinian Revolt." *Foreign Affairs* 80, 1 (January/February 2001), 124–138.

Hertzberg, Arthur. "A Small Peace for the Middle East." *Foreign Affairs* 80, 1 (January/February 2001), 139–147.

Hertzog, Michael. "Can Hamas Be Tamed?" *Foreign Affairs* 85, 2 (March/April 2006), 83–94.

Makovsky, David. "How to Build a Fence." *Foreign Affairs* 85, 2 (March/April 2006), 50–64.

Ottoway, Marina S. "Promoting Democracy After Hamas' Victory." Washington, DC: Carnegie Endowment for International Peace Publications, March 2006.

Phillips, James. "Hamas Victory: The United States Should Not Recognize or Aid a Terrorist Regime." Heritage Foundation WebMemo 971, March 2006.

Sadat, Anwar. *In Search of an Identity: An Autobiography.* New York: Harper and Row, 1978.

Salem, Paul. "The Future of Lebanon." *Foreign Affairs* 85, 6 (November/December 2006), 13–22.

Viorst, Milton. "Middle East Peace: Mirage on the Horizon?" *Washington Quarterly* 23, 1 (Winter 2000), 41–54.

Waxman, Dov. "Between Victory and Defeat: Israel after the War with Hizballah." *Washington Quarterly* 30, 1 (Winter 2006–07), 27–42.

Weymouth, Lally. "'We Are Ready for Change.'" *Newsweek,* April 17, 2006, 34.

WEB SITES

The Middle East Peace Summit, 2000: http://www.mfa.gov.il/go.asp/MFA

UN documents on Palestine question: http://www.un.org/Depts/dpa/qpal

U.S. policy: http://www.state.gov./p/nea

Israeli positions on conflict: http://www.mfa.gov.il

Palestinian positions: http://minfo.gov.ps

PART III

Economic
Globalization

The spread of the international economy through increased world trade, commonly known as globalization, was one of the distinctive characteristics of the 1990s, and it continues to be a dominant force in the new century. Globalization provided much of the optimism of the early and middle 1990s, but it has been tempered and in some ways submerged by the terrorism-driven conflicts that have dominated the early 2000s. At the same time, the continuing globalization process has produced enough controversy that it is no longer viewed universally as a positive force.

The three case studies in this section look sequentially at three aspects of globalization that frame concerns about the phenomenon. The first case, "Free Trade or Not Free Trade," looks at the substantive and organizational bases of free trade, the most basic underlying dynamic of the globalization process. The chapter begins with an examination of the intellectual history of the idea of unfettered trade and advocacy of creating an international mechanism to support and enforce free trade, beginning with the 1940s advocacy of an International Trade Organization and ending in the 1990s with the World Trade Organization. The case then examines whether moving in this direction was a good idea for the world economy.

The second case, "Debating Globalization," examines the differential impact globalization has had worldwide. The optimism of the 1990s presumed that globalization was a virtually universal virtue, "a rising tide that lifts all boats." The late 1990s and early 2000s suggest this prediction may have been overly optimistic and that globalization clearly benefits some areas more than others. To examine this differential, the case will contrast the impact of what Thomas L. Friedman calls a "flat" world in Asia (notably India) and in Latin America.

The third case, "Evaluating Globalization," examines the actual impact of globalization as manifested in the application of an international agreement justified by its globalizing effect, the North American Free Trade Agreement (NAFTA), after ten years of operation. The retrospective reveals both differences about how beneficial NAFTA has been and about the difficulties of specifying the extent to which NAFTA deserves the credit or blame for changes that have occurred.

CHAPTER SEVEN

Free Trade or Not Free Trade

FROM ITO TO WTO AND BEYOND

PRÉCIS

Free trade is and for a long time has been a controversial concept, as has its institutionalization in the form of an intergovernmental organization. In this case, we begin by looking at the question of promoting free trade historically, from before the early post–World War II advocacy of an International Trade Organization at the Bretton Woods conference through the creation of the World Trade Organization (WTO) in 1995. As events like massive demonstrations against the WTO at Seattle in 1999 and more recently indicate, this institutionalization remains controversial.

Because of this controversy, we then ask the question of whether free trade is a good idea. This in turn leads to breaking the question into two aspects argued by advocates and opponents: the desirability of free trade as an idea and phenomenon, and what kind of institutional structure is most desirable for promoting and enforcing free trade. The case concludes by combining the two aspects and comparing them.

Trading goods and services has been one of man's oldest forms of interchange with other peoples and communities. In ancient times, the purpose of trade was generally to acquire goods that either did not grow or could not be produced locally, such as the importation of exotic fabric like silk, or spices. As the ability of political communities to span greater distances in shorter periods of time increased, trade expanded both in extent and in terms of what was and was not traded. The modern issue of trade probably congealed over whether to import goods and services that were also produced domestically.

That question is near the top of the agenda in contemporary discussions of trade and is manifested in most disagreements on the subject, from questions of barriers to trade to environmental impacts of importation versus domestic production.

It is not a new debate, either internationally or in the United States. The emergence of the capitalist system first in Europe and then worldwide pitted global traders against what we now call protectionists in the form of mercantilists seeking to protect new, infant industries from destructive outside competition. Historically in the United States, advocacy and opposition have been sectional and remain as part of the contemporary landscape. As Michael Lind explains, "From the eighteenth century on, the Southern plantation oligarchy was content for the United States to specialize in exporting agricultural goods and raw materials to more industrial nations, importing manufactured goods in return. Thanks to the dominance of the South and Southwest, what was once the foreign economic policy of the Confederate States of America has become the trade policy of the United States as a whole." In turn, he argues, this has caused the United States to lead "the campaign to reduce or eliminate tariffs worldwide."

Whether to allow the unfettered movement of goods and services internationally (free trade) or to place restrictions of one kind or another on that flow is a central element in contemporary international relations. The removal of barriers to trade was the centerpiece of the economic globalization movement of the 1990s, one of the engines designed to draw countries into closer collaboration by entwining them in the global prosperity of that decade. The global economic downturn at the turn of the millennium and the rise of the global war on terrorism has taken some of the luster from the free trade issue and relegated it to a less prominent place on the international political agenda. Yet, while our attention is diverted elsewhere, globalization continues, and proponents and opponents continue to fight over whether to expand or constrict free trade arrangements.

This debate has a long intellectual and political history. The basic poles have been between those seeking to expand trade (free traders) and those seeking to restrict trade (protectionists). Nestled between the extremes are those who advocate freer, but not necessarily totally free, trade (who often portray themselves as fair traders). While the Industrial Revolution was raging in Europe and later North America, the need to buffer nascent industries from outside competition militated toward restriction, largely under the intellectual banner of mercantilism, as noted. During the period leading to World War II, protectionism ran rampant in a Great Depression-riddled Europe, and economic restrictions were partially blamed for the bloodiest war in human history. The "lessons" of interwar economics, in turn, helped frame the international political debate and its institutionalization, the topics of this case.

The economic aspect of this debate has been, and is, asymmetrical, so that proponents on one side or the other tend to talk past one another, meaning interchange often devolves into monologues. The arguments for free trade tend to be mainly abstract, impersonal, and macroeconomic. Free trade is said to be beneficial because it unleashes basic economic principles like comparative advantage that make overall economies (national or international) stronger and economic conditions within and between countries more vital. Anti–free trade arguments, on the other hand, tend to be specific, personal, and microeconomic. Cries to restrict trade tend to be posed in terms of the adverse impact that opening up trade opportunities has on individuals. Trade is not about economic theories, it is about people's jobs and livelihoods. Fair traders seek a compromise somewhere between the extremes, advocating selective trade reductions in conformance with the principle of free trade but minimizing negative microeconomic impact.

The argument over textiles illustrates the asymmetry in this debate. To pro-free traders, moving clothing manufacturing overseas, where labor costs are lower, makes economic sense. Clothes are cheaper, and the economies of new textile producers are stimulated, which allows them to buy things produced in the United States; and uncompetitive American textile manufacturers redirect their efforts to other production areas in which they can compete successfully (produce better products at lower costs). Moreover, all consumers benefit, because goods are produced at the lowest possible costs, and the savings are passed along to consumers. Moving the manufacture of clothing overseas, in other words, means Americans can buy their clothes more cheaply than they could from domestic producers with higher labor costs in this labor-intensive industry. In the end, it is a macroeconomic win-win situation with the added benefit of drawing countries closer together, thus promoting greater cooperation and reduced international tension.

From the anti-free trade viewpoint, these abstractions are unconvincing, because the effect of moving textile manufacturing overseas is to cost American textile workers their jobs. It is a concern centered on the impact on individuals, not on abstract phenomena. Thus, when free traders extol the removal of barriers and anti-free traders deride that possibility, they are, in a very real sense, not talking about the same thing. In this particular case, fair traders would favor some reduction in barriers to trade, but with limits to minimize individual displacement (scheduled reductions over a period of time, for instance) combined with retraining programs to equip displaced workers to enter alternative industries.

The debate is intensely political at both the domestic and international levels. At the level of American national politics, the asymmetry is reflected between branches of the federal government. Historically, the executive branch of government, more concerned with the overall health of the economy and somewhat more removed from the impact on specific individuals or groups (as opposed to the whole), tends to be more free trade-oriented and macroeconomic. Members of Congress, whose constituents are the people whose jobs are endangered when foreign goods and services are allowed to enter the country more freely, tend to be more microeconomic and opposed.

At the international level, the debate tends to get muddled with preferences for the general orientation toward political interactions with the world. Broadly speaking, two positions have dominated the American experience (and that of other countries as well, to some extent). *Internationalists* generally advocate a maximum involvement of the United States in the international system; in a world where the United States is the remaining superpower in the system, this means advocacy of the United States playing a prominent leadership role working with other countries. Advocacy of free trade and globalization are an extension of that political preference to the economic realm.

The other position, *isolationism,* advocates a much more restrained level of American involvement in the world. This position reached its institutionalized zenith between the world wars, when "splendid isolationism" sought to keep the United States entirely separated from world, and especially European, politics. The belief that the United States could remain aloof from world affairs was, of course, punctured permanently by

Pearl Harbor, and its successor ideology, *neoisolationism,* advocates a restricted level of U.S. interaction from the world, but not total rejection of the world outside American boundaries. In its pure form, isolationists are also protectionist, because protectionism limits international economic interactions.

The terms of the debate are not purely economic. Pro-trade advocates of the 1990s, for instance, argued that the globalization process of which free trade is an underpinning produces political as well as economic benefits. As noted in Chapter 3, one of the major reasons for promoting trade with China is to draw that country more intimately into the global political system. At the same time, anti-free trade arguments have expanded to include strictly noneconomic concerns ranging from environmental degradation to compromises of sovereignty, as well as politico-economic arguments about the effects on different groups within societies, as noted in Chapter 8.

This introduction frames the structure of the case, which has three purposes. The first, and major, purpose is historical, tracing the process whereby free trade has been institutionalized in the international system since the end of World War II. That process has crystallized the principal reasons for advocating and opposing free trade, a discussion of which supports that evolution and is the second purpose of the case. Finally, we will attempt to apply this institutional framework and the positions of the two sides to the current, ongoing debate on the issue.

INSTITUTIONALIZING TRADE

The genesis of the contemporary debate over free trade emerged from the period leading to World War II, the traumatic impact of the world's bloodiest war, and the determination to attempt to do a better job than had been done at the end of World War I to restructure the international system so that those circumstances would not recur. Part of the blame for the war was attributed to economic conditions that had arisen in the 1930s (during the Great Depression) that had produced economic chaos that worsened conditions and made the descent into the maelstrom of global war more likely.

Economic nationalism and protectionism were deemed to be among the chief culprits during the interwar period. As the Great Depression took hold across Europe and North America, governments scrambled to minimize the effects on their own economies and peoples. One way to do this was to attempt to protect national industries from ruinous foreign competition, and the vehicle was the erection of prohibitively high trade barriers to keep foreign goods and services out and thus to keep domestic industries (and the jobs they created) alive. The erection of tariff and other barriers resulted in retaliation and counterretaliation that brought European trade to a virtual standstill. At the same time, currency fluctuations and devaluations became commonplace as a means to prop up failing enterprises. The resulting destabilization was felt especially strongly in Germany, which faced stiff reparations requirements exacted at the Versailles Peace Conference that ended World War I. Unable to meet reparations schedules with foreign exchange from trade that had dried up, the German economy spun out of control as the depression hit that country harder than any other. Beyond the horrible economic privations that these practices created, they also fueled the animosities and hatreds that made the slide to war easier. In that atmosphere, Adolph Hitler arose, promising, among other things, to restore prosperity.

The process of rebuilding the world after World War II began early during the war itself, largely through British and American collaboration. The purpose was to ensure that the mistakes made in 1919 were not repeated and that the structure of postwar peace would prevent a recurrence of another global war. Politically, this collaboration produced thoroughly internationalist constructs such as the United Nations Charter and the North American Treaty Organization. Economically, it produced a series of agreements to restructure the global economy, a construct known as the Bretton Woods system.

The Bretton Woods System and Free Trade

Encouraged and cajoled by the governments of Great Britain and the United States, representatives of 44 countries met in the White Mountains resort town of Bretton Woods, New Hampshire, in July 1944 to plan for the postwar economic peace. The site, at the picturesque Washington Hotel at the foot of Mt. Washington, was chosen both for its splendor and its isolation (the site was accessible by a single two-lane highway). At Bretton Woods, the conferees hammered out a series of agreements that produced international economic institutions that have endured into the twenty-first century and have become staple parts of the system of globalization.

The conferees agreed that the heart of the 1930s economic problem was protectionism, manifested in such international financial and economic practices such as large fluctuations in exchange rates of currencies, chronic balance-of-payments difficulties experienced by some countries, and prohibitively high tariffs. All of these practices had contributed to restriction of international commerce, and the conferees agreed that a major antidote to these practices was the encouragement of much freer trade among countries. This explicitly free trade preference was held most strongly by the United States delegation to Bretton Woods (the British, seeking to protect the series of preferences for members of the Commonwealth through the Imperial Preference System, sought a more restrained form of trade restriction reduction). This preference, coming from the Roosevelt administration, had some opposition domestically from some conservative members of Congress (a dynamic suggested earlier) and from private organizations like the U.S. Chamber of Commerce (a close ally of American businesses and hence protectionism).

The Bretton Woods process was more successful in confronting some of its priorities than others. Two international organizations were created, the International Monetary Fund (IMF) and the International Bank for Reconstruction and Development (IBRD or World Bank). The IMF was originally chartered to deal with the problem of currency fluctuations by authorizing the granting of credits to shore up weak currencies, thus contributing to economic stabilization. The IMF has gradually widened its purview to a variety of other economic matters. The World Bank, on the other hand, was to assist in economic stabilization by granting loans originally for reconstruction of war-torn countries, and later for the development of the emerging Third World.

The priority of freeing trade did not enjoy as successful a fate. Although Bretton Woods produced two organizations, it failed to see the third pillar of its vision institutionalized, an international organization devoted explicitly to the promotion of free trade. Instead, that process became gradual and convoluted, not reaching fruition until the 1990s. The length of time involved is, in important ways, a testimony to the endurance and strength of the anti-free trade position, especially in the United States.

The Road from Bretton Woods to the WTO

Although there was a clear sentiment for the institutionalization of a free trade-promoting international organization at Bretton Woods, there was enough opposition to the idea both internationally (British misgivings about infringements on its Imperial Preference System relationship with the Commonwealth) and domestically to keep such an organization from being part of the Bretton Woods package. That did not mean, however, that there was not active enthusiasm for the creation of an International Trade Organization (ITO). The problem was that the proposal to create the ITO ran into the familiar ambivalence of American politics relating to foreign affairs. For nearly half a century, the United States found itself alternately championing and opposing the creation of an organization to promote free trade, depending on whether free trade or anti-free trade elements held sway in the decision process.

During and shortly after the war, the idea of the ITO largely existed within the executive branch of the American government, and more specifically the U.S. Department of State. When Harry S. Truman succeeded Franklin Delano Roosevelt as president in 1945, he adopted the ITO as his own project. The Truman administration took the leadership role in proposing a United Nations Conference on Trade and Development in 1946, a major purpose of which was to draft a charter for the ITO. That proposal was, however, opposed by powerful elements in the U.S. Congress, and as a result, a meeting was held in Geneva, Switzerland, in 1947 to lay out the principles of a General Agreement on Tariffs and Trade (GATT), as an interim, partial solution to the free trade issue. The proposal for GATT was to be a temporary "fix" while the treaty to create the ITO was being honed and perfected. A meeting was scheduled for Havana, Cuba, in 1947 formally to propose the ITO.

Then American domestic politics got in the way. ITO, like other free trade institutions since, would have done two things of varying controversy. The first of these was to provide an institutional basis to promote the reduction of barriers to trade. Although there were objections to the proposal on this basis from protectionists and others, it was the less controversial aspect. The second, and more divisive, purpose was to create an instrument with jurisdiction and authority to enforce trade agreements, including the capability to levy enforceable penalties against sovereign governments. Opponents of ITO and its successors complained that this enforcement provision represented an unwise infringement on American sovereignty, a position that resonated with both opponents and some proponents of the principle of free trade.

The ITO proposal was undermined by political actions in the United States in 1948. A coalition of powerful elements in the Congress led the way. The major players in this array against the ITO included conservative Republicans backed by protectionist agricultural and manufacturing interests seeking to protect American goods from foreign competition, liberal Democrats who viewed the ITO document as too timid an approach to promoting free trade, and conservatives who feared the sovereignty infringement that ITO enforcement provisions represented.

This Congressional array faced a Truman administration that favored ratification of the ITO statute but that was unwilling to expend scarce political capital in the process. Competing in the foreign policy agenda was the North American Treaty Organization (NATO) proposal. As an initiative to create the first peacetime alliance in American history, NATO was also a controversial concept. The Truman administration reasoned that it could muster support for one or the other of the treaties, and that of the two, NATO was the more critical (the Cold War was heating up at the time). At the same time, 1948 was a presidential election year, and underdog incumbent Truman feared that spirited advocacy of a controversial idea like the ITO could become a negative campaign issue. Thus, the Truman administration backed away from its advocacy of the ITO, and the proposal died. The United States had, not uncharacteristically, both enthusiastically endorsed and helped develop the charter for the ITO and then destroyed it, further evidence of American ambivalence toward international involvements.

The demise of the ITO elevated GATT to a more prominent and permanent position than those who had originally proposed it had envisioned. GATT survived as the banner carrier for international free trade from 1948 until the WTO came into existence in 1995. Those who oppose free trade in principle or effect were unenthused by GATT, but felt less threatened by it than by the ITO.

The reason GATT was less objectionable than the ITO was that it lacked the second characteristic of the ITO, an enforcement capability. GATT, in effect, was not an organization at all, but rather a series of negotiating sessions (called "rounds" and normally named after wherever a given round's first session was held) among the sovereign members. The result of these sessions was to create international agreements on different free trade issues, but these were less threatening than the ITO. For one thing, GATT was not an organization and thus lacked more than a modest staff; therefore, it had no investigating capability. Moreover, GATT was never granted any enforcement authority, and all of the agreements reached during GATT negotiations had to be ratified by all participating countries before its provisions affected them. Thus, those who feared institutionalizing free trade on sovereignty grounds had little to fear from the GATT process.

Although it lacked the foundation of a permanent international organization, GATT was not useless. Indeed, the outcomes of the various rounds did produce a series of principles and practices that have been incorporated into the WTO. At heart, the principal thrust of GATT action was centered around the *most-favored-nation* (MFN) principle: the idea of providing to all trading partners the same customs and tariff treatment enjoyed by a country given the greatest trade privilege—the most-favored country. Thus, if one country lowers its tariffs on a particular good to another country, it should extend that same tariff treatment to all GATT members. John Rothgeb argues that the GATT experience can be categorized around four distinct principles flowing from the MFN precedent. They are: *nondiscrimination* (the promotion of MFN status among all countries regardless of status); *transparency* (the unacceptability of secret trade restrictions and barriers); *consultation and dispute settlement* (resolution of disputes through direct negotiations); and *reciprocity* (the idea that all members should incur balanced obligations).

The last, or Uruguay, round of GATT included among its proposals the establishment of the World Trade Organization (WTO). In a very real sense, the WTO is the ITO reincarnated, because it combines the two basic elements of the ITO again within a permanent international organization: the promotion of free trade, *and* mechanisms to enforce trade agreements and the legal authority to penalize members of the organization who violate international trade agreements.

When the WTO was first proposed in 1993, it did not produce the same volume of objection that the ITO did in 1948. The same basic opposed interests, if with different representatives, were against the WTO. Protectionists disfavor the principle of free trade; in 1948, these were mostly business-related Republicans, but in 1993 they were mostly union-supporting Democrats. Some again objected on the grounds that the organization was too timid—in this case the objectors were principally environmentalists concerned the WTO would not aggressively protect the environment. Others raised objections on the grounds of infringements of national sovereignty. These problems are discussed in the next section.

The WTO statute was ratified by the United States Congress on December 1, 1994. It was not submitted as a treaty (requiring the advice and consent of two-thirds of the Senate), but instead as an economic agreement under the provisions of so-called *fast track* procedures (now known as trade promotion authority). Treating the WTO as an economic agreement meant it had to pass both houses of Congress, but with only a simple, rather than a weighted, majority. Designating it under fast track (a provision to facilitate the passage of trade agreements) meant there were limits on congressional debate on the matter and that it could only be voted up or down in its entirety (the authority to amend it was removed). The date is important because it came after the November 1994 off-year elections but before the newly elected Congress was inaugurated (qualifying it as a lame duck session). Critics wailed at the timing and procedures (some maintained, for instance, that had WTO accession been presented as a treaty that it never would have gotten a two-thirds majority), but their cries of "foul" were in vain. Nearly fifty years after its principles were first proposed, institutionalized free trade became reality in 1995.

The WTO has now been in existence for well over a decade. Its membership has increased from approximately 70 in 1995 to 149 as of December 11, 2005 (according to its Web site). In addition, 35 nonmember countries participate in the organization (observers have five years to apply for full membership), including Russia, Iraq, Saudi Arabia, and Vietnam. The headquarters, including the secretariat, are located in Lausanne, Switzerland. The WTO has established itself as a leading international economic organization in the process.

Its brief tenure has also been filled with controversy and a great deal more visibility than functional international organizations (those that deal with a specific policy area rather than generalist organizations like the UN) usually attract or desire. In some ways, the acceptance of or opposition to the WTO reflects the status of globalization, whose central principle of free trade it exemplifies. When the charter came into effect in 1995, globalization was at its apex and the new WTO only activated its most ardent opponents. By the end of the 1990s, on the other hand, globalization was less in vogue, and the WTO has become more controversial. This controversy became extremely public during widespread and highly destructive demonstrations at its 1999 convention in Seattle, Washington, leading the organization to hold its 2001 meeting in Doha, Qatar, and its 2003 meeting in Cancun, Mexico, presumably more easily secured locations that would attract less attention.

IS INSTITUTIONALIZED FREE TRADE A GOOD IDEA?

This is really two separate but related questions, and there is disagreement on both aspects. One aspect has to do with whether free trade itself is a worthy goal, and it has as a subtext the question whether free trade *as it is currently defined and being pursued* is a good idea. One can, for instance, believe that the general principle of removing barriers to trade is a good idea, but disagree that the overarching implementing principle of removing "barriers to trade" should override other principles, such as the promotion of human rights. The other aspect of the question is whether free trade advocacy and implementation should be institutionalized, and that question has the subtext of whether the WTO *as it is currently organized and with the authority it has* is a good idea. Many of those who believe in free trade as a principle and accept the idea that it needs some institutional base, for instance, disagree with the current structure of the WTO and advocate a more open, democratic structure for the organization. Clearly, those who oppose free trade (in principle or in its present guise) oppose the WTO as well.

The WTO has become a lightning rod on the free trade issue. Those who oppose free trade, generally on the basis that its effects are not as desirable for individuals or societies as its advocates suggest, clearly oppose an advocating institution, and especially one with mandatory authority to impose its values on individuals and countries. Proponents of free trade generally support the idea of an institutional base from which to promote their advocacy, but may or may not like the structure they have. To make some reasonable personal assessment on the issue of free trade requires unraveling and reaching some personal conclusions on each aspect.

Free Trade or Not Free Trade?

The generalized defense of free trade rests on the macroeconomic benefits it brings to countries and the microeconomic benefits it accords to individuals and groups. Both benefits are controversial. Free trade is the international application of the Ricardian principle of comparative advantage. By removing barriers to the movement of goods and services across national boundaries, the most efficient producers of goods and providers of services will come to predominate the markets in the areas of their advantage, to the benefit of consumers who will receive the best goods and services at the lowest prices from these providers. Presuming all countries can find products or services at which they have such advantages, all will find markets, and the result will be a general and growing specialization and prosperity. The application of free trade internationally is the handmaiden of the process of economic globalization, because the result should be the gradual widening of participation in the global economy, as more and more countries find and exploit areas in which they have or can develop a comparative advantage.

Freeing trade has the added benefit of promoting a more cooperative, peaceful environment, according to its champions. The major conceptual vehicle for this dynamic is *complex interdependence,* the idea that as countries become increasingly reliant on one another for essential goods and services, their ability and desire to engage in conflict, and especially war, becomes more remote—either because the desire to fight is decreased by proximity and acquaintance, or because the intertwining of economies makes it impractical or impossible to fight.

This macroeconomic argument is abstract and intellectual, and its dynamics are not universally accepted. It argues that free trade improves the general lot of peoples, and thus increases the prosperity of individuals: "a rising tide lifts all boats," to borrow a phrase. As an abstract matter presented in this way, it is difficult to argue with the virtue of free trade, although some do. At a slightly less abstract level, proponents of free trade also point to largely macroeconomic indicators, especially from the middle 1990s, that demonstrate growth in the global economy and within individual countries, phenomena they attribute to free trade-driven globalization. Despite these arguments, when these statistics are applied at more specific levels—to those of individuals or even sectors of economies within countries—the case is not as clearly positive.

The major objections to free trade come not from these abstract principles, but from the way they are applied. In the current debate about free trade, many of the objections go back to the conjunction of free trade and the values of market economics in fact if not in theory. It is the effects of the kind of free trade that the advocates put forward that is the problem.

Without seeking to be comprehensive, two examples can be given. The first, which has already been raised, is microeconomic. The process of responding to the need for competitive advantage creates privation and displacement for those whose livelihoods depend on ventures that prove to be uncompetitive and thus must be eliminated. The theory of comparative advantage, of course, holds that those displaced will somehow be reabsorbed into more competitive enterprises that possess comparative advantage. The principle, however, is much easier to implement in the abstract than it is in real cases. To return to the example cited earlier, it is not an easy or automatic process to transform a lifelong textile worker into a high-tech employee in the computing industry. Those who are displaced by the evaporation of old, uncompetitive jobs and cannot be absorbed into new industries are hardly likely to become ardent supporters of the abstract beneficial effects of free trade—at least not as it affects them.

A second example regards the effect of institutionalized free trade on the economic development of poor countries. Because of the basis of free trade in the MFN principle, opponents argue that poor countries that are members of the free trade regime are vulnerable to be flooded with goods and services across the range of economic activity. Virtually by definition, poor countries lack comparative advantage in producing anything. Their inability to protect nascent economic activities means that indigenous development will be systematically undercut by the free trade regime and domestic industry and thus development will be retarded. The net impact of being exposed to MFN has been, according to critics, to contribute to greater economic inequality between the rich and poor countries, the very opposite of what the proponents of free trade argue.

For the "turtles," as Thomas Friedman labels the countries that cannot compete in the free trade environment, there are two options, as in the example above. One is to stay outside the WTO framework, as its principles and rules only apply to members. Notably, almost all the countries that have not joined WTO are extremely poor, and although the WTO has tried to develop outreach programs to these nonmembers, they have not been successful at overcoming these objections. The other alternative is to join the WTO and suffer the consequences of assault on the domestic economy in the hopes that doing so will help "lift" the national boat.

The policies that implement free trade can have similar effects. As we will see in Chapter 8, joining the free trade-driven globalizing economy requires adopting both macroeconomic and microeconomic policies that require individual privation and thus engender popular political opposition both to the policies and to the governments that advocate them. The result, seen most keenly in Latin America, has been a considerable backlash against globalization.

The WTO: Problem or Solution?

The WTO is the final fulfillment of the dreams of the planners of the post–World War II global economy who convened at Bretton Woods. Freeing trade was a central part of the remedy they saw for the international economic ills associated with protectionism and its contribution to the war. When the idea was first presented, American objections prevented the first institutional form, the ITO, from coming into being. In 1995, the proponents succeeded, but the controversy remains. Is the WTO the answer, or the problem?

Assessing whether the WTO helps or hinders the progression of free trade can be broken into three separate questions. The first has to do with the kind of free trade that the WTO advocates. To its opponents, the WTO is little more than a handmaiden to the large multinational corporations (MNCs). Global Exchange, a Web-based research organization that is very critical of the WTO, calls it an "unaccountable, corporate-based government" that reflects the values of the MNCs at the expense of virtually everyone else. At least to some extent, this should come as little surprise. The globalization process of which free trade is an implementing device is based in the promotion of capitalist, free market economics, of which corporations are a prominent part. Moreover, much of the economic resources on which the spread of globalization is based is in the form of foreign direct investment (FDI) by private sources, and entities like international banks and multinational corporations provide most of the FDI. Because they do so out of a profit motive and not from a sense of philanthropy, it stands to reason that these entities would have an interest in helping to shape the philosophies and policies the WTO promotes. As indirect evidence of the success of the MNCs in this regard, it might be remembered that corporations within the United States were major opponents of the ITO because of protectionist motives, but have by and large been equally strong supporters of the WTO.

The advocacy of free trade and the promotion of its implementation through the WTO thus entails two substantive judgments. One is whether there is an alternative economic philosophy that could be attached to free trade that would make it more palatable to those who oppose the idea or its consequences. Is there some alternative to a market-economy-based, free trade-driven globalized economy? The second judgment flows from the first: If there is no acceptable alternative underpinning, are the positive outcomes of institutionalized free trade better or worse than the absence of such a system? The analogy of the rising tide and the boat is sometimes used to frame this question. Pro-free traders admit that not everyone benefits equally from free trade, but that everyone does benefit to some extent and thus everyone is better off under a free trade regime (the tide lifts all boats). Opponents argue the benefits are so inequitably distributed that gaps are actually widened to the point that some are left relatively worse off (some boats get swamped).

The second question revolves around the structure of the WTO itself. To reiterate, the WTO has two basic functions: the promotion of free trade and the enforcement of free trade agreements. The enforcement mandate is and always has been the more controversial aspect of WTO. The mechanism for enforcement was agreed on during the Uruguay round of GATT in the form of the Dispute Settlement Understanding (DSU). Under the DSU, the WTO is authorized to establish and convene the Dispute Settlement Body (DSB). The Geneva Briefing Book describes the considerable authority of the DSB, "which has the sole authority to establish such panels to adjudicate disputes between members and to accept or reject the findings of panels and the Appellate Body, a standing appeals body of seven independent experts. The DSB also . . . has the power to authorize retaliation when a member does not comply with DSB recommendations and rulings."

These powers are not inconsiderable and include both the power to identify alleged violations; to convene and prosecute those alleged violations; and then to issue binding rulings and penalties and to enforce those penalties, ostensibly without recourse to an outside, independent source of appeal (all appeals are internal to the process). The membership of these panels is chosen by the WTO itself, and, according to Global Exchange, "consist of three trade bureaucrats that are not screened for conflict of interest."

To critics that span the ITO–WTO debate, a chief objection to this arrangement is its effect on national sovereignty. The rulings of the DSU process have the effect of treaties on the countries against which they are levied, which means that they can overturn the effect of those laws. This is particularly a concern in the United States where, as noted, there is particular sensitivity over intrusions on state sovereignty. In the specific case of WTO rulings, these have disproportionately affected the United States. According to the Geneva Briefing Book, "From the advent of the WTO, in January 1995, until October 1, 2003, the United States has been a party in 56 out of 93 WTO dispute settlement panel reports and 36 out of 56 Appellate Body reports." The source does not indicate how many of these involved judgments against the United States, but it is likely at least some of them did.

The third question regards what unforeseen consequences the institutionalization of free trade has had, and whether those consequences are acceptable. As one might expect, most unforeseen outcomes that have been identified are negative and are expressed most vocally by opponents of the process and its outcomes. Two in particular stand out as examples: the alleged antilabor bias of the WTO, and its negative environmental impacts. Unsurprisingly, these two arguments have been raised by two of the most prominent and visible opponents of the WTO, neither of which was evident in the 1940s but are today. Both touch on the dual questions of whether free trade itself or the way it is institutionalized is the problem.

Objections to free trade on the basis of being antilabor contains both elements of objection. Free trade is, of course, the culprit among those people working in industries and services that do not enjoy comparative advantage and can only compete if protected by some form of trade barrier. The textile industry cited earlier is a prime example. Labor unions also contend that the way in which the WTO operates to remove barriers to trade provides incentives for corporations to move their businesses to places that engage in unfair labor practices (everything from low wages and benefits to child labor) thereby creating an unfair environment within which to compete. Moreover, they believe that the corporatist mentality they say reigns supreme within the WTO encourages foreign direct investors to nurture and create these unfair practices as ways to create comparative advantage. These allegations are parallel to older domestic arguments about union busting and scab labor practices. Because these are extremely emotional issues among trade unionists, it helps explain the depth of their animosity toward the WTO and the prevalence of trade unionists in anti-free trade, anti-WTO demonstrations.

Environmentalists' objections to free trade and the WTO are parallel. The need to establish conditions of comparative advantage drives some countries to rescind environmental regulations that add to the cost of production (dumping hazardous chemicals used in processing materials into the environment rather than rendering these chemical harmless before release), thereby making their industries more competitive than industries in the United States that must meet environmental standards that add to production costs. Critics cite cases in Latin America (especially Mexico) in which environmental standards have indeed been relaxed or done away with to attract industry.

The environmentalist objection is also applied directly to the WTO. Environmentalists contend that most corporations resist environmental restraints philosophically and only accede to environmental regulation reluctantly and unenthusiastically. Because the WTO is alleged to be largely controlled by corporate interests and reflects corporate values, they are thus predisposed to be suspicious of the organization on those grounds. Environmentalists are also generally conspicuous at demonstrations against the WTO.

CONCLUSION

Whether to advocate or oppose free trade and its institutionalization is not an easy or straightforward proposition. At the abstract, theoretical level of international macroeconomics, the case for free trade is very convincing, and it is not surprising that many of the defenses of free trade spring from these theoretical arguments. At the applied level of the impact of free trade on individuals and groups (the microeconomic level), the proposition is more ambivalent. Certainly, individuals as consumers benefit when comparative advantage produces goods and services at lower cost and higher quality through free trade than from less efficient, protected domestic industries. Imagine, for instance, the impact on Christmas gift spending if all goods from China were eliminated. At the same time, removing protection can terminate employment for those in the less efficient industries, and although the theory of comparative advantage says that people so displaced should find alternative employment in more competitive fields, doing so is almost always easier said than done. When these dislocations affect large portions of a society, there may also be a negative political reaction both to the phenomenon of globalization (and hence free trade) and to those politicians who are supporters of free trade.

The question of institutionalizing free trade is a related but not synonymous matter, because one can reasonably take one of three positions on the desirability of free trade per se: one can favor free trade unconditionally, one can oppose it equally unconditionally, or one can favor free trade some but not all of the time, a position usually called freer (or fair) trade. For the "pure" positions, the answer to whether some organization should be established to promote and enforce free trade is fairly straightforward. If one believes free trade is comprehensively desirable, then a free trade-promoting institution is clearly a desirable instrument to that end (although the kind and extent of enforcement capability may be debatable). Conversely, if one opposes free trade across the board, then it would be nonsensical to support any instrumentality that promotes or enforces a rejected idea.

That leaves the "fair traders," who support expansions in trade through the reduction of barriers to trade, but who believe there should be exclusions or limitations on the extent and degree of trade promotion. Such an advocacy attempts to finesse the dichotomy between free trade and protectionism by advocating some of both, depending on the context. This position is politically tenable as well, because it allows general support for free trade (which, in the abstract, most people favor) with restrictions to protect politically significant victims of free trade.

The advocacy of freer trade leads to three questions that can be applied to the dual thrusts of free trade and its institutionalization. The first is, "How free should trade be?" The general criterion for answering the question is how much of the benefits and costs of free trade is one willing to bear, and the answer one determines will, in turn, vary with the level of personal benefit one (or one's group, or country) derives from various levels of free trade.

The second question is, "What kinds of values should underlie a free trading system and, especially, the institution that supports and promotes it?" If the current free trade-based system of globalization is based on the values of market-based, capitalist economics, as it at least partly is, this leads to one form of organization based in pure economic competition in which the less government regulation exists, generally the better. If, as alleged, the WTO is dominated by people with these values and interests, then the *kind* of free trade system that evolves and is institutionalized will reflect those values. On the other hand, if one enters values such as equity (fair trade) and social consciousness (environmentalism) into the values underlying a free trade system, it probably looks different than the current system.

The third and final question is, "What kind of enforcement mechanism is most desirable?" The answer, of course, begins with the level of enthusiasm one has about free trade in the first place: The more enthusiastic one is, the more enforcement one is likely to favor. But the answer also incorporates how one has answered the second question: One's enthusiasm for enforcement may depend on what kinds of values are being enforced and whether one supports those values. In a favorite example cited by critics of the current system, the American ban on tuna fishing using mile-long nets that also ensnare and kill dolphins was overruled in a judgment by the WTO. In an action brought by Mexico, the WTO said the law, when applied to American territorial waters, was a barrier to trade. Does a free trade regime need to lead to that kind of conclusion?

The question implied in the title—"free trade or not free trade?"—turns out to be more complicated than the simple dichotomy suggests. Whether, or to what extent, free trade, its advocacy, and its institutionalization are desirable are not simple matters, but involve questions and subquestions, the answers to which are not always as easy as they may seem at first blush. But then, that is why the question has endured for over a half century and will undoubtedly remain on the agenda for the foreseeable future.

STUDY/DISCUSSION QUESTIONS

1. What is free trade? Why is it an issue, both historically and in the contemporary context? What are the basic disagreements about the desirability of free trade? What basic positions do people take on the trade issue?

2. Describe the process of institutionalizing free trade from the Bretton Woods conference of 1944 to the ratification of the World Trade Organization in 1995. Why did the International Trade Organization fail to come into existence in 1948 but the WTO succeed in 1995? What was the role of the General Agreement on Trade and Tariffs in this evolution?

3. What are the principal arguments for and against free trade? How do the disputes over intellectual property rights and the impact of free trade on development of the poorest countries illustrate this debate?

4. What are the major controversies surrounding the WTO? What values does it promote? What powers does it have? How do labor and environmental objections illustrate this controversy?

5. Answer the three questions posed in the conclusion: How free should trade be? What kinds of values should it promote? What kind of enforcement mechanism is most desirable? After determining your personal answers to these questions, do you consider yourself a free trader, an anti-free trader, or somewhere in between (a fair trader)? Why?

READING/RESEARCH MATERIAL

Barshefsky, Charlene. "Trade Policy in a Networked World." *Foreign Affairs* 80, 2 (March/April 2001), 134–146.

Bauman, Zygmunt. *Globalization: The Human Consequences.* New York: Columbia University Press, 1998.

Dierks, Rosa Gomez. *Introduction to Globalization: Political and Economic Perspectives for a New Era.* Chicago: Burnham, 2001.

Dregner, Daniel W. *U.S. Trade Strategy: Free versus Fair.* New York: Council on Foreign Relations Press, 2006.

Friedman, Thomas L. *The Lexus and the Olive Tree: Understanding Globalization.* New York: Farrar, Straus and Giroux, 1999.

Landau, Alice. *Redrawing the Global Economy: Elements of Integration and Fragmentation.* New York: Palgrave, 2001.

Lind, Michael. *Made in Texas: George W. Bush and the Southern Takeover of American Politics.* New York: New America Books, 2003.

McBride, Stephen, and John Wiseman (eds.). *Globalization and Its Discontents.* New York: St. Martin's Press, 2000.

"Measuring Globalization." *Foreign Policy,* March/April 2004, 46–53.

O'Connor, David E. *Demystifying the Global Economy: A Guide for Students.* Westport, CT: Greenwood Press, 2002.

Panagariya, Arvind. "Think Again: International Trade." *Foreign Policy,* November/December 2003, 20–29.

Park, Jacob. "Globalization after Seattle." *Washington Quarterly* 23, 2 (Spring 2000), 13–16.

Rothgeb, John M. J. *Trade Policy: Balancing Economic Dreams and Political Realities.* Washington, DC: CQ Press, 2001.

Schaeffer, Robert K. *Understanding Globalization: The Social Consequences of Political, Economic, and Environmental Change.* Lanham, MD: Rowman and Littlefield, 2003.

"World Trade Organization." *The Geneva Briefing Book.* Lausanne, Switzerland: World Trade Organization, 2004.

WEB SITES

The text of GATT online

GATT at http://farnsworth.mit.edu/diig/NII_info.gatt.html

Critical views of the World Trade Organization

Global Exchange at http://www.globalexchange.org/campaigns/rulemakers/topTenReasons.html

Summaries of international trade law

International Trade Law Monitor at http://itl.irv.uit.no/trade_law/

The home page of the World Trade Organization

http://www.wto.org/Welcome.html

Information on worldwide trade

Global Trade Watch at http://www.citizen.org/pctrade/tradehome.html

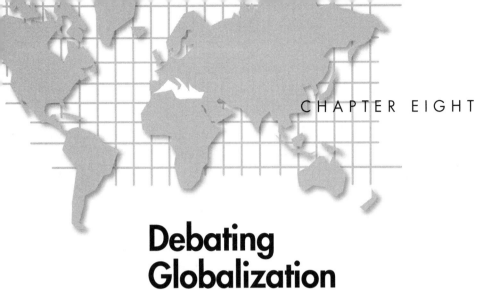

Debating Globalization
INDIA AND VENEZUELA

PRÉCIS

The economic system of globalization has continued to spread in the early 2000s, although not with the flair or attention it attracted before the 2001 terrorist attacks on the United States diverted attention from globalization as a, if not the, primary dynamic of international politics. The spread of globalization has not been uniform nor has it occurred without residual controversy. A number of points of controversy surround the process and thus make uneven the continuing phenomenon in the world.

This case study examines the debate about globalization. It begins by looking at basic questions that help frame the debate. That discussion leads to an examination of the basic dynamics of globalization that condition how or whether different states and regions adopt the values of a globalized world. The cases used to show how this debate plays out in different parts of the world are India, which is one of the most enthusiastic acolytes of globalization, and Venezuela, where globalization was heartily embraced but where negative economic and political effects have caused it, and a number of Latin American countries, to retreat from their commitments to the process.

Globalization is controversial. Despite the concentration of international attention on terrorism since the September 11, 2001, attacks on the United States, the process of globalization remains one of the strongest trends within the global system, and in the absence of the terrorist phenomenon, it would likely occupy center stage among world phenomena, as it did for a good deal of the 1990s. During that decade, globalization emerged as the leading light of economic activity and expansion in much of the world. Parts of the globe, however, were left behind, while others flirted with and even embraced the phenomenon, only to have an adverse reaction later on. It is the response, adaptation, and in some cases rejection of globalization that is at the center of debate in the second half of the 2000s.

There are a number of sources of controversy surrounding globalization, five of which we will raise in this introduction. The first is that globalization is a distinctively Western construct, based on theories of economic activity that are Western at base and that reflect Western economic and political preferences and practices. The symbol of globalization is something often called the *Washington consensus,* which represents a set of rules of economic practice that govern participation in the globalized economy. These rules reflect strongly Western economic and political values, and are especially heavily influenced by the United States, which has been the leading apostle of globalization since it began to emerge as a leading force in the 1990s. In order to become a full-fledged member of the globalization system and thus to reap the primarily economic benefits that it promises (largely reflections of the material prosperity of the West, and especially the United States), countries are effectively required to adopt the values and practices of the Washington consensus, which some countries and areas find inconsistent with their own values and situations.

The other sources of controversy flow from the Western intrusiveness of the first. The second controversy surrounds the cultural impacts of embracing the Washington consensus. Becoming part of the global system inevitably entails becoming *like* the countries that are members of the system: capitalist, consumer-oriented societies that eventually adopt both the cultural aspects of the West and many of its outward trappings. A prime necessity of membership in the globalization system is opening societies to outsiders for economic purposes, including foreign investment. Foreign investors in turn bring with them preferences for how things should be done that their money helps allow them to influence: If you become part of the globalization system, the friendly arches of McDonalds are likely not to be far behind.

This opening and cultural assault is of greater or lesser import from region to region of the world. The trade-off it requires—sacrificing established values and practices that are dysfunctional in a globalized society for values that are compatible with globalization—is more acceptable in some places than in others. The Islamic Middle East, for instance, has been more reluctant to make this bargain than other parts of the world, but even in places like parts of Latin America that initially embraced globalization, there has been a backlash against some of its effects.

The third and fourth sources of controversy are related to one another. The third is the difficulty of making the transition from a noncapitalist economy to the capitalist model built into the Washington consensus. In general terms, the consensus requires putting in place macroeconomic and microeconomic practices (detailed below) that are difficult and that can require considerable sacrifice and even privation during the transition process. As an example, one macroeconomic requirement is reduction of government expenditures in order to create something like a balanced budget that will create a healthy economic condition for low inflation and investment, among other things. Such practices may make good long-term economic sense, but they also generally entail reductions in benefits to citizens that occur in the pursuit of reduced government spending and thus cause economic privation and political opposition to the process.

This description suggests the fourth source of controversy, already raised in Chapter 7, which is the differential macro- and microeconomic impact of globalization. As noted in the discussion of free trade, most arguments made in favor of globalization are macroeconomic in character, referring to the overall benefits to societies that become part of the globalization system. While in theory such benefits accrue to individual members of the society as well (the "rising tide that lifts all boats"), those benefits are highly differential (some boats are raised more than others), and there are individuals whose boats are not only not raised, but which may be swamped and sunk in the process. Although its champions argue that globalization overwhelmingly produces winners (people become better-off), it also produces losers, and those losers become the opposition. If their numbers become large enough, the result may be political shock waves that raise the controversy to significant levels. This has become the case in a number of Latin American countries like Venezuela, as we shall see.

The fifth controversy surrounds whether the debate is purposive. The heart of this controversy is whether the process of globalization is inevitable, and whether there are meaningful, non-self-destructive choices that can be exercised as to whether one participates in globalization or not. In some parts of the world, globalization has been almost wholeheartedly embraced and the question is moot, because there is no question about whether participation is valuable or not. In other parts of the world, however, the question is lively, because there is reluctance to embrace either of the core values of globalization. In places like the Islamic Middle East, this reluctance may be the result of indecision about adopting the basic rules of globalized societies (free-market capitalism or transparent banking laws, for instance), or because the secondary and tertiary effects of globalization (secularization and Westernization) are deemed undesirable. At the same time, the transition to globalization may be politically or economically so difficult that some societies believe it should or needs to be avoided, either in principle or because preliminary experience with globalization has been disillusioning.

Whether globalization is optional or inexorable is thus an important question for many countries and areas that are either outside the network of states that are partners in globalization or that have only begun to adopt some of the trappings of membership in the globalized world. Do countries have a *meaningful* choice in this matter? If globalization is indeed inexorable, as its most vocal champions (Friedman, for instance) loudly proclaim, then resistance to accession is akin to relegating one's country to the poor peripheries of the future. In that case, the "choice" is hardly meaningful, because a negative determination is openly self-destructive. If, on the other hand, there *is* a meaningful choice to be made, then the calculation differs. Can a state or region, for instance, stay completely outside the globalization system? Can it adopt some of the trappings of globalization but not all of them? Or is globalization, as Thomas Friedman has asserted in *The Lexus and the Olive Tree,* a "one size fits all" proposition in which one must buy in altogether or be completely excluded?

The answers to these problems, and especially the last one, help to determine both *whether* there is a real debate about globalization and *what* the parameters of that debate might be. To this point, these questions remain only partially answered, and the answers are, to some extent, contradictory. Before looking at how different places have reacted to globalization, it is necessary to first examine the nature of globalization and thus at the parameters of what it means to join the globalization process.

THE BASES OF GLOBALIZATION

Globalization is almost exclusively a product of the evolution of the most advanced states on the globe—what is often called the developed or First World—that have provided both the technological possibility and basic values that define the system. The unfolding process of making globalization universal is thus largely a question of how to spread the globalization system and its benefits to countries outside what President William J. Clinton called the "circle of market democracies," or the developing or Third World. Some areas and countries have embraced this process more enthusiastically than others. Asia (other than Islamic southwest Asia), for instance, has by and large been the most receptive, Africa has hardly been approached about membership, and the response in Latin America has been decidedly mixed.

What has differentiated responses? At the risk of oversimplification, one can look at two sets of factors, which also describe the nature of globalization. One involves the nature of globalization from a technological vantage point. The vast motor of globalization has been the result of the information technology revolution, and some places are better equipped to contribute to and absorb that phenomenon than others. The second are the values, notably those included in the Washington consensus, that countries entering the globalization system must agree to conform to, and this includes accepting or rejecting the political, social, and economic consequences of those choices.

Globalization and Technology

According to *New York Times* columnist Thomas L. Friedman, we live increasingly in a "flat world" whose flatness is largely technologically defined and that has basically altered the economic climate in the world. The great advances in technology that have emerged in the last third of a century and that continue to evolve and become more pervasive have been the necessary precursors for developing a truly global economy in which more and more countries and regions participate. A discussion of the nature and dynamics of the telecommunications revolution that is at the heart of this development goes well beyond present purposes, but some of the impact and possibilities it has created do not.

The telecommunications revolution has condensed both the time and space in which we interact in the world, and this has had enormous impacts on the dynamics of the international economy, both in terms of how international commerce is conducted and how the production of goods and services occur. Each is worth briefly exploring.

One impact of telecommunications has been the globalization of financial markets to an extent unthinkable as little as twenty years ago. It is now possible (and even seems routine to those whose major experience is with this reality) for investors around the world to buy and sell stocks and other financial instruments 24 hours a day by virtue of electronic access to various markets (stock, commodities, etc.) around the globe in real time. These transactions can involve the movement of enormous amounts of capital instantaneously without the ability of sovereign governments to interfere with, and in some cases even monitor, the volume and nature of transactions. This ability in turn creates a high level of international interest in high-quality information about conditions worldwide in which investment may be contemplated, and a desire on the part of investors to have uniform (and understandable for them) conditions around the world to increase their confidence in investments they might make. Realizing this, countries seeking outside investment as a way to stimulate their economies are put under pressure to produce an investment environment that those investors with electronic funds to invest (what Friedman called the "electronic herd" in *The Lexus and the Olive Tree*) will find attractive. Because many of the investors are American or influenced by the United States, the result has been pressure to build a common model of economic activity to attract investment—the Washington consensus.

The internationalization of production offers a second example. Internationalization occurs in two ways. One is the movement of firms into countries with a favorable economic climate (low wages, favorable tax structures, etc.) to manufacture goods at comparative advantage (see discussion in Chapter 7). Apparel and toys are examples of this activity at the lower end of the production cycle; electronic devices are an example at the higher end. The other method of internationalization occurs in the manufacture of complex products like automobiles from parts made in various countries (where the parts can be produced at lower costs than elsewhere) for assembly elsewhere, generally where labor costs are not onerous. The effect of both of these permutations is to create a climate whereby countries compete with one another for the investment opportunities and incomes that accompany either form of investment, and those who judge the competition inevitably do so on the basis of their particular economic values.

In his 2005 book, *The World Is Flat,* Friedman argues that a new dynamic has crept into the globalization dynamic. A variety of developments in the telecommunications revolution, from universally available Web browsers to excess fiber optic networks broadly available worldwide, has had an egalitarian effect on the ability to become part of the cutting edge of the high-technology phenomenon. In the early days, the defining edge of technology was the proprietary characteristic of those with the most advanced computers and educationally based centers—the "Silicon Valley" phenomenon. If one lacked access to the most advanced computers and the brightest minds, one was relegated to being a consumer of technology or, at best, a conveyor and adapter of that technology.

The "democratization" of technology through greater access to information has reduced that advantage to the point that almost any person or group with access to educational facilities and computers can access the most advanced information and knowledge and thus become part of the technology producing leadership in the globalization process. At this point, the countries that seem to be taking the greatest advantage of this phenomenon are places like India, which noncoincidentally also has made some of the greatest investments in science and technology education (China is not far behind). The result is that the gap between the most advanced, First World countries and ambitious Third World countries is narrowing, meaning the competition for leadership and success in a globalizing world is changing as well.

Does technological change make globalization inevitable? Certainly, technology has created the necessary underpinning for this particular historical round of globalizing and helps define the nature of the system and competition within it. It has been a competition in which the most advanced countries have had the major advantage, because they have had both the knowledge base on which the system operates and also the necessary capital to provide the economic incentives. The former advantage (knowledge) may be changing as the nature of the telecommunications revolution changes as well. Certainly the competition among states that are currently part of the system is changing. Whether the same dynamic applies to countries that have not accepted altogether the values of this system is a matter to be explored in the case examples.

Policy Bases: The Washington Consensus

Countries aspiring to full "membership" in the globalization system must adopt the underlying values and rules that informally govern the relationships between the members. Adherence to the norms contained in those rules facilitates the flow of capital between members, and especially from the rich, developed countries to the less developed aspirants. The major incentive for states to accept (or at least live by) these rules is the reasonable promise that doing so will result in greater prosperity for the country and its citizens. Remaining outside the globalization system does not necessarily relegate nonparticipating states to a lessened economic status, because other dynamics (the possession of petroleum wealth, for instance) may provide an alternative means to achieve something like the prosperity that adherents to the Washington consensus enjoy.

The Washington consensus is the composite of a set of economic practices that reflect both the positive and negative aspects of the American experience over the past quarter century or so. These rules have evolved across time, heavily influenced by the values of privatization (turning over previously publicly performed economic functions to private enterprise), deregulation (removing governmental restrictions from economic activities), and free trade (the removal of international barriers to the movement of goods and services across national boundaries).

There is no definitive, official list Washington consensus of rules that a country must adopt to gain membership in the globalizing economy. In *The Lexus and the Olive Tree,* however, Friedman lays out a list of practices under the rhetorical device of what he calls the "golden straitjacket" that fairly represents the basic requirements involved. Friedman provides a reasonable list of requirements and points to why adoption of the rules may be easier for some places than for others. There are sixteen total requirements.

Ten of the criteria flow directly from deregulation and privatization. According to Friedman, they apply to states seeking to join the system:

1. "Making the private sector the primary engine of its economic growth;
2. "Maintaining a low rate of inflation and price stability;
3. "Shrinking the size of its state bureaucracy;
4. "Maintaining as close to a balanced budget as possible;
5. "Privatizing state-owned industries and utilities;

6. "Deregulating capital markets" to facilitate capital flow;

7. "Deregulating its economy to promote as much domestic competition as possible;

8. "Eliminating government corruption, subsidies, and kickbacks as much as possible;

9. "Opening its banking and telecommunications systems to private ownership and competition;" and

10. "Allowing its citizens to choose from an array of competing pension options and foreign-run pension and mutual funds" as a means to protect savings.

The straitjacket also contains six criteria associated with promoting free trade:

1. "Eliminating or lowering tariffs on imported goods;

2. "Removing restrictions on foreign investment;

3. "Getting rid of quotas and domestic monopolies;

4. "Increasing imports;

5. "Making currency convertible;" and

6. "Opening its industry, stock and bond markets to direct foreign ownership and investment."

Regardless of the virtues of any of these rules or all of them collectively, they can be very difficult to adopt. They were formulated in the 1990s, when, for instance, the United States conformed to most of the rules; the same is hardly true with regard to prominent privatization/deregulation rules today (a balanced budget, for instance).

Countries can face at least three different kinds of problems adapting to the straitjacket. First, the rules may be contrary to accepted practices in regions or countries. Opening up national economies to outside competition, for instance, directly contradicts policy in much of Latin America aimed at avoiding having their economies swamped by the United States by restricting imports and relying on often inefficient domestic production (a policy known as "import substitution"). Second, implementation of the policies requires an austere approach to economic policy, including a reduction in government spending, the enforcement of high savings rates, and the like. The result can be a (hopefully temporary) belt-tightening that causes consumer pain and discomfort, which can be politically difficult. Third, if countries lack comparative advantage in any significant areas, reducing barriers to trade can create a flood of imports that drains revenues but is uncompensated for by income from competitively produced domestic goods.

In the early and middle 1990s, many of the problems that have emerged in moving toward globalization were submerged in the general prosperity that seemed to be sweeping the world, and resistance was largely isolated to particular groups displaced by the process (American textile workers, for instance) or countries and regions (most of Africa) that could not compete. When the Asian financial crisis of 1997 and 1998 hit and was accompanied by downturns in a number of other areas at the turn of the millennium, more questions began to be raised about whether globalization is an equally appealing prospect for all countries and regions. The result is a debate about globalization.

THE GLOBALIZATION DEBATE: INDIA VERSUS VENEZUELA

Reactions to the continuing unfolding of globalization have been both area and country specific. In general terms, much of the enthusiasm for globalization was originally manifested in Asia, and a good bit of that enthusiasm continues. One of the countries that is most committed to that evolution is India. Other regions were less at the forefront of globalization and engaged themselves in the process later and more tentatively. Latin America, watchful because of the overwhelming influence of the "colossus of the North" in the process, falls into this category, and it is thus not surprising that some of the countries that are now expressing reservations about and reversing trends toward globalization come from the Western Hemisphere. Venezuela is a prime example.

The two countries, of course, differ in more ways than geographic location. India, with a population estimated by the *CIA World Factbook* in 2006 at just under 1.1 billion, is the second-most populous country in the world, is the world's largest democracy, and depending on what definition one uses for classification, has the world's largest middle class (estimated at 300 million). India features a very high economic growth rate (7.6 percent in 2005), but still has enormous differentials in income and living standards by region of the country. Venezuela, by contrast, is a physically much smaller country, with an estimated 2006 population of 25.7 million. Thanks to high petroleum revenues, it sustained a 9.1 percent economic growth rate in 2005, and the fact that 80 percent of its export income comes from petroleum insulates it from some competitive aspects of the globalization process.

The two countries also have developed very different attitudes toward globalization. India has become one of the most enthusiastic, successful advocates of globalization, fueled largely by its preeminence in the area of high technology. Venezuela, on the other hand, embraced globalization during the 1990s but, stung by the impact of conforming to the rules of the straitjacket, reacted negatively in 1999, electing (and in 2006 overwhelmingly reelecting) Hugo Chavez, a vocal opponent of globalization and champion of a return to socialism, as president.

India and Venezuela, for different reasons, represent the reactions to and thus the debate about, the continuing phenomenon of globalization. A brief examination of each case demonstrates some of the dynamics and tensions associated with globalization.

India

Particularly in the past few years, India has been portrayed as the "poster child" of globalization, the country where, more than virtually anywhere else, the values of globalization have taken hold, are spreading, and are bringing with them the benefits that globalization can promise for improvement in the human condition (a reputation earned despite the fact that India still maintains vestiges of a preglobalization profile in areas such as tariffs). The explosion of India onto the international globalization scene has, for instance, been the major impetus for unabashed globalization enthusiast Friedman to reexamine the evolution of globalization for a second time in his 2005 book, *The World Is Flat,* because it is Indian entrepreneurship that has provided much of the evidence of how technology generation has spread across the globe, thereby flattening both access to and the ability to produce technology.

The statistics of Indian economic growth are substantial and impressive. As *Newsweek* reported in its March 6, 2006, edition, for instance, India has had the world's second-fastest-growing economy over the past fifteen years, and that growth expanded to an annual rate of 7.5 percent in 2005. The result has been an unprecedented growth both of personal income and entrepreneurial activity that has helped expand the middle class in India to over 300 million, and this group has the second-highest consumption rate in the world, trailing only Americans in terms of the amount of income they expend. Estimates reported by the magazine suggest that if current trends continue (always a risky proposition), India's economy will be larger than Italy's in ten years or Great Britain's in fifteen years. By 2050, the Indian economy could be five times that of Japan's.

Long-term economic projections can be very incorrect, but even if the details are questionable, the fact that India has experienced and likely will continue to experience the kinds of growth that make it one of the world's true superpowers in the future is clear. It is also unquestionable that India has enjoyed its remarkable growth at the same time that it has adopted the values of globalization and become a leader of that movement.

The question is, what has caused India to become such an active and successful partner in globalization? India is such an enormous, diverse, and complicated place that simple explanations do not capture its dynamics. India is, for instance, about one-third the physical size of the United States, but it has a population more than three and a half times the American population. It is a place of enormous ethnic, linguistic, and religious diversity (there are, for instance, sizable numbers of adherents of virtually all the world's major religions practicing in the country). In addition to English and Hindi, there are 14 additional officially recognized languages in India. The 300 million estimated members of the Indian middle class are matched by at least that number who fall below the world's standard for destitution, surviving on less than $2 a day per capita. Ethnic divisions have resulted in open or smoldering violent conflict in places as diverse as the Tamil lands of the south and Kashmir in the north. At the same time, the country is beset by one of the few remaining active Marxist wars of national liberation, a small but persistent guerrilla movement dedicated to establishing a communist regime in the country. All of this diversity occurs within a framework of the world's largest political democracy.

India's entrance into and place in the globalizing economy is largely the result of its growing preeminence in the high-technology sector that helps define globalization's parameters. Many countries have embraced and become part of globalization essentially by becoming consumers and appliers of the growing economic possibilities that globalization provides. India does that too, but its unique place comes from India's position increasingly as both a consumer *and* producer of technology.

The city of Bangalore has become the symbol of India's evolving place in the globalization system. Often referred to as India's Silicon Valley, it has become synonymous with India's entrance into the global economy and as a gathering spot for the large numbers of scientists and engineers produced by India's higher-education system who come to this highly modern, cosmopolitan city to engage in the kinds of technological innovation and entrepreneurial activity that we associate with the San Francisco Bay Area and places like North Carolina's research triangle, the Boston area's Route 128 corridor, and other concentrations of high-technology activity in the United States. Bangalore serves both as technological innovator and consumer, as it is also the location in which much of the highly publicized "outsourcing" of lower-end technology jobs from the United States (telemarketing, service contractors, etc.) is found. Indeed, Bangalore (and other Indian sites like it) have become competitive with American enterprises both in terms of their work output and their competition for highly trained and motivated scientists and engineers who used to be drawn inexorably to locations in the United States.

How does one explain how a country like India can embrace globalization as successfully as it has, when other countries have not? As noted, the complexity of India makes any easy, glib answers suspect. However, we can identify several characteristics that are often raised in the literature about India and globalization.

One factor is that India has emerged from an economically repressive past during the 1960s and 1970s that left the country poised for a leap forward in activity once the opportunity arose. As Amitabh Pal explains in a *Global Policy Forum* paper, during the period before the 1990s (when India jumped on the globalization bandwagon), the country had "a closed, protectionist economy with scarcely any foreign goods, especially consumer goods, available." This was the case because "tariffs on imported goods were among the highest in the world," and were combined with extremely progressive tax schedules that effectively stifled entrepreneurial activity. This was particularly the case under Prime Minister Indira Gandhi, who purported a kind of socialist economic philosophy that "the Indian upper-middle class perceived . . . as a straitjacket." The country, in other words, failed on both aspects (privatization/deregulation and free trade) of Friedman's golden straitjacket, and the result was a very confined economic condition. The economic situation came to a head due to policies pursued by the government of Rajiv Gandhi that depleted Indian foreign exchange and caused a crisis that resulted in reform. Those reforms, begun in 1991, were aimed both at privatizing and deregulating economic activity and at opening the country to outside influences and came as a significant reaction to the overmanagement of the economy that had been characteristic of the 1960s and 1970s. What has become progressively an Indian "economic miracle" dates to these reforms, which have continued but are not entirely complete (India still has relatively high tariffs on certain classes of goods).

Several other indigenous and exogenous influences have helped stimulate the Indian transition. One of these is that India has a societal structure that helps support the growth of a vital private sector. The structure includes, according to *Newsweek,* "a real and deep private sector, a clean, well-regulated financial system and the sturdy rule of law." All of these amount to what Friedman calls "corruption-free economic governance" that is a necessary underpinning of a globalizing society. Another characteristic that derives from this is the Indian democratic culture that, when combined with an entrepreneurial work ethic, combines to create what Max Singer and the late Aaron Wildawsky refer to as a "quality economy" (one that has the requisite characteristics for growth because it provides the economic and political incentives for people and groups to work hard and to innovate significantly).

In addition to these advantages, there were at least two others. One, which is both indigenous and exogenous, is the Indian commitment to quality education. At least for those classes with access to it, India has some of the best schools and colleges in the world in the area of science and technology. The Indian Institute of Technology, for instance, is a global leader in this field, and its graduates are heavily recruited worldwide. Historically, many of these highly educated Indians have migrated to the United States, where they have been a mainstay of American technological preeminence. In the process, they have been Americanized and adopted many of the values of American society. Increasingly, thanks to outlets like Bangalore, many of these émigrés are returning to India (creating a potential reverse "brain drain" for the United States), but they return with a highly Americanized view of the world, including an adherence to most of the values included in the Washington consensus. As evidence of this attraction, Indians remain among the most pro-American people in the world, at the interpersonal if not necessarily at the intergovernmental level.

India's headlong plunge into globalization has not been entirely smooth or devoid of criticism, although the level of opposition remains moot. The major criticism is one that is familiar throughout the globalizing world, that globalization may indeed increase the prosperity of the country as a whole, but that improvement is not at all uniform. Macroeconomic benefits to India, in other words, are incontestable and demonstrable in any number of measures of the economy; microeconomic benefits to individual Indians are not so uniform. The rising tide may be raising all boats, but it is raising some boats much higher in the water than others.

The anomaly of growing inequity has already been suggested in the new demographics of India: The country has the world's largest middle class with 300 million purported members, but it also has one of the world's largest concentrations of desperately poor individuals at around 300 million as well. Due to the tradition of societal castes in India's past, this disparity has not yet produced a sizable backlash, as the dispossessed have not—at least to this point—asserted the unacceptability of their much more meager existence. The fact that India is fast becoming two countries economically—an emerging member of the wealthy, sophisticated globalization system and a parallel society that contains some of the world's most wretched people—creates an anomalous situation for Indian governance. On one hand, policies that allow and encourage the accumulation of wealth as a necessary way to stimulate the entrance of India into the global economy preclude significant government intervention and revenue redistribution to ameliorate the living conditions of those worst-off in Indian society. On the other hand, a serious movement toward social egalitarianism would deeply drain Indian resources to the point of jeopardizing India's continuing movement into the globe's upper economic reaches.

The result has been a debate within India that is currently largely confined to the upper classes of Indian society. Defenders of Indian globalization argue a kind of Reaganomics that suggest that the benefits of economic growth will "trickle down" to the poor eventually and that efforts to redistribute wealth will shut off that trickle altogether. In more extreme cases, the poor are even blamed for their condition, because, among other things, they have too many children. Pal, quoting Indian columnist Dilip D'Souza, counters, "Proponents of globalization say wait for 10 years. But the poor can't wait. They have waited for 53 years (since independence). We have to have urgent measures to help them."

This theme of inequality and how to deal with it helps explain the difference in reaction to globalization in India and in Venezuela. In India, the very poor are also politically unorganized and weak, and as long as they remain so, macroeconomic justifications of globalization will overwhelm and swamp their microeconomic woes. In Latin America, advocacy—sometimes sincere, sometime questionably so—is a much more potent source within the political system, as an examination of the Venezuelan reaction to globalization demonstrates.

Venezuela

Like many other Latin American countries, Venezuela adopted the values of the globalization centered around the Washington consensus in the 1990s. Unlike the case of India, however, the results have not been entirely positive in either an economic or a political sense. The strictures of the consensus on many national economies caused higher levels of economic inequality than had previously been the case, and the restrictions fell especially heavily on the lower classes in many countries, relegating people to even more wretched lives than they had experienced before, lowering standards of living for many people at the lower end of the economic continuum. Such a short-term phenomenon is not an uncommon microeconomic characteristic of the early stages of globalization. It happened to occur, however, in the very late 1990s and early 2000s, when the worldwide economic slowdown was having adverse effects almost everywhere, and these dynamics particularly deflated some of the bubble economies in Central and South America, leaving, for instance, Argentina on the brink of literal bankruptcy. The result has been a political backlash against globalization in a number of states, including Venezuela, that is much stronger than the concern about the poor in India.

The Indian and Latin American cases offer both similarities and differences. The most strikingly obvious similarity is that globalization blossomed as a reaction to heavy state involvement and control of economies that had effectively stifled economic growth in both cases. In the Latin American case, the impetus for state control was different than in India, in that a major impetus to state management was to avoid the economic stranglehold of the United States. The fear was that if the economies of most states in the region were open to outside competition (notably through the free trading of goods and services) that U.S. goods and services would overwhelm local markets and thus destroy native structures. The most obvious manifestation of the protection that most countries displayed was the policy of "import substitution," in which local manufacture of the kinds of goods that could be bought from the United States were subsidized and protected from outside intrusion, thereby substituting local for foreign goods and services. The effect of import substitution (and other forms of government intrusion into the economy) was to make those economies weak and uncompetitive globally and to suppress the ability of citizens to consume world-class goods at competitive prices.

Both India and numerous Latin American countries were thus receptive to international economic reform when the winds of globalization began to blow in the early

1990s. Old socialist, statist governments were swept aside and replaced by regimes that promised reform and prosperity. During the early and middle 1990s, growth occurred in most places, and the opening of economies produced increased trade and economic activity that seemed to benefit all. Latin American boats were lifted as were those from other regions.

This process, which seemed inevitable, inexorable, and overwhelmingly beneficial, took a negative turn as the 1990s wore down. The initial warning, discussed earlier, was the East Asian economic crisis of 1997–1998, which, among other things, revealed economic weaknesses that would become more pronounced as the millennium approached. India rode out and crested the storm of reaction, maintaining its adherence to and participation in the globalizing economy. Many Latin American economies were swamped and determined to abandon ship.

The reaction has been dramatic. Writing in *The Nation,* Greg Gandin describes it: "Today, roughly 300 million of Latin America's 520 million citizens live under governments that either want to reform the Washington consensus—a euphemism for the mix of punishing fiscal austerity, privatization and market liberalization that has produced staggering levels of poverty and inequality—or to abolish it altogether and create a new, more equitable global economy." The emphasis of this reaction is decidedly microeconomic— the impact on the Latin American masses—rather than the macroeconomic benefits that are much more prominent in Indian discussions.

The response in much of Latin America has been political and taken the form of a resurgence of the popularity of political movements that are putatively socialist in their orientations. In India, socialism tends to be the province of intellectual classes with a more or less open noblesse oblige basis. In Latin America, however, these movements are much closer to the grassroots of populations whose support is necessary for the success of these movements, and their appeal thus tends to be much closer to the microeconomic, personal level. As Jorge C. Castenada explains it in a recent *Foreign Affairs* article, "The left . . . stresses social improvements over macroeconomic orthodoxy, egalitarian distribution of wealth over its creation, sovereignty over international cooperation, democracy over governmental effectiveness."

Within the Latin American context, there are two distinct strains that have reemerged. One is traditional and Marxist, and as Castenada explains, it is attempting to reconstruct the "formerly radical left" by emphasizing social policy that "usually attempts to deepen and broaden democratic institutions." The other strain is more strictly populist, promising economic equality as a means to promote support for a particular leader or movement. A common phenomenon in Latin America, this strain is most closely associated with supporters of the late Argentine president Juan Peron (Peronism).

Both strains of socialist resurgence have taken clear aim at globalization and its strongest regional manifestation, the proposed Free Trade Area of the Americas (FTAA), an idea first adopted in 1994 as a way to create a hemisphere-wide free trading area. When the prosperity of the 1990s was benefiting all parties, there was at least rhetorical support for the FTAA, despite the overwhelming preponderance of the U.S. economy in the region. The arrangement would be, at least in many Latin American eyes, of primary value to the United States, and as such has been the bull's eye for opposition to both the United States and the globalization that FTAA represents. As Grandin puts it, "The

FTAA is the U.S. government's gambit to turn things around. It is meant to do for Latin America what the North American Free Trade Agreement did for Mexico: ratify its status as a U.S. province within an increasingly globalized economy." The language of the quote is arguably hyperbolic; the fear is not. We will examine the impact of NAFTA on Mexico in Chapter 9. At any rate, the region's response to the FTAA has left it a very badly, if not mortally, wounded construct.

Venezuela's experience is both representative of Latin America's disenchantment with globalization, but with uniquely Venezuelan characteristics as well. Michael Shifter condenses the Venezuelan experience through the vantage point of its charismatic president, Hugo Chavez: "Chavez's appeal cannot be explained without acknowledging the deep dissatisfaction with the existing political and economic order felt by much of the population in Venezuela, and throughout much of the rest of Latin America." Much of Chavez's appeal is couched in opposition to the current American administration (Chavez makes a point of professing his warm feelings for average, and especially disadvantaged, Americans) that manifests itself in both anti-Americanism and opposition to globalization (and hence FTAA) that, in their context, is more or less a seamless whole. Shifter describes it as "an eclectic blend of populism, nationalism, militarism, and, most recently, socialism."

Chavez, of course, is a particularly controversial politician, and has been a constant thorn in the side of the Bush administration on a number of fronts, including globalization and the FTAA. His open friendship with Fidel Castro's Cuba and its socialist economy and his active opposition to the implementation of FTAA are major sources of confrontation between the American Bush administration and his regime. He was elected originally in 1999 and reelected to a second term in a special election in 2004 and another six-year term in December 2006. In the process, he has amended the constitution to ensure his continuing rule, to the chagrin of the American administration. Chavez's style, which is openly populist and charismatic, has been analogized with that of the late Peron, and his willingness to stand up to the Americans wins him widespread support both within his own country and the region.

The phenomenon of Chavez is one of the unique aspects of Venezuelan reaction to globalization; Venezuela's oil is the other. Petroleum is Venezuela's economic lifeline, accounting, according to the *CIA World Factbook,* for one-third of gross domestic product and 80 percent of export earnings, and over half of government revenues are derived from oil revenues. Venezuelan oil plays a significant role in American imports, providing roughly 11 percent of American imports in 2006, and Venezuela has in the past been an important backstop for the United States when Middle Eastern members of the Organization of Petroleum Exporting Countries (OPEC) have threatened to or have actually withheld petroleum from the American market. The most recent estimates are that Venezuela produces about three million barrels of oil per day, of which it exports about 2.1 million barrels. In a tight world market for oil (see Chapter 13), this provides the Venezuelan government considerable leverage and makes it easier for Chavez to take controversial international positions.

Being an oil-rich country provides Venezuela with two major advantages in dealing with the globalizing system that are not enjoyed by many other countries in Latin America or elsewhere in the world. One of these is that it allows Venezuela to provide tolerably for the welfare of its citizens without undergoing the kinds of painful reforms associated with implementing the Washington consensus. The other is that it frees Venezuela from what it views as unacceptable economic pressure from the United States.

Oil wealth, in other words, provides economic options for the Venezuelan government that countries lacking such wealth do not enjoy. Chavez, for instance, has been able to use petroleum profits to provide subsidies for the lower classes that suffered under the globalization regime that a country like India simply cannot provide. By ameliorating peasant discontent, Chavez is also bolstering his populist political base and thereby increasing his political popularity and durability. Friedman, however, warns that this ability (which he says is shared by many oil-exporting countries) has a darker side: Because the Chavez regime can effectively buy off the public by simply shoveling money at problems, it can (and does) avoid engaging in the kinds of fundamental reforms that are necessary for the long-term viability of the economy. Oil wealth, in other words, evades the painful strictures of the golden straitjacket, but that avoidance may simply be a form of deferring the problem for the future.

Oil wealth also allows Chavez to pursue foreign policies independent of American pressure, and especially the pressure to globalize. Chavez has emerged as a leading force in opposition to the FTAA, and he is able to influence other Latin American states by the promise of providing or withholding assistance to compliers and noncompliers with his preferred anti-American stance. In the contemporary oil market, where the withdrawal of as little as a couple million barrels a day (more or less Venezuela's output) can have a major impact on supply and demand, there is very little leverage that the United States or others can wield over Chavez.

CONCLUSION

The turn of the twentieth century into the twenty-first has produced a differential response to the spread of globalization. During the heyday of the 1990s, there was virtually no debate about whether countries should seek admission to the ranks of the globalized and globalizing: Joining the global economy was viewed as both inevitable in order to avoid relegation to the ash heap of international economics, and the effects of globalization were so uniformly positive that this inevitability was not viewed as a burden on states.

That is no longer universally the case. Experience has shown that the benefits of globalization are not uniform across or within societies. Some states clearly benefit from globalization more than others, and globalization both positively and adversely affects groups within the societies it enters. At the macroeconomic level, there is not a great deal of debate about whether globalization is a good thing; at the level of individual states and especially at the microeconomic level of impacts on groups within states, the universality of benefit is no longer accepted carte blanche. The result is a debate about globalization, both its benefits and liabilities, and based on that assessment, a judgment about whether globalization should be embraced or avoided if possible.

India and Venezuela provide examples of the two responses to the debate. India remains an ardent globalizer and is moving steadily forward to gain an increasingly prominent role in the globalization system. Venezuela, mirroring a more general Latin American reaction, has become skeptical of the process and resistant to accepting the strictures of the Washington consensus. Unlike some other Latin American countries, oil literally lubricates a fairly painless process of resistance for the Venezuelans; others suffer more obviously from trying to resist.

Why have these countries chosen different paths? The analysis is undoubtedly incomplete, yet our brief case studies suggest at least three interrelated points of difference. A more in-depth analysis of the two cases or analysis of a broader set of cases might yield a different set of conclusions.

The first contrast has to do with the processes involved in moving toward globalization, which in turn reflects the different political contexts of the two countries. Both emerged in the 1990s from a largely unsuccessful experience with state control, even socialized economies that had underperformed and thus created an atmosphere for promoting change. Both entered the globalization process, but India has stayed on course whereas Venezuela has not. Part of this reflects different political cultures: an Indian culture steeped in British adherence to the rule of law and a tradition of "staying the course" versus a much more volatile political culture in Venezuela with a notable populist underpinning. The two influences provided the countries with different capacities to accept and weather the early, difficult stages of the transition. In both countries, globalization widened wealth divergences: in India, that was tolerable; in Venezuela, it was not. Thus India could more easily politically persevere down the globalization road than could Venezuela.

The second, and related, difference flows from the first. Globalization magnifies resource inequalities within societies: All boats may rise, but the boats of the rich rise much faster and higher than those of the poor. In India, the tradition of inequality is well enough established and the poor are sufficiently politically impotent that their continued impoverishment is not enough to derail a process from which its adherents argue the poor will eventually benefit (whether they believe that sincerely is a different question). The poor, in other words, can be ignored politically. The Peronist influence in Latin America finds much of its cause in support of the same poor peasants that the Indians ignore. Whether concern for the poor is any more honestly felt in Venezuela than in India, politically, support for the poor is part of the populist calculus—and a shibboleth that can turn into opposition to the symbols of continuing suffering, like globalization.

Finally, India and Venezuela have different resource bases. India's great strength does not lie in its sheer numbers, which are potentially a drag on future growth, but in its highly educated, entrepreneurial class. India has a citizen base in its emerging middle class that is tailor-made for the globalization revolution, and India's ability to harness that resource (rather than see it trickle away to the United States) is a major part of its past and future success. Venezuela, by contrast, has no equivalent of the science and engineering class found in India, but it does have an abundance of one of the world's most valued commodities, petroleum. As long as the world's major energy source is petroleum, Venezuela has an effective prophylactic against encroaching globalization. Avoiding globalization may in the long run prove detrimental to Venezuela, but in the short run it can afford to eschew the phenomenon. Lacking an equivalent to oil, India is impelled much more strongly along the globalization path.

 STUDY/DISCUSSION QUESTIONS

1. Why has globalization become controversial? What are the major sources of controversy? Describe each.

2. What are the major bases of the globalization phenomenon? Describe each. How are the influences of each factor evolving and changing?

3. What is the Washington consensus? Describe its major underpinnings and effects. How do its characteristics define embrace of or opposition to globalization?

4. India has been a leading proponent and success story for globalization. Examine how and why.

5. Venezuela is part of Latin America's resistance to globalization. Describe the reasons for this resistance. What are the unique aspects of Venezuelan resistance?

6. Why has India embraced globalization whereas Venezuela (and other Latin American countries) has resisted?

READING/RESEARCH MATERIAL

Abdelal, Rawi, and Adam Segal. "Has Globalization Reached Its Peak?" *Foreign Affairs* 86, 1 (January/February 2007), 103–114.

Blinder, Alan S. "Offshoring: The Next Industrial Revolution." *Foreign Affairs* 85, 2 (March/April 2006), 113–128.

Castenada, Jorge C. "Latin America's Left Turn." *Foreign Affairs* 85, 3 (May/June 2006), 28–43.

Corrales, Javier. "Hugo Boss." *Foreign Policy*, January/February 2006, 32–41.

Friedman, Thomas L. *The Lexus and the Olive Tree: Understanding Globalization.* New York: Farrar, Straus and Giroux, 1999.

———. *The World Is Flat: A Brief History of the 21st Century.* New York: Farrar, Straus, and Giroux, 2005.

Grandin, Greg. "Latin America's New Consensus." *The Nation,* May 1, 2006, 23–29.

Pal, Amitabh. "The Great Divide: India Confronts Globalization." *Global Policy Forum,* September 3, 2001.

Shifter, Michael. "In Search of Hugo Chávez." *Foreign Affairs* 85, 3 (May/June 2006), 45–60.

Singer, Max and the Late Aaron Wildawsky. *The Real World Order: Zones of Peace, Zones of Turmoil* (revised edition). Chatham, NJ: Chatham House, 1996.

Talbot, Strobe. *Engaging India: Diplomacy, Democracy and the Bomb.* Washington, DC: Brookings Institution Press, 2004.

Wolf, Martin. *Why Globalization Works.* New Haven, CT: Yale University Press, 2004.

Zakaria, Fareed. "India Rising." *Newsweek,* March 6, 2006, 24–42.

WEB SITES

General Sources

http://www.globalpolicy.org/globaliz/econ.htm

http://www.theglobalist.com/DB.web

http://yaleglobal.yale.edu

Venezuelan experience

http://www.venezuelanalysis.com/articles

CIA World Factbook

http://www.cia.gov/cia/publications/factbook/print/ve.html

Evaluating Globalization

NAFTA AFTER A DECADE

PRÉCIS

It began as an intensely politically controversial proposal that was one of the highlights of the 1992 presidential election in the United States between President George H. W. Bush, Governor William J. Clinton, and Texas millionaire H. Ross Perot. The North American Free Trade Agreement (NAFTA) proposed an economic union between the major states of North America— the United States, Canada, and Mexico. Who would benefit and who would suffer under its provisions was a matter of considerable controversy and expansive claims surrounding its negotiation, its initial implementation starting on January 1, 1994, and its long-range benefits or dangers. Over a decade after it came into being, advocates and opponents are still cheering and bemoaning this edifice to globalization and free trade.

The effects of NAFTA are important both in understanding the dynamics of globalization and in assessing the impact that future schemes designed to promote a globalized world will have on individual countries, regions, and the globe. When it was announced, it was heralded as the first step in creating what would be the world's largest free trade area in terms of population included under its umbrella and potentially in the volume of trade it created. It was the "deepest" arrangement in terms of the extent of obligations that the United States government had reached in the economic area and thus was viewed as a harbinger of how the leading proponent of globalization would respond to changing international issues. It was also seen as the stalking horse for the broader economic integration of the Western Hemisphere in the form of the Free Trade Area of the Americas (FTAA), which was proposed

147

later in the same year NAFTA came into force and which has since been the subject of considerable controversy in its own right.

NAFTA is now over a dozen years old, and most of the same controversies and disagreements that were present and discussed at the time its approval was being debated are still present today. At first glance, one would assume that over a decade of experience would have removed most of the doubts about NAFTA one way or the other, but they have not. As a result, it is impossible to construct a clean, clear assessment on which all—or even a large percentage of—observers could agree. If anything, the effects of NAFTA remain as amorphous and controversial today as they were in 1994. Because no consensus has emerged, it becomes the burden of this case study to examine both why disagreement about NAFTA continues and then to assess the agreement's impact in terms of the substantive bases of disagreement. The reader looking for a clear, decisive conclusion should be forewarned that no such conclusion is possible without distorting or ignoring the data available.

THE CONTROVERSY OVER NAFTA

There are two broad, and interconnected, reasons for disagreement about the impact NAFTA has had. The first has to do with the context in which the disagreement arises, and includes both political (verging on theological) disagreements on globalization and free trade and methodological difficulties of reaching conclusive determinations. The second source of disagreement is the rather sizable and diverse set of supposed impacts of NAFTA that have to be assessed and that in turn are subject to highly emotional differences of fact and opinion, and thus discord about the substance of the effects of NAFTA.

The Context of Disagreement

Much of the problem of dealing with the impact of NAFTA on its members and the international system is that the arguments become entangled in the broader context of support for and opposition to globalization and, especially in the case of NAFTA, its principal handmaiden, free trade. Some of the common contours of those debates and disagreements have been raised in the two previous case studies and need not be repeated here. Suffice it to say that NAFTA, as a very comprehensive, ambitious globalization proposition, immediately energized political and ideological forces on both sides of the general free trade argument and elicited the support and opposition of those groups that generally are supportive of or in opposition to free trade as a general proposition.

As in the general debate, the coalitions of supporters and opponents represented a mixed bag. The supporters in the United States included Eastern liberal internationalists (mostly Democrats), conservative businesspersons (especially those affiliated with large multinational corporations who expected to benefit from the arrangement and who were mostly Republican), and Southerners (who, as pointed out in Chapter 7, have historically supported the free trade concept) of both political stripes. It is, for instance, probably not coincidental that the concept was first proposed by President George H. W. Bush, an adopted Texan whose roots are in the Eastern liberal, if Republican, tradition; and was pushed through to completion by an Arkansas Democrat, William J. Clinton.

Opposition also came along reasonably predictable political lines. Traditional, mostly Republican conservatives (as opposed to religious, largely southern "conservatives" who have formed much of the Republican, pro-NAFTA base in the 2000s) generally opposed the agreement as an unwanted extension of governmental authority and as an intrusion on American sovereignty. They were joined by traditional Democrats (principally labor unionists who feared that jobs would be lost to Mexico) and Democratic-leaning environmentalists fearful that the implementation of NAFTA would result in greater environmental degradation due to the movement of polluting industries to Mexico, which has lower environmental standards.

In some ways, the debate over NAFTA was indeed a stalking horse, even a training ground of sorts for the debate over globalization that would grow and mature during the remainder of the 1990s over the spread of globalization through organizations including the World Trade Organization (WTO), the Asia-Pacific Economic Cooperation (APEC), and even the G-8 economic summits. The discussions about NAFTA served both as a precursor to some of these debates and were influenced by them, particularly in the context of the arguments surrounding the formation of NAFTA and a retrospective on its performance after a decade or more.

The debate about globalization has become almost theological in its nature, and NAFTA has become one of the altars on which the disagreement is played out. While it may be offensive to partisans on both sides, there has become a near knee-jerk reaction on both sides about any globalization, free trade proposition, including its NAFTA incarnation. NAFTA itself is a stereotype of this theological debate with aspects that are sui generis: It is unique, for instance, in the sense that other free trade proposals do not include a significant aspect of their surrounding debate that centers on the question of illegal immigration, as NAFTA does. Nonetheless, it is important when looking at the arguments commentators make about NAFTA to realize that these sometimes reflect, intentionally or implicitly, underlying assessments that are really about globalization and free trade generally and that may or may not apply directly to NAFTA.

The other problem is methodological and has to do with the problem of demonstrating whether either beneficial or harmful events that have occurred between the time NAFTA was implemented in 1994 and any present time can be attributed to the influence of NAFTA or might be the result of other, possibly quite unrelated reasons.

This problem arises from the nature of scientific proof. That subject may be arcane and is certainly beyond definitive presentation here; it is nonetheless a sufficient conditioner on what can and cannot be said about the impact of NAFTA on the world. The methodological problem deals with the question of necessary and sufficient causation and the danger of committing the logical fallacy of affirming the consequent. These terms may seem obtuse and confusing, but they are basic to making sound arguments, in our case about the impact of NAFTA on the world.

We begin with brief definitions (which may offend methodological purists). Causation (roughly, what leads to or causes one thing—an effect—to happen) can be of two kinds: necessary and sufficient. Necessary causation is a situation in which something must occur for something else to occur: The cause is necessary for the effect. Thus, for instance, it is impossible to hit a home run in baseball if you do not make contact with the ball. Making contact is thus a necessary condition for hitting a home run. Clearly, however, a home run is not the result every time someone hits the ball: No home run will occur if, for instance, you swing and miss, but the simple act of making contact is not enough—it is not sufficient—to result in a home run. To hit a home run, you must also meet all the conditions necessary for a home run: a proper swing, placing a proper charge on the ball, achieving a proper trajectory for the ball, even having an outfield fence the right distance from home plate for the ball to clear. All or some of these conditions are necessary for a home run to be hit, and collectively some or all of them are sufficient (adequate) for the result. The problem is that there are generally multiple sufficient causes or combinations of necessary causes that will produce the effect (an upper-cut swing on a hanging curveball or a flat swing at a fastball down the middle over a short fence, for instance).

The problem is simple when there is a single cause, or combination of causes, that are individually necessary and collectively sufficient to create the effect. In that case, if we observe the effect (whatever it may be) we know what caused it, and an assessment is both easy and straightforward. In the real world, however, that is rarely the case; rather, there are almost always multiple sufficient causes—different reasons why changes may have occurred, and it is logically impossible to attribute the effect (the result) to one possible cause or another.

The fallacy of attributing a particular cause to an effect when there are multiple possible explanations is known as affirming the consequent. An admittedly frivolous example may help explain this concept. It involves a frog sitting in Times Square in New York. The frog is hitting two sticks together, and someone comes up to the frog and asks why he is doing so. The frog replies, "To keep the elephants away." The person asking the question looks surprised at the answer, and the frog continues, "See any elephants?" And, of course, there are no elephants. So, is the frog the explanation for the absence of elephants on the scene?

The clear answer is that it is not. Even if one admits that the frog and his sticks might ward off elephants (a dubious proposition), there are clearly other sufficient causes of the absence of elephants as well. The most obvious is that elephants are prohibited in the Time Square area, other than when the circus may be playing at Radio City Music Hall or Madison Square Garden, and there are doubtless others as well (the skyscrapers of midtown Manhattan are obviously a poor habitat for elephants, for instance). In formal, argumentative terms, the problem is that the frog may be a sufficient reason for the absence of elephants (it *can* be the reason for the absence of elephants), but clearly there are other plausible causes. When one observes the consequent (no elephants), one does not know why. To attribute that reason to one sufficient cause or another goes beyond the evidence, and thus commits the fallacy of affirming the consequent (attributing one cause to a phenomenon that can have several competing causes).

What has this to do with measuring the effects of an economic arrangement like NAFTA? The answer is that when one concludes that NAFTA is to be credited or blamed for some change in the economic conditions of the member states (or anything else), one must commit the same logical fallacy involved in saying the frog is the reason there are no frogs in Times Square. As we shall see, various analysts have argued that NAFTA would make the overall economies of the region and those of various member states stronger, weaker, or that it would have a mixed effect (some improvements, some worsening of conditions). It does not matter which outcome one predicts.

If one looks at the situation since NAFTA was instituted, what one can observe is improvement/worsening/a mixture. The problem is *what* caused whatever change one observes. Hypothetically, for instance, if the economy of the United States grew at an above-average rate since the institution of NAFTA, does that mean NAFTA was the reason? Certainly one could cite supportive evidence (e.g., increased exports to Mexico), but are there not other plausible reasons for growth (or, in other words, other sufficient conditions to explain the phenomenon)? Of course there are, and despite the elegance and weight of evidence that may be brought to bear to demonstrate the cogency of NAFTA as an explanation, one can only assert that conclusion by implicitly stating that the existence of NAFTA rather than other sufficient causes is the reason for the expansion. That additional step involves going beyond the evidence by selecting one explanation over the others, and doing so inevitably requires committing the fallacy of affirming the consequent.

The debate over NAFTA (or many other contentious issues, for that matter) is rarely put in these terms. Why not? Part of the reason is that most of those who make arguments on any side of this or other issues are not trained in formal logic and are probably unaware of the methodological "sin" they are committing. Most analysts recognize that they are treading on uneasy ground when they make inferences on these kinds of matters, but manage to enshroud their uncertainty and the ambiguities they inevitably confront with mountains of supporting data that can make for very convincing preponderances of evidence that amount to little more than support for choosing one sufficient cause over another but do not negate the basic flaw in their argumentation. At a darker methodological level, the problem may also be the theological nature of the argumentation already noted: Many analysts have a priori conclusions they wish to support, and are not going to be troubled by the shakiness of their own or others' methods of reaching conclusions.

The obfuscation of conclusions suffers from another source that should be mentioned in passing: the nature and extent of evidence available. For better or worse, economic arguments tend to be reducible to numerical, statistical values. Placing such values in this form adds a kind of authority and elegance to the arguments they are used to support: The "numbers don't lie." That may be true, but they may well fib or mislead. The problem is that there is a veritable mountain of numerical data available to support nearly any economic argument, and sometimes that data can be—and is—used very selectively. Statistics that show the overall economy of the United States has grown at an accelerated rate, for instance, may be cited to demonstrate the benefits of NAFTA (despite the possibility that other dynamics may have caused the growth). Meanwhile, increased income distribution inequality resulting from that growth may be equally cited to demonstrate that the impact of NAFTA is not so positive.

This somewhat lengthy discussion is intended to provide a conditioning framework within which to examine the arguments that are made about NAFTA (and about other similar phenomena as well). The arguments that are made on all sides of this contentious issue are forceful, eloquent, and often persuasive, citing elaborate supporting evidence. Those arguments, however, are often made for partisan purposes based in preexisting views of globalization generally and NAFTA in particular, and their arguments and evidence are not as unassailable as the champions of one side or another will contend. These arguments should be viewed exactly as what they are: positions intended to elaborate and convince, not scientific explanations. Most of the time, the analyses are honestly put forward rather than sophistic devices, but the conclusion remains that the analyses will not yield simple, clear-cut, and definitive answers to the basic questions about NAFTA. Our quest will thus be for the most convincing arguments, not the definitive answers that remove all questions and doubts.

Substantive Arguments

Because NAFTA is a large and encompassing arrangement that has an impact on a large and diverse set of phenomena in the countries where it is in force, it has resulted in many substantial areas of controversy. If economic conditions affect just about everything about life and NAFTA has a wide-ranging, even profound effect on the economic condition, we should expect it to cause an impact and thus concern over a number of policy areas.

In a case study of this scope and length, it is impossible to deal even cursorily with the entire range of concerns about and effects of NAFTA. Instead, we will look selectively at five impact areas that are often cited and about which a maximum amount of controversy has arisen. These areas are: the overall economic impact of NAFTA on the affected economies and, by extension, broader regional and world economies; the impact on jobs, both domestically and across borders; the relative distribution of the economic impacts of NAFTA on different groups from the viewpoint of growing or shrinking income equality or inequality; the environmental impact of implementation both on the member states and the global ecosystem; and the impact of NAFTA on immigration, including illegal immigration, across member borders (particularly the flow of undocumented aliens entering the United States). Collectively, these five issues reasonably represent the range of concerns usually attributed to NAFTA. Some, such as income distribution effects, are generic to the impact of globalization and free trade schemes generally. Others, notably the impact on illegal immigration, are to this point unique to NAFTA. In this section, we will very briefly introduce each of these concerns, and then will apply them to the argumentation about what was expected from NAFTA and what it has produced.

Impact on Overall Economy. What difference the institution of the NAFTA framework of obligations has on the overall economies of its affected parties is, of course, the most basic and consequential macroeconomic question about it, and as a result, it has been the subject of the most vigorous and extreme claims and debate. NAFTA can be viewed as a kind of applied referendum on the question of globalization and as a precedent to be applied further or to be avoided elsewhere, either in the exact form of the NAFTA arrangement or generally. To champions of globalization, NAFTA embodies and accentuates its most basic dynamic, free trade. If free trade can be made to work within the NAFTA framework, then there is reason to support its extension in the hemispheric region or its transference to other regions. If it fails, on the other hand, then proposals for extension or transference are dampened or extinguished. Thus, the stakes are quite high on all sides of the issue, as reflected both in terms of stated prospects for NAFTA and in assessments about its impact. Because arguments about NAFTA as a general proposition tend to be macroeconomic in nature, supporters tend to argue general, in this case national, levels of supportive evidence rather than more specific impacts.

Impact on Jobs. How NAFTA has an impact on jobs is a more obviously microeconomic concern, and an area that is more politically volatile and contentious, because it involves the livelihoods of individuals. As such, one would expect the jobs question to attract the most controversy and the most expansive claims on all sides regarding whether NAFTA is a net job creator or destroyer, or if the effect of NAFTA on jobs is mixed, and one would not be disappointed.

As we shall see in the next section, the question of how NAFTA would impact jobs was a major question in the 1992 election, during which the wisdom of NAFTA was a prominent foreign policy issue. As might be expected, incumbent President George H. W. Bush, whose administration had been a cosponsor of the NAFTA idea, argued that NAFTA would create more jobs than it would destroy and was thus a net plus. Bush's fellow Texan, H. Ross Perot, argued that the result would be a massive movement of jobs south of the border to Mexico, making NAFTA a job destroyer. Democrat William J. Clinton argued that NAFTA would be a mixed bag of job losses and gains. This issue has remained high on the economic agenda ever since, especially within the context of illegal Mexican immigration into the United States.

Income Inequality. A major criticism of globalization in general has been that the process widens the wealth gap between the rich and poor in countries where globalization takes hold, and the NAFTA region has not been exempt from that general criticism. It is a demonstrable aspect of globalization that disparities between the rich and the poor do in fact tend to increase as the processes of privatization and deregulation occur. Defenders of the process make the familiar argument that everyone benefits from globalization ("a rising tide lifts all boats"), but tend to downplay that it lifts some boats considerably higher than others. From the vantage point of the champions of globalization, the macroeconomic arguments tend to override any negative distributional outcomes (microeconomic effects). From the opposite viewpoint, the underlying capitalist values on which the Washington consensus is firmly grounded tend to favor the wealthy over the poor in areas like taxation, and thus globalization and its handmaiden, free trade, are simply devices by which the wealthy exploit the poor. When income inequalities become politically intolerable, as they have in Latin American countries like Venezuela (see Chapter 8), the result can be a decisive reaction against the process.

These arguments have been prominent in the debate over NAFTA as well. One major argument in favor of the agreement was that it would lift the standards of living of

Mexican peasants, who would benefit from the higher-paying jobs that would flow southward and thus reduce the disparities between the richest and poorest in that country (and also, as we shall see, reduce the incentives for immigration across the Mexican-American border). In the United States, it was argued that very low-paying jobs (in the textile industry, for instance) might be lost, but these would be replaced by higher-paying jobs in newer, more technologically sophisticated industries. It is, however, a fact that income inequalities in the United States have increased dramatically during the period in which NAFTA has been in force. How much of that increase can be attributed to the impact of NAFTA and how much is the result of other causes is a part of the ongoing debate about both NAFTA and income distribution.

Environmental Concerns. As noted in Chapter 7, environmentalists have been part of the antiglobalization coalition since the beginning of the 1990s. The basic concern that activates environmentalists is the belief that the movement of goods and services, and especially the migration of some, normally primitive and environmentally unsound, industries from the most developed countries to Third World countries aspiring to join the globalizing economy will be accompanied by relaxations in environmental standards that will be harmful to the global ecosystem. Many industries, particularly in areas such as petrochemicals, produce considerable ecological waste that must be treated if environmental degradation is to be avoided. "Cleaning up" the by-products of industrial process is normally expensive, and requirements to treat wastes to acceptable levels represent one of the (not inconsiderable) expenses that firms in the developed countries incur. The environmentalists fear that Third World countries, which typically have minimal environmental regulations, will achieve comparative advantage in dirty industries by bypassing the cleanups that add to costs for industries in the developed world. This particular case has been particularly prominent in NAFTA, as a number of chemical processors have moved into Mexican border towns to conduct business, threatening to make true cesspools of these towns, with waste seeping into the United States. Dealing with this problem resulted in a 1993 protocol to NAFTA even before it took force, but environmentalists remain skeptical and leery of actions being taken anyway.

Illegal Immigration. The final issue is illegal immigration across the Mexican border into the United States, a politically volatile domestic question in the United States and a major irritant in U.S.-Mexican relations. At the time NAFTA was negotiated, undocumented worker immigration into the United States was steady, but had not achieved such a level that it was considered a major problem. At that time, much of the immigration was impermanent, notably migrant workers entering the United States for short periods of time to engage in activities such as picking crops and the like. It was only in the 1990s that large numbers of people from Latin America, but especially Mexico, began to enter the United States and remain indefinitely.

NAFTA was advertised as a way to reduce the flow of undocumented workers into the United States. Although the argument was not as prominent in discussions as it might be were the debate to occur now, the basic idea was that NAFTA would raise the standards of living across the board in Mexico, including the standards of poor Mexicans living in rural areas to the point that they would no longer need to trek to the United States to earn enough money to support their families. Rather, rising income levels would provide enough revenue so that poor farmers could either work in imported industries and earn a livable income or could afford to buy their own plots of land, from which they would be able to support their families. In fact, something like the opposite has happened as income disparities have widened, peasants have seen their property foreclosed and taken over by Mexican equivalents of agribusinesses, and the fate of poor Mexicans has become so desperate that they are fleeing across the border in record numbers in order simply to survive. Whether NAFTA or some other cause (for instance, the substantial impact of narcotics money) has been the reason for increased disparities and economic desperation remains contentious.

These are, of course, not the only things about NAFTA that are matters of disagreement, but they are prominent factors and are representative of the controversies that continue. Two points about these areas of disagreement should be made that will become obvious when we look retrospectively at the impact of NAFTA. First, most of the arguments about NAFTA are extensions of larger arguments made about globalization and free trade generally, and as a result, the argumentation on either side of the NAFTA question reflects the broader arguments and arguers in the general debate. Second, partisans on both sides of the NAFTA issue tend to ascribe both the good and bad effects of changes in the issues since NAFTA was implemented to the impact of NAFTA-created changes, but doing so is bedeviled by the problem of necessary and sufficient causation that we have already described: It is demonstrable that the economies of the three original members of NAFTA either have grown or not; it is not entirely certain that NAFTA is the reason for that change.

ASSESSING NAFTA

The NAFTA framework has now been in place for over a dozen years. In that period of time, there have been major economic changes in the economies of all three major members, some of which can probably be fairly attributed to NAFTA and some of which probably cannot. During the early years of its existence, NAFTA was part of the general expansion of the world economy, and the economies of its members expanded as part of the global phenomenon. In those circumstances, there was not much interest in determining how much of the change was the direct, measurable effect of NAFTA and how much was part of the spreading general prosperity. As the global economy slowed at the end of the millennium, NAFTA began to come under some increased scrutiny, and the connection of NAFTA to the immigration crisis in the United States recently has put a spotlight on U.S.-Mexican, and thus NAFTA, relations as well. We are now concerned with what difference NAFTA makes.

NAFTA has always been controversial, just as globalization generally provokes controversy. At the time it was negotiated, it managed to avoid most of the public glare because other matters were higher on the public agenda. It is, however, useful to look at least briefly at the gestation of NAFTA before turning to an assessment of its performance over the past decade plus.

The Genesis of NAFTA

The basis of NAFTA was negotiated by the administration of President George H. W. Bush. The agreement was actually the expansion of an arrangement between the United States and Canada, the Canada-U.S. Free Trade Agreement of 1989. President Bush and Canadian prime minister Brian Mulroney, both free traders, sought to deepen the relationship between the countries, trade between which had always been open on most items (there have been exceptions, such as the export of Canadian timber to the United States), and the expansion included Mexico. In October 1992, shortly before the 1992 presidential election in the United States, Bush, Mulroney, and Mexican president Carlos Salinas initialed the agreement, subject to ratification by the legislatures of each country.

NAFTA was a natural proposal for George H. W. Bush. The president, as already noted, came from two political traditions that made him sympathetic to the idea of free trade: His ancestors came from Connecticut, where they were part of the liberal Eastern establishment with heavy trading ties to Europe, and he had adopted Texas and its pro-free trade values as well. A staunch internationalist, the idea of a dramatic gambit into the area of free trade seemed an entirely natural idea for the forty-first president of the United States. The approval of the agreement got caught up in the election campaign, and it was only through the active intervention of new president William J. Clinton that it was passed by the Congress as a "congressional-executive agreement" requiring the assent of both Houses of Congress rather than as a treaty requiring a weighted majority of the Senate. Public Law (PL) 103–192 passed the U.S. Senate by a vote of 61 to 38 and the House of Representatives by a bipartisan vote of 234 to 200 and came into force on January 1, 1994.

The negotiations of NAFTA were overshadowed by other foreign policy events, notably the crisis in the Persian Gulf that precipitated the American-led effort to evict Saddam Hussein's Iraq from Kuwait in 1991. By the time of the presidential debates of 1992, however, the sheen had worn away from the Gulf War issue, and attention turned at least briefly to the matter of NAFTA.

The positions of the three candidates in the 1992 election on NAFTA were encapsulated in an interchange during the second debate of that year on October 15. In response to the first question in the town hall format used for the debate, each of the three candidates took one of the three basic positions possible on the impact of NAFTA, and their responses are thus worth considering as predictions about what NAFTA would and would not do, as reflected in the official transcript of the debate.

President Bush, who had proposed NAFTA, predictably took the most positive view of its impact. Declaring that he was a supporter of "free and fair trade" (see distinctions in Chapter 7), Bush declared that the impact would be overwhelming positive and would help move the United States and the world at large from the global economic slump that ultimately contributed to his defeat. He argued that "the thing that saved us in this global economic slowdown has been exports, and what I'm trying to do is increase our exports. . . . And so I have just negotiated the North American Free Trade Agreement, and I want to have more of these free trade agreements, because new jobs are increasing faster than any jobs that may have moved overseas." At the macroeconomic level, in other words, NAFTA would strengthen the economy.

Texas businessman and independent candidate H. Ross Perot took the exact opposite position, arguing that the implementation of NAFTA would cause a loss of American jobs to the cheaper labor market of Mexico, thus creating a negative impact on the economy. He illustrated his point with a hypothetical example: "If you are paying $12, $13, $14 for a factory worker, and you can move your business south of the border, pay $1 an hour for labor, have no health care, have no environmental controls, no pollution controls and no retirement benefits," the choice will be simple for businessmen. They will relocate to the cheaper places to do business, and the result will be the famous "job-sucking sound to the south." NAFTA, in other words, would be a microeconomic disaster for the United States.

Governor Clinton, whose background was more in the microeconomics of job losses and gains at the grassroots level, took a more moderate position, suggesting that free trade arrangements like NAFTA carried mixed benefits and costs. "The trick," he argued, "is to expand our export base and to expand trade on terms that are fair." He suggested three ways to accomplish this end. The first was fairness in trade, "to make sure that other countries are as open to our markets as our markets are to them." Second, he suggested that the U.S. tax code should be modified, because under then current regulations, "there are more deductions for shutting down plants and moving overseas than there are for modernizing plant equipment here." Third, he argued the educational code should be revised to "stop the federal government's program that now give low-interest loans and job training funds to companies that will actually shut down and move to other countries, but won't do the same thing for plants that stay here." He summarized his position as favorable to "more trade but on fair terms." Free trade, in other words, was a mixed proposition that had to balance the macroeconomic benefits with microeconomic guarantees that would produce fairness.

The controversy surrounding NAFTA goes back to its beginnings and has never subsided altogether. At the time of its negotiation, its most ardent supporters came from the transnational business community, who believed that NAFTA, as an example of institutionalized free trade generally, would result in greater profits for them, at least partly because it would allow them to move their enterprises to places where they could gain comparative advantage. The provisions of NAFTA favored corporations, resulting in one of its first crises over Chapter 11 of NAFTA, which allows corporations to sue national governments in the NAFTA region if they perceive that governmental actions discriminate against them. This advantage increased the suspicion of other groups, notably labor unions, who feared that some of the actions might include labor agreements. Labor and major corporations have been on opposite sides of the NAFTA debate ever since.

Two specific areas raised earlier became early subjects of NAFTA concern. One of these was the environmental impact of the agreement, and the result was a supplement to the NAFTA accord, the North American Agreement for Environmental Cooperation (NAAEC), which sought to mollify environmentalists by creating several mechanisms to deal with environmental concerns: a North American Commission for Environmental Cooperation (NACEC) to address trade and environmental issues; a North American Development Bank (NADBank) to fund investments in pollution reduction; and a Border

Environment Cooperation Commission (BECC) between the United States and Mexico to deal with border problems (e.g., Mexican industrial pollution caused by NAFTA seeping into American border towns). To deal with labor-related problems, the North American Agreement on Labor Cooperation (NAALC) was created to promote cooperation between labor organizations in the member countries. Both of these supplements were negotiated in 1993 to mollify objections to ratification in the member countries (notably the United States), and while they were successful enough to help get NAFTA through the American Congress, they did not remove all concerns about the impact of NAFTA.

NAFTA in Retrospect

As noted, NAFTA has now been in existence for over a dozen years. How has it done? Has it met the glowing expectations of Bush, the dour predictions of Perot, or the positive but guarded assessment of Clinton? Or has it done some of each? To try to answer that question, we will assess the impact of NAFTA in terms of the categories laid out earlier.

Impact on Overall Economy. Trying to determine the impact of NAFTA by looking at and trying to rationalize the assessments of observers on all sides of the issue is inherently difficult. Most defenses of NAFTA tend to be at the macro level, and to concentrate on matters such as increases in trade among the three members of the agreement. Indeed, the numbers, regardless of which set one chooses, do support the contention that, for instance, American trade measured by exports with Canada and Mexico have increased much more than has trade with other parts of the world—a sign the advocates argue demonstrates the viability and positive effectiveness of NAFTA on the economies of the member states. Most of this analysis is made by Americans about the effects on the American economy, and critics point out that increased American exports have more than been equaled by increased American imports from those same countries, with a net negative effect. One study, for instance, concludes that the American trade deficit with other NAFTA members now accounts for more than 17 percent of the overall American trade deficit.

In one particularly troubling example, proponents of NAFTA argued at the time of its ratification that a primary beneficiary of the agreement would be the American automotive industry, which would be able to sell more vehicles in Mexico with the removal of trade barriers in place before NAFTA took effect. In fact, just the opposite has occurred: In 1993, for instance, the United States imported a little over 200,000 automobiles from Mexico and sold nearly 500,000 to the world at large. In 2005, the United States imported about 700,000 cars made in Mexico and sold slightly less than 500,000 automobiles to the rest of the world—hardly figures meeting the more optimistic projections.

The problem with extrapolating from any particular case is threefold. First, the proponents tend to speak at the macroeconomic level, where they argue that, in the words of A. Ellen Terpstra, the U.S. Agriculture Department's Foreign Agricultural Service Administrator, testifying before a subcommittee of the U.S. Senate Foreign Relations Committee on April 20, 2004, "NAFTA is an unqualified success" in the agricultural area. At the gross, aggregate level, this is true: Volumes of agricultural commodity export to Mexico have indeed increased dramatically under NAFTA. At the same time, most of the profits from this trade have gone to large agribusinesses (which were among the great champions of NAFTA when it was proposed), whereas small farmers have not benefited much, if at all. Because American farm exports are subsidized by the U.S. government (a point of contention and negotiation with the NAFTA partners), those foodstuffs often are cheaper than domestically produced commodities in Mexico (corn is a primary example), and the result has been bankruptcy for many small Mexican farmers, with consequences that include increased illegal migration into the United States.

Second, there is the question of how much of the good and bad effects can be attributed to NAFTA. David Datelle, for instance, wrote in 1997 in a defense of the impact of NAFTA on jobs (especially negative impacts) that, after all, "it is very difficult to isolate the effects of NAFTA on the U.S. economy." The reason? The short duration of the agreement at that time. Writing in 2002, Dan Griswold of the Cato Institute (a consistent supporter of NAFTA), agrees, saying, "NAFTA was never going to have much of an impact on the domestic economy."

Third, most of the negative reactions to NAFTA, as to free trade schemes generally, come from the microeconomic level, at the places directly affected by plant closings and job migration, for instance. Writing in the *New York Times* in December 2003, for instance, Tim Weiner catalogues negative impacts in places as diverse as Goshen, Indiana; Cuidad Acuna, Mexico; and Durham, Ontario; and concludes that rather than raising living standards "from the Yukon to the Yucatan," as its most expansive champions maintained, it has instead created "jarring dislocations" for individuals and communities. Weiner quotes Gary Hufbauer of the Institute for International Economics: "NAFTA-related job loss and lower income may be small, but the echo is very large because of all the other jobs lost to globalization. Nafta is a symbol of all that pain."

What emerges from analyzing these impacts is a very mixed, selective message. Proponents tend to extol the broad, macroeconomic benefits of NAFTA, which they admit are not enormous. In the process of minimizing those positive impacts, they also shield themselves from overly expansive criticisms based in dire economic consequences, in effect arguing that NAFTA may not have done enormous good, but neither has it done much harm. As such, their arguments mirror the more general debate about globalization and free trade. Critics, on the other hand, argue the pernicious microeconomic effects that NAFTA has, also reflecting more general positions on free trade. Anyone seeking a clear-cut, unequivocal, nonpartisan statement that the overall impact of NAFTA is either beneficial or is not is likely to be frustrated.

Impact on Jobs. The general debate on NAFTA's impact on the economy is closely reflected in analyses of its impact on jobs. Once again, most analyses tend to be focused on the effects in the United States (where most of the studies have been conducted). The impact on jobs has been the leading shibboleth of the critics, from Perot's "great sucking sound" to microeconomic studies on the impact on various adversely affected communities. Proponents, predictably, emphasize the larger picture of overall job impacts rather than those on specific jobs.

There are two points of contention about the jobs' effects of NAFTA: whether it has increased employment (including the extent to which increases in overall employment can be attributed directly to NAFTA); and the quality of jobs that have been destroyed and created, both in the United States and other NAFTA countries. There is, of course, disagreement on both points.

Timothy Kehoe and Kim Ruhl, in a 2004 paper covering employment from 1990, before NAFTA, to 2000, summarize the general employment picture during that period, including the first six years of NAFTA. They found the overall employment rate in the United States rose by 3.7 percent, in sharp contrast to the negative results predicted by Perot (largely based on projections by economist Pat Choate). The authors, predictably, hedge NAFTA's impact on these figures one way or the other: "NAFTA has not been the sole cause of increased employment and rising labor productivity during the period 1994–2000. . . . The point is, rather, that it is difficult to argue that NAFTA has resulted in falling employment or income levels in the United States." They add the standard qualified prediction that NAFTA's "macroeconomic impact would be small" to further hedge the impact. There was, in other words, no expectation that NAFTA would have a dramatic effect on the U.S. economy because it is so much larger than the economies of the other members.

Whether NAFTA has produced better (higher-paying, more skilled) jobs is also a matter of considerable difference, particularly focusing on the flow of manufacturing jobs from the United States to Mexico and the kinds of U.S. jobs that would replace those losses. Once again, the evidence is largely anecdotal, with positive responses based in general theoretical expectations using comparative advantage and negative responses citing particular communities where there has been an adverse impact.

Income Inequality. There has been relatively little discussion of the income distribution of NAFTA, especially among its most ardent supporters. This is not entirely surprising, because it is generally admitted (grudgingly, by the supporters of free trade arrangements) that an increase in income inequality is one of the concomitant effects of globalization, and NAFTA is no exception to this principle. To supporters, this greater divergence between the rich and the poor is no more than a logical extension of the greater economic prosperity that globalization brings: Profits from expansion accrue disproportionately to large (and presumably more efficient) corporations—including the multilateral corporations—which then translate into profits, dividends, and the like, which are disproportionately held by the wealthier segments of society. Growing disparities are then justified on the basis that everyone benefits to some extent, thus making free trade a net benefit to everyone.

Not everyone sees this tradeoff as acceptable. As the Weiner article in the *New York Times* points out, "By every measurable standard, the gap between the rich and the poor in Mexico widened. Unemployment is up and real wages are flat or down for millions of workers." One result, as we shall see, has been increased pressure for immigration to the United States to compensate for these conditions. The Economic Policy Institute draws a parallel for the United States: "NAFTA has contributed to rising income inequality, suppressed real wages for production workers, weakening of workers' collective bargaining powers and ability to organize unions, and reduced fringe benefits." This latter assertion highlights the very real philosophical/theological basis of the debate over free trade and hence NAFTA: These losses from the vantage point of workers are often seen as benefits for capitalist corporate interests. The losses that workers have allegedly suffered, for instance, sound very much like the incentives that have caused a number of foreign automobile companies (Honda, Daimler/Chrysler, Hyundai) to choose to locate assembly plants in the American southeast.

The problem with assessing income inequality figures is twofold. On one hand, there is disagreement about whether it exists and whether it is good or bad. NAFTA proponents maintain that, at a theoretical level, the losses of jobs in one sector will be offset by the creation of better-paying jobs in other sectors, whereas opponents maintain with equal or greater ferocity that the jobs tend to be replaced by lower-paying jobs in service industries, and there is little comprehensive data on either side. On the other hand, how much of the effect can be attributed to NAFTA will always be debatable (the affirming-the-consequent problem). Income inequality measured as the gap between the richest and poorest Americans has increased markedly during the George W. Bush years. Is NAFTA a significant contributor to that inequality, or is it the Bush tax cuts of 2001, or some other cause? Answers tend to reflect the theological position one takes on free trade generally and thus on NAFTA specifically.

Environmental Concerns. Environmental opposition has been a mainstay of general opposition to free trade arrangements, and environmentalists posed a major roadblock to the approval of NAFTA by the American Congress, to the point that then-new president Clinton felt it necessary to negotiate the NAAEC and its associated organs to mollify environmentalists' concerns with the arrangement.

Beyond the normal objections that environmentalists have to free trade arrangements, NAFTA engendered a series of specific objections. These are summarized in a generally hostile analysis by Roberto Salinas-Leon for the heavily pro-NAFTA Cato Institute. As a matter of balance, his list of what he calls "green herrings" can serve to illustrate these concerns without appearing to advocate them. There are five arguments:

1. "NAFTA will drive large numbers of U.S. firms south of the border to reap the advantages of lax environmental regulations and enforcement.

2. "NAFTA's settlement mechanisms will compromise U.S. health, safety, and environmental regulations (by allowing corporations and others to ask for exceptions from NAFTA regulators to rules that threaten their corporate existence).

3. "NAFTA's trade liberalization will force the United States to weaken its 'clean' environmental standards to increase its competitive advantage.

4. "Free trade will bring about greater environmental degradation in Mexico.

5. "The increase of economic activity along the U.S.-Mexican border will intensify the already grave problems of cross-border pollution."

All of these arguments deal primarily with bilateral U.S.-Mexican relations and can be summarized in the notion that Mexico's efforts to benefit from NAFTA will create pressures to loosen already less-than-stringent environmental efforts and that this will cause tension both along the border (where increased Mexican economic activity will increase pollution that will flow into the United States) and pressure to reduce American standards to avoid the loss of comparative advantage.

These questions are ongoing. NAFTA defenders argue against environmental concerns on two grounds, one more compelling than the other. First, they point to the fact that NAFTA is the most environmentally sensitive of free trade arrangements anywhere, as witnessed by emphasis in its charter (its preamble contains the statement that signatories pledge to "undertake (trade change) in a manner consistent with environmental protection)" and the creation of the NAAEC and other organs designed to protect the environment. Second, Salinas-Leon argues that environmental concern is part of free trade: "[M]ore trade generates economic growth, which stimulates the demand for a healthier environment and thus leads to sustainable (i.e., environmentally nondestructive) development." One can, of course, counter that when environmental concerns and the profits associated with economic growth collide it is rarely, if ever, environmental concerns that prevail.

How has NAFTA done in environmental matters? An authoritative assessment was put forward by Victor Shantora, then acting executive director of the Commission on Environmental Cooperation (an organ created under the NAAEC). Free trade has brought about advances in technology and management practices that have made positive environmental changes. On the other hand, in some circumstances, free trade since NAFTA has also been linked to environmental degradation. It is clear that trade liberalization accompanied by robust environmental policies can help achieve sustainable development—just as freer trade without adequate environmental safeguards can trigger degradation. Gary Hufbauer of the Institute for International Economics reflects this conclusion, stating that "NAFTA's environmental record is mixed. Anyone who expected a rapid improvement in conditions along the U.S.-Mexican border is disappointed." Like everything else about NAFTA, there is no definitive judgment on environmental impact.

Illegal Immigration. The causal relationship between NAFTA and the illegal immigration of Mexicans into the United States that became a major political issue in 2006 may be NAFTA's dirty little secret. When NAFTA was first proposed, one of its primary selling points was that it would *reduce* the flow of undocumented Mexicans into the United States. In fact, this supposed reduction was a critical element in House passage of the NAFTA legislation. The reason immigration would decrease was that the agreement would stimulate economic prosperity and thus better-paying jobs in Mexico, thereby undercutting the incentives that Mexicans had to cross the border into the United States.

That prediction could hardly have been more wrong. Bill Richardson, the Latino current governor of New Mexico and majority whip in the House of Representatives when NAFTA passed in 1993, summarizes the problem. "The whole idea that Nafta would create jobs on the Mexican side and thus deter immigration has just been dead wrong. That was oversold."

What happened? The short answer is that immigration from the south, in the words of a Center for Immigration Studies (CIS) report, "exploded during the 1990s, from 4.2 million to 9.2 million, reaching a whopping 10.5 million by 2004." Unlike other aspects of the NAFTA assessment, this is one factor that can be laid fairly firmly on the agreement's doorstep. As Mark Krikorian argues in the CIS study, "the massive growth in immigration pressures from Mexico in the 1990s was not a failure of NAFTA, but an inevitable consequence." That inevitability, which some predicted, was ignored at the time, only to resurface.

The problem is rooted in the agricultural sectors in both the United States and Mexico. In reducing trade barriers across the board, one area where reduction has occurred (and will continue to occur) is in agricultural goods. Food grains and corn are produced at comparative advantage in the United States (with controversial subsidies) by large agribusiness, which gained access to the Mexican market and quickly swamped the competitiveness of Mexican corn grown by small Mexican growers, who were small landowners. Many of these farmers were forced into bankruptcy by the impact of imports from the United States, and legislation passed in Mexico as part of NAFTA implementation also allowed their lands to be confiscated and seized by large landholders to meet incurred debts. Thus, upwards of 10 million Mexican farmers were displaced by the impact of NAFTA. Desperate to make ends meet, many of these farmers migrated to where they hoped they could find jobs. A prime target were the so-called *maquiladora* manufacturing plants that sprouted up along the Mexican-American border. Jobs at these plants paid much better than traditional Mexican jobs, but there were not enough opportunities for the volume of displaced farmers, and the result was to fulfill one of Perot's 1993 predictions: As manufacturing in northern Mexico expands, hundreds of thousands of Mexican workers will be drawn north. They will quickly find that wages in the Mexican maquiladora plants cannot compete with wages anywhere in the U.S. Out of economic necessity, many of these mobile workers will consider illegally immigrating into the United States. In short, NAFTA has the potential to increase illegal immigration, not decrease it.

And that is exactly what happened, although it arguably did not have to do so. Krikorian, for instance, says the reaction was predictable. "Economic development, especially agricultural modernization, *always* sets people on the move, by consolidating small farms into larger, more productive operations." The problem, he argues, is that this migration was not correctly channeled by policies contained within the NAFTA transition. "The fact that development cuts peasants loose from the land and compels them to move to cities doesn't tell us *whose* cities they're moving to. The problem with NAFTA was that neither country did anything meaningful to make sure that the excess Mexican peasantry moved to Mexico's cities instead of ours." Krikorian thus concludes "that free trade agreements must be accompanied by muscular immigration controls" and that "the suspicion of some conservatives that free-trade pacts are the first step toward open borders is not without foundation." There is virtually no refutation of this causal link, although the general unpopularity of current immigration practices and laws makes emphasis of the NAFTA link one that its proponents are understandably at some pains to avoid.

CONCLUSION

The major conclusion about the assessment of the impact of NAFTA is that it is virtually impossible to reach any valid, overarching conclusions at all. That conclusion in itself is certainly not very satisfying, both because it offers so little guidance about future endeavors like NAFTA and because it tests and, arguably, overcomes the elegance of our analyses. Yet, the very complexity that makes authoritative assessment virtually impossible is of some instructive value in trying to place simple, decisive assessments on complex, ambiguous enterprises.

Ironically, the clearest impact of NAFTA—the stimulation of illegal immigration of displaced Mexican peasants to the United States—is the effect least discussed. The impact of NAFTA on immigration is rarely included in discussions of the virtues of NAFTA, and it is essentially never raised as part of the debate about "solving" the illegal immigration problem. On the surface, at least, NAFTA as a cause of the surge in illegal immigration remains a dirty little secret.

The bottom line in assessing the impact of NAFTA is that it is virtually impossible to do so objectively. NAFTA and economic change have coincided, but how much of that change can be attributed to NAFTA is a matter of speculation; in the case of the impact on the U.S. economy, its effect is, even according to its supporters, very small. To make anything like sweeping generalizations, one must go beyond the data in terms of interpretation, probably falling back to what we have called "theological" beliefs about free trade and selectively applying the data to support whatever basic belief one wants to support. This suggests that one should treat any broad, decisive interpretations (e.g., "NAFTA is a resounding success" or "NAFTA is an abject failure") with equal suspicion. Truth undoubtedly lies somewhere in between the extremes. Moreover, when the NAFTA experience is cited to support or oppose future similar schemes, one should look very carefully at the data and interpretations on which arguments are based.

STUDY/DISCUSSION QUESTIONS

1. What are the bases of disagreement about NAFTA? Discuss each and how it creates problems in assessing NAFTA's impact.

2. Discuss and assess the general arguments about free trade. How has the NAFTA debate reflected the general debate?

3. Discuss the methodological problem of NAFTA assessment, emphasizing necessary and sufficient causation and the fallacy of affirming the consequent.

4. What five substantive arguments are made about the impact of NAFTA? Discuss each, including the macroeconomic and microeconomic bases of each.

5. Discuss how NAFTA came into being, including the competing claims about what impacts it would create. What particular areas of concern caused modification of the agreement before it was ratified?

6. Discuss the impact of NAFTA on the overall economy, jobs, and income inequalities. Compare and contrast the arguments about each. How do they reflect the schism between macroeconomic and microeconomic analyses?

7. Discuss the environmental impact of NAFTA and how an assessment of environmental impact reflects general ambivalence about NAFTA.

8. The clearest impact of NAFTA has been on illegal immigration of Mexicans to the United States. Discuss the dynamics of this phenomenon. Should it have been (or was it?) anticipated? How should an understanding of the NAFTA link be included in solutions to this problem?

9. What does the NAFTA experience demonstrate for advocacy or opposition to future free trade proposals?

READING/RESEARCH MATERIAL

Cameron, Maxwell A., and Brian W. Tomlin. *The Making of NAFTA: How the Deal Was Done*. Ithaca, NY: Cornell University Press, 2000.

Griswold, Dan. "NAFTA at Ten: An Economic and Foreign Policy Success." *Free Trade Bulletin No. 1,* December 17, 2002.

Hastings, Paul. *North American Free Trade Agreement: Summary and Analysis*. Albany, NY: Matthew Bender, 1993.

Kehoe, Timothy J., and Kim J. Ruhl. "The North American Free Trade Agreement after Ten Years." University of Minnesota: Center for Urban and Regional Affairs, 2004 (http://www.econ.unm.edu/~tkehoe)

Kennedy, Kevin C. (ed.). *The First Decade of NAFTA: The Future of Free Trade in North America*. Ardsley, NY: Transnational, 2004.

Krikorian, Mark. "Bordering on CAFTA: More Trade, Less Immigration." *National Review Online*, July 28, 2005 (http://www.cis.org/articls/2005/mskoped072805.html).

Metz, Allen. *NAFTA: A Bibliography*. Westport, CT: Greenwood Press, 1996.

Rosenberg, Jerry M. *Encyclopedia of the North American Free Trade Agreement*. Westport, CT: Greenwood Press, 1995.

Rockenbach, Leslie J. *The Mexican-American Border: NAFTA and Global Linkages*. Abingdon, Oxford, UK: Routledge, 2001.

Salinas-Leon, Roberto. "Green Herrings: NAFTA and the Environment." *Regulation: The Cato Review of Business and Government*, 1994.

Scott, Robert E. "The High Price of 'Free Trade.'" Economic Policy Institute: EPI Briefing Paper #147, November 17, 2003.

Terpstra, A. Ellen. "Statement before the Senate Foreign Relations Committee, Subcommittee on International Economic Policy, Export, and Trade Promotion." Washington, DC: April 20, 2004.

Weiner, Tim. "Free Trade Accord at Age 10: The Growing Pains Are Clear." *New York Times,* December 27, 2003.

WEB SITES

NAAEC, Commission on Environmental Cooperation
  http://www.cec.org/news
Interpretation on jobs effects (David Datelle)
  http://www.ppionline.org/ndol/print.cfm?contentid=1391
NAFTA and environment (Institute for International Economics)
  http://www.iie.com/publications/papers
Commission on Presidential Debates
  http://www.debates.org/pages/trans92bl.html
Public Citizen NAFTA at Ten series (Public Citizens Global Trade Watch)
  www.tradewatch.org

PART IV

The Altered Face of Security

Along with globalization, some of the most dramatic changes in the post–Cold War environment have occurred in the areas of national and international security. The Cold War security system was overshadowed by the prospect of nuclear war between the superpowers, a cataclysmic possibility before which other problems paled in comparison. Certainly, there was no shortage of other problems, it was just that they were subordinate to avoiding a possibly nuclear World War III.

Although a nuclear inferno is still a physical possibility, it is now considered far less likely to occur. This has allowed consideration both of some old problems that existed before the end of the Cold War but which received less concern then, but especially some matters that have arisen since the Cold War ended. Much of the change is connected to technological possibilities that did not exist before, which have turned traditional patterns of warfare on their heads.

The cases selected for this part of the book reflect this continuity and change. Chapter 10, "Future War," looks broadly at what warfare may look like in the future and how well our anticipation of the future of war in the past century affects our confidence about judging the shape of war in a new century. The focus is on the contrasting impact of military technology on two eras, the period between the two world wars and the present. Planning in the 1920s and 1930s produced differential refinements in thinking about conventional, European-style, or symmetrical warfare. Technology today has produced such imbalances between the most capable militaries and others that planning must concentrate on unconventional, or asymmetrical warfare. Adjusting to the dictates of the "new kind of war" is a major challenge.

The other two cases are instances of contemporary problems, the origins of which are in the Cold War. Chapter 11, "The Perils of Proliferation" deals with the problem of proliferation of new weapons to states that currently do not possess them and about which there is some agreement that they should not be allowed to possess them. In the Cold War, which will provide the context for the case, the emphasis was almost exclusively on the spread of nuclear weapons to nonpossessing states, and the major instrument for achieving that end was the Nuclear Non-Proliferation Treaty (NPT). The contemporary application is the spread of so-called weapons of mass destruction (WMDs)—nuclear *and* biological and chemical weapons—to nonpossessors and currently focuses on nuclear weapons programs in Iran and North Korea.

Chapter 12, "Who Cares about Kashmir?" examines a basic problem of Indo-Pakistani relations that dates back to the partition of the Indian subcontinent in 1948. The princely states of Jammu and Kashmir have been points of contention ever since, but now the problem has been made more dangerous by the addition of the "new teeth" of nuclear weapons on each side. The case looks at how this new "variable" may affect Kashmir in the future, and whether this conflict, often viewed as nearly as intractable as the Israeli-Palestinian conflict, may be capable of resolution.

CHAPTER TEN

Future War

FROM SYMMETRICAL TO ASYMMETRICAL CONFLICT

PRÉCIS

Anticipating the nature of future conflict and preparing for that form of combat has always been a primary responsibility for those charged with national and international security. Doing so is always a difficult process involving extrapolation of the past into the future.

The difficulties of preparing for future wars is the central theme of this case study. It is presented in a comparative fashion. The first part of the case deals with preparation for World War II during the two decades after World War I, in terms of four questions: What would the conditions be like (conflict environment)? How would war be fought (structure of war)? Who would fight (likely enemy)? And what would the ensuing peace be like (postconflict environment)? The basic problem was extending the prospects of war between two similar groups of countries fighting in a similar manner, what we all symmetrical warfare. The second part of the case looks at the contemporary military planning problem. Unlike the gradual changes in warfare that faced the World War II planners, contemporary planners face a world increasingly dominated by asymmetrical warfare, where competing sides fight in a dissimilar manner under different rules and with ever changing concepts and execution. This part of the case describes asymmetrical warfare, and attempts to answer the same questions asked of the interwar period.

Anticipating and preparing for the next war is an age-old problem that has concerned politically organized entities throughout history. Whether states or other political organizations thought about the problem, knowing who one's enemies are and how they are likely to provide a menace can mean the difference between victory and defeat, even survival or destruction. Understanding the threats present in the environment and acting appropriately to defuse them can also lead to the avoidance of war, clearly the best outcome.

It is, and always has been, a difficult problem. Future wars, by definition, are projections into a period of time that does not yet exist and which, by definition, we cannot know entirely in advance. Will the same kinds of weapons be available in the future as there were in the past? If there are new weapons, what will they be like, how will they be used, and what will be their effect? Who will have the new weapons, and who will not? How will weapons balances affect patterns of war? For that matter, who will the enemy be? Where will I have to fight the next adversary?

Because we cannot precisely know the answers to any of these questions in advance, uncertainty becomes a major part of the operational universe of the military planner. Uncertainties produce an environment laced as well by an aura of conservatism and seriousness. It is conservative because reckless innovation and lack of preparedness can lead to vulnerability that can have potentially devastating consequences. It is serious because the wrong decisions—the failure to prepare properly or adequately—can literally endanger national existence. Because of these potential consequences, there is a built-in propensity to overprepare—to anticipate more threats than realistically exist. Conservatism and the seriousness of making mistakes also predispose planners to emphasize ways of doing things that have worked in the past—to stay "inside the box"—rather than to embrace change and its uncertainties. The result is a tendency to prepare "to fight the last (most recently concluded) war."

The problem of gauging the future of war is especially acute today. There are some clear reasons why many states are grappling very seriously with the future. For one thing, the period that marked the Cold War also marked the "long peace" of the second half of the twentieth century. Much of the preparation that states undertake in planning for war is in fact an extrapolation of their most recent experience; that means our useful experience, at least in the desperation of a major war that threatens national existence and thus forms what is known as the "worst case," is now over sixty years old. What is the continuing relevance of the most recent experience to the future?

It depends. One of the most important aspects of preparing for future war is anticipating against whom one is likely to have to fight. Although many Americans sought to ignore the warning signs during the 1930s, it was pretty clear that World War II would find the United States on one side and countries like Germany and Japan on the other (at least retrospect suggests that structure of the conflict). During the Cold War, it was absolutely clear that the enemy against whom we had to prepare was the Soviet Union and its communist allies. The structure of the system dictated the content of the planning process.

Not all planning has such a clear focus. In August 1990, Iraq invaded and quickly conquered Kuwait. This act of aggression would ultimately bring together a coalition of over twenty-five states, none of whom had given much if any thought to the possibility of war with Iraq as little as a few months before the invasion occurred. The lesson was that some problems can be easily anticipated; others cannot. The largely unanticipated terrorist attacks of September 11, 2001, redouble the point.

There is another factor that influences the process today that was a lesser concern in the past: technological change. In the historical past, warfare generally did not change greatly. As chroniclers of war like Bernard and Fawn Brodie (see the readings) have suggested, with the exception of an occasional innovation like the catapult or gunpowder, warfare during much of the second millennium did not change a great deal, and most of the changes were gradual and incremental rather than revolutionary and dramatic. Once in a while, a traditional enemy might fashion some new weapon—such as the crossbow— that would make accepted ways of conducting war dangerous or suicidal. At the same time, an outsider might present a military problem with which a society had no idea how to cope—the massed mounted cavalry of Genghis Khan's Golden Horde, for instance. But generally, the problem of physical preparation remained relatively the same.

The Industrial Revolution and its adaptation to warfare in the nineteenth century accelerated the impact of technology, and its impact has grown steadily ever since. Our twentieth century past involved applying inventions like the internal combustion engine to warfare. The twenty-first century looks at a battlefield environment more reminiscent of science fiction motion pictures than of warfare in the past. The control and manipulation of information has become a critical element that adds further to the uncertainty of a future where tomorrow's enemies, like the Iraqis in Kuwait in 1990 and the Iraqi resistance of 2007, are more difficult to anticipate.

Most of the past century or more was dominated by a style and philosophy of warfare that was heavily Western and which culminated in the way World War II was fought, what we now call symmetrical warfare (both sides fight in the same manner and basically by the same rules). Since early in the post–Cold War world, that has changed, Arguably, warfare is changing fundamentally from the confrontation and clash of mass armies to a more asymmetrical form in which weaker foes seek to negate Western styles with non-Western variants on war in which the two sides are dissimilar in organization and purpose and do not fight honoring the same rules and conventions. September 11, 2001, may be remembered as the harbinger of this change in the nature of warfare.

Thus, the problem of preparing for future war boils down to four basic considerations. The first is the *conflict environment,* and the main factor in that environment is the nature of the adversaries one may encounter in the future, including why and how one may have to or want to fight them. In the past, war was between the organized armed forces of states. Contemporary conflicts often pit traditional armed forces against so-called nonstate actors, forces with no territorial base nor governmental affiliation. The second consideration is the *physical structure of warfare,* which consists of the means available for adversaries to fight one another and the degree to which the means available are appropriately adapted to achieve military ends. In the contemporary era, the means are widely disparate for different foes, creating the basis for asymmetrical approaches for the disadvantaged. The third concern is determining *against whom one might have to fight* in a major power environment that was remarkably tranquil for over a decade and that has not witnessed a major war in over a half century; and where possible enemies are difficult to anticipate in conventional ways. The fourth, and often incompletely considered, factor is the *postwar peace:* What conditions will be created in what we now call the "postconflict environment." Failure to consider this aspect adequately can result in the old trap of "winning the war and losing the peace."

Military technology is a major influence in these calculations. Between the world wars, new technologies were "weaponized" by both sides, and more efficient applications were rewarded. The competition, however, was essentially over who could harness the same technologies to becoming "best" at symmetrical warfare. Today, technological levels have become so imbalanced that the nonpossessors of modern technology have no reasonable chance engaging the opponent symmetrically and must fight asymmetrically to have any prospect of success.

These observations form the rationale for the rest of the case. In the following pages, we will examine the problem of preparing for future war through two "mini-cases." The first will be historical, how planners in the 1930s prepared for the likelihood of a second major war in the first half of the twentieth century. Looking at the four basic categories of concern, the conflict environment was, or could have been, fairly clear, but the physical structure of conflict was not. While some argued that war with the Soviets was more likely than war with Germany or Japan and others felt it could be avoided altogether, the combatants were basically locked in by the latter part of the 1930s. Although the last major war was only twenty years in the past, the planners had to grapple with adapting to a number of weapons—tanks, for instance—that were introduced during the Great War (as World War I was known at the time) but not used to maximum effect, and ultimately atomic weapons.

Planning for the wars of the twenty-first century is different. For one thing, there are no obvious major, conventional adversaries in the system, due in large measure to the ideological harmony among the major powers in the current international system. The answer to the question, "preparing to fight whom?" is especially fraught with uncertainty regarding who to prepare to fight and how to prepare to fight them. The long gap between major wars has allowed the accumulation of many militarily relevant technologies that have greatly enhanced the conventional capabilities of those who possess them. Some of the electronically based innovations have been employed in "shooting galleries" like the Persian Gulf War and Operation Iraqi Freedom in 2003, and the primary lesson these victims seemed to have learned is not to fight the West (especially the United States) on its terms. The imbalance in symmetrical capabilities has in effect done two things: It has made the development of asymmetrical, technology-negating methods the primary dynamic of the present, and it has arguably rendered symmetrical warfare archaic because no one will fight that way. Finally, fighting against unconventional opponents complicates the task of planning and executing stable postconflict peace arrangements.

PLANNING TWENTIETH-CENTURY STYLE: ANTICIPATING WORLD WAR II

Imagine the world from the viewpoint of a military planner in 1919, shortly after the end of World War I. The bloodiest military conflict in human history to that point had just been concluded. It had been a war that had been poorly anticipated; as late as the early 1910s, there was still the widespread belief that economic interdependence had rendered war between the major powers functionally impossible or at least highly unlikely.

The war had started almost accidentally, as the assassination of Archduke Franz Ferdinand of Austria and his wife by Bosnian Serb terrorists had activated a string of alliance commitments that brought the major combatants into confrontation. As the crisis grew, little was done to defuse it. Some attribute that failure to mediocre leadership in the major capitals (see Stoessinger in the readings). There was even positive sentiment for war, based on the belief that European youth had gone soft in the interim since the last large European conflict, the Franco-Prussian War of 1870. A war, so the argument went, would infuse Europe with a reinvigorating discipline and sense of national duty and sacrifice.

The greatest tragedy was that Europe had so poorly anticipated the kind of war that it was going to get. From warfare in the nineteenth and early twentieth centuries, there were two models available about what war in the future would be. One model was that of the Franco-Prussian War, in which lightning strikes by offensively oriented armies led to rapid and decisive warfare. The other model combined the experiences of the American Civil War and the Russo-Japanese War of 1904–1905. Both these wars, conducted 40 years apart, were extremely hard fought and costly in terms of blood, and both featured the increasing dominance of defensive tactics over the offense. The planners chose the wrong model as the harbinger of World War I. They dismissed the American Civil War, which one German observer described at the time as "two armed mobs chasing one another around the country, from which nothing can be learned," and the Russo-Japanese precedent was similarly dismissed because the combatants were either Asian or Eurasian, and hence inferior to European troops. Instead, their preparations and predictions reflected the belief that the war would be short and decisive like the Franco-Prussian War: Everyone anticipated a relatively bloodless reprise of the Franco-Prussian War.

All of these projections were, of course, erroneous, and planners looking at the scene in 1919 could only shake their heads at the wreckage and begin to plan for the future, hopefully fashioning a system that would prevent a future war, or, failing in that, assuring that the conduct and outcome would be very different than what they could survey from the last war. That meant examining the likely environment in the future and the physical structure of the next war.

Largely lost in the bitterness surrounding the environment in 1919 was rebuilding a durable peace that would make a repeat unlikely. In retrospect, World War I had been avoidable if the combatants had tried to avoid it, but they did not. Woodrow Wilson had sought a durable peace through the League of Nations, but U.S. Senate rejection of the peace treaty and vindictive, bitter sentiments in Europe and elsewhere pushed war avoidance to the back burner. Inadequate concern for the postconflict environment would make a second world war inevitable a short generation later.

Conflict Environment

The conflict environment facing military planners and political leaders in 1919 bore both similarities to and differences from the prewar environment. The map, for instance, had changed somewhat, but the major players were still intact. The Austro-Hungarian and Ottoman Empires had disappeared from the map, and the Russian Empire had been refashioned as the Soviet Union. Germany was disarmed and had contrition forced on it by the terms of the peace treaty, but would rise again in the 1930s to great-power status. France and Great Britain were physically and financially exhausted by the war, and sought to retreat from major commitments and to recover. In the Pacific, Imperial Japan was showing signs of the militarism that would lead to its imperial expansion and the road to war in the Pacific. The United States, of course, was in the process of its retreat into "splendid isolationism."

The geopolitical environment was not entirely unlike the prewar environment. Germany was prostrate and held down by provisions of the Versailles Treaty officially ending the war, but Franco-German animosity remained, and the geopolitical question that had dominated Europe since the Napoleonic Wars, which country would dominate the continent, had clearly not been permanently resolved. The major innovation in the system was the new League of Nations, the twentieth century's first attempt at organizing the peace around an international organization.

Although it is easier to make projections with the assistance of "20–20 hindsight," the geopolitical environment in which conflict might emerge had to be basically familiar to planners in 1919. One might or might not have been able to project with precision what country or countries one might have to fight sometime in the future, but the next war was likely to be between the major European states fighting in familiar ways. Force planning, in other words, was likely to be an extrapolation from the geopolitical past rather than any major deviation from that past. It may have been more difficult to anticipate the growing rivalry between the United States and Japan over the Pacific region, although some historians have argued that war between the two countries was probably made inevitable by American colonization of the Philippines in 1898, since the Philippines archipelago was a clear barrier standing in the way of Japanese expansion in east Asia.

Physical Structure of Warfare

World War I had been a technologically interesting event, as a number of new weapons based on technologies developed in the years leading to the conflict were introduced to the battlefield. As is so often the case, the new technologies were often not employed in the most effective way, nor were they employed in support of warfare in the same ways they would be in the future. For military planners in the years between the world wars, the task was to assess these innovations and how they might be better utilized in a future war.

There were two categories of innovation introduced between 1914 and 1918. One of these was in firepower, and it was represented by two kinds of weapons in land warfare: rapid-fire military rifles that could fire up to 20 bullets per minute; and the first reliable machine guns, which could fire as many as 200–400 rounds per minute. These weapons were, however, heavy; the machine gun and its mount weighed about 100 pounds, meaning it had to be placed in a stationary position, generally with entrenchment or some other form to protect the machine gunner. The other land innovation was improvement in heavy artillery. The artillery pieces employed in World War I could fire large shells over long distances at the rate of 6–10 shots per minute. As the name implies, their weight made them largely immobile, and the result was that large-scale artillery exchanges took place as each side tried to silence the other's big guns.

The tactics associated with the war did not adequately compensate for this change in firepower. The offensive orientation that both sides had adopted before the war put them on the attack as the doctrinally proper way to fight. When the trench lines hardened (and were aided by other innovations such as razor-sharp concertina wire), attacks against these rapid-fire weapons systems were nothing short of suicidal. Planners, however, remained wedded to their ideas, and sent wave after wave of increasingly cynical, disillusioned young men to their deaths at the hands of the machine gunners.

Transportation also changed, inspired by the invention and application of the internal combustion engine and the storage battery to warfare. The internal combustion engine produced three vehicles of war; the truck, the tank, and the heavier-than-air airplane. The battery made the submarine possible. Each changed the nature of warfare, although with different effects.

The truck provided a way to transport troops and supplies to the battlefield. It increased military flexibility, because trucks could go anywhere there were roads. The tank was first introduced into the war by the British in 1916. Its promise was as a weapon system that could smash through German trenches and open spaces through which troops could advance, thereby breaking the deadlock and recreating movement on the front. The tank did not, however, fulfill its promise in World War I. The early tank designs were very slow, leaving them vulnerable to artillery fire, and their treads often came off, leaving them immobile sitting ducks. The internal combustion engine also made feasible flight by heavier-than-air flying machines. The airplane was introduced into the war with little advance indication of what its role would be. The first air warriors were used as observers, flying over enemy positions and performing reconnaissance missions. Gradually, airplanes became engaged in air-to-air combat and some limited bombing, but their impact on the war's outcome was minimal.

Finally, the storage battery made the submarine a plausible naval weapon. Their major purpose was attacking Allied shipping across the Atlantic, and especially between the United States and the Western Allies. Fortunately for the Allies, the Germans manufactured relatively few U-boats, because the kaiser was discouraged from putting his resources into so-called commerce raiders by the writings of American naval strategist Alfred Thayer Mahan.

Determining Opponents

The coalition that would ultimately fight World War II did varying jobs of sizing up their potential opponents. The Japanese understood that their expansion ultimately would bring them face-to-face with the United States, but they underestimated the enormous power the United States would bring to bear against them. Similarly, Hitler underestimated the task of subduing the Soviet Union. Had his hatred for Slavs been less consuming, he might have maintained an uneasy accommodation with the Soviets, in which case the war might have ended very differently. On the Allied side, none of the major powers prepared adequately for war; and when it came, they had to build up their capabilities, thereby almost certainly prolonging the fighting.

Postconflict Peace

Ultimately, the purpose of war is to create some better set of political circumstances than existed in the prewar environment, and achieving the "better state of the peace" is the political purpose that gives war its meaning. This Clausewitzian truth (see discussion in Snow and Drew) is captured well by British analyst Colin S. Gray: "War is *only* about the peace that follows. It should be waged in such a style that the subsequent peace is not fatally mortgaged." Because of this centrality, Wesley Clark reminds us, "Planning military operations in war must take into account planning for the aftermath. . . . Achieving victory requires backward planning, beginning with a definition of postwar success and moving backwards."

Because World War I was essentially accidental, there had been little thought given to the postwar peace. Rather, the incredible carnage created such bitterness that the victorious Allies dictated a harsh, punitive peace settlement that the losers could not possibly embrace and which would become the basis for the second war. Planners in the 1930s could see what a lack of postconflict planning could create; their job was to fashion a more durable peace for the next time around.

Interwar Planning

Each of these factors underwent reevaluation during the interwar years. Revisions in hardware and tactics became part of the backbone of the military machines that prepared for and fought World War II. In the case of each technology, there would be some disagreement about what those roles would be, and only the crucible of war itself would validate some ideas and invalidate others.

Military planning incorporating the new technologies affected all three media on which warfare could take place: on land, in and under the water, and in the air. Land warfare, especially as it would be applied again in Europe, came to reemphasize the offense in warfare through mobility. The fruits of the internal combustion engine led the way, as tanks, armored personnel carriers, and the like became the spearheads of land campaigns, with infantry acting in a supportive role to armor, rather than the other way around, as had been the case in World War I.

Some of these developments were anticipated in World War I. The German general Oskar von Hutier experimented with highly mobile special forces that infiltrated Western trench lines by avoiding the most heavily defended areas and attacking isolated places instead. These ideas would, however, bear fruit in World War II and were, according to Clark, central to the American rush to Baghdad in 2003.

Some countries anticipated these possibilities and planned accordingly better than others. The German general staff was at the forefront, developing principles of mobility and movement into what became known as *blitzkrieg* (lightning war). Other countries, notably France and Poland, continued to rely on mounted cavalry and gave inadequate attention to mechanization of the war machine. When war came, those who had failed to understand the change in warfare suffered the most.

Naval warfare was transformed as well. Prior to World War II, naval warfare was typically between surface combatants, where the object was to attack and sink the opponent and where the largest and most heavily armed vessels normally prevailed. Technological advancements also rendered battleships highly vulnerable and increasingly obsolete. The battery systems (and internal combustion engine for providing propulsion on the surface and for recharging the batteries) that made submarines practical in the first war were improved considerably, and the torpedo-armed submarine became a long-range platform that could lurk beneath the surface and put the largest battleships at its mercy. More fundamentally, the airplane transformed the way naval warfare would be fought in the second world conflagration. In the years between the world wars, the centerpiece in naval warfare ceased being the battleship and became instead the aircraft carrier. In World War II, carrier-based aircraft became the principal weapons of naval warfare, with other ships relegated largely to the role of protecting the carrier from attack (a principle that remains largely intact today).

The enthusiasts of the airplane were amongst the most active and ambitious planners between the world wars. People like Mitchell, the Italian Guilio Douhet, and Great Britain's Hugh Trenchard led the way, arguing that the ability to attack from the air would ultimately make other forms of warfare obsolete. In the future, they argued, it would not be necessary to defeat an enemy's army or navy to attack the homeland; aircraft would simply fly over the battlefield and attack the enemy with impunity. The airmen's claims proved to be excessive, and the supremacy of airpower remains a contentious issue. Airpower eventually did reduce Germany's war industries to rubble, but the detractors counter that Germany had essentially lost the war anyway by the time bombing succeeded in destroying Germany's vital centers. In the Pacific, the atomic bombing of Hiroshima and Nagasaki by the U.S. Eighth Air Force relieved the United States of the need to launch a sure-to-be-resisted invasion of the Japanese home islands, but at a terrible cost in civilian deaths.

Planners for the postwar world were not left on the outside this time. Early in the war the process of creating a stable postwar environment based on the United Nations and ensuring that the losing states would be reintegrated into the new international system on satisfactory terms was instituted. Only the question of whether Soviet-American wartime collaboration could be sustained after the war remained an (admittedly very important) question.

PLANNING TWENTY-FIRST–CENTURY STYLE: ANTICIPATING FUTURE WARS

The process of anticipating and planning for war during the first half of the last century has a certain comfortableness and familiarity about it. For the most part, wars were fought for traditional reasons between traditional adversaries in basically familiar ways. The same basic coalitions, after all, fought both world wars in Europe, with only the war in the Pacific between the United States and Japan adding novelty to the cast of characters and motivations. The basic function of planning was the adaptation of new technology to its most efficient ends. In effect, the planners were fine-tuning and adapting a style of warfare with which they were familiar and comfortable—symmetrical warfare.

Those conditions are not so clearly evident today. If we put ourselves in the shoes of a military planner in the year 2007, the continuities of the past are not always obvious.

All the elements of the planning process have changed, the conflict environment and the physical structure of warfare, the composition of likely enemies to be deterred or, if necessary, fought, and the nature of stable postconflict environments.

Two major factors have changed things: the end of the Cold War and the rise of new forms of opposition. The collapse of the Cold War left the United States as the only traditional military great power. American technology-based power has continued to grow absolutely and relatively to the rest of the world, no new opponent has replaced the Soviet Union as an opponent, and the result is a chasm in traditional military power between the United States and the rest of the world. As that power has increased, however, it may have lost some of its relevance. American conventional military capability has become so overwhelming as to be unchallengeable. No one can or will fight the United States the way the United States is prepared to fight. The rise of new opposition emerges in this context. Middle Eastern, fundamentalist Islamic opposition to Western values based in nationalism cannot confront the West head on, and has reverted to less direct, more traditionally Eastern forms of asymmetrical warfare that are rapidly adapting to American responses. The terrorism of September 11, 2001, and the Iraqi resistance may be the future with which planners must contend.

Conflict Environment

Traditional geopolitics has clearly taken a beating since the end of the Cold War. Two politico-military alliances facing one another is the stuff of traditional calculation, but that basis has evaporated. The first victim of the end of the Cold War has been the structure of adversarial relationships that provides concrete military problems against which to prepare. At least among the major military members of the international system, that structure has utterly disappeared.

In some ways, this is a considerable improvement over the past. It means that for now, at least, there is virtually no likelihood of major war between the most powerful countries of the world on the scale of the world wars but made more potentially devastating by the addition of nuclear weapons in the arsenals of antagonists. Certainly the tools for such a war are still available, but it is difficult to conjure the circumstances that would ignite such a conflagration. There are a few places in the world, for instance the Indian subcontinent, where adversaries might become involved in a war of fairly large proportions, but none of those places would raise the distinct likelihood of drawing in other major actors on opposite sides and thus widening the conflict to anything like the scale of World War III (the major planning case of the Cold War).

The conflict environment is different in two distinct ways. First, the imbalance in conventional capability between the United States and the rest of the world is so great that no one is likely to confront the United States in large-scale conventional warfare. This means, however, that those who oppose the United States must devise new ways to do so. As Bruce Berkowitz puts it, "Our adversaries know they cannot match the United States in tanks, planes, and warships. They know they will most likely lose any war with us if they play according to the traditional rules." This innovation is the second new characteristic of the environment: the adoption and adaptation of asymmetrical ways to negate the advantages of overwhelming military capability and the emergence of new categories of opponents, such as non-state actors. Asymmetrical approaches are intended, Berkowitz's terms, "to change the rules to strategies and tactics that avoid our strength head-on and instead hit us where we are weak." This problem is progressive, because the core of asymmetrical warfare is constant adaptation, meaning the problem is never exactly the same from instance to instance. Moreover, traditional warfare is directed at state-based political opponents, and it is not clear how one subdues an opponent who lacks such a base.

Asymmetrical warfare is not new. As Renee de Nevers points out, asymmetrical wars are "perhaps better understood as reversions to very old wars." The Thirty Years' War, for instance, featured marauding bands we would now call nonstate actors, and nineteenth-century resistance to colonialism certainly featured highly mismatched forces. It is different in terms of the problems for which it is conducted; how those who carry it out think and act; and in terms of the motives of the asymmetrical warrior. Asymmetrical warfare is not only militarily unconventional, it is intellectually unconventional as well. Asymmetrical warriors often lack any clear military hierarchy, are prone to use ambushes or acts of terror to achieve their goals, and may act from motives that seem strange, even bizarre to outsiders.

The United States' first major encounter with asymmetrical warfare was in Vietnam. (We had previous limited experience in places like the Philippines at the turn of the twentieth century, but on a much smaller scale.) Vietnam mixed symmetrical and asymmetrical characteristics. In terms of its purposes, it was quite conventional: The North Vietnamese and their Viet Cong allies sought to unify Vietnam as a communist country, and the South Vietnamese and the Americans sought to avoid that outcome. In terms of conduct, however, the war was unconventional. The North Vietnamese concluded early in the American phase of the war that they could not compete with the United States in symmetrical warfare because of visibly superior American firepower. Instead, they reverted to tactics of harassment, ambush, and attrition, the purpose of which was to produce sufficient American casualties to convince the American people that the cost of war was not worth the projected benefits. The North Vietnamese could not have succeeded fighting by the American rules. Their only hope was to change the rules and fight in a way that minimized American advantage and gave them a chance. It worked.

The heart of asymmetrical warfare is not a set of tactics or strategies, but instead is a mind-set. The potential asymmetrical warrior always begins from a position of military inferiority, and the problem, as Berkowitz points out, is how to negate that disadvantage. Adaptability is at the heart of asymmetrical approaches to warfare. If one asymmetrical tactic does not work, try another. Vietnam was a primer for those who may want to confront American power, but an organization like Al Qaeda or the Iraqi resistance to the American occupation could not succeed simply by adopting Vietnamese methods (for one thing, there are no mountainous jungles into which to retreat after engagements). Instead, the asymmetrical warrior learns from what works and discards what does not. Iraq is a case in point.

In 1990–1991, Iraq attempted to confront the United States conventionally and was crushed for its effort. It apparently learned from this experience that a future conflict with the United States, the prospects of which Iraq faced after September 11, 2001, could not be conducted in the same manner as before without equally devastating results, which included the decimation of Iraqi armed forces.

What to do? The answer, largely unanticipated by the United States, was to offer only enough resistance to American symmetrical force application to make the Americans think they were prevailing, while regrouping with important parts of the military structure to resist an occupation that they were powerless to avoid. Thus, the limited form of irregular warfare (ambushes, car bombings, suicide terror attacks) became the primary method of resisting the Americans, aimed, apparently at the same goal the Vietnamese attained thirty years earlier—convincing the Americans that the costs of occupation were not worth the costs in lives lost and treasure expended.

Whether this was some carefully modulated plan formulated in advance of the invasion by the Iraqis or not is not the point (and it is a point for which adequate evidence is un available anyway). What is hardly arguable is that the United States underestimated the likelihood of such an asymmetrical response in planning the invasion in the first place. In postinvasion analysis, the argument is frequently made that American planning was flawed in, among other ways, its failure to allocate sufficient troops to the effort. The criticism is valid but somewhat misses the point. The troop numbers *were* clearly adequate for a symmetrical invasion and conquest, which is apparently all that was anticipated. The troop levels were (and are) inadequate for a protracted resistance to occupation, which was an asymmetrical response that was not anticipated. If asymmetrical actions are likely in the future (and the success of the Iraqi resistance has to be encouraging to potential asymmetrical warriors), it is necessary to look at the physical dynamics of these kinds of situations.

Physical Structure of Warfare

What is absolutely clear about the future of warfare involving the United States is that we are uncertain about its face. Part of the reason is the changing nature of the face of war. A primary characteristic of future conflict is that it is itself changing. Vietnam was a prototype, but the experience in Vietnam became the baseline from which others would adapt, changing the problem the next time we encountered it. Similarly, the next asymmetrical challenge will incorporate elements of Iraq, but it will not be identical. Preparing for the next war has become very perilous.

The other problem is finding a conceptual frame for organizing looking at the future. Writing in 1995, then U.S. Army Chief of Staff Gordon Sullivan and Anthony M. Coroalles analogized the problem to "seeing the elephant," a phrase borrowed from the American Civil War (the idea of deriving what the initial exposure to combat was like from descriptions by others—like having an elephant described). They wrote, "Our elephant is the complexity, ambiguity, and uncertainty of tomorrow's battlefield. We are trying to see the elephant of the future. But trying to draw that metaphorical elephant is infinitely harder than drawing a real one. We don't know what we don't know; none of us has a clear view of what the elephant will look like this time around."

We have learned some of the language to describe the new elephant, if not the dynamics of asymmetrical warfare. As an American Marine officer in Iraq has been quoted as saying: "The enemy has gone asymmetric on us. There's treachery. There are ambushes. It's not straight-up conventional fighting." In other words, it does not conform to the accepted rules of symmetrical warfare.

In trying to determine the shape of the new elephant of asymmetrical warfare, one can begin by looking at predictable problems that the asymmetrical warrior will present in the future. With no pretense of being exhaustive, at least five stand out. Undoubtedly there are more.

First, political and military aspects of these conflicts will continue to merge, and distinctions between military and civilian targets and assets will continue to dissolve. The asymmetrical warrior will continue to muddy the distinction for two reasons. One is that he is likely to see conflicts as pitting societies against societies, such that there is no meaningful distinction between combatants and noncombatants. A second reason is that imbedding conflict within the fabric of society facilitates removing some of the advantage of the symmetrical warrior. Urban warfare, for instance, can only be waged symmetrically by concentrating firepower intensity on areas where civilians and opponents are intermingled, meaning such applications of firepower create maximum civilian casualties for which the symmetrical warriors are blamed. If fighting can be reduced to the street-by-street, door-to-door level, much of the symmetrical warrior's advantage is undercut.

Second, the opposition in these kinds of conflicts will increasingly consist of nonstate actors often acting out of nonstate motivations and without state bases of operation. International terrorist organizations, for instance, often carry out operations that cannot be tied to the advantage of any state, and are not clearly based in any state. This creates a problem of response for the symmetrical warrior. Who does he go after? Who does he attack and punish? If the asymmetrical warrior remains in the shadows (or mountains or desert) and the government plausibly denies affiliation or association, then the lever of using force against the opponent is weakened, and the symmetrical warrior is left ungrounded. This is a major problem Israel faced in opposing Lebanon-based Hiz'ballah.

Third, the opposition posed by asymmetrical warriors will almost certainly be protracted, even if the tempo and intensity of opposition varies greatly from situation to situation. The reason for protraction flows from the weakness of the asymmetrical warrior compared to his symmetrical foe. Since direct confrontation is suicidal, the alternative is patient, measured application of force not designed to destroy the enemy, but instead to drag out the conflict, testing the will and patience of the opponent. The United States first saw this dynamic in Vietnam and is seeing it again in Iraq. The antidote is recognition of the tactic and a considerable degree of patience, generally not the long suit of the United States.

Fourth, these conflicts will often occur in the most fractured, failed states, where conditions are ripe for people to engage in acts of desperation that include things like suicide bombing. In situations of high desperation and deprivation, the systemic problems will be extraordinarily difficult to address and try to rectify. The problem is recognizing the multifaceted nature of the wants and needs of the people. The difficulty of rectifying these problems is having the patience and level of physical (including financial) commitment to remove the festering problems that give rise to violence in the first place. The situation in Afghanistan is an excellent example of this kind of problem.

Fifth, we have only seen the tip of the iceberg of what asymmetrical warfare will look like in the future. The problem of Iraq is more than overcoming the Iraqi resistance, it is a matter of defeating and discrediting its methods, so it will not form the basis for the opposition of others in the future. From the vantage point of potential asymmetrical warriors, the resistance has already been successful enough that parts of it will be imitated. Can anyone doubt the next asymmetrical warriors will come armed with improvised explosive devices (IEDs) to be detonated against symmetrical opponents? Or that hostage taking and execution will be employed to force occupiers out of the next occupation? The trick is figuring what else will be learned from the experience to be countered and what new and unique elements will be added.

Determining Opponents

Virtually by definition, asymmetrical warfare will take on a variety of forms in the future. Asymmetrical warfare is, after all, an approach rather than a method, and some variant will occur whenever a technologically inferior force confronts an opponent so superior that it cannot be confronted directly. In this section we will look at three current variants. One is hybrid symmetrical-asymmetrical conflicts, of which Afghanistan is a prime example. Quasi-military situations involve attacks on states generally by non-state actors, whereas internal wars involve factions within a state. Each poses a different planning problem. Hybrids are likely to be confused as symmetrical wars, quasi-military situations are likely to be overly militarized, and internal wars raise vexing questions of interests and solutions.

Symmetrical-Asymmetrical War. One of the most difficult aspects of dealing with asymmetrical war situations is recognizing them for what they are. The United States faced this recognition problem in Vietnam in the 1960s and concluded, after the first major encounter between American and North Vietnamese regulars in the Ia Drang Valley, that the war was conventional, a symmetrical conflict between two similar foes that could be prosecuted in a conventional manner.

The problem was that the strategy of the Vietnamese contained both symmetrical and asymmetrical elements. After the battle of the Ia Drang, the North Vietnamese concluded they could not match American firepower and switched their method to guerrilla-style warfare, one of the classic forms of asymmetrical warfare. Their purpose was to harass and drain the Americans sufficiently to cause them to give up the fight as unwinnable at acceptable cost. After the United States abandoned the war, they returned to conventional, symmetrical warfare against a South Vietnamese opponent that they could defeat conventionally. American experiences in Afghanistan and Iraq suggest the United States continues to confuse this hybrid form of warfare.

In 2001, the United States entered an altogether symmetrical civil war between the Taliban government of Afghanistan and a coalition of opposition clans known collectively as the Northern Alliance. Both sides relied heavily on guerrilla warfare tactics, but because both sides used the same rules, the situation was symmetrical. The role of the United States was to aid in the overthrow of the Taliban government that was providing sanctuary to Al Qaeda—an extension of the war on terrorism. The American military role was to provide strategic airpower against the Taliban forces facing the Northern Alliance. The tactic was successful, because the Taliban could not abandon their lines and take cover without ceding vital territory to the rebels. As a result, their forces were decimated, their government was forced to flee, and victory was proclaimed. The problem was that crushing the extant armed forces of the opposition did not destroy their will to resist, and in a postconflict environment in which conditions have not improved for most Afghans, the Taliban and other warlords have returned.

The Afghan precedent is important, because it demonstrates that modern war is more than simply crushing the organized armed forces of an opposition country. In fact, conceptualizing contemporary war in conventional military terms, as in Afghanistan, oversimplifies how one views the problem and leads to incomplete responses. In many ways, the American effort in Iraq is quite similar: a crushing symmetrical warfare victory followed by a long, inconclusive campaign against an asymmetrical opponent whose existence and methods were apparently unanticipated. Yet, this hybrid form of war, partly symmetrical and partly asymmetrical, is likely to be a prominent part of the future pattern of warfare in developing world countries, for the simple reason that it appears to work.

Quasi-Military Situations. A second set of circumstances in which military force may be employed in the future is in quasi-military unconventional roles and missions. Some of these are outgrowths of the struggles between the haves and the have-nots within developing countries and finds vent in things like terrorist acts either within the society or against outsiders, with the objects normally being the major powers (the African embassy bombings against the United States in 1998, and most dramatically, the attacks against New York and Washington, D.C., in 2001). Others are extensions of the general decay of some of the failed states and often manifest themselves in activities such as criminality (the "war" over control of the diamond fields in Sierra Leone is an example). Attempts to deal with the prospects of potential WMD attacks also fit into this category. What these phenomena share is that they are only semimilitary, even quasi-military, in content.

The Western, and specifically American, problem with Usama bin Laden illustrates the problem of terrorism. For a variety of reasons that he has publicly stated (see examples in Chapter 16), bin Laden blames the United States for a large number of the problems afflicting the Middle East and is consequently devoted to inflicting as much pain and suffering on the United States and Americans as he can through the commission of acts of terror committed by his followers and associates. The campaign to eradicate Al Qaeda since 2001 has in fact decimated much of the ranks and leadership of the original organization, but it has also spawned a series of spin-off, copycat, and affiliated organizations that make the terrorist threat much more Hydra-headed than it was before (this problem is discussed in Chapter 16). These successful actions have, by and large, been the result of intelligence and law enforcement efforts, as in the June 2006 assassination of Abu Musab al-Zarqawi in Iraq.

The other problem is dealing with the criminalization of societies in states broadly described as failing. In the contemporary world, there is no better example than Colombia, where elements associated with the illicit narcotics industry have destabilized that country to the point of making Colombia a virtually lawless land. Worse yet, Colombia's criminalization is spreading across borders and infecting neighboring countries like Venezuela and Ecuador. There is a danger of greater or lesser severity (because the phenomenon is fairly new, it is hard to gauge which) that effectively criminalized countries will also destabilize their neighbors. More or less predictable consequences include migration of those who can afford to do so out of the country and the dangers of living in a lawless society.

Internal Wars. The third kind of environment in which asymmetrical warfare will certainly occur is in the *new internal wars* of parts of the developing world. These wars became a prominent part of the landscape of violence in the 1990s after the end of the Cold War. Although overshadowed by the conflicts spawned by responses to terrorism since 2001, they will continue to produce "opportunities" for the application of force by countries around the world, generally for the purpose of ending the violence. During the 1990s, major international efforts were made in places such as Somalia, Bosnia, Kosovo, and even East Timor (where violence broke out again in 2006), while similar outbreaks were ignored in places such as Rwanda and the Democratic Republic of Congo (former Zaire).

There are several characteristics of these situations that make them problematic as sites for the application of force, especially by major powers. Many of these characteristics are shared by terrorists and by other asymmetrical warriors. Five of these are worth mentioning in the current context.

First, they will always display dramatically the gaps in capability between opponents. Generally speaking, the protagonists in these civil conflicts will be armed with little more than hand-carried weapons or light artillery; will be loosely organized militarily if they are organized at all (the participants will generally be "fighters" as opposed to trained "soldiers"); will engage in hit-and-run attacks and terror directed at the civilian population; and will not stand and fight against organized military units intervening to stop the killing. By contrast, intervening forces will be technologically sophisticated, firepower-intensive, and will emphasize high mobility and an emphasis on airpower. Because the countries where these wars occur will often be equatorial and mountainous, many of the advantages of the technologically superior will be of dubious utility.

Second, the decision to become involved in these situations will always be difficult for outside parties, because generally the potential peacemakers will have few if any concrete, geopolitical interests in the situation important enough clearly to justify intervention. Most of the time, the answer to the operational question, "how will my interests be affected by any possible outcome?" will be "not very much."

Third, there is a growing consensus in the developed world that involvement when important interests are not involved must be relatively bloodless to be tolerable. This idea was especially evident during the NATO intervention in Yugoslavia, where particular attention was paid to ensuring that allied pilots engaged in the bombing campaign were not shot down and killed. The absence of casualties has been a major factor in allied efforts in Bosnia and Kosovo as well. Strategies that begin with the avoidance of casualties as a first requirement, of course, very severely limit the kinds and quality of military action that can be undertaken.

Fourth, the absence of major interests also dictates that interventions will be multilateral affairs, in which coalitions of intervening states provide "burden sharing" by major actors and the problem of the "free rider" (the actor that does not participate in but benefits from an action) is avoided. The failure to engage in preconflict cooperation can have an adverse impact later. As Clark explains, the result can be "difficulties of postwar burden-sharing." The other side of this problem is that these coalition actions are generally militarily inefficient and sometimes fraught with major operational problems. In the NATO Kosovo Force (KFOR) operation, for instance, all the national units report to their home defense ministries before accepting orders from the mission command, and occasionally those orders are refused.

Fifth, the outcomes of these missions are highly problematical. International involvement in the internal affairs of countries predates the post–Cold War period (UN interventions in Cyprus and the Belgian Congo during the 1960s, for instance), but those earlier instances did not produce a pattern or a "model" for how to drop in and "solve" these problems. If the goal of intervention is both to stop the fighting and reasonably assure peace and tranquility after the mission is completed (which it usually is), it can fairly be said that no humanitarian intervention has unqualifiedly succeeded. Some may, but none have.

Postconflict Peace

Planning for the peace that follows these highly fluid asymmetrical conflicts is easily as difficult as their prosecution, and partly as a result, tends to be underemphasized in the planning process. Nevertheless, no durable peace is likely to ensue unless there are concrete plans to alleviate the conditions that gave rise to the violence in the first place or that were created by the violence.

This means wartime planning must work backwards, in Clark's terms. Most asymmetrical conflicts begin with prominent internal bases that must be addressed after the fighting in what Clark calls the "four-step minuet" of planning (development, deployment, decisive [military] operations, postconflict operations). Describing Afghanistan, former minister of the interior Ali A. Jalili argues the need for "human security, which assumes the sustainability of the peaceful environment . . . Freedom from fear and freedom from want lead to human security, and they require more than building the state's security forces." He cites good governance, social security, economic development, and protection of human and political rights as additional needs. This realization leads backward to military operations, as Gray points out: "The primary objective in counterinsurgency is protection of the people, not military defeat of the terrorists-insurgents." It is not clear that adequate attention to these kinds of concerns was present in American prewar planning for Afghanistan or Iraq.

CONCLUSION

Planning for the wars of the future has always been a difficult business. During man's bloodiest century, the twentieth, the problem of seeing into the future and determining what kinds of wars to prepare for clearly evolved greatly. As the first part of this case study demonstrated, the exercise was more linear in the first half of the century: The protagonists remained relatively constant, and the major problem was adapting the emerging weapons technologies to their most efficacious applications. Planning for World War II was not that much different than planning for World War I. Only the scale of violence escalated.

Planning for the future wars of the twenty-first century does not offer the same apparent continuities. The Cold War structure and military planning problem was familiar and represented the kind of continuity that World War II planners faced; the structure of who provided the opposition was the major difference. But the collapse of the communist world and the threat it presented has fundamentally altered the landscape of possible future violence. There are few concrete, compelling, state-based enemies (or even potential adversaries) that provide the grist for planning grounded in concrete problems. Instead, we face a shifting set of shadowy potential opponents, the nature of whom and the threats they pose being largely speculative and ever changing. Who will the next terrorists be, and where and why will they strike? What can be done to prepare for that contingency or others that may emerge? How will experience in the last war temper the approach to the next war and thus complicate our counter asymmetrical warfare strategy problem? *Should* we interfere in the fratricide that has become so common in so much of the developing world? The answers to these questions are not clear at all. What is clear, however, is that these are characteristics of the environment in which future war will occur. They all seem more compelling today than they did before September 11, 2001.

 ## STUDY/DISCUSSION QUESTIONS

1. The past case of military planning between the world wars and today offer points of similarity and contrast. One of these is in the nature of planning; for the familiar in the 1930s, and the unfamiliar now. Discuss these similarities and differences. Which would be a more comfortable planning environment?

2. Put yourself in the position of being a military planner looking at weapons for the future based on the experience of the past. What kinds of military capability would you like to have to deal with the universe you see ten or fifteen years in the future?

3. What is asymmetrical warfare? Contrast it to symmetrical warfare. Why has it arisen as the major military problem of the twenty-first century? Is it likely to continue to be the dominant problem?

4. Should it be a major priority of the most advanced countries to involve themselves in trying to ameliorate internal violence in the developing world? If so, what kind of criteria should be adopted to guide involvements? If not, what should we prepare for?

5. Predict where and in what kind of conflict the United States is most likely to be fighting ten years from today? Try to devise the basic principles for a counter asymmetrical warfare strategy to deal with that future.

6. What are the postconflict environment and operations? Why are they so critical to success both in symmetrical and asymmetrical warfare? Why do they tend to be underemphasized?

READING/RESEARCH MATERIAL

Berkowitz, Bruce. *The New Face of War: How War Will Be Fought in the 21st Century.* New York: Free Press, 2003.

Brodie, Bernard, and Fawn M. Brodie. *From Crossbow to H-Bomb: The Evolution of Weapons and Tactics on Warfare.* Bloomington: Indiana University Press, 1965.

Clark, Wesley. *Winning Modern Wars: Iraq, Terrorism, and the American Empire.* New York: PublicAffairs, 2003.

De Nevers, Renee. "Modernizing the Geneva Convention." *Washington Quarterly* 29, 2 (Spring 2006), 85–98.

Gannon, Kathy. "Afghanistan Unbound." *Foreign Affairs* 83, 3 (May/June 2004), 35–46.

Gray, Colin S. "Stability Operations in Strategic Perspective: A Skeptical View." *Parameters* XXXVI, 2 (Summer 2006), 4–14.

Jalili, Ali A. "The Future of Afghanistan." *Parameters* XXXVI, 1 (Spring 2006), 4–19.

Lind, William S., et. al. "The Changing Face of War: Into the Fourth Generation." *Marine Corps Gazette,* October 1989, 22–26.

Scales, Maj. General Robert H. Jr. *Future War: Anthology.* Carlisle Barracks, PA: U.S. Army War College, 1999.

Snow, Donald M. *When America Fights: The Uses of U.S. Military Force.* Washington, DC: CQ Press, 2000.

———, and Dennis M. Drew. *From Lexington to Desert Storm and Beyond: War and Politics in the American Experience,* 2nd ed. Armonk, NY: M. E. Sharpe, 2001.

Stoessinger, John. *Why Nations Go to War,* 9th ed. New York: St. Martin's Press, 2003.

Sullivan, General Gordon R., and Anthony M. Coroalles. *Seeing the Elephant: Leading America's Army into the Twenty-First Century.* Boston, MA: Institute for Foreign Policy Analysis, 1995.

Van Creveld, Martin. *The Transformation of War.* New York: Free Press, 1991.

WEB SITES

Research projects on national security issues conducted by the RAND Corporation for the U.S. defense establishment

National Security: Research and Analysis at http://www.ran.org/natsec_area

Reports on future trends in terrorism

Federal Research Division: Terrorism Studies at http://www/loc.gov./rr/frd/terrorism.htm

Leading organization studying military matters

The International Institute for Strategic Studies at http://www.iiss.org

Alternate visions of defense issues

Stockholm International Peace Research Institute at http://www.sipri.se

CHAPTER ELEVEN

The Perils
of Proliferation
IRAN AND NORTH KOREA

PRÉCIS

Nuclear proliferation, a subject of concern since the dawn of the nuclear age, returned to the world agenda with a vengeance in late June 2006. Two states, Iran and North Korea, occupied the spotlight because of actions they had taken or were contemplating taking with strong overtones for the world's nuclear balance. Iran and much of the West were engaged in negotiations regarding the potential of that country's nuclear power industry being upgraded to include the possibility of producing nuclear weapons. North Korea, which almost certainly already has a small number of nuclear arms, was threatening to test a ballistic missile delivery system possibly capable of delivering payloads to parts of the continental United States, among other places, and did test a nuclear bomb. Both countries denied any wrongdoing; the United States led international condemnation and threatened possible retaliation if the actions of either went forward. Proliferation was on our minds again.

The spread of different categories of weapons to states that do not possess them and whose possession concerns other states is not a new phenomenon. Trying to place limits on the numbers and types of weapons that states possess goes back to the period between the world wars in modern times (the Washington Conference on naval fleet sizes and the Kellogg-Briand Pact, both of which were negotiated in the 1920s) were early prototypes of the concern we now call proliferation, and dealing with the spread of nuclear weapons has been a concern virtually continuously since the early 1950s.

The post–World War II concern with the spread of nuclear weapons reached a crescendo with the negotiation of the Nuclear Non-Proliferation Treaty (NPT) of 1968. The NPT prohibited additional states who did not already have nuclear weapons from acquiring (or trying to acquire) them and required current possessors from aiding in the spread of nuclear weapons and made them promise to reduce and eliminate their own arsenals. As we shall see, the NPT has enjoyed a mixed level of success.

Concern about proliferation has ebbed and flowed across time. When the membership in the nuclear "club" (the counties that possessed the weapons) was very small during the 1950s and 1960s, there was great concern about additional countries acquiring the weapons, and the body of nuclear proliferation theory was developed to deal with that contingency. During the 1970s and 1980s, that level of concern became more muted, both because the number of nuclear states did not grow perceptibly despite the dire warnings of proliferation theorists whose entreaties increasingly had a kind of "cry wolf" quality, and because of concern with other matters, including the demise of the Cold War and the need to adapt to that change.

Interest in proliferation has returned since the turn of the millennium. The revived interest has been tied closely to the problem of international terrorism, because of the fear that terrorists might acquire and use nuclear or other weapons (so-called weapons of mass destruction or WMDs), a concern important enough that the 2006 *National Security Strategy of the United States* intoned, "There are few greater threats than a terrorist attack with WMD."

The current emphasis on WMD has two basic sources that culminate in the possibility of terrorist acquisition and use of proscribed weapons. The first has to do with the countries that might acquire such weapons, and it focuses currently on countries such as Iran and the Democratic People's Republic of Korea (DPRK or North Korea). Each is a problem for somewhat different reasons, as we shall see. The second source of concern is the various types of WMD that might be acquired. Ultimately, the WMD that most matters are nuclear weapons because of their enormous destructive capacity, but other forms are of importance as well.

This case study seeks to clarify and apply the problem of proliferation. It begins with a discussion of the general problem as it has evolved through scholarly and policy concerns, including the nature of the problem and how the international system has attempted to deal with it. Proliferation is a real and vital current problem, and the case then applies the general principles to the two most important current potential nuclear proliferators, Iran and the DPRK, looking both at attempts to prevent their joining the nuclear club and the dynamics that have made such conformance difficult to achieve.

THE PROLIFERATION PROBLEM

Proliferation is a delicate international problem, in large measure because its underlying aim is both discriminatory and condescending to those at whom it is aimed. In the modern context, the desire to limit possession of nuclear and other proscribed weapons has come from countries that already possess those weapons and is aimed at those who do not possess them. Thus, current efforts to prevent countries like North Korea and Iran from obtaining nuclear weapons are made most loudly by countries like the United States and Britain, which already have them.

The delicacy of the situation comes from rationalizing why it is all right for some states to have, for instance, nuclear weapons whereas other states should not. Saying some states should be allowed to have nuclear weapons but others should not is, of course, inherently discriminatory, and the question that must be answered is, why some but not the others? Invariably, the answer to that question comes back to an assertion regarding responsibility: Those who have the weapons, it is asserted (usually by those countries) can be trusted to act responsibly with the weapons (which basically means they will not use them). Others, however, are not necessarily so trustworthy and, by def-inition, have no track record of responsible possession. This logic is convincing to the countries already possessing the weapons but not necessarily to those who do not, and who argue that the assertion is inherently, and from their vantage point, unjustifiably condescending. This dynamic, to which we will return later in the section, is a major conceptual barrier to enforcing proliferation policies.

The proliferation problem is also complex. To understand and be able to analyze current cases such as the DPRK or Iran, we must look at the structure of the problem. We will do so by raising and trying to answer three questions: What is the nature of the problem? Why is it a problem? And what can you do about the problem? The answers collectively form the context for analyzing the two case applications.

What Is the Nature of the Proliferation Problem?

The roots of the contemporary proliferation problem are in the Cold War, when the major dynamic was to prevent the spread of nuclear weapons to states that did not have them, and also to limit the size and destructiveness of the arsenals of possessing states. These two intents were related to one another. In addition, there was concern about the destabilizing impact of burgeoning nuclear possession, which in turn spawned two addi-tional concerns. One was about the kind of capability that one was attempting to prolif-erate, and the other was the mechanics of how proliferate could occur (and thus what steps had to be taken to prevent it from happening).

There are, essentially, two forms of proliferation that were identified and targeted during the Cold War: *vertical* and *horizontal*. Vertical proliferation refers to incremental additions of a particular weapons system by a state (or states) that already has the weapon. It is a concern both because additional increments of weapons add to the potential deadli-ness of confrontations and because those increments can spawn arms races in which addi-tions by one side cause the other to build more, resulting in an arms spiral. Efforts to control vertical proliferation generally aim at curbing or reducing levels of particular arms (arms control). Most of the nuclear arms treaties negotiated by the United States and the Soviet Union during the Cold War (the Strategic Arms Limitations Talks—SALT—and the Strategic Arms Reduction Talks—START—are examples) were attempts to limit ver-tical proliferation.

Contemporary proliferation concerns center on horizontal proliferation: the spread of nuclear or other weapons to states that currently do not possess them; generally, when we use the term *proliferation* in contemporary discussions, it is shorthand for horizontal proliferation. The two forms are linked because many of the calls for limiting horizontal proliferation have come from states (like the United States and the former Soviet Union) who were engaged in vertical proliferation (nuclear arms races) that made their entreaties to others to self-abnegate attempts to gain the weapons seem disingenuous and created demands to link the two (see discussion of the NPT below).

What kinds of capabilities were being proliferated was also a concern that created independent efforts to curb each kind of capability. The kinds of weapons that may be proliferated are (and were) WMDs, which generally are categorized into three groups captured by the acronym NBC: nuclear, biological, and chemical weapons. Though all are of concern, the dangers they pose are differential. Nuclear weapons are arguably the only unambiguous weapons of *mass* destruction, because of the size and destructiveness of nuclear explosions. Biological (or agents of biological origin, ABO) and chemical weapons can cause large numbers of deaths that are often particularly hideous, but their extensiveness of destruction is more limited. On the other hand, biological and especially chemical weapons are much easier to construct than nuclear weapons. In an era when terrorist possession and use is a major concern, chemical and biological weapons take on added importance because they are the kinds of weapons that terrorists are more likely to be able to obtain (or make) and use. Efforts to contain proliferation, especially in the cases we will highlight, have centered on nuclear weapons. In addition, there is also concern about how WMDs might be delivered to target. The most dramatic form of WMD (and especially nuclear) delivery is by ballistic missiles, because there are no current reliable means of engaging in highly effective defenses against ballistic missiles.

The mechanics of producing (and avoiding the production) of these capabilities has also been a matter of major concern, centering on nuclear weapons and ways to get them to target. The problem of nuclear weapons production is straightforward and has two components. The first is the knowledge of how to fabricate a nuclear device. Nuclear physics has been taught openly for about 60 years now in the world's (and notably the United States') universities, so that knowledge is widely available both to most governments and undoubtedly to some private groups as well. The knowledge genie is clearly out of the bottle. The other requirement for building nuclear weapons is possession of weapons-grade (i.e., highly enriched) isotopes of uranium/plutonium, which generally are byproducts of nuclear reactions in power generators and the like. Access to such materials is highly guarded and restricted, and aspirants to nuclear weapons either have to come into possession of nuclear reactors that produce weapons-grade materials, or they must purchase or steal such material from those who possess it. Nonproliferation efforts have been concentrated on denying access to weapons-grade material to potential proliferators.

The other, somewhat less publicized, aspect of nuclear proliferation surrounds the ability of proliferating states to deliver those weapons to targets—specifically those in the United States and other Western countries. Terrorist horror scenarios center on clandestine shipment of assembled bombs via cargo ship and the like to places like New York or the dispatch of so-called suitcase bombs (small nuclear devices contained in luggage or other parcels) or dirty bombs (conventional explosives coated with radioactive materials dispersed with detonation of the bomb). More conventional analyses deal with the ability of nuclear pretenders to build or buy ballistic missiles to deliver these weapons, because a country that can deliver weapons over only a short distance creates much less of a problem than a country that can deliver the same weapon over intercontinental ranges. As we shall see, the question of ballistic delivery systems is a problem in dealing with the DPRK much more than in dealing with Iran.

Why Is Proliferation a Problem?

The short answer to this question is that one has much less to fear from a weapons capability that one's actual or potential adversaries do not possess than from a capability that they do possess. In the classic, Cold War seedbed of thinking about nuclear proliferation, the problem was conceptualized as the difficulty of keeping additional *sovereign states* from achieving nuclear capability. The more such additional countries obtained the weapons, the more "fingers" there would be on the nuclear "trigger," and thus as a matter of probability, the more likely nuclear war would be. That problem remains central to the contemporary problem, but is augmented by the fear that some of the potential proliferating states might share their capabilities with terrorist nonstate actors, who would allegedly be more difficult to dissuade from using those weapons than would state actors.

In classic terms, the problem of the spread of nuclear (or other) weapons to nonpossessing states is known as the *N+1 problem*. The idea is straightforward. In the formulation, *N* stands for the number of states that currently possess nuclear weapons and to the dynamics among them. *Plus 1,* on the other hand, refers to the problems that would be created for the international system (notably the states that form *N*) by the addition of new (*+1*) states to the nuclear club.

The problem is that the current members (*N*) and potential proliferators (*+1*) see the problem essentially from opposite ends of the conceptual spectrum. The current members generally believe that the current "club" represents a stable, reliable membership (even if earlier members opposed the addition of some others before they were members). Viewed this way, the emphasis of the club is on the problems that will be created by new members, and the criterion for concern is the likelihood of destabilization of the system created by new members. Looking from this perspective, it is not surprising that members of *N* tend to find sources of destabilization that should be opposed.

Members of *+1*, however, see the problem differently. The nonmember does not see his own acquisition of nuclear weapons as destabilizing and is righteously indignant at the notion that his acquisition would have a detrimental effect on the stability of the system. The accusation of destabilization is a backhanded way of suggesting that the new member would be a less responsible possessor than those who already have the weapons. Put more bluntly, the imputation that a new state would destabilize amounts to accusing such a state of a greater likelihood of *using* the weapons than those who already have them and have refrained from doing so. If you are a member of the government of Iran, for instance, you would like an explanation of exactly why a United States that has invaded your next-door neighbor (Iraq) should be treated as somehow more responsible with weapons of mass destruction than you are.

Indeed, in the current context, nonpossessors are more likely to make the argument that their membership in the nuclear club will actually *stabilize* their situations, because it is a fact (even if the causality is arguable) that no state that possesses nuclear weapons has ever been the victim of an aggression against it. As we shall see in the next major section, one of the arguments that both Iranians and North Koreans (among others) have made in recent years is that gaining nuclear weapons capability is a useful—even necessary—means to avoid being attacked by an aggressive United States. Would, for instance, the United States have attacked Iraq if Iraq actually had, rather than being accused of trying to get, nuclear weapons? Some nonpossessing countries argue the American attack would have been less likely and that Saddam Hussein's major error was in not getting the kinds of capability *that would deter the United States.*

There is a further irony that attaches to the *N*+ *1* problem—it is generally only viewed as such by the current nuclear club. A country that aspires to become a member (a + *1* country) may be viewed as a problem before it gets the capability, but once it has and has demonstrated its "responsible possession" of the capability, it ceases to be a part of the problem and instead views other aspirants as part of the problem. Thus, for instance, when only the United States and the Soviet Union had nuclear weapons, we viewed the addition of the third member (Britain) as a potential problem. When Britain obtained the weapons, it ceased to be a problem, but viewed the addition of other countries (France, China) as destabilizing prospects. When those countries joined the club, they became part of *N* and thus looked at other prospective members as part of the problem.

The proliferation problem is obviously worse the more nuclear powers there are, but one obstacle to sustaining international momentum has been that proliferation has not occurred at the pace that those who most fear the prospects have projected. The nuclear club as we know it was pretty well established by 1964, when China obtained nuclear weapons and pushed the number to five—in order of acquisition: the United States, the Soviet Union, Great Britain, France, and China. At the time, there were fears that the number, unless constrained, might jump to 20 or 30 or even more nuclear states, but that simply has not happened. Since the 1960s, only four states have gained nuclear capability. One state (Israel) does not formally admit it has the weapons (it also does not deny it), one state obtained and then renounced and destroyed its weapons (South Africa), and two countries openly joined the club in 1998 (India and Pakistan). The total number of nuclear states thus stands at eight, which is far less than the doomsayers would have it. In the current debate, four states have been mentioned with varying levels of likelihood of attempting to join the club: Iran, Iraq, North Korea, and Syria. The American invasion of Iraq precludes that country's membership, and international pressures effectively curb any Syrian ambitions. That leaves Iran and North Korea as the most likely new members.

What activates the level of contemporary concern is thus clearly not the *quantity* of states that may join, but rather it is the *quality* of new aspirants. The DPRK and Iran are regularly accused of being unstable and bellicose and raise fears on those grounds. Particularly in the case of Iran, there is the additional fear that the Iranians might share nuclear weapons with terrorists groups that would be less likely to be constrained against using them. The question thus arises of what can and should be done to try to keep proliferation from occurring, thus avoiding the possibility that nuclear weapons might be shared with terrorists.

What to Do About the Problem?

Once again, because the roots of thinking about the control of nuclear weapons have their origins in the Cold War, so too does thinking about how to prevent proliferation. The key concept in dealing with nuclear weapons in the Cold War context was the idea of *deterrence,* and that concept dominates contemporary discussions of proliferation as well.

The problem of deterrence has changed with the end of the Cold War system. In the past, nuclear deterrence was among states with very large arsenals of nuclear weapons—principally the United States and the Soviet Union—and the dynamic of deterrence, captured in the idea of assured destruction, was that any nuclear attack against a nuclear-armed superpower would be suicidal, because the attacked state would retain such devastating capabilities even after absorbing an attack as to be able to retaliate against the attacker and destroy it, making any "victory" decidedly Pyrrhic (costing far more than it was worth). Because potential attackers were presumably rational (or at least not suicidal), the prospects of a counterattack that would certainly immolate them was enough to dissuade (or deter) an attack in the first place. The same logic applies to the continuing viability of the NPT, the major international regime on proliferation.

Deterring Proliferation in a Changed World. That situation has changed in two important respects. First, the possession of such large amounts of nuclear power is now unilateral: Only the United States has the unquestioned ability to launch a devastating nuclear attack against anyone in the world, and because of recent improvements in American capability and degrading of the capabilities of historic possible opponents, Kier Lieber and Daryl Press argue in a recent article that "it will probably be possible for the United States to destroy the long-range arsenals of Russia or China with a first strike." This means that the old system of mutual deterrence (i.e., the United States and the Soviet Union deterring *one another*) has disappeared. More important in the current context, the threats in the contemporary environment come from states that will, at best, have a small number of nuclear weapons at their disposal but may not be dissuaded by the same threats that deterred the Soviets during the Cold War. Thus, as Joseph Pilat puts it, "There are real questions about whether old, Cold War–vintage concepts . . . really address the needs of today."

What was the structure of deterrent threats that were available both to dissuade states from acquiring nuclear weapons and to convince states that had those weapons not to use them during the Cold War? Answering that question is logically a precondition to assessing whether such mechanisms will work in the current context.

In a text published originally in 1996, Eugene Brown and I laid out a reasonably comprehensive framework for categorizing types of mechanisms that could be used to deter unwanted nuclear behavior. Within this framework, arms proliferation can be dealt with in two ways, *acquisition* (or front-end) and *employment* (or back-end) deterrence means. Acquisition deterrence, as the name implies, consists of efforts to keep states from obtaining nuclear weapons in the first place. The effort consists of two related and, for many purposes, sequential, activities. Persuasion, or convincing states that gaining nuclear weapons is not in their best interests (often accompanied by the promise of related rewards for nonproliferation or punitive threats if compliance does not occur), seeks to cajole possible proliferating states into not doing so. In contemporary terms, efforts through the United Nations and the European Union to dissuade Iran from making a positive nuclear weapons decision fall into this category. If persuasion does not work, then coercion (threatening or taking punitive—including military—action to prevent proliferation) may occur. The attacks by Israel against an Iraqi nuclear reactor in 1981 are an extreme example of coercive options.

The other form of dissuasion is employment deterrence. If efforts to keep states from gaining nuclear weapons fail, then one must turn to efforts to keep them from using the weapons they do acquire. Once again, there are two mechanisms that can be employed. One is the *threat of retaliation* against any nuclear possessor who may choose to use its weapons against another state (and particularly the United States). The threat is to retaliate with such devastating—including assured destruction—force that it would not only be suicidal for an attacking state to use its weapons (there is an argument that this deterrence could also apply to attacks with other forms of WMD), but that the suicide would occur without having inflicted comparable damage to the retaliating state. Thus, a possible North Korean attack against the United States would consist of lobbing a handful of weapons against American targets and inflicting severe but not fatal damage; North Korea would be destroyed in the U.S. retaliation. The question that is raised about the extension of this form of deterrence in the current context is whether potential proliferating states' leadership are sufficiently rational (i.e., nonsuicidal) that this form of threat will be effective against them. The other form of employment deterrence threat is *denial,* the promise that if an attack is launched, it will fail because the potential attacked state has the capability to defend itself from an attack. The question here is whether the claim to be able to deny an attack is credible given the wide variety of means by which someone could attack, say, the United States with nuclear weapons.

The mechanism by which nonproliferation has been enforced is the Nuclear Non-Proliferation Treaty. The NPT was negotiated in 1968 and went into effect in 1970. Most countries of the world are or have been members of the regime—Iran and North Korea, for instance—and the question is whether the treaty will remain a viable means to avoid more proliferation in the future.

The Role of the NPT. The NPT was, and still is, the most dramatic, open international attempt to prevent the spread of weapons of mass destruction around the world. Conventions exist banning the production, use, and sale of chemical and biological weapons and their components, and the Missile Technology Control Regime represents an effort by the major powers (it was initiated by the G-7 powers) to control the spread of missile delivery technology, and all have been reasonable successes. The crown jewel of proliferation control, however, has been the effort to prevent the spread of nuclear weapons in the world, and the instrument has been the NPT.

The NPT was not the first international agreement that had horizontal proliferation as a purpose, but it was the first treaty to have proliferation as its sole purpose. In

1963, the United States, the Soviet Union, and Great Britain negotiated the Limited Test Ban Treaty (LTBT), which prohibited the atmospheric testing of nuclear devices, and this was supposed to have a secondary proliferation effect, because the technology at the time virtually required nuclear weapons aspirants to explode a nuclear device in the atmosphere to achieve adequate confidence such a device would work.

The same three states cosponsored the NPT. Its major purpose was to create a nuclear caste system on the basis of nuclear weapons possession. Nuclear weapons-possessing states party to the NPT are allowed to keep their nuclear weapons, but agree not to share nuclear technology with nonpossessing states and to work toward disarmament of their arsenals, as noted earlier. These provisions, one should quickly note, require very little action on the part of possessors, and are thus generally innocuous. Nonpossessing states, on the other hand, incur real obligations, because they agree, as long as they are members of the treaty (and there are provisions to renege on one's membership), not to build or seek to build nuclear weapons. Among the nonweapons states who have signed the NPT, this creates a varying obligation. Some states (Sweden, for instance) have never had any intentions to build nuclear weapons and so could join the treaty regime without noticeable effect. Other states (more of the states of sub-Saharan Africa, for instance) lack the wherewithal to even think of developing the weapons, and thus they sacrifice little by joining, either.

There is, however, a third category of states: Countries that do not have nuclear weapons but might want the ability to exercise the option sometime in the future. For these states, the NPT creates a real potential problem, because ratifying the NPT means giving away the right to exercise the nuclear option as long as one is a member of the regime. States can withdraw from the treaty and thus free themselves from its restrictions, but doing so is traumatic and would brand whoever did so as a potential aggressor. As a result, only one state that has signed NPT has ever left it (North Korea in 2003), joining Israel, Cuba, India, and Pakistan as nonmembers among the world's major countries.

States desiring to retain the nuclear option have two ways to deal with the NPT. One is not to sign it, thereby avoiding its restrictions. The most prominent states not to do so have included Israel, India, and Pakistan. Other states with potential nuclear aspirations have signed the agreement and either complied fully with it or have engaged in activities that come close to noncompliance but stop short of that level. Iran and North Korea fall into this category.

Suspicion that some countries are not living up their NPT obligations has led to additional steps to try to enforce the deterrence goal of acquisitions deterrence. The Bush administration, for instance, created something it called the Proliferation Security Initiative (PSI) among like-minded states to, in Andrew Winner's words, "aggressively interdict weapons of mass destruction (WMD), their components, and their delivery systems." The PSI originally consisted of 11 members (Australia, France, Germany, Italy, Japan, the Netherlands, Poland, Portugal, Spain, the United Kingdom, and the United States) and has, according to the 2006 *National Security Strategy of the United States (NSS),* attracted the interest of over 70 countries.

The nonproliferation enterprise remains a work in progress. Since the NPT was launched over a third of a century ago, there has been little overt nuclear weapons proliferation (India and Pakistan have been added, South Africa subtracted from the list).

Yet, proliferation has emerged in the post–September 11 world as a major concern, fueled by the fear some rogue state—some member of the "axis of evil"—might acquire such weapons and either use them personally or through some terrorist surrogate. Whether this fear is real or fanciful is not the point; that this perception fuels international concern is the point. Within the crosshairs of international concern, two states currently stand out—Iran and North Korea. The study thus moves to those states.

THE PROLIFERATION PROBLEM APPLIED: IRAN AND NORTH KOREA

The two countries most prominently in the proliferation spotlight in recent years are Iran and the DPRK. Both share several characteristics. First, both have significant foreign policy differences with the United States (although of different natures and for different reasons) and have been categorized among America's adversaries. Second, both possess the technology and expertise to produce nuclear weapons and either have or reasonably easily could have access to the weapons-grade plutonium necessary for bomb construction (this commonality separates them from other worrisome states). Third, both deny any interest or desire to build, and especially to use, nuclear weapons, claims that are widely disbelieved in policy circles, especially in the United States. Fourth, although both are or have been members of NPT, they are deemed to be untrustworthy, rogue regimes whose word cannot be trusted at face value. This web of perceptions helps form the context for considering each case.

They are also different in an important respect already identified. Iran is not currently a nuclear power: There has never been verification that it has fabricated a nuclear weapon, and its regime denies any interest in doing so. As such, it poses a problem of acquisition (or front-end deterrence) for those countries that seek to avoid the spread of nuclear weapons. North Korea is different. According to former assistant secretary of defense Ashton Carter and former secretary of defense William J. Perry (both under President Clinton) in a June 22, 2006, column in the *Washington Post,* the DPRK "openly boasts of its nuclear deterrent, has obtained six to eight bombs' worth of plutonium since 2003 and is plunging ahead to make more." A 2003 article in the *Bulletin of the Atomic Scientists* went so far as to state that "North Korea has apparently become the world's ninth nuclear power." Thus, the problem posed by North Korea is one of employment (or back-end) deterrence. The world in other words, is, trying to keep Iran from obtaining nuclear weapons; it is attempting to get North Korea to avoid using its weapons (as well as dismantling the stocks it has already obtained). The two countries thus represent bookends of the overall range of the perils of proliferation.

Iran

The context and content of Iran's nuclear program depends on the perspective from which one begins. From an Iranian viewpoint, any incentive they may have to develop WMDs is regional in nature. The prime focus arises from Israeli unilateral possession of nuclear weapons, which the Iranians, along with many others in the Middle East, find unacceptably threatening and in need of balancing. This motivation is important enough to lead Michael Donovan to conclude in a Center for Defense Information Terrorism Report, "The Israeli nuclear arsenal will continue to drive Iranian . . . WMD acquisition efforts for the foreseeable future." (American support of Israel's status as sole nuclear power in the area is seen as suspicious at best.) At the same time, fellow Islamic (but not Shiite) Pakistan has nuclear weapons, and neighboring rival Iraq has possessed and used other forms of WMD against Iran and at one time had a nuclear weapons program. Iran, the inheritor of the mantle of Persia, believes itself to be a prime power in the region and thus, if any state in the Middle East should be nuclear weapons capable (either possessing the weapons or able to fabricate them), they believe it should be Iran. Because the Persian Iranians are not Arab, this sentiment is not universally accepted in the region.

The perspective changes if one adopts the American vantage point. As the world's remaining superpower, the United States considers itself the self-appointed arbiter of proliferation and sees the problem both in global terms and as it affects American security interests. From an American vantage point, the possible accession of Iran is a classic application of the $N+1$ conundrum: Iranian possession of nuclear weapons is troublingly destabilizing, both because those weapons might be used against American "ally" Israel and because it is alleged Iran might make its nuclear weapons, if it had them, available to Al Qaeda or some other terrorist organization.

The American–Iranian relationship over nuclear weapons reflects the deep schizophrenia of relations between the two countries. Prior to the Iranian Revolution of 1979, Iran was the United States' closest Islamic ally in the region, and the Shah of Iran was one of America's most steadfast friends and allies. In that status, Iran willingly signed the NPT on July 1, 1968, and ratified it on February 2, 1970, thus becoming one of its original members. In 1974, the Iranians initiated a nuclear power program without American opposition, although there were reports at the time that it had a potential weapons component. The Shah of Iran was, after all, America's friend.

After the Iranian Revolution that all changed. The Shah of Iran was replaced by a violently anti-American regime whose titular head was Ayotollah Khomeini, and the United States went from Iran's close friend to the "great Satan." When Iran reinstated its nuclear program in 1984, including a possible weapons component, it was considered a problem. Iran's elevation to the forefront of proliferation concerns came in President Bush's 2002 State of the Union address, where he famously declared the "axis of evil" with Iran as one of its spokes.

Whether, or the extent to which, Iran poses a proliferation problem once again is a matter of perspective. Iran itself denies vociferously that it has any intention ever of possessing nuclear weapons and asserts that it considers the possibility of nuclear weapons usage to be amoral and unacceptable (a view ascribed to Ayotollah Khomeini in 1984, when he reinstated the program "reluctantly," according to Donovan). To this end, Ayotollah Ali Khamenei, the religious head of the country, signed a *fatwa* (religious edict) prohibiting the production, stockpiling, or use of nuclear weapons on August 9, 2005. Between 1992 and 2002, Iran freely allowed inspection of all its nuclear facilities by inspectors from the International Atomic Energy Agency (IAEA), and on December 18, 2003, signed a protocol to the NPT allowing IAEA inspections of all facilities on request of the IAEA.

Concern about Iranian intentions were piqued within the Bush administration in 2002 when American intelligence learned of the existence of two secret Iranian nuclear facilities at Natanz and Arak, one of which was a uranium enrichment facility and the other a heavy water power production plant (heavy water facilities are necessary to produce weapons-grade fissile material). Iran denied that these facilities were linked to weapons production or research and quickly opened them to inspection. Their existence and potential, however, were enough to raise international—especially American—suspicions about what Iran was up to.

The problem was and is the *dual use* nature of nuclear facilities and research. Efforts to develop nuclear power capabilities also have value in nuclear weapons research and development, so that a country may contend its nuclear program is entirely for peaceful power-producing purposes (and thus quite within the bounds of NPT requirements), but that effort may also be contributing to the base of a nuclear weapons program. After its experience in the Iran-Iraq war during the 1980s, the Iranians were chastened by their vulnerability to WMDs, and, arguably this experience caused Iran to redoubled its efforts to develop weapons of mass destruction and ballistic missiles. To a suspicious Bush administration, this translates into a direct and compelling threat. In the words of the 2006 *NSS*, "We face no greater challenge from a single country than from Iran." In addition to the worst-case face it places on the Iranian nuclear program, the Bush document adds that Iran "sponsors terrorism, threatens Israel, seeks to thwart Middle Eastern peace, disrupts democracy in Iraq, and denies the aspirations of its people for freedom." In possession of nuclear weapons, the Iranian regime would presumably be in a more powerful position to pursue each of these alleged policy objectives.

No one alleges that Iran currently possesses nuclear weapons. In fact, there is considerable disagreement as to whether they even intend to build the weapons. Three possibilities exist. One is that the regime is indeed aggressively pursuing nuclear capability and will build the weapons as soon as it can unless it is restrained from doing so. Efforts by Russia and the European Union have been underway to steer the Iranian nuclear program unambiguously toward a peaceful uses' program, for instance, by offering Iran light water power reactors (that do not generate weapons-grade material) in return for an Iranian open reaffirmation of its NPT obligations. The United States has opposed this offer on the grounds that it rewards Iran's "bad behavior" in the nuclear area. The second possibility is that the Iranian nuclear program is entirely peaceful and power-generation oriented, in which case there is no cause for concern. The dual-use nature of the Iranian nuclear program probably makes this a disingenuous and reckless assumption to make because its falsity could prove dangerous if Iran suddenly broke out and built nuclear weapons.

The third possibility is that Iran is indeed pursuing a dual-use research program, but that it will only activate the weapons component if it feels the need to do so. The 2002 CDI study by Michael Donovan suggests this conclusion, arguing "such an approach allows for a practical military program to be rapidly instituted" if the need arises. Pike explains the dynamics of this approach. "Iran appears to be following a policy of complying with the NPT and building its nuclear power program in such a way that if the appropriate political decision is made, know-how gained in the peaceful sector (specialists and equipment) could be used to produce nuclear weapons." This dual-track approach at the research and development levels while deferring the acquisition decision and process has precedence in the actions of India, which had an active nuclear program for well over a quarter century before "going nuclear" in 1998. Moreover, staying below the threshold of actual nuclear weapons development and procurement means Iran stays in technical compliance with its NPT obligations, even if they may be violating the spirit of those obligations not to seek nuclear weapons capability. It would also facilitate a breakout should the Iranian government so choose, whereby Iran withdrew from the NPT and then went ahead with nuclear weapons procurement.

This leaves three pivotal questions about the Iranian nuclear program to be answered. The first is how close Iran is to being able to build nuclear weapons, which is another way of asking the imminence of whatever threat such acquisition poses. The second is what would motivate the Iranians to make the decision to break out of their abstinence from nuclear weapons, move from an acquisitions to an employment deterrence problem, and become part of *N* rather than *+1*. The third is what difference such a decision would make for the stability of the system. These questions are all about future situations and are necessarily progressively speculative. The menace and dread of the prospects (or its absence), however, affects one's assessment.

Estimates vary about how soon Iran could have nuclear weapons if it chose to activate its weapons program. The Israelis, who would be among the few affected countries actually under the gun if Iran fielded a nuclear weapon, are the most pessimistic: Donovan, for instance, reported in 2002 an assertion by Israeli defense minister Binyamin Ben-Eliezer that they could achieve such a status by 2005, a claim that has proved false. The problem is that there is a difference between when a state, Iran or anyone else, *can* fabricate a bomb (have the material and knowledge to do so) and when they *do* build one. While Iran may be near the point of collecting the requisite material for bomb fabrication, there is little evidence it has built one (or more), and the Iranians fervently deny they are, or have any intention of, doing so. Moreover, building a workable nuclear explosive and being able to wed it to a ballistic missile with which to launch it against Israel or anywhere else is an additional and difficult step: Most primitive, first-generation devices are too large and heavy to be placed on ballistic missiles. In late 2005, American director of national intelligence (DNI) John Negroponte publicly estimated that Iran could build a nuclear device between 2010 and 2015, a date sufficiently far in the future that, if wrong, most people will have forgotten by the time it proves false.

Why would Iran decide to move forward and build nuclear weapons? The United States, of course, responds that such a decision is consistent with the aggressive, antagonistic role it ascribes to Iran, and even if one rejects that typification as overly extreme, a positive weapons decision would certainly alienate large portions of the international community, including the European Union, which has led attempts to mediate the situation. Iran, of course, knows this and even its mercurial president, Mahmoud Ahmadinejad, has gone out of his way to assuage the Europeans and to seek a peaceful resolution in which the world is reassured of Iran's peaceful intentions but in which Iran is not forced to take down its nuclear industry, which is a point of considerable national pride.

Beyond an aggressive intent, what might influence the Iranian decision process? Two, more defensive, possible motivations stand out. One is Israeli unilateral possession of nuclear capability in the region. Being effectively under the Israeli nuclear gun is humiliating for Islamic states, and they all find American support for this continuing condition enigmatic and unfortunate, to put it mildly. To a state with the proud Persian heritage of Iran, this humiliation is particularly difficult to accept, and a latent ability to go nuclear as a deterrent to possible Israeli-threatened or actual aggression will always be an attractive policy option difficult to give away. The other motivation is to deter a possible American attack on Iran. The Bush doctrine of preemption may or may not be a dead or dying letter in the lame duck portion of the second Bush administration, but the administration has certainly proved willing to use force to resolve its problems in the Persian Gulf region and has, as indicated, identified Iran as a major threat and as a possible target for "regime change" Iraq-style. Nuclear weapons possession might provide a deterrent to American aggression; at least it is possible from an Iranian vantage point to consider that possibility.

If Iran is, as argued, an acquisition deterrence problem, what tools are available to influence their decision? According to our analysis in the last section, there are both positive and negative incentives. The attempt to convert the Iranian power industry to light water reactors that do not produce weapons-grade residues represents the positive incentive; at this writing in mid-2007, that track was being actively pursued by the EU and the Iranian government. The other form of reaction, of course, is coercion, and the United States has led that approach, threatening UN Security Council sanctions and other possible actions should Iran not comply completely with international efforts to halt its weapons-potential program.

What effect would a positive Iranian nuclear decision have on the international system and, more specifically, the nuclear balance among the N and $+1$ countries? It is, of course, impossible to answer that question authoritatively, and predictions range from the apocryphal to the mundane. The history of proliferation suggests that an impact somewhere between the extremes is probably prudent. Before each proliferation that has occurred since proliferation was identified as a major problem, there have been dire predictions of systemic effects, and essentially none of them have proved true. Most recently, there were terrible projections about what nuclear-armed India and Pakistan would do to one another and by extension to the world. These dire predictions included the possibility that an "Islamic bomb" would fall into the hands of terrorists. Yet it has not happened. Similarly, it is postulated that a Shiite Iran that would earn itself the near universal designation of pariah state by producing nuclear weapons might do so and then share these with Sunni-based terrorist organizations. Is such an assertion reasonable or sustainable?

One other factor regarding Iran should be raised at this time, although it will be examined in more detail in Chapter 14. Iran is a major oil-producing country, and that fact affects its relations, including the nuclear component, with the rest of the world. The fact that Iran pumps over 2.5 million barrels of oil a day makes it a major player in global energy markets. This standing leads the Bush administration to argue Iran has no need for nuclear power because it can produce all the power it needs by burning oil, and thus its nuclear program should be abandoned. The possibility of Iran withholding its oil from the global market (a decision that would have strong negative impacts on Iran and the world at large), however, produces a degree of leverage for Iran in its negotiations with the Europeans and Americans, for instance.

The Democratic Republic of Korea (DPRK or North Korea)

The proliferation problem regarding the DPRK is different than that surrounding Iran. The link between the two is their mutual inclusion in the Bush axis of evil, although it is not clear whether the composition of the troika of axis members was rhetorical or had a deeper geopolitical meaning at the time. North Korea, of course, poses a more advanced problem than does Iran, because of its presumed possession of a small number of nuclear weapons and its development of long-range missile systems. Indeed, its threat to test fire a Taepodong 2 missile with a reported intercontinental range was the precipitant for international concern in summer 2006.

The rift between Pyongyang and Washington is far longer and deeper than it is between Tehran and Washington. The DPRK is the only country to withdraw from the NPT, and it has been much more recalcitrant about its weapons programs, including both nuclear weapons and ballistic delivery systems. Moreover, the Korean peninsula's location in the heart of east Asia gives it a great deal of geopolitical importance. On the other hand, North Korea has no oil and is one of the most destitute countries on the globe. It also shares with Cuba the distinction of being the only remaining avowedly Marxist-Leninist (communist) regimes in the world (the other putatively communist states, China and Vietnam, have long since renounced Marxist economics).

The history of the North Korean nuclear program—and concerns about it—is long-standing and is largely framed in terms of U.S.-North Korean relations. The United States and the DPRK have, of course, been antagonists since the Korean War (1950–53) in which they were primary opponents. Aside from the general antagonism this confrontation created, it may have provided the impetus for North Korean nuclear pretensions. As Robert Norris put it in his 2003 *Bulletin of the Atomic Scientists* article, "The fact that North Korea was threatened with nuclear weapons during the Korean War, and that for decades thereafter U.S. weapons were deployed in the South, may have help motivate former President Kim Il Sung to launch a nuclear weapons program of his own." Regardless of whether one accepts this explanation at face value, the North Koreans have been consistent over time that they need to maintain the *option* to develop nuclear weapons (and they have never publicly admitted anymore than that prior to their summer 2006 nuclear test) to deter a potential American attack against them. The DPRK program is normally dated to the early 1960s, and the country joined the NPT in 1984. At six-party talks about their program, the North Koreans insisted in December 2006 that they be treated as a nuclear power.

The genesis of the current crisis goes back to the Clinton administration. A May 1992 inspection of North Korean nuclear facilities by IAEA inspectors headed by Hans Blix concluded the North Koreans might be engaged in weapons activity (converting spent nuclear fuel into weapons-grade plutonium). This precipitated a crisis in which the North Koreans threatened the until-then unprecedented step of withdrawing from the NPT in March 1993. At this point the Clinton administration intervened, entering into direct talks that produced a negotiated settlement to the problem known as the Agreed Framework. Under its provisions (reference to the complete document is found in the suggested readings), the North Koreans agreed to freeze and eventually to dismantle its nuclear weapons program under IAEA supervision. In turn, it would accept light water nuclear reactors to replace those capable of producing weapons-grade materials and would receive heavy fuel oil for electricity and heating purposes. In addition, Norris adds, "political and economic relations would be normalized, and both countries would work toward a nuclear weapons-free Korean peninsula and strengthen the nuclear proliferation regime."

How well this arrangement worked was primarily a partisan political question in the United States. Republican critics—notably neoconservatives—of the Clinton policy underlying the Agreed Framework argued that the North Koreans were cheating on the letter and spirit of the agreement in terms of their handling of materials from their light water reactors, a claim vigorously denied by Selig Harrison in a 2005 *Foreign Affairs* article, who equates the intelligence reports of violations in North Korea to distortions similar to those coming out of Iraq in 2002.

At any rate, the current crisis was precipitated when the Bush administration cut off the flow of heating oil to North Korea and terminated the Agreed Framework in December 2002. The DPRK responded by announcing on January 10, 2003, that it was withdrawing from the NPT, which it did after the mandatory 90-day waiting period after the announcement of intent. Following saber-rattling on both sides in the ensuing months, six-party negotiations (the DPRK, South Korea, Japan, Russia, China, and the United States) opened on August 28, 2003, at which point North Korea announced it was prepared "to declare itself formally as a nuclear weapons state (which, as noted it did in December 2006)," and added that it possessed the capability to deliver these weapons to target by ballistic means.

The North Koreans have always viewed the six-nation format for negotiations (an American construct) unacceptable, preferring bilateral negotiations the Bush administration refuses to accept. On September 9, 2004, an explosion occurred at a nuclear site (Ryanggang) in North Korea that may have been a nuclear test, although the North Koreans denied that the test was of a nuclear device. The North Koreans announced on February 10, 2005, that they had developed nuclear weapons for self-defense purposes and suspended participation in the six-party talks. In a direct reversal that illustrates some of the flavor of the ongoing relationship, the six-party talks resumed in September 2005 and produced an agreement whereby the DPRK agreed to dismantle its nuclear weapons program in return for economic assistance. In June 2006, as the Taepodong crisis unfolded, Carter and Perry declared that "the six-party talks . . . have collapsed."

The summer 2006 brouhaha over North Korean missile tests emerges from this context. North Korea has for some years had a missile development program, and its potential ability to deliver WMD by ballistic means distinguishes the DPRK from other proliferators. The last missile crisis occurred in 1998, when the DPRK tested a Taepodong 1 missile that passed over Japan and created an international incident. The Clinton administration exacted a moratorium on missile testing from the North Koreans in 1998, which, according to a June 21, 2006, *Los Angeles Times* report by Barbara Demick, it renewed in 2002. The North Koreans, in keeping with their nuclear tradition of denying they are engaged in

WMD activities while asserting their right to do so if they choose, maintain the current Taepodong 2 test is intended to see whether North Korea can insert a satellite into space, while arguing they retain the right to develop military missiles.

Is the missile dispute just another round of U.S.-North Korean bickering or something more serious? Carter and Perry, who were officials during the 1990s when agreements were reached with the DPRK, believe the crisis is real and that the United States should consider a preemptive strike against the missile launch site if the North Koreans fail to decommission the missile. Alarm is raised because the Taepodong 2, especially if equipped with a third boost stage—which the purported test does not include and which the North Koreans have never done successfully—could reach targets in the United States (purportedly the current version could hit Hawaii, Alaska, and possibly parts of the West Coast of the United States). On the other hand, the Taepodong series of missiles are old technology, very vulnerable liquid-fuel rockets that take literally days to fuel at above-ground launchers and could hardly be used for a sneak attack against the United States or anywhere else. They are also very vulnerable to being attacked and destroyed during the fueling process, as Carter and Perry admit. "The multi-story, thin skinned missile filled with high-energy fuel is itself explosive—the U.S. airstrike would puncture the missile and probably cause it to explode." There is no reliable public information available on the accuracy of such missiles; presumably, they are fairly inaccurate.

One is left with what to make of the North Korean nuclear "threat." If, as they imply, they are nuclear-capable, the question is what would keep them from using their weapons? It is difficult to conjure reasons why North Korea would launch an offensive, preemptive nuclear strike against anyone, given the certain response would be its own utter and certain destruction. Using the nuclear weapons most observers say they have—and that the North Koreans do not strongly deny (a la Israel)—may make little sense, but *possessing* such weapons may make sense if North Korea believes they help deter the United States from attacking them. The idea that the United States needs to be deterred may seem outlandish to most Americans. In February 2007, both sides in effect "blinked." The DPRK agreed in the six-party talks to suspend its nuclear weapons program in return for the same kinds of incentives offered in 1994 by the United States.

CONCLUSION

The title of this case study, "The *Perils* of Proliferation" was chosen purposely, because it suggests a level of uncertainty and disagreement. Is proliferation a problem? If so, what kind of a problem is it? More important, how great a problem is it? And what should be done about it?

No one, except potential proliferating countries that are part of *+ 1*, argue that the spread of nuclear and other weapons of mass destruction to nonpossessing states is in principle a good idea that should be encouraged. On the other hand, the empirical evidence of the impact of individual proliferations (when individual countries joined the nuclear weapons "club") hardly provides incontrovertible proof of the most dire perils that have been predicted. What is the evidence, for instance, that the world is a less stable place because Israel, India, or Pakistan have the bomb? We might contend it would be better if they did not, but the peril remains theoretical, not demonstrated.

We are now concerned with the possibility that Iran and North Korea will become the next uninvited, unwanted members of *N,* and dire predictions accompany that prospect. Are those predicted perils reasonable and prudent, reflexive and hysterical, or somewhere in between? More to the point, what can we do about these prospects—of Iran getting the weapons, of North Korea's continuing possession and possible use—that is prudent and does not make matters worse? Declaring the situation highly dangerous, as the U.S. *National Security Strategy* does, is inflammatory but ultimately not very helpful. Dismissing the problem out of hand is probably also neither responsible nor acceptable. If the answer to how we should treat the problem was entirely obvious, it would not be a problem. But then, real problems are seldom so transparent and thus solvable.

STUDY/DISCUSSION QUESTIONS

1. What is the basis of the current international concern for nuclear proliferation? How do Iran and the DPRK exemplify this problem?

2. Why is proliferation a "delicate" problem? Distinguish between types of proliferation, including what kinds of materials and capabilities are being proliferated and what difference each makes.

3. What is the *N+1* problem? Define it and why it suggests the delicacy of the proliferation problem. Why is it so difficult to resolve?

4. What means are available to deal with proliferation? Distinguish between acquisition and employment deterrence. How does each work? How does the Proliferation Security Initiative contribute?

5. What is the Nuclear Non-Proliferation Treaty (NPT)? How does it work? What categories of states are there in regard to the treaty? How are they different?

6. Compare and contrast the proliferation problems created by Iran and the DPRK. How are they similar and different? What is the status of each? What problems does each present?

7. Define Iran in proliferation terms. What is the status of the problem? What efforts have been and are being applied to it? Why would Iran elect to go nuclear or to abstain from doing so?

8. Define the DPRK in proliferation terms. What is its status? How has it evolved to where it is? How serious is it to international stability, and what can be done about it?

READING/RESEARCH MATERIAL

Arnoldy, Ben. "How Serious Is North Korea's Nuclear Threat?" *Christian Science Monitor* (online edition), August 27, 2003.

Carter, Ashton B., and William J. Perry. "If Necessary, Strike and Destroy." *Washington Post,* June 22, 2006, A29.

De Bellaigne, Christopher. "Think Again: Iran." *Foreign Policy,* May/June 2005, 18–26.

Demick, Barbara. "Few Moves Left with N. Korea." *Los Angeles Times* (online edition), June 21, 2006.

Donovan, Michael. "Iran, Israel and Nuclear Weapons in the Middle East." *CDI Terrorism Project* (online), February 14, 2002.

Harrison, Selig S. "Did North Korea Cheat?" *Foreign Affairs* 84, 1 (January/February 2005), 99–110.

Lieber, Kier A., and Daryl G. Press. "The Rise of U.S. Nuclear Supremacy." *Foreign Affairs* 85, 2 (March/April 2006), 42–54.

The National Security Strategy of the United States of America. Washington, DC: The White House, March 2006.

Norris, Robert S. "North Korea's Nuclear Program, 2003." *Bulletin of the Atomic Scientists* 59, 2 (March/April 2003), 74–77.

Pilat, Joseph F. "Reassessing Security Assurances in a Unipolar World." *Washington Quarterly* 28, 2 (Spring 2005), 59–70.

Snow, Donald M., and Eugene Brown. *The Contours of Power: An Introduction to Contemporary International Relations.* New York: St. Martin's Press, 1996.

Specter, Arlen with Christopher Walsh. "Dialogue with Adversaries" *Washington Quarterly* 30, 1 (Winter 2006–07), 9–26.

Winner, Andrew C. "The Proliferation Security Initiative: The New Face of Interdiction." *Washington Quarterly* 28, 2 (Spring 2005), 129–143.

WEB SITES

Country Profile on Iran and Nuclear Weapons
   http://www.nti.org/e_research/profiles/Iran/print/index_1772.prt

Status of Iranian Nuclear Program (Global Security):
   http://globalsecurity.org/wmd/world/iran/nuke.htm

North Korean Weapons Program Summary (Wikipedia)
   http://en.wikipedia.org

Text of U.S.-DPRK Agreed Framework of 1994
   http://www.carnegieendowment.org/static/npp/agreed_framework.cfm

CHAPTER TWELVE

Who Cares about Kashmir?

AN OLD PROBLEM WITH NEW TEETH

PRÉCIS

Some politico-military problems are so deep and fundamental that they appear to be irreconcilable and incapable of solution. The situation between Israel and Palestine depicted in Chapter 6 is one of those kinds of conflicts. The struggle between India and Pakistan over control of the strategically and emotionally important princely state of Jammu and Kashmir (Kashmir for short) is similar. Given the depth and diametrical opposition of the various sides, it is also an irresolvable conflict.

This case develops the problem in two ways. The first is historical, looking at the evolution of the problem from the partition of the Indian subcontinent after World War II to the present. The second, and more fundamental, purpose is to look at the prospects for ending the fighting and coming up with a peaceful solution with which all parties can live. This involves examining the underlying interests of the major players and their desired outcomes. Why do India and Pakistan believe control of Kashmir is vital to their national interests? Why do some Kashmiris believe that independence is the only acceptable option? Finally, the problem acquired "new teeth" in 1998 when both India and Pakistan publicly demonstrated nuclear weapons capability. That new variable has changed their relations, as have other events such as the 2005 earthquake in the region.

It is a war that has been fought literally at the top of the world, in a land that is home to some of the world's tallest mountains and most awesome vistas that have earned it the nickname the "Switzerland of the East." The battlefields are the high Himalayan

Mountains, often at altitudes of 16,000–17,000 feet above sea level where the air is so oxygen-poor that normal military activities by combat forces are physically impossible to perform even were it not for the icy, snow-covered, rugged terrain. Given the conditions, much of the fighting consists of long-range artillery duels between the contending sides. The front has long since stabilized along a high barbed-wire fence marking the Line of Control, which has become a de facto international border between Indian- and Pakistan-controlled segments of Kashmir. A mutually acceptable end to the dispute seems as elusive as peace between Israel and Palestine.

The place is the northern tip of the Asian subcontinent, where India, Pakistan, Afghanistan, Tajikistan, and China meet in the world's tallest mountain range. The *CIA Factbook* calls it "the world's most highly militarized territorial dispute." Forming the geographic cap for the new country of India when independence came to the subcontinent, the point of contention is the princely state of Jammu and Kashmir (hereafter Kashmir), a territory about the size of Utah annexed by India when the subcontinent was subdivided in the latter 1940s as Great Britain dissolved its long-held colonial empire there. Because the population of Kashmir is about 70 percent Muslim, the new government of Pakistan never recognized Indian control and has, through Kashmiri "freedom fighters" whom India accuses of being agents of the Pakistani government (a charge denied by Pakistan), been contesting sovereign political control ever since. On at least two occasions, Kashmir has been a major battleground in wars between India and Pakistan. The rest of the time, Kashmir is the site of a low-level war of attrition with considerable explosive potential for the region and possibly beyond.

Why highlight a seemingly parochial dispute over some physically awe-inspiring but economically impoverished territory very far from the center of the international political scene? On the face of it, the answer to who cares about Kashmir would seem to be not much of anyone except the people who live there. Such a conclusion, however, would not be warranted.

What has revived, or for much of the world, created international interest in Kashmir, quite simply, are the "new teeth" demonstrated by India and Pakistan in 1998 when they both exploded nuclear weapons and thus made official the spread of the nuclear arms race to that part of Asia. Kashmir is the most likely flash point that could lead to wider war between India and Pakistan, and dealing with the Kashmir problem was one of the major reasons that President Clinton traveled to the subcontinent in early 2000. Prior to leaving on that trip, he referred to Kashmir as "the most dangerous place in the world today." The emergence of India as a major international economic power makes the dispute more relevant to international politics generally than it was a decade ago.

Defusing the Kashmir conflict as a means to help lower the likelihood of nuclear war on the subcontinent would seem enough to establish its importance, but there is more. On one hand, the outcome of the dispute, particularly if it resulted in independence for Kashmir or attachment to Pakistan, would provide a significant territorial precedent in the region in at least two ways. Indian possession of Kashmir has been compared to Chinese possession of Tibet (which is not far away physically). At the same time, Kashmir's secession could provide encouragement for other areas within India (or even Pakistan) with centrifugal tendencies.

In addition, there is another significant aspect of the Kashmir situation for the study of international relations. In a world where American power seems to be a factor nearly everywhere, the crisis also demonstrates the limit of the United States to influence events. The United States has always had very limited influence on the subcontinent and especially with the government of India, a lack of affinity that might seem strange between the world's two largest political democracies and prominent leaders of a globalized world. Part of the problem has been that the United States has been more interested in improved relations with China, and that has "tilted" U.S. policy more toward China's ally, Pakistan. India, in turn, felt the necessity to be closer to the Soviet Union during the Cold War to counterbalance China, and especially after the Soviets took a leading role in mediating the outcome of the 1965 Indo-Pakistani War. Even with the Cold War over, however, U.S. influence on the subcontinent, and especially with India, remains minimal. The United States' de facto alignment with Pakistan over the 2001 war in Afghanistan (in which India has also offered assistance) has increased American visibility and presence in the region. Any long-term change in influence remains to be seen. Although India is one of the few bastions of pro-American sentiment in the mid-2000s, the United States is not clearly an important "player" in resolving the tensions over Kashmir.

The Kashmir conflict is an extremely intractable situation that has proved very difficult—to this point impossible—to resolve, and it may remain so. To understand both the nature of the problem and the barriers to its solution, we will begin by looking at the historical basis of the disagreement and how it has evolved, including the effects that "nuclearization" has had on it. We will then examine the interests of the various parties to the dispute, and how those interests have served to preclude particular outcomes. We will then look at a series of options for settling or managing the dispute and the political and other barriers to implementing them. We will conclude with some assessment of where the dispute may head in the future.

EVOLUTION OF THE PROBLEM

Kashmir became an international problem with the breakup of the British Raj (the British colonial administration) on the subcontinent after World War II. Before World War II, there were several independence movements on the subcontinent. One of these, the Muslim League headed by Muhamad Ali Jinnah, represented the interests of the Islamic minority, while the interests of the Hindu majority were represented by the Indian Congress, headed by Mohandas Gandhi. Between the world wars, the activism was sufficient to force the British to pass the Government of India Act of 1935, promising independence for the subcontinent. That process was interrupted by the outbreak and conduct of World War II. After the war, it would return and have to be faced.

Subdividing the Subcontinent

After World War II ended, a high-level British delegation under the leadership of British war hero Lord Mountbatten was dispatched to the Indian subcontinent. Its purpose was to subdivide what had been a single colonial unit (the *Raj*) into independent units that represented some reasonable form of self-determination along ethnic and communal lines. The problem was that the subcontinent before (and after) colonialism is an incredibly diverse physical and political place, made up of numerous nationalities and religions that have, through history, been more or less antithetical to one another. To get some feel of the extent of this diversity, 562 "princely states" had to decide their political destiny for partition to be complete.

The basic form of partition was conceptually simple enough. The subcontinent would be divided into a predominantly Muslim state (Pakistan) and a Hindu state (India). The basic criterion for drawing the map between the two would be territorial: Areas that were overwhelmingly Muslim would become part of Pakistan, and predominantly Hindu areas would accede to India. For a variety of ethnic, cultural, religious, and historical reasons, such a basic subdivision was both necessary and sensible.

No political boundary line could perfectly partition the two groups, and as a result, at independence several million Muslims were left in India and vice versa, causing a panicked migration across the borders that remains the largest such event in human history (most of this occurred in the Punjab region of western India and West Pakistan) and resulted in high levels of tension and fighting there as populations migrated from one side of the frontier to the other. In addition, the principle of territorial majority also meant that the Muslim state would be divided into two physically distant parts of Pakistan, the Punjabi-dominated West Pakistan and Bengali-majority East Pakistan separated by 1,000 miles of Indian territory. In 1971, East Pakistan splintered away from Pakistan to form the independent country of Bangladesh.

The princely states were given two choices. They could accede either to India or to Pakistan; they could not choose independence. Further, states that were not predominantly Muslim would become part of India. Based on religion and other factors, most had little difficulty reaching a decision under what was known as the Transfer of Power. In the vast majority of cases, accession to one state or another was accomplished either through popular vote or by an act of accession by the government of the princely states and India or Pakistan. The Transfer of Power guidelines did not specify which method would be used.

The accession process went well for all areas except Jammu and Kashmir, which, along with the states of Janagadh and Hyderabad, had not decided their fate when the Transfer of Power took place on August 15, 1947. All three states eventually became part of India over the protests of Pakistan; of the three, Kashmir has remained the major point of contention since 1947.

The situation in Kashmir was the mirror image of Jungadh in the Punjabi western part of the subcontinent. In Jungadh, 80 percent of the population was Hindu, but the region's ruler was a Muslim. At the insistence of the Indian government, the issue of accession was submitted to a plebiscite, and the population voted overwhelming to become part of India. This line of action would not provide a precedent when it came time to decide the political fate of Kashmir.

In Kashmir, the demographics and geopolitics were reversed: About three-quarters of the population of four million in 1947 were Muslims, whereas the ruler of the state was a Hindu, Maharajah Sir Hari Singh. The maharajah's instinct was to press for independence, but this option was unacceptable to any of the other parties. In 1947, Muslim "freedom fighters" invaded Kashmir to force union with Pakistan, and the fighting became part of the general war on the subcontinent between India and Pakistan that broke out in October of that year. Unwilling to submit the fate of Kashmir to a referendum he knew he would lose, the maharajah reluctantly acceded to joining India in 1948. The state of Pakistan refused to recognize the accession and demanded a referendum that was authorized by the United Nations in 1949. The Indian government refused to hold the referendum, maintaining Kashmir had legally become part of India by intergovernmental agreement. The basis for the ongoing dispute was established by this Indian action.

The Bases of Dispute

On the face of it, the case for allowing Kashmir to be a part of Pakistan rather than part of India would appear to be a strong one. Writing in 1991, Alastair Lamb summarizes these bases of the Pakistani claim to Kashmir: "First, the State of Jammu and Kashmir was a region with an overwhelming Muslim majority contiguous to the Muslim majority region of the Punjab, which became part of Pakistan. Second, the economy . . . was bound up in what was to become Pakistan. Its best communication with the outside world lay through Pakistan, and this was the route taken by the bulk of its exports. Third, the waters of the Indus, Jhelum, and Chenab [Rivers], all of which flowed through Jammu and Kashmir territory, were essential for the prosperity of the agricultural life of Pakistan" (p. 105).

These reasons are emotional, pragmatic, and geopolitical. Clearly, the desire to have coreligionists united with their religious brethren is a deeply emotional question that has helped fuel continued Muslim activism over the decades of the conflict and that formed the original rationale for partition. Particularly given that India insisted on popular self-determination in other cases in which Hindus were in the majority, it contributes to the ongoing sense of distrust and hatred between the people of the country and the Pakistanis that, among other things, precluded a meeting between heads of states of India and Pakistan between 1947, when partition occurred, and 2000, when meetings that are ongoing took place. The pragmatic, economic argument, of course, has been overcome with time, as the commercial patterns that formed its base in the 1940s have been supplanted with a reorientation of the Kashmiri economy toward India.

Although it is less often emphasized, the geopolitical argument about the Indus rivers, which contains an emotional element as well, may be the most sustaining part of the Pakistani contention other than religious kinship. The basis of this importance is the enormous reliance on the waters from these rivers to sustain Pakistani agriculture, which depends on them for irrigation.

As the accompanying map shows, essentially all the river water flowing into Pakistan has its source in the mountains of Kashmir. Of a total of six rivers, three (the Indus, Jhelum, and Chenab, collectively known as the western rivers) flow directly from Kashmir to Pakistan, while the other three (known as the eastern rivers) flow from Kashmir into the Indian state of Rajasthan, and then into Pakistan. Prior to the partition of the subcontinent, the Indus river system had formed part of the oldest irrigation system in the world, providing irrigation waters for what would become Pakistan and India. When the Mountbatten mission provided its final plan for partition, the boundary line cut through

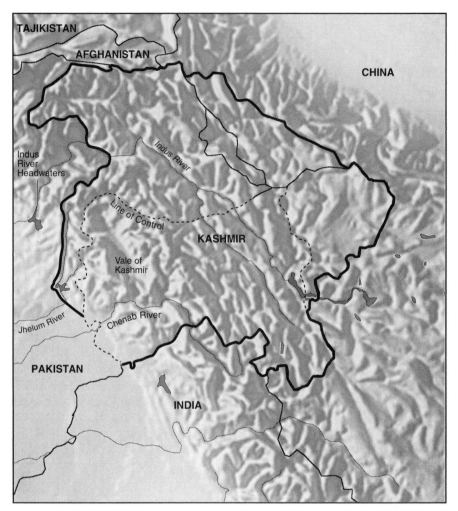

Map 12.1 Map of Kashmir

the irrigation system, leaving ambiguous which states would continue to have access to the waters.

The crisis that brought home to Pakistan how vital control of the headwaters of the rivers in Kashmir was occurred in the spring of 1948. The Indian government, arguing it needed the extra water to sustain Hindu immigrants who had fled from Pakistan into Rajasthan, cut the flow of the eastern rivers for six weeks at a critical period just prior to harvest, nearly ruining the crops in Pakistan that relied on the rivers. Although the flow was restored after international intermediation, a Pakistani government already suspicious of Indian intentions took the lesson to heart that access to the water could never be interrupted again.

The issue is clearly an emotional one for the Pakistanis as well. Pakistan's need for water from the rivers is undeniable; most of the Punjab region of Pakistan (West Pakistan) is very arid, with an average annual rainfall in the 10–15 inches per year range (about the same as eastern Colorado), and a good deal of that falls in spate during the monsoon season. Without a reliable source of irrigation water during the year, much of Pakistani agriculture is at peril. The geopolitics of Pakistani survival and prosperity are clearly at work.

Recognizing this problem and attempting to solve it, the International Bank for Reconstruction and Development (IBRD or World Bank) helped India and Pakistan negotiate the Indus Waters Treaty of 1960. The provisions of the agreement included dividing claims to the waters so that India received all the water from the eastern rivers (a fraction of the total flow), whereas Pakistan got all the water from the western rivers. Hydroelectric dams were built in Kashmir to create reservoirs that would allow control of the flow of the rivers into Pakistan, and canals were built to redirect water from the western rivers to irrigate parts of Pakistan formerly supplied by water from the eastern rivers.

This agreement would seem to have solved the water problem, but it has not. Because the headwaters of the western rivers continue to rise in Indian-controlled Kashmir, the Pakistanis continue to worry about another interruption and thus insist on de facto control of those headwaters by Azad Kashmir (Free Kashmir) rebels. Their position is more emotional than rational in this regard because the geography of the mountains through which the waters flows makes it physically impossible to divert any of the water into India without boring tunnels through the mountains to redirect the flow, and such a diversion goes well beyond Indian physical or financial assets.

The Indian position on Kashmir is more straightforward. As far as India is concerned, there is no conflict over the status of Kashmir, because that was settled in 1948 with Kashmir's accession into India. Thus, the fracas that flares from time to time is strictly an internal matter, although one that is aggravated by what they see as illegal Pakistani interference in support of "rebels" and pro-independence freedom fighters or terrorists (depending on what side one is on) that India considers as agents of Islamabad.

The Indian position has a geopolitical side as well. Part of their reason for insisting on continuing control of Kashmir is based in geography. Located as it is literally as the "cap" of India, Kashmir also sits astride historic invasion routes into India, notably from China (which occupies a small part of Kashmir known as Aksai Chin). A Kashmir totally controlled by a Pakistan in official or informal alignment with China poses a very real military threat to India. At the same time, the idea of Kashmir breaking away from India has a precedent value for India, as it does for China over Tibet. Although the fear is not as great as it once was, the government of India worries that a breakaway by Kashmir could encourage other similarly inclined areas to follow its lead.

STATUS OF THE PROBLEM

The dispute over Kashmir sporadically breaks out into more or less intense violence, with even the "peaceful" interludes marked by some intercommunal fighting and terrorist attacks. Kashmir was a major object of the first war fought between the two countries shortly after independence was granted in 1947, a conflict that ended on January 1,

1948, with a United Nations mandate to hold a plebiscite that never, in fact, occurred, as already noted. In 1965, war broke out again between India and Pakistan at a barren area along the border between West Pakistan and India known as the Rann of Kutch; initial Pakistani success in that encounter emboldened them to try unsuccessfully to seize Kashmir. In 1971, war broke out again, and although its major focus was the secession of East Pakistan to form Bangladesh, much of the tension during the conflict centered on Kashmir as a potential second front in that war. Nuclear saber rattling accompanied returned violence in 2001.

Kashmir has thus been a major focus in each of the three full-scale wars fought between the two subcontinental powers since their independence. A truce line drawn after the war in 1971 gave de facto control over portions of western Kashmir to the Pakistanis and their Kashmiri brethren, thereby creating a lull in the violence for a time. Kashmiri dissidents under the banner of Azad ("Free") Kashmir resumed the armed struggle in 1988, and regular Indian and Pakistani units began exchanging fire in 1990. Although violence was suspended in summer 2000 as part of the first-ever meeting between the heads of state of the two countries, tensions remain high and terrorist attacks continued to be reported into 2001. Inconclusive talks have continued to the present, and there has been some limited cooperation, as in coordinated relief efforts after the massive October 2005 earthquake struck in parts of Pakistan-controlled Kashmir.

The potential for resumed fighting remains. It is not, for instance, entirely clear what the relationship is between the Pakistani government and Azad Kashmir, and hence the degree to which the Pakistanis can control the actions of their "allies." If Indian descriptions of that relationship are to be believed, Azad Kashmir is no more than a puppet organization of the Pakistanis, who recruit, equip, train, and even provide some of the "freedom fighters" that make up the force. Pakistan, of course, vehemently denies these charges, maintaining the rebels are an independent body seeking independence for Kashmir from India and long-term union with Pakistan.

Part of the problem is that the status quo, while minimally acceptable, pleases neither side. The "line of control" or truce line established in 1971 provides de facto Pakistani control over most of the western portion of Kashmir, giving them (through Azad Kashmir) physical possession of the headwaters (or sources) of the western rivers of the Indus system. As long as Kashmir remains legally a part of India, however, that possession is not as firm as Pakistan would like, given the dependency Pakistan has on the irrigation waters from the river system for its survival. Moreover, some of the hydroelectric dams created by the settlement of the Indus Waters Treaty to provide electricity and to store monsoon rains for later use are also in the zone. India, on the other hand, maintains physical control of the mountainous regions and thus the geopolitically important passes along its border with China. The fact that part of its sovereign territory is effectively outside its sovereign control is annoying to the Indian national ego and creates the motivation to alter the line of control.

The issue of Kashmir was revived in international consciousness by the public display of nuclear weapons capability by India and Pakistan in 1998. On May 11 and 13, India conducted five underground nuclear tests in the desert of Rajasthan, announcing the reason for the tests was growing concern about the Chinese nuclear threat and alleged nuclear cooperation between China and Pakistan. On May 28, Pakistan also exploded five devices underground at the Chagai test site.

One interesting aspect of the Kashmir dispute and its nuclear extension is the impotence of the United States to affect the situation one way or the other. A hallmark of the post–Cold War 1990s was American global activism in brokering peaceful settlements of international disputes, often through the personal efforts of President Clinton. The most notable instances of this success were in negotiating agreements on aspects of the Arab-Israeli conflict (not including Palestine) and in Northern Ireland.

The United States has been notably unsuccessful in influencing events on the subcontinent. The United States was, for instance, not even informed ahead of time about the nuclear tests by either India or Pakistan (partly because both countries knew the United States would object), and American intelligence was apparently caught completely off guard and failed to predict the explosions. When Clinton visited the subcontinent in April 2000, going first to India and then to Pakistan, he was largely unsuccessful in moving the peace process along. Besides "photo ops" in front of the Taj Mahal and other Indian sites, he made little headway with the Indian leadership on the nuclear weapons question and was virtually given the cold shoulder by the leaders of Pakistan. Given the centrality of the United States in other parts of the world, this void means, in K. Shankar Bajpai's words in *Foreign Affairs,* "there are no positive pressures whatsoever in Indo-Pakistani relations."

PROSPECTS FOR RESOLUTION

Why has the conflict over Kashmir been allowed to fester for over a half century? One possible explanation is that the issues involved are so intractable and the possible outcomes so emotionally charged that none is possible, a situation not unlike the Palestinian question in the Middle East. Another possibility is that resolution of the matter is insufficiently important for the parties to make the necessary sacrifices to achieve closure. Yet a third possibility is that there has been no outside force that has the level of interests or leverage involved to mount an effective effort to mediate the differences. Finally, the situation may be troublesome and the lack of resolution discomfiting, but the status quo may be less unacceptable than the alternatives.

The Problem Reformulated

Until 1998, some combination of intractability, insufficient local interest or outside interest or leverage or lack of urgency explained why the dispute was not resolved. But things have changed. Most notably, the explosion of nuclear weapons has added Kashmir to the list of conflicts in the world over which a nuclear war might begin. Whether the public demonstration of nuclear capability by the two major regional powers has made any war between them more or less likely is an open question. What that demonstration *does* mean is that nuclear war between them is now physically possible. The aspect of the Indo-Pakistani relationship that has most often resulted in war has been Kashmir; the next battle over Kashmir could become far more deadly, both to the principals and the international system as a whole.

Other things have changes as well. India has emerged as a global economic power in the last decade (see Chapter 8), and its prosperity and the growth of its international stature stand in sharp contrast to neighboring Pakistan. The geopolitics of the subcontinent have tilted sharply in India's favor. The violent showdown of 2001 also provided both with a harbinger of conflict escalating, possibly to include nuclear exchange, a sobering prospect for each. The specter has helped create a state-to-state dialogue between Pakistani president Musharaff and Indian prime minister Singh that could break the roadblock on a number of issues, including Kashmir. Moreover, the Kashmir earthquake of October 2005 created an enormous international humanitarian relief effort in that part of Pakistan-controlled Kashmir where the epicenter was located, including some limited Indian-Pakistani cooperation (barriers along the Line of Control were opened at five points to allow relief workers to traverse from Indian to Pakistani-controlled areas).

The situation seems more conducive to outside mediation than it has since 1947, but little progress has been made. One reason may be that international mediation efforts have been on the wane in recent years. Here the equation of Kashmir with Palestine suggests a negative precedent: The failure of American-led efforts to resolve the Palestine imbroglio may have soured sentiments regarding similar efforts elsewhere. Moreover, Kashmir has been pushed down the list of international concerns by responses to 9/11 in the form of the war on terror. Both India and Pakistan have sought to portray themselves as good warriors on terrorism, thus making it hard to depict the conflict as a theater of the war on terror. As long as the criteria for international activism begins with the terrorism problem, Kashmir will stay in the wings of international concern.

What commends Kashmir to serious consideration is the uncertainty created by nuclear weapons. The fact is that nuclear weapons have never been used in war when both sides possessed them and could use them against their enemies. Over the years of the nuclear age, we have devised "rational" constructs about how countries should act in different nuclear situations, but given our total lack of experience in the circumstances surrounding the nuclear escalation process, they remain no more than elaborate, articulate speculations.

That means the answer to the question, "what happens to the rest of the world if India and Pakistan engage in a nuclear exchange during the next Kashmir crisis?" must be "there is no way to know." Rationally and analytically, the prospect of escalation to the system as a whole would seem to be fairly remote; what the major—including nuclear—powers *probably* would do would be to marshal as much international pressure as possible to end the nuclear fighting at as low a level of death and suffering as possible. That would make sense, if sensibility were to prevail.

But we do not know that would happen. Everyone might act calmly and rationally, or they might not. What we *do* know for certain is that the most certain way to avoid finding out the answer is to avoid there being another war over Kashmir that could escalate to nuclear exchange. Thus, the search for a suitable option to resolve the dispute takes on added meaning when the "new teeth" are present.

There is yet another possible effect that nuclearization of the subcontinent could have on the Kashmir issue. It is also possible to argue that the overt possession of nuclear weapons will have a calming, sobering, and even stabilizing effect on both India and

Pakistan. Both countries are now fully aware that *any* war in which they might face one another is a potential nuclear exchange with incalculable consequences for both of them. This realization forces either side to include in its decision process the question of whether any objectives in any contemplated conflict are worth the risk of nuclear escalation, no matter how small that risk might appear to be in any given situation. It might or might not have much or any impact in any particular encounter, but it is also true that no two states both of which possess nuclear weapons have ever fought one another. That may be the result of coincidence rather than of the weapons. But it is nonetheless true and can lead to the conclusion that nuclear weapons will stabilize rather than destabilize the subcontinent in the future. Ongoing negotiations between the two sides on the issues that divide them at least suggests some salience to this possibility.

Options for Resolution

The possibility that another war over Kashmir could escalate to a nuclear exchange may make resolution a more important priority although, as noted above, it may also make a renewed war less likely, since both sides presumably recognize what could happen now and may avoid actions with escalatory potential. Regardless of which of these arguments one makes, the clearest way to avoid finding out if Kashmir has nuclear dynamics is to settle the problem in such a manner that the reversion to war is no longer a real prospect—if it is possible to find such a solution acceptable to the parties.

A variety of schemes for settling the problem have been put forward over time. Not all have been formal proposals, nor have any of them enjoyed universal support. What has bedeviled all the proposals is that none have, to date, been acceptable to the three principal groups to the conflict: the Indians, the Pakistanis, and the Kashmiris. The crux of the difficulty is that each interested party sees the outcomes in absolute and mutually exclusive terms, as a kind of zero-sum game in which one side's gains are inevitably the other side's losses. The Indians optimally want to reassert their sovereign authority over all of Kashmir. The Pakistanis and Kashmiris want that sovereignty reversed, either by accession of Kashmir to Pakistan (the Pakistani preference) or independence for Kashmir (the preference of at least some Kashmiris). None of these outcomes has been acceptable to the others.

The proposals for settling the dispute have generally followed these preferred outcomes. In *The Crisis in Kashmir,* Sumit Ganguly has summarized seven proposals, three of which would reinforce India's continued claim of sovereign control, two of which represent compromises in which each side receives some but not all of what it wants, and two of which support the Pakistani/Kashmiri desire to remove Indian sovereignty. As Ganguly points out in a 2006 *Foreign Affairs* article, it has so far proved impossible to impose any solution: "[N]either war nor negotiations has brought the issue any closer to resolution, and there has been no significant change in the territory's status since the two sides first exchanged shots nearly 60 years ago." In addition, we will explore an eighth outcome, which is a more or less permanent stalemate that results in continuation of the status quo.

The Pro-Indian Options. The three pro-Indian options involve changing the political composition of Kashmir so that some semblance of pro-Indian legitimate control can be manifested. One possibility, which violates current Indian law and thus cannot be formally advocated, is called *ethnic flooding:* to encourage massive Indian immigration into Kashmir to tip the population balance to the Indians, thereby allowing something like a plebiscite in which the new Indian majority might prevail and legitimize Kashmir's status as an Indian state. Seventy percent of the seven million current citizens of Kashmir are Muslim, so this would require a very large influx of people who would patently not be welcomed by the current citizenry. Implementation of the strategy would require amendment of the Indian constitution, a provision of which (Article 370) prohibits, among other things, the sale of immovable properties in Kashmir to non-Kashmiris. Moreover, it is impossible to imagine that organizations like the Jammu Kashmir Liberation Front (JKLF), which seeks independence for the state, would sit idly by while the population flood occurred.

The other two pro-Indian solutions involve military actions, the purpose of which would be to destroy the armed resistance to Indian rule. Each strategy is based on a precedent that India has employed elsewhere in the country to quell dissent, although the situations from which the precedents derive are arguably too different to be applicable. Also, it is hard to imagine that Pakistan would accede to the reduction and destruction of groups with which it has had, at a minimum, close relations for a half century. Military solutions almost certainly increase the risk of more general war on the subcontinent, with all the dangers that might entail.

One military solution is the *mailed-fist strategy.* This option, which is the most bellicose of any, has not received any formal endorsement within the Indian political system. The idea, based on a strategy used earlier to pacify the Punjab, would require greatly increased military action against the dissidents, the purpose of which would be to crush the armed resistance completely, as was done to the Sikhs in the Punjab. With the rebels defeated and removed from the scene, the idea is that elections could be held that would hopefully endorse Indian hegemony. History suggests that Kashmiri resistance to such a campaign would be considerably greater than that which occurred in the Punjab, making the possibility of success more problematical.

The other military solution, applied in India's northwestern region in the 1960s and 1970s, is a *wear-down strategy* of attrition. The idea in this case is that a patient strategy of military pressure may literally wear down the dissident Kashmiris by using "superior military might," according to Bajpai, to the point that they simply tire of the contest and fade away. This suggestion runs in the face of a long-term, tenacious opposition within Kashmir that has shown considerable resilience over a long period of time.

Compromises. As in any situation in which all parties have strong claims to the object at hand, compromise is always an attractive possibility, especially if a compromise can be arranged whereby each party can argue that they prevailed. This is especially the case in an emotionally charged situation in which almost any concession will be viewed by some partisans as an unacceptable sellout of a deeply held preference. Finding a compromise with which all feel they can live has proved elusive to this point.

Two ideas, one territorial and one jurisdictional, have been put forward. The territorial solution involves *cessation of the Vale of Kashmir to Pakistan.* This region is in the western part of Kashmir, thus contiguous to Pakistan, and it is also the region through which the rivers flow (the Jhelum in particular traverses the valley). The tradeoff would be Pakistan's relinquishing claims to other parts of Kashmir, and notably the mountainous areas so important to Indian security. It is a solution with conceptual ties to Israel relinquishing the West Bank and Gaza as part of the price of peace with the Palestinians. The problem is that it is politically unacceptable.

There are several objections to this compromise raised by the various parties. First, it is argued that formally ceding *any* part of Kashmir to Pakistan after a half century of resistance to just such an outcome would be political suicide for any Indian government that might suggest it. Doing so might be interpreted in Islamabad as a sign of Indian weakness, which was a perception that many Indians believed contributed to Pakistani aggression into Kashmir in 1965. Further, the concession might embolden Pakistan to try to annex all of Kashmir. The solution would also be unacceptable to the JKLF, which will accept nothing less than total independence for the province. There is also the objection that the concession would be morally unacceptable for India because it would involve abandonment of pro-Indian citizens who are residents in the valley.

The other proposed compromise, little more than a fuzzy suggestion at this point, is *shared sovereignty*. The basic idea here would be somehow to come up with a scheme whereby India and Pakistan would jointly control Kashmir, presumably with some participation by the Kashmiris themselves. Details of how this would work—for instance, would there be parts of the country administered by one country and parts by the other?—have not been talked through, and it is difficult to imagine how two countries with as long and bitter a relationship of animosity could suddenly agree to the extraordinary levels of cooperation that any form of joint administration would require. There is also the question of whether Kashmiri separatists would agree to anything less than full autonomy.

Pro-Pakistani Solutions.   The last two solutions favor Pakistan or Kashmir. One of these is to hold a *plebiscite* to let the Kashmiris decide their own fate. This was, of course, the solution favored by the United Nations in 1948, and it has been endorsed in subsequent UN resolutions as well. The Pakistanis would clearly be most enthused about this option, particularly if the options for voters were limited to those available under the Transfer of Power guidelines crafted in 1948: union with Pakistan or union with India. The problem is that independence for Kashmir has entered the discussion and would be advocated by a large number of natives of Kashmir (and probably opposed by Pakistan). Short of a campaign of ethnic flooding that preceded a vote, the Indians would oppose any form of plebiscite: Regardless of whether the voters favored union with Pakistan or independence, they would clearly vote for disunion with India.

The final option is *Kashmiri independence*. It is opposed by everyone except those Kashmiris who want an independent state. The Indians and Pakistanis oppose the creation of such a state for geopolitical reasons: India would lose control of strategically vital territory in the north of Kashmir, and Pakistan would lose control of the equally vital headwaters of the Indus rivers. In addition, both countries have other regions whose continuing desire to remain part of India or Pakistan is suspect. The creation of an independent state of Kashmir could only serve as an encouraging precedent for separatists elsewhere on the subcontinent. Even neighboring China joins the chorus on this point, because the success of Kashmir's independence movement might also encourage similar sentiments in Tibet.

Formalized Stalemate. None of these solutions seem especially promising, and it may be that the situation is so intractable and the unwillingness of the parties to compromise so deeply held that no mutually acceptable outcome is possible. Because the imposition of a solution by military force is largely ruled out by the nuclear possibility, Kashmir may be a problem that cannot be solved but instead only managed in a way least objectionable to most.

The triangular relationship between the Kashmiris, Pakistanis, and Indians over the political control of Kashmir may be similar. All three sides have irreconcilable positions about who should be sovereign, and none is willing to compromise its preferred outcome. Even if the Kashmiri separatists and Pakistan could somehow reach agreement (the only possible compromise), the Indians would disapprove and block implementation.

Thus, managing or even institutionalizing a perpetual stalemate based on the status quo established in 1971 may be the only attainable solution. Although de facto control of the headwaters provides less security for Pakistan than sovereign control, it is better than Indian control. India wants the whole issue to go away, but it will not and at least they control the invasion routes. Ganguly (2006) suggests such a solution. "For an accord to be viable, it would need to address the growing grievances of the Kashmiri Muslims in Indian-controlled Kashmir without granting them territorial sovereignty. . . . It would have to move toward making the Line of Control a permanent international border while allowing contacts between communities across the divide." The Kashmiri separatists, who are incapable of seizing independence, at least do not have their hopes snuffed out altogether. It is by no means the best solution; but it may be the best *possible* solution.

CONCLUSION

Two things have change about the Kashmir situation since the latter 1990s: the nuclearization of the subcontinent in 1998 and the opening of discussions between the Indians and Pakistanis on a variety of matters dividing them, including Kashmir, in 2002, talks that continue to be held. The two phenomena are related. The "new teeth" added to the relationship have dampened any bellicose sentiments both sides hold due to the sobering possibility of escalation to nuclear war. That prospect, in turn, has produced the realization that those disagreements most likely to lead to war need to be contained or resolved. Kashmir heads that list, and while resolution remains as elusive as ever, at least the two sides are talking.

Despite ongoing talks and symbolic events like a 2003 cricket match between the Indian and Pakistani national teams and limited cooperation in responding to the 2005 earthquake, the situation continues to be intractable. Each side has distinct positions that have survived for nearly sixty-five years. The Indian accession of 1948 was of shaky legality and was and continues to be condemned by the United Nations as a rather clear violation of the principle of self-determination that was supposed to dictate the political affiliation of the princely states at the time of partition. Still, accession to India remains a fact.

Positions have hardened, and circumstances have changed. The longer Kashmir has been part of India, the more Indians think of it as Indian territory as a result; ceding Kashmir (or even a part of it) to Kashmir would be a politically heinous crime on the order of giving New Mexico back to Mexico. No Indian politician or government could survive such an event. Moreover, the transfer might be seen as an act of weakness by the hated Pakistanis, and if the territory ceded included the passes between India and China, could be a geopolitical disaster. Any compromise by India would require an enormous act of political courage by any Indian politician proposing it.

The Pakistani position is equally hardened. Pakistan has made itself the principal advocate of Muslim Kashmiris for over a half century and is no more likely to abandon that position than are the Indians to turn their backs on Kashmir's Hindu minority. Politically, the Pakistanis have less to lose by movement toward a settlement, because any solution is likely to come at physical Indian expense (giving away sovereign control over some of Kashmir), which is a net gain for Pakistan. As long as pro-Pakistani elements control the regions of Kashmir that control access to water, the status quo is tolerable if not optimal. The only outcome (other than the reassertion of Indian hegemony over all of Kashmir) that could cause Pakistan potentially to suffer would be independence for Kashmir.

The independence movement is one important way things have changed in the Kashmir situation. As stated earlier, independence for the princely states was ruled out as an option by the British when the subcontinent was divided. It is still opposed by all parties except the Kashmiri separatists, notably the JKLF. Any settlement that does not give at least some consideration to separatist demands may well be resisted violently within Kashmir itself by those who see Kashmiri independence as the only acceptable outcome.

Finally, there is the matter of outside efforts to achieve a lasting peace in the region. Such efforts were minimal during the Cold War, from a combination of lack of interest and of embroiling the area as yet another Cold War battleground. Cold War reluctance has given way to concern with the possibility of nuclear war on the subcontinent. Is the need to remove Kashmir from the list of potential nuclear battlegrounds sufficiently great to make an attempt to mediate the dispute more attractive than it has been in the past? Does the international effort in Afghanistan make the region more geopolitically important than before?

There is precedent for an international effort about Kashmir, the Indus Waters Treaty of 1960. In that instance, the principal outside mediator was the World Bank, which negotiated a division of the waters that provided India with secure access to the waters of the eastern Indus rivers to irrigate Rajasthan, and Pakistan with control of all the western rivers, including diverting some of that flow to irrigate areas previously watered by the eastern rivers. Hydroelectric and storage dams to produce power and regulate the flow of the rivers were an added incentive.

Would a parallel effort work to settle the dispute in Kashmir? If so, who would lead it? As noted at the beginning, American lack of clout in the region is one of the distinguishing characteristics of the conflict. Should the lead role go to some other state, such as the old colonial power, Great Britain? Is there enough interest in settling the problem to produce the funding for some kind of solution, some way to escape the current zero-sum mentality? Ganguly (2006) argues that outside involvement is critical: "Without some form of subtle but firm outside intervention, such a settlement is unlikely." Thus, is there some mutually acceptable solution that will still the guns at the top of the world?

STUDY/DISCUSSION QUESTIONS

1. There are four possible long-term outcomes to the crisis in Kashmir: continued union with India, annexation to Pakistan, partition between India and Pakistan, or Kashmir independence. Compare and contrast each. As an outsider with no vested interest in the outcome, which would you recommend?

2. The problem with each possible outcome is the objection that other interested parties have to each solution. Using the four options in Question 1, to whom is each outcome unacceptable? Weigh the objections. Which have the most and least merit?

3. Assume the role of an outside mediator. What would be the position on settling the dispute from which you would begin negotiations? What concessions would you have to be prepared to make to reach a compromise solution? What would be the costs of a solution?

4. Think of yourself as an outsider viewing the problem. How much difference does the possession of nuclear weapons by India and Pakistan make to you? Does the addition of nuclear weapons create enough interest to become involved? If, as is likely, a settlement will require lubrication with outside funds, how much is a settlement worth?

5. The other possibility is that nuclear weapons actually stabilize the situation by making both sides realize the consequences of escalation. Defend and critique the ideas that nuclear weapons make negotiating a settlement more and less important to the subcontinent and the international system at large.

6. Eight potential solutions were suggested as possibilities for solving the crisis over Kashmir. Rate them by two criteria: desirability and practicality, for each party. Is there any basis for optimism? Does perpetual stalemate emerge as the least objectionable solution?

7. Is there any way to create a positive-sum atmosphere in the Kashmir conflict that parallels the Indus Waters Treaty in 1960 and allows agreement to be reached?

READING/RESEARCH MATERIAL

Bajpai, K. Shankar. "Untangling India and Pakistan." *Foreign Affairs* 82, 3 (May/June 2003), 112–126.

Ganguly, Sumit. *The Crisis in Kashmir: Portents of War, Hopes of Peace.* New York: Cambridge University Press, 1997.

———. "Will Kashmir Stop India's Rise?" *Foreign Affairs* 85, 4 (July/August 2006), 45–56.

Habibullah, Wajahat. "The Political Economy of the Kashmir Conflict: Opportunities for Economic Peacebuilding and for U.S. Policy." Special Report No. 121. Washington, DC: United States Insitute for Peace, June 2004.

Jha, Prem Shankar. *Kashmir 1947: Rival Versions of History*. New Delhi, India: Oxford University Press, 1996.

Krasner, D. Stephen. *Sovereignty: Organized Hypocrisy*. Princeton, NJ: Princeton University Press, 1999 (see especially Jose Joffe, "Rethinking the Nation-State").

Lamb, Alastair. *Kashmir: A Disputed Legacy, 1846–1990*. Hertingfordbury, Hertfordshire, UK: Roxford Books, 1991.

Schofield, Victoria. *Kashmir in the Crossfire*. London, UK: I. B. Tauris and Co., Ltd., 1996.

Widman, Stan. *Kashmir in Perspective: Democracy and Violent Separation in India*. London: Routledge, 2002.

Wirsing, Robert G. *Kashmir in the Shadow of War: Regional Rivalries in a Nuclear Age*. Armonk, NY: M. E. Sharpe, 2004.

WEB SITES

Oldest and most widely circulated newspaper of Kashmir

   The *Kashmir Times* at http://www.kashmirtimes.com

Annotated, current record of electronically distributed sources on Kashmir

   Kashmir Virtual Library at http://www.clas.ufl.edu/users/gthrusby/kashmir

Views on the situation from Pakistan

   Islamic Republic of Pakistan: Kashmir at http://www.pak.gov.pk/public/kashmir

Views on situation from Kashmir government, India

   Jammu and Kashmir at http://jammukashmir.nic.in

Organization publicizing Kashmir's desire for independence

   Kashmiri American Council at http://www.kashmiri.com

Sociocultural, political events, and current affairs on Kashmir

   Kashmirnet at http://www.kashmir.co.uk

Overview of the 2005 Kashmir earthquake

   http://en.wikipedia.org/wikikashmir_earthquake

The CIA Factbook

   www.us.gov/cia

PART V

Transnational Issues

The book concludes with a discussion of a relatively recent emphasis in international relations, something called transnational issues (technically, they are transstate or trans-sovereign issues because it is states that deal with them, but the term *transnational* has become conventional in describing them). These issues are defined as problems that transcend international borders in ways over which governments of individual states have little control and that generally cannot be solved by the actions of individual states working alone.

In most of the literature, the discussion of transnational issues focuses on a few familiar problems such as various environmental difficulties, the human condition (human rights or the rights of certain groups of people), and man-made problems like drugs, to name some of the most obvious. In an attempt to broaden and extend the discussion, this part addresses three different areas that meet the criterion of transnational issues or which attempt to address transnational issues that are not so commonly found in the literature, as well as the problem of international terror.

Chapter 13, "Warm and Getting Warmer," examines one of the most serious and controversial transnational issues, global warming and efforts to deal with it. The issue is controversial in two ways not dissimilar to the issue of free trade. One controversy surrounds the international effort to control global warming and has centered on the Kyoto Protocol of 1997. The other controversy surrounds the nature and severity of the problem and thus what needs (or does not need) to be done about it. The two come together around the question of whether the Kyoto Protocol is needed.

The second chapter in the section, Chapter 14, "Let Them Drink Oil," looks at the transnational issue of resource scarcity in the new century. The problem is not new—imbalances of, access to, and control of scarce resources are an ancient problem. In the contemporary period, two resources dominate that concern—water and petroleum—and both have strong connections to the Middle East and adjacent areas. After exploring the general, interrelated nature of this problem (from which the title is derived), the study looks at two specific cases in which water and petroleum have special geopolitical importance and implications.

Chapter 15, "Worse Than the Bubonic Plague," is a case study of the AIDS pandemic in Africa. Beyond the reiteration of the enormous social and physical consequences of the problem (projections suggest more people will die from AIDS than perished in the bubonic plague of the Middle Ages), local and world attention (or inattention) will be presented as a model for how the international system deals with the problem that "disease knows no frontiers" (the motto of the World Health Organization), with particular emphasis on the possibility of an avian flu virus epidemic.

Finally, Chapter 16, "Beyond September 11, 2001," looks at the problem of global terrorism six years after the attacks of 9/11. The case will concentrate on how the terrorist problem has changed and grown since 2001, what creates and motivates terrorists, and what can be done about the problem in the future, including suggestions for a comprehensive strategy for what the Bush administration calls the Global War on Terrorism (GWOT).

CHAPTER THIRTEEN

Warm and Getting Warmer

GLOBAL WARMING AND THE FATE OF THE KYOTO PROTOCOL

PRÉCIS

Global warming represents one of the clearest, yet most controversial, transnational issues. It is clearly a transnational issue because it is clearly a problem that cannot be solved by the individual efforts of states, but must be done collectively if it is to be done successfully at all. It is controversial because there is substantial disagreement both about the nature and severity of the problem and over the structure and content of proposed solutions to climate change that is the clear byproduct of global warming.

This case study looks at the problem from two related vantage points that are similar in structure to the case on free trade in Chapter 7. The first vantage point is an examination of the controversial process surrounding international efforts to deal with global warming, the lightning rod for which has been the Kyoto Protocol of 1997 and attempts to implement that treaty (which have largely focused on the United States as a prime opponent of the initiative since its 2001 withdrawal from the protocol). The second is on the nature and extent of the problem and thus what does and does not require controlling. The two emphases are related because the nature of the problem has a clear relationship to the kinds and extent of remedies that are proposed for it.

The issue of global warming—the extent to which the climate of the Earth is gradually increasing in temperature due to human actions or natural processes—is one of the most controversial, divisive, and yet consequential problems facing international relations in the twenty-first century. No one, of course, favors a gradual or precipitous change in global climate because the consequences could be catastrophic. Having said that, amateurs and experts, some disinterested, some self-interested, disagree on almost everything about the phenomenon. Some question whether global warming exists at all, whereas others predict apocryphal consequences unless drastic measures are taken to curb the contributors to warming (mostly the burning of fossil fuels in support of a broad variety of human activities). There are significant differences on the parameters of the problem (exactly what will be affected and how much), and on the quality of the science underlying claims on either side (especially when extrapolations are made far into the future).

Regardless of how serious the problem is, global warming is clearly a classic, full-blown transnational issue. As Eileen Claussen and Lisa McNeilly put it, "Climate change is a global problem that demands a global solution because emissions from one country can impact the climate in all other countries." Global warming, in other words, will be curbed internationally or not at all.

The underlying dynamic, if not its seriousness, can be easily stated. Global warming is the direct result of the release of so-called greenhouse gases into the atmosphere in volumes that are in excess of the capacity of the ecosystem to eliminate them naturally. Although there are a number of these gases, the vast majority of the problem comes from the burning of fossil fuels such as petroleum, natural gas, coal, and wood. Burning these fuels releases carbon dioxide, methane, and nitrous oxide (what the Kyoto Protocol calls the "three most important" contributors to pollution) into the air in large quantities. The natural method of containing the amount of carbon dioxide (which is the major culprit) in the atmosphere is the absorption and conversion of that gas in so-called carbon sinks, which separate the two elements (carbon and oxygen) and release them harmlessly back into the atmosphere. In nature, the equatorial rain forests have been where these sinks have historically done most of the work.

The problem of excessive carbon dioxide comes from both sides of the production and elimination process. The burning of fossil fuels, which are essential for much energy production and thus economic activity worldwide, has increased steadily over the last century (and at current rates will continue to do so). Thus, there is more carbon dioxide in the atmosphere than there used to be, and because carbon dioxide has a half-life of roughly a century, that which is emitted today will be around for a long time. At the same time, cutting down trees in the rain forests has reduced the number and quality of natural sinks, thereby reducing nature's ability to capture and convert carbon dioxide into innocuous elements.

The cumulative effect is that there is more carbon dioxide in the atmosphere than there used to be, and it acts as a greenhouse gas. What this means is that as heat from the sun radiates off the Earth and attempts to return as an adequate amount into space to maintain current climate, carbon dioxide acts as a "trap" that retains the heat in the atmosphere rather than allowing it to escape. This blanketing effect keeps excess heat in the atmosphere, and the result is a warmer atmosphere and the phenomenon of global warming—net increases in atmospheric temperatures in specific locales and worldwide.

Responsibility for causing global warming and thus primary liability for doing something about it is also controversial. Significantly, the problem has become a mainstay of the global debate between the more industrially developed countries mostly located in the Northern Hemisphere and the less developed countries, many of which are located in the Southern Hemisphere. One aspect of this debate has to do with causation of the problem and hence responsibility. Fossil fuel burning is at the heart of warming; clearly, much of the problem was created in the North, which has already gone through an industrializing process for which fossil fuel–based energy was and remains an important component. From the vantage point of developing countries that aspire to the material success of the developed countries, this creates two points of contention. On one hand, they view developed countries as the cause of the problem and thus believe those countries should solve the problem by reducing emissions or by other means. At the same time, developed countries ask them to refrain from the same kind of fossil fuel–driven growth that they underwent, because doing so will simply make the greenhouse gas effect worse. The call for self-abnegation (under the banner of "sustainable development") by those countries that were fossil fuel self-indulgers strikes many in the developing world as hypocritical, to say the least. In some ways, this entreaty to self-denial is parallel to nuclear proliferation appeals raised in Chapter 11.

This North–South dimension is undeniable and critical to any solution to the global warming problem. At the most obvious physical level, both the developing and developed world have to contribute to any solution: the developed world by reducing its emissions to something like sustainable levels (levels that can be absorbed and converted naturally by the ecosystem), and the developing world by minimizing the destruction of carbon sinks, the natural means of abating excess gases.

At the political level, the debate over global warming, like virtually all transnational issues with a developed–developing world context, get tied inextricably into the debate over development and the obligations (if any) of developed countries to assist in the development of the less developed countries. The dialogue takes on a tit-for-tat character. Developed countries insist that efforts aimed at economic development be conducted within the context of sustainable development, by which is meant developmental processes that do not use more of resources than can be restored by natural processes. Thus, in the case of greenhouse gases, fossil fuel consumption should not exceed the ability of carbon sinks to absorb it. These self-imposed limits were not constraints on the already-developed states, of course, and developing states insist that their compliance with such restrictions be accompanied by developmental assistance both to speed growth and to help underwrite compliance with sustainable growth requirements. Thus, the issue of global warming becomes something of a pawn within a wider international debate.

The Kyoto Protocol of 1997 (so named after the city where it was finalized) is the most visible symbol of this process and has become the lightning rod of the procedural and substantive debate over global warming. The protocol is a very technical, complicated document (see the next section), the heart of which is a series of guidelines for the reduction of emissions by various countries according to a timetable established in the document. The requirements of the protocols have raised controversy because of the differential levels of reduction they impose; this has been especially true of the United States. Support for or opposition to the Kyoto Protocol has also become, in many quarters, emblematic of how one feels about the issue of global warming.

This introduction has laid out some of the basic underlying issues about global warming and the Kyoto Protocol as its symbol. In the next section, we will briefly examine the process by which the international community moved to the formalization of the effort to contain and reverse global warming. Since the urgency (or even the need) to engage in such a process depends on whether or to what extent the problem exists, positions on global warming are then presented. The case concludes by looking at the prospects for global warming and the institutionalization of efforts to contain it.

THE ROAD TO KYOTO—AND BEYOND?

Although the Kyoto Protocol is the most visible symbol (or target, depending on one's perspective), it was in fact an evolutionary step in a process that was begun well before the protocol was adopted and has continued to evolve since. Kyoto became the lightning rod for support or opposition because it provided the most comprehensive set of regulations and guidelines that had occurred to that point; in a very real sense, the rhetoric of global warming turned into a concrete plan and program in 1997.

Several points can be made about the road to Kyoto by means of introduction. First, concern about climatic change had been going on for a long time before the protocol was adopted, and the formal international process that resulted in the document began almost 20 years earlier. Second, the document and its requirements are complicated and technical, making a detailed description impossible within the confines of this case format. We will, however, discuss the highlights, including those that the Bush administration has found most objectionable. Third, the United States has had a special role in the evolution of this process, as is so often the case in international initiatives. In this case, the United States has, as in the case of the International Criminal Court, vacillated on the issue, with one administration serving as a major architect and its successor reversing that position completely. At the same time, the United States is the world's largest producer of greenhouse gases, and thus the protocol's provisions have questionable effectiveness in attacking the problem of global warming in the absence of American participation. Fourth, the protocol is nearly a decade old, and some critics maintain that it is based in science that has been overcome by events, meaning its provisions are of declining relevance.

The Kyoto Process

The chronology of global warming as a formal international concern is described by the United Nations Framework Convention for Climate Change (UNFCCC) Secretariat in a 2000 publication, *Caring for Climate*. According to that document, the first step in the process occurred in 1979, when the First World Climate Conference was held. That meeting brought together international scientists concerned with the effects of human intervention in the climate process and the possible pernicious effects of trends that they observed. This meeting also provided the first widespread recognition of the greenhouse gases phenomenon, which was largely known only within the scientific community before then.

Although not directly related to global warming, interest in atmospheric degradation and its effects on the human condition was further publicized in 1987 by the Montreal Treaty dealing with chloroflurocarbons (CFCs). The problem of CFCs was their relationship to ozone depletion and notably the emergence of holes in the ozone layers over the North and South Poles (that, it was argued, contributed to the melting of polar ice caps). A more specific problem than carbon dioxide, the CFC problem was the result of several chemicals mostly used as aerosol propellants in consumer goods (e.g., hair sprays) and for air conditioning systems (e.g., freon). The treaty negotiated a gradual elimination of CFCs and served as a model for the more ambitious pursuit of an agreement on global warming.

The international momentum began to pick up in 1988 with two events. First, the United Nations General Assembly adopted a resolution, 43/53, urging the "protection of global climate for present and future generations of mankind." The resolution was sponsored by Malta. In a separate action, the World Meteorological Organization (WMO) and the United Nations Environmental Programme created the Intergovernmental Panel on Climate Change (IPCC) and charged this new body with assessing the scientific evidence on the subject. As requested, the IPCC issued its First Assessment Report in 1990, concluding that the threat of climate change was real and worthy of further study and concern. Also in 1990, the World Climate Conference held its second meeting in Geneva, Switzerland, and called for a global treaty on climate change. This call in turn prompted the General Assembly to pass another resolution, 45/12, which commissioned negotiations for a convention on climate change to be conducted by the Intergovernmental Negotiating Committee (INC). This body first met in February 1991 as an intergovernmental body. On May 9, 1992, the INC adopted the UNFCCC, which was presented for signature at the Rio De Janeiro United Nations Conference on the Environment and Development (the Earth Summit) in June 1992. The requisite number of signatures was obtained in 1994 and the UNFCCC entered force on March 21, 1994. The process leading to the Kyoto Protocol was thus officially launched.

One express feature of the UNFCCC was an annual meeting of all members of the Convention (which numbered 188 in 2002) known as the Conference of the Parties (COP). The first COP was held in 1995 in Berlin. The third COP was held in Kyoto, Japan; the result was the Kyoto Protocol.

The Protocol

The Kyoto Protocol is a complicated document (references to the whole treaty can be found in the Web Sites section of this chapter) the details of which go beyond present purposes. Several elements can, however, be laid out that provide a summary of what the protocol attempts to do and, based on those purposes, the objections that have been raised to it.

The overarching goal of the protocol, of course, is a net reduction in the production and emission of greenhouse gases and thus the arrest and reversal of the adverse effects of climate changes caused by these gases (as a sort of baseline, the Intergovernmental Panel on Climate Change predicts a rise of 1.4 to 5.8 degrees Centigrade in global surface temperatures during this century if present trends continue). For this purpose, the protocol identifies six gases for control and emission reduction. As noted, the protocol specifies three of these gases as "most important": carbon dioxide (CO_2), methane (CH_4), and nitrous oxide (N_2O). This importance comes from the large relative contribution of these gases to the problem: Carbon dioxide accounts for fully half of "the overall global warming effect arising from human activities" in UNFCCC's language, followed by 18 percent for methane and 6 percent for nitrous oxide. For the United States in 2002, the percentages were 83% carbon dioxide, 9% methane, and 6% nitrous oxide, according to David Victor. The other three specified categories, the "long-lived industrial gases," are hydroflurocarbons (HFCs), perfluorocarbons (PFCs), and sulfur hexafluoride (SF_6).

The goal of the protocol is a global reduction in the production of targeted gases of 5 percent below the baseline year for measuring emissions, 1990, by the period 2008–12. The baseline year establishes how much each developed country contributed to emission levels. These levels are then used for two purposes: to determine how much reduction each targeted country must accomplish, and to provide a measuring stick for determining when the protocol comes fully into effect. For determining these contributions, the protocol further divides the countries of the world into three different categories (what it calls Annexes) in terms of the obligations that are incurred.

Since the source of greenhouse gases is fossil fuel consumption (gasoline, coal, and natural gas) for energy production for economic activity and transportation, it comes as no surprise that the countries most clearly identified and targeted are those in the developed world, and indeed, Annex I contains these countries. Using 1990 baseline figures for CO_2 emissions as its yardstick, these countries are listed by the amount of emissions they produced and the percentage of the world's total emissions this amount represents. Leading the list by a wide margin is the United States, which was responsible for 36.1 percent of global emissions. Aggregated as a whole, the European Union followed with 24.2 percent, followed by the countries of the Russian Federation with 17.4 percent, and Japan with 8.5 percent (for a total of 86 percent of global emissions). The next largest polluter after these was Australia with 2.1 percent.

The countries in Annex I are divided into two subcategories in terms of determining contributions to greenhouse gas reductions. Most of the countries are full members and must use the 1990 baseline figures to determine the amount of their reductions. However, because 1990 was a year of transition in the status of the countries of the communist world, these countries (including the Russian Federation and other former Soviet republics and Eastern Europe) were designated Economies in Transition (EIT) Parties, which meant they could choose a different baseline year against which to measure their reductions.

The protocol also created two other Annex categories. Annex II contains all the members of the Organization of Economic Cooperation and Development (OECD) but excludes the EIT countries (it is, in other words, the Annex I countries minus the old communist world). Countries designated in Annex II are "required to provide financial resources to enable developing countries to undertake emissions reduction activities and to help them adapt to adverse effects of climate change," according to the UNFCCC. The final category are Non-Annex I countries. These are the developing countries whose economies are not yet developed enough to contribute meaningfully to global warming (although some of them could become part of the problem in the future) and are thus excluded from participating in reduction activities. This category contains some significant economic powers (South Korea, for instance) and the world's two largest countries in population, China and India, whose potential contribution to the global warming problem are enormous.

The baseline for Annex I countries provides the specifications for reductions of emissions levels. These differ by country. Switzerland, most central and eastern European countries, and the European Union are targeted at 8 percent reductions (individual EU countries have different standards to reach the total); the United States' target is 7 percent; and Canada, Hungary, and Japan have 6 percent targets. Russia, New Zealand, and the Ukraine are ordered to stabilize their emissions at 1990 levels, and Norway, Australia, and Iceland can actually increase their emissions levels.

The baseline serves an additional function. Rather than creating a standard for coming into effect based on how many countries ratify the protocol (which is the standard method by which international treaties take effect), the standard for the Kyoto Protocol is the percentage contribution to the baseline of all countries that ratify. The standard set is 55 percent of emissions. This reflects the truly transnational nature of global warming by saying that reduction can only be meaningful if most of the real pollution falls under the protocol. It also reflects the enormous importance of American participation in the protocol: American ratification means 36 of the necessary 55 percent is accomplished; conversely, American refusal to participate means that only 64 percent of emissions can fall under the protocol if all other Annex I parties accede. The 55 percent threshold was reached in 2004 without American accession.

If all these provisions are not complicated enough, the protocol adds another source of complications in terms of what UNFCCC calls "three innovative mechanisms" for meeting goals by means other than straight reductions. These are joint implementation, the clean development mechanism (CDM), and emissions trading. Each deserves at least brief mention, if only to illustrate the convoluted nature of the entire process.

Joint implementation (technically, emission reduction units in the protocol) allows Annex I countries to gain credits against their emission reduction quotas by undertaking projects with Non-Annex I countries either to help those countries reduce their emissions or increase carbon sinks. The CDM provides emissions credits for Annex I countries that invest in projects in Non-Annex I countries, especially in the private sector, that contribute to emissions reductions or in other ways that support the general principle of sustainable development (developmental projects that do not add to pollution of the environment). Emissions trading allows countries that exceed (purposely or as the result of a downturn in their economies) their emissions goals in effect to sell that excess to Annex I countries, which can then apply the excess purchased toward reaching their own required reductions.

As this discussion suggests, the mechanisms and procedures included within the Kyoto Protocol process are indeed complicated and intricate, creating very different requirements for different states and categories of states, as well as complicated means of compliance through the addition of the "innovative" methods discussed directly above. As a result, it should not be surprising that this process has also resulted in a certain level of controversy. That controversy, in turn, centers on the United States, which has emerged as the most vocal and important opponent of the protocol.

American and Other Objections

Both because of extent of American contribution to greenhouse gas emission (about 25 percent of all the affected gases as opposed to 36 percent of carbon dioxide) and the related formula for implementing the Kyoto Protocol, American participation in the effort is virtually a sine qua non for the global warming effort to succeed. When the movement began, the United States was an enthusiastic participant in the process leading to Kyoto, and the Clinton administration was among the early signers and supporters of the protocol and its implementation.

That position changed when the Bush administration entered office. During the 2000 campaign, Bush favored legislation that would require power plants (one of the major sources of carbon dioxide, along with transportation vehicles) to reduce their emissions by adding "scrubbers" to emissions leaving plants and entering the atmosphere. After he assumed office, he quickly changed course, siding instead with power industry opponents of Kyoto and announcing on March 13, 2001, that he no longer favored U.S. participation in the Kyoto Protocol. In the process, the administration publicly stated that it would not send the treaty signed by Clinton to the Senate for ratification. As a result, the United States remains the most important country in the world that is not a party to the protocol and thus does not consider itself subject to its requirements, although it remains a party to the UNFCCC.

American objections to the protocol tend to focus on two basic themes. The first is cost and burden to the United States. Although some other countries have higher percentage reduction quotas than the United States, the mathematics of bearing 7 percent of 36 percent of the total required reductions is odious, in the view of opponents of the treaty. In addition, U.S. emissions were already 15 percent above the 1990 level by the end of the millennium and, according to Victor, rising at 1.3 percent per year, thereby demanding further reductions. Thus, the United States is being asked to do too much proportionately to the rest of the world. This is particularly true of the burden that would fall on the power and transportation industries in the United States, which would be forced to take actions to reduce most of the carbon dioxide reduction requirements. In the view of administration and other critics, compliance would be economically ruinous in terms of the additional expenses of doing business and the loss of comparative advantage to industries in other countries that are not regulated by these requirements because of the additional costs they add to production. Conformance to Kyoto standards that do not apply universally thus unfairly imbalances the "playing field" of economic competition.

This leads to the second objection, which is the exclusion of developing countries from the requirements of the protocol. In most cases, this exclusion is innocuous, as most of these countries neither do nor will contribute meaningfully to greenhouse gas in the foreseeable future, when circumstances could be much different due, in part, to the effects of the protocol. At the same time, there are exceptions to that basis for exclusion.

The Bush administration has directed its criticism of developing-world exclusion principally at two countries, China and India. China, it is alleged, is becoming a major greenhouse gas emitter (some estimates maintain it is already the second-largest emitter in the world), and that this situation will continue and intensify as China further develops (thereby requiring additional energy) and as China continues to promote automobile ownership among its huge population base. India does not pose quite as urgent a threat, but with a population roughly the size of China's and an emerging technological and industrial capacity, the sheer magnitude of the country's potential suggests it should be part of the solution before it becomes an overt part of the problem. The contrary argument—that inclusion of these countries would impede their ability to develop and become competitive economies—is simply further evidence of the inequitable set of rules the protocol creates.

A third, more contemporary objection to the protocol is that it is essentially dated. The argument here is the march of technology and change may have simply outgrown its provisions. John Browne, writing in a recent *Foreign Affairs,* summarizes this argument: "First, Kyoto was simply the starting point of a very long endeavor. Second, we have improved, if still imperfect, knowledge of the challenges and uncertainties that climate change presents. . . . Third, many countries and companies have had experience reducing emissions that have proved that such reductions can be achieved without destroying competitiveness of jobs. Fourth, science and technology have advanced on multiple fronts. Finally, public awareness of the issue has grown."

A fourth objection, related to the third, is that the protocol and all its provisions are simply too complicated and unwieldy to be administered in any enforceable, objective way. The various "innovative" ways of substituting means of compliance discussed earlier are a case in point. This complexity suggests to some critics of the protocol that the effort should be scrapped and a new, comprehensive approach grounded in contemporary realities should replace it (this argument is often made by Bush administration supporters with energy industry credentials). Environmentalists argue this is essentially a cop-out to avoid implementing greenhouse gas emission standards. As Fred Krupp, executive director of the private advocacy group Environmental Defense, puts it, "It is bad for America's interests for the United States to be seen as the rogue nation of greenhouse gas pollution. By simply opposing the Kyoto Protocol rather than seeking to improve it, the administration would have effectively blocked the only binding international agreement for fighting global warming, while offering no alternate path to protect the planet."

Finally, there is an objection from the other end of the spectrum that says the fatal flaw of the Kyoto Protocol is not that it requires too much of countries and the world but that it requires too little. In this argument, the problem is not the degree of sacrifice demanded, but the need to cut greenhouse gas emission much more drastically, in the range of 50 percent rather than the roughly 5 percent demanded in the Kyoto Protocol.

Just how compelling these arguments surrounding the Kyoto Protocol are and thus how vital universal compliance with the document should be is a matter of conjecture. As might be guessed, American objections to Kyoto are at least partially grounded in an assessment of the consequences of greenhouse gas contamination that is significantly less dire than the estimates made by those who argue the problem is serious and pressing. For that reason, it is necessary at least to raise some of the questions that occur in the debate about global warming

WARM AND GETTING WARMER: BUT HOW MUCH?

There are at least three related factors that make a calm, rational debate over the extent and consequences of global warming difficult to conduct. The first is the absence of immediate consequences of whatever change is occurring. Over the past quarter century or more, climate change in the form of warming has indeed been occurring worldwide, but the effects have been so gradual and generally miniscule that either they have gone unnoticed by most people or have not been easily attributable to the phenomenon. Were there dramatic events that could be associated with climate change (or equally convincing absences of predicted changes), it would be easier to make the case one way or the other. But such immediate effects have not, by and large, occurred—even if they are predicted by many scientists who believe some apocryphal event is inevitable somewhere in the not-too-distant future.

Second, there is abundant scientific disagreements about the parameters of the problem and its solution. Some of the disagreement is honest, some possibly self-interested (for instance, studies of carbon dioxide's effects funded by the petroleum industry), but for every dire prediction about future consequences, there is a rebuttal from another part of the scientific community. This debate often becomes scientifically shrill and accusatory, leading to confusion in the public about what to believe. In this confusion, the citizenry has a difficult time making reasoned assessments and consequent demands on policymakers to adopt standards.

Third, almost all the projections are sufficiently far in the future to allow considerable disagreement and to discourage resolution. One can argue the scientific evidence to date is very strong one way or the other on various consequences of warming; the actual consequences are distant enough, however, that the extrapolation is subject to sufficient variation that scientists can take the same data and reach diametrically opposed conclusions. These extrapolations are often 50 or even 100 years in the future, when most of the people at whom they are aimed will not even be alive to witness or be held accountable for them. Is it any wonder there is difficulty mobilizing the population in these circumstances?

The often acrimonious debate over the melting of polar ice caps provides an example of this disagreement. There is no disagreement over the fact that ice caps are melting; the disagreement is about why and what this means. Those most worried about global warming argue the burning of fossil fuels is the culprit, and the consequences include rising ocean levels (mostly from melting in Antarctica) and ecological change (especially in the Arctic). Critics contend there is little evidence that the changes are not natural and dispute the notion of an accelerated rise in sea levels (they argue, for instance, that most of the melting is of floating ice—ice already in the water—that does not affect ocean levels one way or the other). Environmentalists counter that greater melting of floating ice accelerates the melting of ground ice (ice on land), which *does* raise ocean levels, and so on. How is the layman to gauge these arguments?

If all this is abstract to most people, what if there was a real example with which people could relate? For instance, the furor over Hurricane Charley in July 2004 revealed how dangerously low-lying most of Tampa Bay was. Large parts of the waterfront of Tampa, for instance, lies at five feet or less above sea level, making it a prime candidate for eventual inundation in the next century, when some projections say sea levels will rise *over* five feet. Does that alarm citizens of Tampa Bay, or will it take some violent occasion (such as the surge that was predicted had Charley come ashore at Tampa Bay) to convince people to take the problem seriously? It is not an easy case to make.

Getting Too Warm?

That global climate is changing is not contested on any side of the debate over global warming. The Intergovernmental Panel on Climate Change (IPCC) has investigated the extent to which this has happened in the past and has concluded that the average surface temperature of the Earth increased by about one degree Fahrenheit during the twentieth century and "that most of the warming observed over the past 50 years is attributable to human activities." (Much of the IPCC material in this section is from the 2001 report of Group I-III of the IPCC, cited in the suggested readings.) Extrapolating from trends in the last century, the IPCC predicts additional warming between 2.2–10 degrees Fahrenheit (1.4–5.8 degrees Centigrade). The primary culprits are the greenhouse gases cited in the Kyoto Protocol that result from deforestation (and its destruction of carbon sinks), energy production from the combustion of fossil fuels (natural gas, oil, and coal), transportation (primarily cars and trucks, but also trains and other modes), cattle production (methane gases), rice farming, and cement production.

A variety of effects have been observed and attributed to these changes. In some areas, birds are laying eggs a few weeks earlier than they used to, butterflies are moving their habitats farther up mountains to avoid lowland heat, and trees are blooming earlier in the spring and losing their leaves later in the fall. Any of these changes can be dismissed as of low relative concern, but there are more fundamental changes alleged with more obvious consequences. Warming, the IPCC II reports, show that snow accumulation is decreasing worldwide, as is the global supply of ice pack. At the same time, glaciers are retreating worldwide (some of the most dramatic American examples are in places like Glacier National Park in Montana), sea levels and ocean temperatures have risen, and rainfall patterns in many regions have changed as well. In addition, there is evidence that permafrost is thawing in the polar regions, that lakes are freezing later and thawing earlier, and that even some plant and animal species have declined and may disappear due to changes in climate.

If these trends continue, the results could be dramatic. As an example, tropical diseases that have heretofore been confined to tropical lowlands could spread to previously impervious areas such as plateaus and mountains and might even extend to temperate regions of the globe that have previously been too cool for them to survive. Although there is widespread disagreement on the details, it is likely that a large number of fragile animal and plant species will become extinct (one study estimates between 15 and 37 percent in some regions will be vulnerable).

Some of the most dramatic examples involve the effects on coastal regions. The projected problems arise both from the gradual rise of oceanic levels and the warming of ocean waters. Both are a concern because of the large and growing portion of populations residing in coastal locations (it is, for instance, a major demographic reality in the United States that the population is gradually moving out of the central parts of the country toward more temperate coastal regions).

The extent of these effects, of course, depends on the amount of change caused by global warming. IPCC II data project an average rise of between 6 and 36 inches in sea levels by 2100. Using the higher figure, the impact on some countries would be dramatic. A 36-inch rise would inundate territory in which 10 million people live in Bangladesh alone, forcing their relocation to scarce higher land. The same increase would cover 12 percent of the arable land of the Nile River delta in Egypt, which produces crops on which over seven million people are dependent. Some estimates suggest the island country of Vanuatu in the South Pacific would simply disappear under the rising waters. Worldwide, it is estimated that 45 million people would be displaced.

Warming of ocean water could also have dramatic effects, for instance, by affecting ocean currents that now have an influence on climate in various parts of the world. The Atlantic Gulf Stream, for instance, could be affected by warmer water coming from polar regions, changing patterns for the coastal United States and Europe. As an example, Gulf Stream effects that tend to keep major hurricanes off parts of the American coast (e.g., the South Carolina Lowcountry) could be diverted, resulting in a new pattern of hurricane, tornado, and storm patterns. Large-scale changes in patterns of ocean circulation are possible worldwide. The cumulative effect, according to the IPCC, could be "a widespread increase in the risk of flooding for human settlements (tens of millions of inhabitants in settlements studied) from both increased heavy precipitation and sea level rise" (IPCC II).

Not So Fast

Scientists disagree about the accuracy of these projections and the direness of the consequences that they project. There is little disagreement about the historical record (e.g., the amount of climate change in the last century) because that is based on observable data that can be examined for accuracy, although there is some disagreement on the precise causes of change (e.g., scientists affiliated with the power industry tend to downplay the impact of energy production). There is, however, disagreement on projections of trends and effects extrapolated into the future. The main source of this disagreement is the fact that any projections are based in observations of effects in a future that has not yet occurred, but are instead based on projections of historically grounded observations (and hence scientific inference) into a future the exact dimensions of which cannot be known or entirely predicted. Extrapolation becomes more uncertain the farther predictions are cast into the future, and thus there is an increased level of disagreement the farther into the future one goes. The deleterious effects of global warming are argued to be cumulative and thus more serious the farther into the future one projects; the basis for lively, at times acrimonious, discussions are thus built into the debate.

Without delving into great detail, there tend to be three criticisms of global warming scientists that can be phrased in terms of questions. The first is the factual content of the warnings: How much effect will global warming have? A second, corollary question is how much those effects will accumulate under different assumptions about natural and man-made adjustments to these effects? Third, how difficult are the solutions?

These are good questions that, depending on how they are answered, define both the dimensions of the problem and the urgency and forms that dealing with it should take. The question of how much is clearly the driving dynamic here: If the amount of change will be great and the consequences large and damaging, that makes the problem urgent and sacrifices to solve it both urgent and important.

The problem, of course, is that there is disagreement on these matters. Take, for instance, the projections on how much average surface temperatures will warm in this century if action is not taken. As noted, they range from one to ten degrees Fahrenheit, and that is a considerable range in terms of the consequences to the world and mankind. If the actual figure is at the upper end of that spectrum, then things like snow pack, glacier, and polar ice cap melting will be considerable, with oceans rising at the upper limits of predictions (around three feet). Parts of Tampa Bay and New Orleans, among other places, will be under water unless levees are constructed to keep the water out, and Vanuatu may become the next Lost City of Atlantis (an analogy often made by global warming scientists). On the other hand, if the rise in mean surface temperature is closer to or at the lower extreme (a degree or so), then the consequences are probably far less dire.

Who knows which part of the range is correct? The answer is that with any scientific certitude, no one does. The amount of warming is necessarily an extrapolation into a future that does not exist, not an observation of something that does. Clearly, it is in the interests of those who either do not believe in the more severe projections or who would be most adversely affected by concerted efforts to reduce emissions to believe in the lower projections and thus to deny the more severe reactions. At the same time, those who believe the problem to be dire have an interest in accepting the higher estimates, either as a hedge against uncertainty (if one plans for the worst, then anything else may be more manageable) or because of a sincere belief in the higher numbers.

The layman is left up in the air. Because the effects are not immediate and unambiguous, the average person has little way to answer the second question: What does all this mean? Are we headed for an environmental catastrophe if we do not do something to slow, stop, or reverse global warming? The scientists on both sides of the issue are passionate and self-convinced, but they have not, by and large, made a case to the world's publics that is compelling, understandable, and convincing—one way or the other. In a world of more instantly consequential problems, it is hard to bring oneself to develop the passion that the advocates, regardless of scientific credentials, have on the issue.

This brings us to the third question, which brings the concern full circle and returns us to the Kyoto Protocol: What should we do about the problem? The immediate answer, of course, is that it depends on how bad the problem is. Most of the world has accepted the basic science of those warning about the more dire consequences of not solving the global warming problem, and the United States remains virtually alone among major powers (and greenhouse gas emitters) in denying or downplaying the problem and resisting the

Kyoto solution. Admittedly, the major source of official U.S. objection is not the veracity of global warming science, but is instead directed at the differential obligations for solving it that Kyoto prescribes: reductions with economic consequences that would make the American economy less competitive and the exclusion of developing-world countries with large pollution potentials from regulation. If, however, the American government fully accepted the direst projections of the consequences, these objections would probably pale in comparison to the dictates of solving the problem. Implicitly or explicitly, American opposition to the Kyoto Protocol also reflects a belief the problem is not great (or, more minimally, that the solution can be deferred without significant consequences).

There is, of course, a hedge in answering the third question that reflects a deep American trait in viewing problems. That hedge is a belief that technology will somehow find a way to ameliorate the problem, either by finding a way to decrease the emission of greenhouse gases or to increase the ability to absorb and neutralize those gases and their consequences. That is the position often taken by the American energy and transportation industries, and it is an approach that has worked to solve other problems at other times. Whether adherence to that belief is a blind leap of faith or a sound scientific prediction is, like so much of the debate over global warming, a question of perspective.

CONCLUSION

No one disagrees that global warming is taking place or that its effects are not pernicious to some degree. There are no pro-global warmers. However, there is, as we have seen, considerable reluctance to attack and eradicate the problem, especially in the United States, whose participation in the effort is absolutely critical to its solution. Why?

The answer lies in two phenomena, one only hinted at to this point and one discussed more fully. One problem is the contrast between the short term and the longer term regarding global warming and its effects. In the short term (say, the next 10 to 20 years), it is not absolutely clear that there will be major negative worldwide or local events that can be attributed unambiguously and consensually to global warming. If, as many maintain, the spate of extremely destructive hurricanes of 2005 (Katrina and Rita) could unambiguously be tied to global warming, we might be moved to act. But is warming clearly the cause? Those who warn about the prospects of global warming are, quite correctly from their viewpoint, insisting that remedial actions need to be taken now to avoid disastrous effects in the short and longer term. These actions include personal and societal sacrifices on the altar of cleaner air, including reductions in omissions from power plants, automobiles, and the like which will incur costs that will be passed along to all of us. We are, in other words, being asked to sacrifice at a time when we will not be able to see the beneficial effects that warrant our sacrifices; instead, we are asked to sacrifice today to serve an abstract future.

The longer view reverses this perspective. According to those most concerned with the damaging effects of global warming, the failure to act in the short run condemns those who will experience the negative effects. As cities are inundated a hundred years from now, for instance, it will likely not be difficult at all to convince people they need to make those sacrifices as the water laps at their front doors, but by then it may be too late to take the corrective actions that need to be taken now to prevent that future fate.

Can we reconcile these two contrasting perspectives? In the abstract, we can. If we *knew* that the failure to take action today would condemn those who follow (or if we are young enough, ourselves) to a specific negative fate, then we might be able to agree to make those sacrifices. That reconciliation flies in the face of the second phenomenon, uncertainty of the nature of the future and a consequent reluctance to act when we are not entirely certain why we need to act.

The first part of this difficulty has been discussed extensively already and need not be reiterated. The simple fact is that there is indeed disagreement about the parameters and severity of the global warming problem, and those who are reluctant to counsel sacrifices that would be politically unpopular can and do use that uncertainty to justify inaction. Those who warn of global warming counter the irresponsibility of ignoring what they are convinced is inevitable, but such arguments fall on at least partially deaf ears in the absence of incontrovertible evidence that the warnings are true.

Until that undeniable evidence is produced, there is precedent to believe we will simply defer the problem. In some ways, the global warming problem and its solution are like deficit spending. No one believes spending more than we take in is good and responsible policy, and everyone knows in the abstract that some time in the future, someone else is going to have to pay off the debt that is being accumulated as we operate literally on borrowed money. At some point, we will have to "pay the piper," but exactly when this will occur and what exactly the piper will exact are matters of disagreement that help us justify not taking the corrective action of balancing budgets. Why should we expect global warming to be any different?

At the beginning of the case study, global warming was described as a true transnational issue, and one with unique aspects. That uniqueness has at least three significant angles. First, global warming is truly a global issue that affects the entire planet and can only be solved by essentially universal actions by the world's countries. This observation accentuates the role of American opposition to the Kyoto Protocol; if global warming is indeed the problem it is advertised to be, the United States will bear unique responsibility globally if we fail to address and solve it. Second, responding to global warming will have direct impacts on two of the most important motors of the global economy: energy production and use, and transportation. Disruptions to either or both of these industries could have catastrophic economic effects for the world generally. The problem of global warming, in other words, is important to all of our well-beings. Third, global warming is the only environmental change problem that intensifies or is intensified by other major environmental problems. Rising water levels affect the ability of the Earth to produce food, and desertification is increased by warming, to cite two problems created. The effects of global warming are, in other words, pervasive.

How warm is the world getting, what does that matter, and what should or must be done or not done about it? These are the questions that we have asked throughout this case study, and they are all questions that have potentially vital answers for the good of all of us individually and collectively. What, then, are those answers?

STUDY/DISCUSSION QUESTIONS

1. Describe the global warming problem. What causes it? What are the short-term and long-term consequences of global warming?

2. Describe global warming as a North–South political and climatic problem. Who bears responsibility for creating and solving the problem?

3. Describe the process leading to the Kyoto Protocol. What are the major provisions of the protocol? Which provisions are most controversial? Why?

4. Why does the United States have a unique place in the global warming and Kyoto Protocol process? What are the major United States objections to the protocol? Why can the protocol not be effective without American participation in its implementation?

5. What are the major claims made by those who believe that global warming is a major worldwide problem? How do skeptics counter these assertions?

6. Explain the major dilemma of the global warming debate in terms of short-term and long-term effects. Are the prospects sufficiently dire that you believe we should endure short-term sacrifices to guard against long-term dangers?

7. Why is global warming unique as a transnational issue? Explain.

READING/RESEARCH MATERIAL

Ackerman, John T. *Global Climate Change: Catalyst for International Relations Disequilibria*. PhD Dissertation. Tuscaloosa: University of Alabama, 2004.

Anderson, Terry, and Harry I. Miller (eds). *The Greening of U.S. Foreign Policy*. Stanford, CA: Hoover Institution Press, 2000.

Beyond Kyoto: Advancing the International Effort Against Climate Change. Arlington, VA: Pew Center on Global Climate Change, 2003.

Browne, John. "Beyond Kyoto." *Foreign Affairs* 83, 4 (July/August 2004), 20–32.

Claussen, Eileen, and Lisa McNeilly. *Equity and Global Climate Change: The Complex Elements of Global Fairness*. Arlington, VA: Pew Center on Global Climate Change, 2000.

Diehl, Paul R., and Niles Peter Gleditsch (eds). *Environmental Conflict*. Boulder, CO: Westview, 2001.

Gupta, Joyeeta. *Our Simmering Planet: What to Do about Global Warming?* New York: Zed Books, 2001.

Intergovernmental Panel on Climate Change. A Report on Working Groups I–III. *Summary for Policymakers—Climate Change 2001*. Cambridge, MA: Cambridge University Press, 2001.

Luterbacher, Urs, and Detlef F. Sprinz (eds). *International Relations and Global Climate Change*. Cambridge, MA: MIT Press, 2001.

Michaels, Patrick J., and Robert C. Balling Jr. *The Satanic Gases: Clearing the Air about Global Warming*. Washington, DC: Cato Institute, 2000.

Pirages, Dennis C., and Theresa Manley DeGeest. *Ecological Security: An Evolutionary Perspective on Globalization*. New York: Rowman and Littlefield, 2004.

Schelling, Thomas C. "The Cost of Combating Global Warming: Facing the Tradeoffs." *Foreign Affairs* 76, 6 (November/December 1997), 8–14.

Victor, David G. *Climate Change: Debating America's Options*. New York: Council on Foreign Relations, 2004.

Wirth, Timothy. "Hot Air Over Kyoto: The United States and the Politics of Global Warming." *Harvard International Review* 23, 4 (2002), 72–77.

WEB SITES

Assessment of state of environment

Yale Center for Environmental Law and Policy at
http://www.ciesin.columbia.edu/indicators/ ESI

Text of Kyoto Protocol at http://unfccc.int/resource/convkp.html

Third Assessment Report of IPCC at http://www.ipcc,ch

UNFCCC Guide on Kyoto Protocol at
http://unfccc.int/resource/guideconvenkp-p.pdf

U.S. State Department Report on Climate at
http://epa.gov/globalwarming/publications/car/index.html

CHAPTER FOURTEEN

"Let Them Drink Oil"

RESOURCE CONFLICT IN THE NEW CENTURY?

PRÉCIS

The desire, even necessity, to control natural resources, and conflict over those resources, are as old as human history. Major wars have been fought over access to precious gems, metals, food, and exotic spices, to name a few examples. In the second half of the twentieth century, the most well-publicized resource conflict was over access to the oil reserves of the Persian Gulf region. What types of resources will cause what kinds of conflicts in the first part of the twenty-first century?

This case examines the general parameters of the problem as it appears early in the twenty-first century, when the primary resources competitions center around access to adequate supplies of two commodities, water and petroleum. Shortages of each of these vital commodities affect different countries and regions, although the two problems come together in the volatile Middle East and adjoining regions. In this case study, we will begin by tracing the general international problem surrounding these resources in physical and geopolitical terms. We will then focus on two "mini-cases" demonstrating some of the characteristics of each. The first deals with access to water in the Middle East, and it is primarily a conflict between Turkey and downstream riparian states within the Tigris-Euphrates river system and, to a lesser degree, between Syria and Israel over the headwaters of the Jordan River. The second mini-case deals with petroleum, but within the context of the large oil reserves of the Caspian Sea area. This case combines the desire to exploit the oil with the geopolitical struggle to determine how the oil will be moved from central Asia to potential consumers.

Conflict and war over the ability to control, monopolize, or deny access to valued resources is as old as recorded human history. Men have fought and died, armies have swept across countless expanses, and empires and states have risen and fallen in the name of precious resources. Whether it was control of the silk route across Asia or the exotic foodstuffs of the Spice Islands, the diamonds and gold of southern and central Africa, El Dorado in the new world, or the petroleum wealth of the Middle East, the struggle for natural, scarce, and valuable resources has been a recurrent theme of human history and the relations between individuals and groups.

How will this historic theme be enacted in the early twenty-first century? What is striking is that the resources over which there is the most competition are also among the most basic resources for the human condition. At the head of the list is water (more specifically, potable water). With 70 percent of the earth's surface covered in water, water per se is hardly a scarce resource, but water that is usable for human purposes (drinking, bathing, agriculture, etc.) is in shortage selectively in the world, and as global population grows, those shortages will likely spread. The other scarce resource is petroleum, which has become the world's most basic source of energy. Whether there is indeed a global shortage of oil is debatable, but like water, petroleum that is easily available for consumption (energy production) is currently close to the point of scarcity.

As has always been the case, resource scarcities are politically important, because political decisions, domestically and internationally, help define scarcities and responses to them. Water, for instance, is reasonably abundant in some places but not in others. Where it is in short supply, the political, including geopolitical, competition between those who have adequate or surplus supplies and those who do not can become acrimonious and be the source of conflict among the haves and the have-nots. Similarly, the worldwide demand for petroleum is growing and will likely continue to do so despite the search for alternate energy sources. As long as demand is increasing and those who can supply those demands can exercise some level of control over how much of the resource is made available to whom, there will be continued controversy when the possessors attempt to maximize the leverage their possession provides and those who desire the resource attempt to find ways to ensure that they (if not necessarily others) receive all they need.

Geographically, these two problems come together in the Middle East, which, as a region, has a surplus of petroleum and a growing deficit (growing because supplies are static and population is expanding) of water. The distribution of the resources is, however, differential: Some countries (Turkey is the prime example) have more water than they need but less petroleum than they would like. Others (Iraq, for example) have surplus oil at least potentially to export (assuming wartime restraints are removed) but not enough water. Petroleum surplus has, until recently at least, been the great lever of power, but the need for water can even trump that. Hence, the title of this chapter ("Let them drink oil") is attributed to an anonymous Turkish diplomat responding to demands from Iraqi officials for greater access to river water that has its source in Turkey, as discussed in the next section.

It is useful to look briefly at each of these dimensions of the resource scarcity problem in order to frame the discussion of the two specific cases, water in the Middle East and petroleum from the Caspian Sea Basin.

The problem of water is the more straightforward resource question. As noted, the problem is not the availability globally of an adequate amount of water, because if seawater is included, water is a virtually limitless commodity (in fact, many observers believe the long-term solution to the world's energy problem involves nuclear fusion based in the use of "limitless" supplies of seawater). The problem, of course, is consumable water: water that is not too saline for use in agriculture and that is pure enough to allow human consumption. Water that meets the criterion of usability is not uniformly available. Some regions have more than other regions, some countries within regions have more generous amounts than others, and within many countries, water availability is skewed toward some areas more than others. The problem of water thus basically boils down to matching demand for potable water with needs given a naturally uneven supply of the resource. This problem would, in principle, be most easily solvable by increasing supply dramatically through the ability to convert seawater into potable water through some form of desalination, but to date, no economically feasible method for doing so has been devised.

The water problem has, of course, centered on the most arid parts of the world, such as the Sahel region of Africa along the southern border of the Sahara desert and in the Middle East. Limited population in the Sahel (partly because there is not enough water to support larger numbers of people) tends to mute the problem there other than under exceptional circumstances, such as the enormous drought in Horn of Africa countries like Somalia in the 1990s and the man-made disaster in Sudan, manifested by massive refugee problems in places like Darfur and Chad. Water has played an important role in the relations both among Middle Eastern Islamic states and in the relations between some of those states and Israel, however, and high population growth rates in a number of Islamic countries will only make both aspects of this problem worse, as the case study demonstrates.

The problem will almost certainly spread in the future as world geopolitics evolves. As is also the case with petroleum, the emergence of China and India as major international players will influence the water problem. The world's two largest countries have different water problems, as Carl Pope explains in a 2005 *Foreign Policy* roundtable: "Water tables of major grain-producing areas in northern China are dropping at a rate of five feet per year, and per capita water availability in India is expected to drop by 50 to 75 percent over the next decade." In China, it is thus the availability of adequate water in the face of a growing population that is the problem. As Zheng Bijian has pointed out in a recent *Foreign Affairs* article, "China's per capita water resources are one-quarter of the world's average." Indeed, a "shortage of resources," including water, is part of what the Chinese leadership has identified as the three major challenges to Chinese development (environmental concerns and the coordination of economic and social development are the others). India's problem is different. As Gurcharan Das points out, "India has a competitive advantage in agriculture, with plenty of arable land (second only to the United States), sunshine, and water." In India's case, the problem is distribution of the water within the country and, as Pope notes, the problem of a shortage of potable water for a growing population.

The problem of petroleum has attracted much more attention. Part of the reason is because petroleum is inextricably tied to the volatile Middle East, meaning that world access to the amounts of petroleum that countries need is, to some extent, tied to the vicissitudes of Middle Eastern politics (currently the situation in Iraq). At the same time, increased demand for petroleum has made the oil market much more competitive and resulted in increased leverage and influence for petroleum exporters, a situation unlikely to improve in the near term (all of the supply-side alternatives that will produce more forms of energy are some years from coming on line). Moreover, the use of petroleum is tied closely to environmental concerns, as discussed in Chapter 13.

In a recent *Current History* article, David L. Goldwyn summarizes the situation. "Energy insecurity is greater today than it has been in nearly 30 years. The global oil market is more fragile, more competitive, and more volatile. The global demand for oil is strong, powered by global economic growth, especially in China and the rest of developing Asia. Global supply has been restrained."

The structure of the contemporary petroleum problem is straightforward. According to recent figures, oil production is at approximately 85 million barrels a day, whereas current consumption hovers around 83 million barrels per day (one can marginally quibble with the exact numbers, but the basic dynamic holds). This means the oil market is extremely "tight," in the sense that a relatively small increase in demand or decrease in supply could make oil a scarce commodity in supply/demand terms. As Leonardo Maugeri points out, this situation is the result of a 20-year trend: "Between 1986 and 2005, the world's spare oil production (the amount produced beyond current demand) dropped from about 15 percent to between 2 and 3 percent of global demand." That margin is currently around two million barrels per day of "spare" production, and a supply decrease or demand increase of over that amount throws supply and demand out of kilter.

There are two major dynamics that affect this tight—and increasingly tightening—market and produce notable problems. The first is that the situation is bound to get worse. The reason, Daniel Yergin argues in a 2006 *Foreign Affairs* article, is that "the last decade has witnessed a significant increase in the world's demand for oil, primarily because of the dramatic increase in developing countries, in particular China and India." Both countries are net oil importers. According to figures provided by Infoplease for 2004, China produces about 3.62 million barrels a day and consumes 6.5 million barrels, about 45 percent of its total is thus imported. According to David Zweig and Bi Jianhai, in 2004 China "accounted for 31 percent of global growth in oil demand," and this figure is likely to continue to grow, although the impact of that growth is a matter of disagreement. (Maugeri, for instance, maintains "even sustained Chinese consumption growth would have only marginal effects on an otherwise normal global petroleum market.") China is currently the world's third-largest importer of petroleum. India reflects this same trend on a smaller scale. Though oil production is expected to increase to about 3 million barrels a day by 2010, there is a current gap of nearly 1.5 million barrels a day that India must import. Continued Indian growth could make this problem more acute.

In addition to increased demand, there is the leverage that oil producers realize they can exercise because of the tightness of the oil market. In 2004 figures, fourteen countries produced 2 million barrels or more a day, meaning if any one of them suspended production of that amount for a sustained period of time, the effects could be profound, because, as Thomas L. Friedman points out, the more prices rise and the possibilities of manipulation of supply exists, "the less petrolists' are sensitive to what the world thinks or says about them." He defines petrolist states as "states that are both dependent on oil production for the bulk of their exports and have weak state institutions or outright authoritarian governments." Azerbaijan, the major subject of the oil mini-case, and Iran are among the states he cites as examples of this phenomenon. As suggested in Chapter 11, the threat to withhold a substantial part of its slightly over 4 million barrels per day production by the Iranians could have a major impact on the global oil market, a fact of which they are well aware and of which those, like the United States, that would influence their behavior are equally cognizant.

These introductory remarks help frame the two case studies that follow. Both are cases about resource scarcity and its consequences. The first case study focuses on the problem of water in the arid Middle East. It has two dimensions: The imbalance between water availability in different parts of the Islamic Middle East pits water-rich Turkey against its more arid fellow Islamic states, notably Syria and Iraq. Who will control the flow of the Jordan River coming out of the Sea of Galilee is a vital (if often underemphasized) aspect of the peace process between Israel and Syria that speaks to the vitality of the water resource. The second case study looks at the need to increase the supply of petroleum worldwide created by the current market as it applies to the Caspian Sea Basin. The instabilities of the Persian Gulf region have made the exploitation of alternative sources of petroleum a major priority and have in particular created a demand to develop the resources of the Caspian littoral, notably Azerbaijan and Kazakhstan. The desire to tap into the oil (and natural gas) reserves controlled by Azerbaijan has, in turn, run into the complex geopolitics of the region, including the desire of both Turkey and Russia to profit from the transshipment of the oil across their territory and even the secessionist movement in Chechnya.

MIDDLE EASTERN WATER

Adequate supplies of potable water to grow food and to provide for basic human needs is clearly a growing global concern for the present and certainly for the future, and many environmental scientists now argue that access to water could be the most important environmental issue of this century. In the arid Middle East, a combination of factors has made the problem a current, rather than a future, area of major concern. In a nutshell, growing populations and increased demands for additional water fueled by both population and economic factors is placing greater and greater demands on a water supply that is finite and, in its present form and projected usage, inadequate for the future. The problem is simple: The demand for Middle Eastern water exceeds supply, and the problem can only get worse as time goes by. Water could supplant oil as the region's most valuable commodity.

In this circumstance, access to and control of water becomes a major geopolitical matter; as the quote in the title suggests, water could also easily supplant petroleum as the major geopolitical concern of states. The oil-producing states have held sway in the region for years, sometimes with considerable haughtiness but by and large, they are the most water-poor states in the region. It is by no means fanciful to suggest they may find themselves digging into their oil profits to buy water in much the same way that other states have had to come to them for oil.

Statement of the Problem

The water problem is endemic to the Middle East. Although the region is surrounded by seas and oceans, their waters are saline and unusable. Within the region itself, there are only two major river systems (if one excludes the Nile, which flows through only two regional states, Egypt and Sudan). These are the Tigris-Euphrates river system, which provides most of the water for Turkey, Iraq, and Syria; and the Jordan River Basin, which contributes to the water supply of Syria, Israel, Lebanon, and Jordan. Most of the region is arid or semiarid.

Of the two systems, the Tigris-Euphrates is the subject of the most immediate physical and geopolitical concern. The Jordan system came into conflict in the 1960s, when the Islamic countries contemplated restricting or cutting off Israeli access to this water source, which was vital to Israel's survival. One major purpose for which Israel fought the 1967 Arab-Israeli war was to gain Israeli control over the river and its tributaries (including the Sea of Galilee and streams flowing into it). This end was accomplished with the occupation of the Golan Heights, which gave Israel secure control over the headwaters of its water supply. Finding a way to reconcile Syrian demands for a return of occupied territories with Israeli insistence on control of vital water access remains one, and possibly the most important, hurdle confronting a Syrian-Israeli peace accord.

The major regional conflict is over the uses of the Tigris-Euphrates system. As the map indicates, the headwaters of both the Tigris and Euphrates are in eastern Turkey, which is the largest and most powerful country in the region. The Euphrates, which at 1,800 miles in length is the longest river in southwest Asia, flows south from Turkey into Syria, and from Syria into Iraq, where it eventually meets the Tigris at the town of al Qurnah, forming the Shatt al Arab waterway that flows into the Persian Gulf and forms the boundary between Iran and Iraq. The Tigris, on the other hand, begins its 1,180-mile flow in eastern Turkey but flows south directly into Iraq (although it briefly forms a boundary between Turkey and Syria).

Water from the Tigris-Euphrates system is important to all three states, although it is not equally vital to all. Access to the waters is particularly important to Syria, and even more so, to Iraq: The system provides the majority of the water each uses for irrigation as well as drinking water, for which there are no ready substitutes. Expansion of the agricultural sectors for each depends on a reliable supply of water, and growing populations in each country place additional stress on current available supplies. Both Syria and Iraq demand that Turkey increase the amount of flow of the rivers out of Turkey and guarantees of the amount available to them.

Turkey is much less dependent on the system, because it enjoys more rainfall than Iraq and Syria and because it has other river systems that run through the country. Although Turkey is classified as having a water surplus, the Turks have claims on and plans for the system that threaten the access of downstream riparian states. For the Turks, the waters of the Tigris and Euphrates river system are an integral part of their plans for

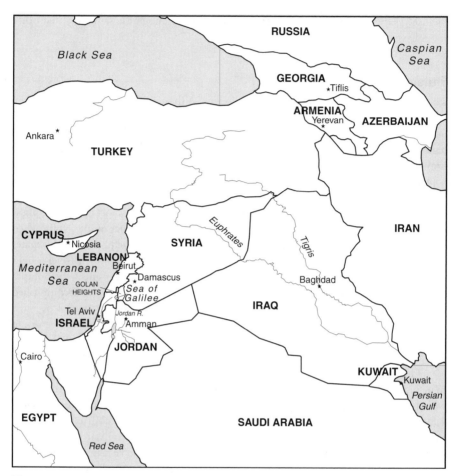

Map 14.1 Map of the Middle East, including the Tigris-Euphrates system and Jordan River

the economic and political development of eastern Turkey. The mountainous area is the site of the Greater Anatolia Project (GAP), and central to that project is the development of a series of hydroelectric dams and reservoirs on the two rivers. In addition to allowing Turkey to control the flow of the rivers, these dams are designed to allow agricultural development of the eastern part of the country through irrigation and also to promote recreational uses of the resulting lakes and thus tourism in the country's poorest region.

The GAP has geopolitical ramifications and purposes as well. The area in which the development is taking place is known to many of its inhabitants as Kurdistan, and the Turkish Kurds have been engaged in a recently suspended, long-term civil war against the Turkish government that has resulted in many deaths and alleged atrocities that have blackened Turkey's eye in international circles (ending the civil war, for instance, has been one of the preconditions for consideration of Turkey's application to the European

Union, a primary objective of the regime in Ankara). Part of the Turkish government's strategy for creating a stable relationship with the Kurds is to make their homeland in Turkey prosperous enough that they will perceive a stake in remaining a part of the country and thus will abandon their secessionist insurrection.

Other regional countries gain a stake in the resolution of the problem in a kind of ripple effect that arises because Syria has claims both against Euphrates and Jordan River waters. In the absence of a satisfactory guarantee that Turkey will keep the water flowing (and Turkey is capable physically of reducing or interrupting the flow altogether), Syria continues to demand a share of the water from the Jordan Basin, which is a matter of considerable concern for Israel, Jordan, and Lebanon (the other users of Jordan River water). To make matters even more complicated, Israel has a nascent alliance with the Turks that may, among other things, result in the importation of Turkish water directly to Israel, providing for them a further interest in Turkey's water situation. Because Saudi Arabia is also a water-poor, oil-rich state that has some interest in importing Turkish water, even it has at least an indirect stake in the problem.

The situation has been intractable, because geopolitics becomes intertwined with the issue of water equity. The issue is clearly defined: Syria and Iraq want and demand concrete, inviolable guarantees to an increasing portion of the water from the two rivers, a demand that reverberates through the interests of the others. Turkey, on the other hand, is perfectly content with the status quo, because that status quo leaves the Turks in control of the situation regarding the supply and control of the water and maximizes their freedom of action.

The problem thus becomes one of claims and counterclaims and leverage. The downstream states base their claims on additional water on demographics like population increases, which no one denies. The Turks, however, counter that the problem is not how much water the Iraqis and Syrians have from the river system, but how they use it. To cite two Turkish examples, the Turks allege that both downstream states grow crops that are inappropriate in their use of water for the amount of water available and given their needs (cotton, for instance), and the Turks allege that downstream riparian states use primitive irrigation techniques that result in a large amount of water being wasted through evaporation. The Turks thus claim that Iraq and Syria receive enough water to sustain themselves if they only use it properly.

With good arguments on both (or all) sides, resolution incorporating change requires leverage to induce agreement. To this point, all the leverage has resided with the Turks. They control the source of the water, they are the most militarily powerful state in the region (thereby ruling out military action to seize the water), and there is nothing that Syria and Iraq have that Turkey needs badly enough to compel the Turks to concede on the water issue. In this region where water is king, the Turks would seem to hold the upper hand.

Possible Means of Resolution

Although discussions have been held periodically between Turkey and the downstream riparian states about the Tigris-Euphrates system, the discussions have not yet approached the point at which anything resembling a solution about equitable distribution has been found. Partly, this is the case because the needs of the downstream states have not become so critical that Iraq and Syria feel the need to try to force the issue. At the same time, both complainants have other, more immediate concerns: Syria has been in the middle of the succession of the late Hafiz al-Assad to his son Bashar, and has the settlement of hostilities (which incorporate a water dimension, of course) with Israel on its diplomatic plate, and more recently it has faced demands to end its occupation of Lebanon and cut its ties to terrorist organizations. The American invasion and occupation of Iraq and the subsequent armed resistance and attempts to reestablish Iraqi sovereignty fills the agenda in Baghdad; any inconveniences caused by water flows from the Tigris and Euphrates pale by comparison. There are no particular outside pressures on Turkey to accommodate either the Syrians or the Iraqis, as both are considered international rogues and have few friends who will bring pressure to bear on them.

What, then, are the possible alternatives that might lead to some form of agreement dividing the waters of the Tigris-Euphrates in a manner that would satisfy all parties. One can safely omit the possibility of military action—an attempted seizure of Turkish land to gain control of the waters, for instance. The armed forces of Turkey are much larger and more powerful than those of either Syria or Iraq (whose military was, of course, disbanded in 2003 and is slowly being rebuilt as a self-defense force). As a member of NATO, Turkish forces are much better equipped than the others. Military threats would be greeted with derision in Ankara.

Although none are very hopeful, there are four other possibilities for bring resolution to the water issue. The first is a *negotiated reallocation* of the current formula for allocating flow from the rivers. Such a negotiation would almost certainly have to be multilateral, probably with outside help provided by some general agency like the United Nations, a regional actor like the Arab League, or a more specialized intergovernmental organization (IGO) like the Water Resources Working Group (WRWG), an organization founded in 1992 to "foster cooperation on water-related issues while creating confidence building measures, and cooperative efforts to alleviate water shortages." The problem with this solution, of course, is the asymmetry of incentives to enter into negotiations; the Turks, after all, see no need to change the formula under which water is currently allocated, and the Syrians and Iraqis can offer few incentives to convince the Turks to change their position. In those circumstances, Turkey would likely be especially unwilling to enter into any discussion, the end result of which might be some mandatory reallocation that it might oppose. In such circumstances, the Turks might well decide that no negotiations are better than negotiations that might provide an unacceptable outcome.

A second approach, advocated vociferously by Turkey, is *improved usage of existing supplies*. As already mentioned, Turkey has maintained all along that the problem Syria and Iraq face is not how much water they receive from the Tigris and Euphrates, but how efficiently and effectively they use it. As noted, Turkish charges are twofold. First, they maintain that neither country has taken sufficient steps to modernize its irrigation system, in which water is allowed to flow through open ditches and to evaporate in the Middle Eastern heat. In the Turkish view, the solution to the downstream water problem is agricultural modernization. Further, they maintain that both countries need to concentrate on growing crops that require less water, such as wheat, rather than crops that require extensive irrigation. These charges are largely valid, but it is not clear where either Iraq or Syria would obtain the resources necessary to engage in the modernization it is alleged they need to undertake. Syria has largely isolated itself from global sources of funding, and the ongoing war continues to dominate and distort the badly disrupted Iraqi economy.

A third approach to the problem is *alternate sources of water*. This supply–side approach is one being pursued throughout various parts of the Middle East—very few states in the region (Turkey, ironically, is one of the few exceptions) have adequate water within their boundaries. Desalinization of seawater has been a popular proposed enterprise (especially in Israel), but has been dogged by problems of expense; if Israel has trouble paying for desalinated water, how could much-poorer Syria and Iraq afford the effort? The fact that Syria is landlocked further complicates its problem—unless it controls Lebanon—and Iraq has only a very short coastline on the Persian Gulf. Bringing water from countries where it is in excess to the Middle East has attracted attention in countries like Saudi Arabia, and Israel and Turkey have been pursuing the possibility of transporting Turkish water to Israel. The problem with both these "solutions" is that they are expensive and thus are available possibilities only for the richer countries of the region; Iraq, and especially Syria, clearly do not fall into that category.

Finally, some have suggested *regional cooperation* as a potential solution. The idea here is that if all the states of the region (probably excluding Israel) could come together and view their mutual water problem as an integral, regional problem, then possibly they could fashion regional solutions from which all would benefit. The problem here is that the incentives to cooperate are, once again, differential. Certainly, mutual cooperation among those who are water deficient might yield benefits. In this particular situation, however, the problem is that Turkey is *not* water deficient, and it is hard to see what benefit they would derive from mutual action and thus what their incentive would be to become involved in the enterprise.

The Prospects

The ongoing barrier to solving the problem of water from the Tigris-Euphrates system is the need to create incentives for Turkey to agree to change. At the moment, they have little incentive other than humanitarian concern for their neighbors, and that is normally insufficient to bring about change, especially when the deprivation being endured by the others is not yet critical.

There is some irony and bitterness in the phrase, "let them drink oil." While Turkey has adequate water supplies, it is not one of the petroleum-rich countries of the region and has not benefited from the prosperity heaped on the oil producers. Now the shoe is on the other foot, and the Turks have to be enjoying the discomfort of their fellow Muslims.

To make progress, Turkey will require some geopolitical incentive to accommodate its downstream riparian states. The hinge may be Turkey's desire to become a prosperous, developed state that can, as Turkey has sought to do for well over a decade, become a full member of the European Union. One requisite for economic development is reliable access to sufficient energy resources to fuel a modern state. In the form of petroleum, that is something the water-poor states (other than Syria) have. A water-for-oil deal may be the best incentive the downstream states can offer. Whether that is attractive enough to whet Turkey's interest depends on whether there are alternative sources for Turkey. One of the most obvious alternatives is the petroleum wealth of the Caspian Sea area, to which the discussion turns as the subject of the second mini-case in this chapter.

THE CASPIAN SEA OIL FIELDS

Petroleum was the most geopolitically potent natural resource of the twentieth century, and especially the latter half of that century, when the concentration of production shifted to the Persian Gulf littoral and the oil-rich states of that region gained control of the wealth under their soil from the major western oil companies (known in the area as the Seven Sisters). Previously poor and underdeveloped countries became strategic prizes in the East–West competition, favor was curried, wars were fought, and American president Jimmy Carter declared the security of the Persian Gulf vital to United States interests. As if to prove the gravity of his assertion in what became known as the Carter Doctrine, the United States led a coalition of over 25 states to expel the invading Iraqis from Kuwaiti soil in 1990–1991.

Western dependence on the Persian Gulf, which possesses nearly two-thirds of the world's known petroleum reserves, for energy has never been entirely comfortable for the oil consumers, and as additional demand from new (e.g., China and India) and existing users continues, this discomfort will almost certainly increase. This dependence ties the consuming, importing countries to the often volatile politics of the region, leaves them subject to periodic extortion when oil supplies are withheld and leads to increased prices at the pump, and necessitates the devotion of military and other resources to a region of the world that would not otherwise warrant the expenditure. The problem and the solution, of course, is how to reduce that dependency.

The basic problem is not, as is sometimes advertised, a shortage of alternate sources of energy. There is, for instance, a large amount of unrecovered oil in the United States, but the cost of extracting it is either too high to make it economical (there is plenty of oil under Texas, but until recently it has not been feasible economically to pay the $60 a barrel or so to recover it), or the effort runs afoul of environmental or other concerns (the current controversy over exploiting the Alaska wilderness, for instance). There are also large reserves in or adjacent to the west coast of Africa, Venezuela, Indonesia, and a number of other places where the politics are nearly as complicated as in the Persian Gulf. There is also, of course, the possibility of reducing dependency by reducing levels of usage and hence demand, a source many governments (especially the United States) have been politically unwilling to embrace and champion seriously. Even questions of global warming from burning fossil fuels enters the equation.

In these circumstances, the desire to break dependence on Persian Gulf oil has led the world's oil consumers to look, among other places, at the small Soviet successor state of Azerbaijan, as well as Kazakhstan. Azerbaijan's capital, Baku, sits on the banks of the Caspian Sea (which is actually a salt lake and the world's largest inland body of water), under which some of the richest deposits of petroleum and natural gas left in the world lie. According to Maugeri, "the proven reserves of Azerbaijan and Kazakhstan stand at about 18 billion barrels, but these countries' total recoverable reserves are estimated to range between 70 and 80 billion barrels." The largest of these deposits are about 60 miles offshore from Baku, making it the focus of concerted exploration and exploitation.

Azerbaijan and Kazakhstan are the two most important Caspian Sea littoral states (other than Russia) with claims to Caspian oil and natural gas (the others are Uzbekistan and Turkmenistan). The situations of the two states are similar but not identical. Kazakhstan is currently the larger exporter, ranking thirteenth globally in 2004 at slightly over one million barrels a day. Because of its location, Kazakhstan has also negotiated and begun constructing a pipeline to China, but the bulk of its eventual exports, like those of Azerbaijan, will be westward (westward options are catalogued in a Department of Energy report listed in the Web sites at the end of this chapter). These alternatives are essentially the same as those for Azerbaijan, which has a more interesting geopolitical situation that will thus be the focus of this case.

The existence of Caspian Sea petroleum is nothing new. In fact, oil was discovered in the area in the second half of the nineteenth century, and by the beginning of the twentieth century, the region supplied most of Russia's oil needs (Imperial Russia completed its annexation of Azerbaijan in 1828). Although Azerbaijan declared its independence in 1918, it was absorbed into the Soviet Union in 1920. During the period when it was a republic of the Soviet Union, Azerbaijan was clearly not an alternative source of petroleum for an increasingly addicted West, however, because of the nature of the Cold War competition and thus Western unwillingness to become dependent on Soviet-controlled petroleum reserves.

The demise of the Soviet Union opened the floodgates for Western entrepreneurs to be drawn to Baku and elsewhere along the shores of the Caspian Sea. When Azerbaijan declared its independence from the Soviet Union on August 30, 1991, the oil companies were not far behind, engaging in a flood of speculation and exploration that many veteran oilmen say had not been seen since the opening of the Texas oil fields in the early 1900s. By the middle 1990s, the Caspian Sea fields were widely being extolled as the means by which the developed world would break the stranglehold imposed by the Persian Gulf oil-producing states. Yet today, little Caspian Sea oil finds its way to the West except from Kazakhstan (through Russia), and the prospects for that situation changing in the short term are unpromising.

Why is this the case? There is certainly no lack of interest among Western governments and the private oil companies in exploiting and bringing to market the petroleum riches lying beneath the Caspian Sea, and there are no major technical or engineering barriers present either. But there are geopolitical problems: One is the political instability of the region; another is the geopolitics of piping the riches to market because of competing routes with different advantages and barriers.

Regional Instabilities

As noted, five states have claims to parts either of the oil or natural gas under or surrounding the Caspian basin. The three northern states (Azerbaijan, Kazakhstan, and Russia) have agreed to a division of the resource contiguous to their shores, but the oil from Azerbaijan still does not flow freely. The reason it does not is most clearly exemplified by the political situation in Azerbaijan.

The major geopolitical liability for Azerbaijan centers on two enclave areas that are points of major contention between Muslim Azerbaijan and neighboring Christian Armenia, Nagorno-Karabakh and Naxcivan (sometimes known as Nakichevan). Of these two disputes, the ongoing conflict over Nagorno-Karabakh has been the more serious and has created the most difficulties for Azerbaijan generally and for exploiting the oil in particular.

Nagorno-Karabakh was an enclave with a majority Armenian population that is located physically in Azerbaijan. There has been a long history of accusations by residents of the enclave that they have been mistreated by their Muslim rulers, and this has accompanied an unease with being physically separated from their Armenian brethren, as the accompanying map shows.

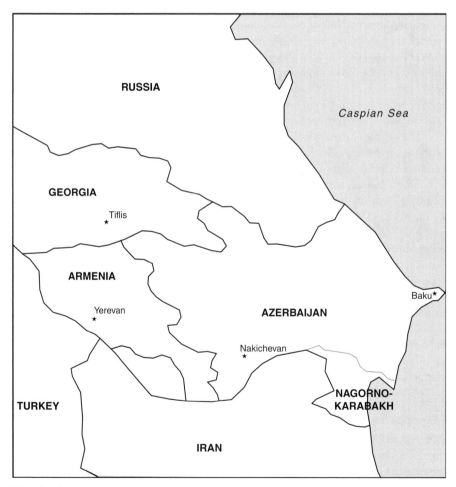

Map 14.2 Map of Azerbaijan and surrounding areas (Armenia, Chechnya, and Turkey)

The contest over the status of Nagorno-Karabakh, which was treated as an autonomous region within Azerbaijan by the Soviets, goes back to the latter days of the Soviet Union. In 1988, the Armenians petitioned Moscow to cede Nagorno-Karabakh to Armenia and were rebuffed by the Soviets. When Azerbaijan declared its independence, it announced that the region would lose its autonomous status and become an integral part of Azerbaijan, an action that sent residents into opposition. War broke out between secessionists from Nagorno-Karabakh and Azerbaijan, and Armenian troops entered the fray in support of the ethnic Armenians. By August 1993, Armenian forces had occupied the area and had also taken control of the corridor linking Nagorno-Karabakh to Armenia. A ceasefire was arranged in 1994, but the issue has never been permanently settled. In the meantime, Armenia remains in control of one-sixth of Azerbaijani territory that constitutes Nagorno-Karabakh and the corridor, and the possibility that fighting will resume remains an ever present likelihood in this undeclared war.

The fighting over Nagorno-Karabakh has left two legacies with which Azerbaijan must struggle. Of the most immediate concern are Azerbaijani refugees from the war zone. It is estimated that the refugees number over a million, which is the largest percentage of refugees (as a part of the population) in any country in the world, and most of them live in the most wretched of conditions within Azerbaijan. Getting the oil to market and hence gaining the revenues that oil will put into government coffers has the potential greatly to ease this problem.

The other legacy is the danger of renewed violence, which affects thinking about where pipelines can be constructed to get the petroleum to the West. The Armenians have made no secret that they are in a physical position to disrupt any lines going near Armenian territory and that they would not be reluctant to engage in disruption if they feel they need to.

The other political problem in Azerbaijan surrounds the government of the country itself. The head of government is Heydar Aliyev, a former first secretary of the Azerbaijan Communist Party who was removed from office by Mikhail Gorbachev in 1987 on charges of rampant corruption. Aliyev returned to the political arena in 1995 as the leader of something called the New Azerbaijan Party (NAP) and was reelected president of the country in 2003. According to the *CIA Factbook 2004,* corruption in the country is "ubiquitous." The 1999 Corruption Perceptions Index, produced by Berlin-based Transparency Inc., rates the Azerbaijan government as the third most corrupt regime in the world after Cameroon and Nigeria and right before Indonesia. In addition, there have been charges of nepotism and cronyism against the Aliyev family. Dealing with the regime is a major source of frustration for the oil industry and casts doubts, among other things, about how much of the projected oil revenue would by applied to problems like the refugees as opposed to lining Aliyev family's pockets.

The Pipeline Problem

The problem of exploiting the Caspian Sea oil and gas fields is not technical in nature; rather, it is almost entirely political, or, more specifically, geopolitical. In the decade or so since the demise of the Soviet Union, the major global oil companies have descended on the Caspian region, generously laden with Western expertise and funds and have transformed the rickety petroleum industry run by the communists into a modern Western-style operation. Although it is true that the Abseron Peninsula on which much of the Baku refining capacity resides has been proclaimed one of the most polluted places on earth, the oil companies are ready and eager to make the oil flow.

The problem is finding a way to get it safely and securely to market, which will help relieve the world's dependence on the Middle East. To this point, there have been three proposals for an Azerbaijani pipeline to the West; none of them meet the dual criteria of security and avoidance of the Persian Gulf. The three routes under consideration go through Russia, Turkey, and Iran. Each is flawed in some political manner.

The Russian pipeline would run across Azerbaijan's northern boundary with Russia and would make its way to the Black Sea, from which it could then be shipped to Western markets. As might be imagined, the Russians are very strong advocates of this route, because they would be able to charge a duty on the petroleum as it is transshipped across Russian territory, thereby providing needed money to aid the transformation and development of the Russian state.

Aiding and hopefully stabilizing the Russian state has considerable support in the West, and especially the United States, but the Russian "solution" raises two objections. The first is that the Russian government has proved so inept and corrupt that it would likely squander the revenues or have them skimmed off by corrupt officials or other criminal elements in the country. Friedman describes Russian President Vladimir Putin as a classic petrolist, because he is using Russia's oil revenues from the Caspian Sea and elsewhere (Russia is currently the world's second-largest oil producer and exporter) to aid the imposition of authoritarian measures by the regime. More fundamentally, however, the pipeline route traverses the rebellious province of Chechnya. The Russians realize that no one is going to endorse a pipeline scheme that could be held hostage by rebellious Chechens, and the recent spate of Chechen terrorism cools a good deal of the enthusiasm for this solution for getting Azerbaijani oil to market.

The Turkish solution has the same kind of problem. The idea here is to build a pipeline across Turkey that would connect to the country's existing oil refineries in the northwest part of the country (which, unfortunately, has been the site of major earthquakes in the past few years). The oil would then be shipped through the Black Sea into the Mediterranean and to market.

The geopolitical problem in this case is that the Turkish pipeline would have to be built across or adjacent to Armenian territory, thereby enmeshing it in the volatile relations between those two successor states. Azerbaijan has no direct border with Turkey. The shortest route to Turkish soil from Azerbaijan is through Armenia (and possibly Nagorno Karabakh, depending on how a route might be fashioned), which is clearly untenable as long as the conflict between the two states exists. The alternatives would be to go around Armenia to the south through Iran, which hardly solves the problem of dependence on the Persian Gulf, or through Georgia. Georgia itself has been unstable, with Abkhazian secessionists periodically causing problems that have led to a Russian army occupation of parts of the country, and it is doubtful the Armenians would hesitate to violate Georgian soil to damage the pipeline if they felt the need to do so.

The Prospects

Because the dual criteria of pipeline security and lessening dependence on Persian Gulf oil have not been met, the Caspian Sea fields remain at far less than peak capacity, certainly not pumping the quantities of oil that could make a difference in worldwide supply and thus price. Other issues remain that contribute to the standstill. There is currently only partial agreement on boundaries in the Caspian Sea among the five littoral states, although the Azerbaijanis, Russians, and Kazakhs have announced an agreement between them on division of rights. Disagreements such as this are not, however, fundamental. What must occur is an agreement on a pipeline route and a guarantee that the route will be secured so that interruptions in supply do not occur.

It is not clear that the principals can make that guarantee at this time. The proximity of Azerbaijan to Chechnya and the Russians' continuing problems there suggest they would have great difficulty providing adequate assurances that Chechen separatists would not act to interrupt the flow. Georgia does not have the might to block the Armenians. Those proposing alternative routes simply lack the leverage to make the necessary assurances to get the pipeline going.

What will have to happen to break the impasse? The probable answer involves extra-regional action. Regional powers cannot or will not act effectively. Russia has been unable to squelch the Chechens (despite the killing of Chechen leader Shamil Baseyev in July 2006), and Turkey is certainly in no political position to suppress Armenian interruptions, given the genocide of the Ottoman Turks against Armenia early in the twentieth century (although Turkey and Armenia met in early 2001 to explore ways to resolve their historical and ongoing differences). That means the impasse will remain until those who have the most vested interest in access to Caspian Sea reserves decide to act themselves. Direct Western involvement opens up so many unpleasant prospects that, for now, it is far easier to dream of the prospects of Caspian Sea oil than to bring it home.

CONCLUSION

Scarcity of natural resources is a continuing source of friction between states that results in geopolitical competition to attain these resources. In some cases, these conflicts can lead to violence, in some instances they can be amicably resolved, and in others, they remain simmering sources of disagreement.

The liveliest resource conflicts in the contemporary world concern potable water and petroleum. Both are scarce resources and will become even more scarce as population increases places greater pressure on available water and new claimants demand greater amounts of petroleum to fuel their continued development. The two mini-cases reflect how these two scarce resources rankle the situations in two particular places. In the Caucasus, the effects of international conflict (Nagorno-Karabakh) and internal strife (Chechnya) complicate and, to this point, make impossible the exploitation of a scarce resource to an outside world anxious for its use. In the region serviced by the Tigris-Euphrates river system, the conflict remains dormant and the geopolitics seem to militate against violence, but tension remains.

The point of the discussion is to highlight the diversity of potential situations in which scarce natural resources have affected worldwide situations in the near past and present, as some indication of the kind of role resource scarcity may play in the future. As the world's population continues to grow, there will be an increasing demand for potable water in an environment of limited elasticity: The supply can be increased by bringing water from water-rich to water-poor areas or by increasing the supply through desalinization, but both are economically prohibitive. As the global economy grows to encompass more states, that participation will place added demands for the energy that undergirds much economic activity. And while it is difficult to detail all the possible areas where resource scarcity will result in political conflict in the future, there is no doubt at all that such conflicts will arise and be troublesome.

STUDY/DISCUSSION QUESTIONS

1. Resource scarcity and its geopolitical implications have not been a prominent topic in international relations to this point. What is the actual and potential problem that scarce resources can have? How might this be a bigger problem in the future?

2. What are the major dynamics of the international competition for water and petroleum? How do countries like China and India contribute to these problems?

3. The possession of a scarce resource may give particular leverage and power to its possessor. Using petroleum as an example, show how this leverage can work. How does Iran provide a particularly good example of how this leverage can provide geopolitical advantage?

4. Describe the problem created by excess demands made on the waters of the Tigris-Euphrates water system (including how it spills over into the Syrian-Israeli debate over the Golan Heights). What is the status of the dispute, how can it be resolved, and why is violence unlikely to be the means of resolution?

5. Why is access to Caspian Sea oil and natural gas such a large international priority? What political factors are interfering with the ability to bring this resource to market? What can be done to break the impasse?

6. Can you discern any patterns from the three mini-case studies included in this chapter? Can you think of other examples of resource conflicts that carry out the same or different themes from those presented here?

READING/RESEARCH MATERIAL

"Azerbaijan." *Microsoft Encarta Online Encyclopedia 2000*. Microsoft Corporation, 2000.

"Azerbaijan," *CIA World Factbook 2000*. Washington, DC: Central Intelligence Agency, 2000. (www.odci.gov/cia/publications/factbook/geos/aj.html)

BBC News. "Q&A: Why Does Nagorno-Karabakh Matter?" BBC News, March 31, 1998.

Bijian, Zheng. "China's 'Peaceful Rise' to Great-Power Status." *Foreign Affairs* 84, 5 (September/October 2005), 18–24.

Das, Gurcharan. "The Indian Model." *Foreign Affairs* 85, 4 (July/August 2006), 2–16.

Elhance, A. *Hydropolitics in the Third World: Conflict and Cooperation in International River Basins.* Washington, DC: United States Institute of Peace Press, 1999.

Friedman, Thomas. "The First Law of Petropolitics." *Foreign Policy,* May/June 2006, 36.

Goldwyn, David L. "Energy Security: The New Threats in Latin America and Africa." *Current History* 105, 695 (December 2006), 441–446.

Homer-Dixon, Thomas. "Environmental Scarcities and Violent Conflict: Evidence from Cases." In Sean Lynn-Jones and Stephen Miller, (eds.), *Global Dangers: Changing Dimensions of International Security,* Cambridge, MA: MIT Press, 1995, 144–179.

Lowi, M. "Bridging the Divide: Transboundary Resource Disputes and the Case of West-Bank Water." *International Security* 18, 1 (1993), 113–138.

Maugeri, Leonardo. "Two Cheers for Expensive Oil." *Foreign Affairs* 85, 2 (March/April 2006), 149–160.

Pope, Carl, and Bjorn Lomborg. "The State of Nature: The *Foreign Policy* Debate." *Foreign Policy,* July/August 2005, 66–74.

Yergin, Daniel. "Ensuring Energy Security." *Foreign Affairs* 85, 2 (March/April 2006), 69–82.

———. *The Prize: The Epic Quest for Oil, Money, and Power.* New York: Simon and Schuster, 1991.

Zweig, David, and Bi Jianhai. "China's Global Hunt for Energy." *Foreign Affairs* 84, 5 (September/October 2005), 18–24.

WEB SITES

Overview of the Tigris and Euphrates damming project from Turkish view
    The G.A.P. Project at http://www.mfa.gov.tr/grup;d/dc/dcd/gap.htm
Information on water resources as well as data on global freshwater issues
    The World's Water at http://www.worldwater.org
Focus on water in the Israeli-Palestinian conflict and Jordan River Basin
    Water and Conflict at http://aternet.rug.ac.be
Analysis of Caspian sea mineral wealth dispute
    EIA: Caspian Sea Region at http://www.eia.doe.gov/emeu/cabs/Caspian.html
World oil production figures from Infoplease at
    http://www.infoplease.com.ipa/AO922041.html
Analysis of Kazakhstan potential oil export routes at
    http://www.eia.doe.gov/emeu/cabs/Kazaexpo.html
Corruption Perception Index at
    www.transparency.org/policy

CHAPTER FIFTEEN

Worse Than the Bubonic Plague
AIDS IN AFRICA AS A TRANSSTATE ISSUE

PRÉCIS

By now, the dimensions of the human tragedy being inflicted on most of the countries of sub-Saharan Africa by the HIV-AIDS pandemic are known to most, at least in general terms. The list of lives lost, and the demographic consequences of those losses for the generations yet to come, have received widespread publicity. The pandemic is real, it is serious, and it is getting worse. Could it be the harbinger of some future horror as bad or worse?

This case study attempts to examine the AIDS crisis from the vantage point of a transstate issue that can only be approached and solved through an international effort. The case reviews the dimensions of the problem and its suggested solutions, a matter made more public by U.S. Secretary of State Colin Powell's adoption of the problem in 2001 and echoed by President Bush in 2003. It then raises the question of whether there is sufficient international will and interest to tackle the problem and whether thinking about this health disaster and its solution is a precedent for dealing with future health disasters (the SARS and avian flu problems serve as examples) might produce an international reaction.

It has been described as the world's most severe health crisis since the bubonic plague ravaged Europe during the Middle Ages, with current projections that more people will die from it than succumbed to the black death. Those who observe its deadly progress no longer refer to it as an epidemic; instead, it is now universally called a "pandemic," because its effects encompass a whole continent and threaten to become a worldwide disaster. Former U.S Secretary of State Colin S. Powell adopted its solution as a personal cause, as did President George W. Bush.

Its effects, which have been widely publicized in recent years, are staggering in their human costs. Left unchecked, several countries that are most affected could see life expectancy, which has been declining for a decade, dip below 30 years within the next decade, according to some projections. A whole generation of children has been orphaned as their parents have died from the disease, and their countries will soon face a ghastly situation in which the leadership the parents of those orphans were supposed to provide will instead be a void, producing a lost generation. We could even see the absolute decline in population on those parts of the continent most adversely affected.

The problem, of course, is AIDS, and the pandemic is at work on the continent of Africa. It is a human disaster with which we all have by now at least a passing acquaintance, due to the tireless efforts of those with an interest in and desire to treat and cure the grisly results. Yet despite a generalized awareness that there is a global problem, AIDS in Africa hardly dents the international agenda. Among the dedicated medical caregivers who seek to lessen the suffering, there is great, even heroic effort both to publicize and to treat the disaster. The international community, including those with the ability to address and ameliorate the problem, basically averts its eyes when asked for help, and, if it cannot completely ignore the cries for assistance, it does less than the advocates say it should. The United States has pledged $15 billion to help cope; even if it all is eventually spent, it will be a small drop in a very large bucket for a problem the treatment of which is estimated to require $38 billion annually.

Why is this the case? One part of the answer almost surely comes from the fact that the disaster is occurring far away, in central and southern Africa, in the most distant and obscure part of the world physically and in terms of consciousness for most people who do not live on or study the continent. The AIDS epidemic in the United States, which the African pandemic absolutely dwarfs as a physical problem, has received massive publicity and the most concerted medical research and pharmaceutical efforts. Africans, suffering monumentally more, have benefited relatively little from these efforts.

Part of the reason for this inattention is economic. AIDS "cocktails," widely available to Western sufferers from HIV and AIDS, typically cost between $10,000 and $15,000 dollars a year, a sum far in excess of the per capita income of most African states, which measure annual per capita income in the *hundreds* of dollars. Even treatments for the side effects of AIDS-caused immunity deficiencies like pneumonia and tuberculosis that cost far less are unavailable in most African countries. In the United States, a person diagnosed with HIV or AIDS has the medical doors opened wide, and the treatment options spelled out. In many African countries, all a doctor who diagnoses a patient with the disease can do is to tell the victim's loved ones to take the patient home to die.

One result has been a virtual scandal between the pharmaceutical firms most heavily involved in HIV-AIDS and Third World drug firms intent on manufacturing cheaper versions of medication, pitting international patent regimes against humanitarian concerns. The drug companies, buffeted by worldwide accusations of profiteering at the expense of massive human suffering, recanted in 2001 and agreed to sell HIV-AIDS drugs at a greatly reduced price (although still well above the means of many in Africa).

International inattention to this horrible plague is difficult to understand, and it is the purpose of this case study to try to shed some light on both the pandemic and how it is a broader concern than for its direct victims. The AIDS pandemic is a classic, although hideous transstate issue, but it remains in the international shadow of more popular international problems like the environment or human rights. We will try to see why. In order to do so, we will proceed in three steps. First, we will examine the AIDS problem in Africa through the lens of the structure of other transstate issues, in the process trying to establish whether African AIDS has the same characteristics as more familiar, orthodox issues spanning the globe and spilling across international boundaries. Second, we will look at some of the characteristics of this particular transstate problem, both as primer (or refresher) for the reader and as a way to see how this issue differs from or is similar to other transstate issues. Third, we will examine how other transstate issues have been addressed internationally, to see whether similar efforts either have been attempted in the AIDS case or might prove helpful in attacking the tragedy of AIDS in Africa. We will conclude by suggesting that what is learned from treating HIV-AIDS as a transstate issue may provide a relevant model for similar international outbreaks of diseases in the future, such as SARS and avian flu viruses, which currently primarily affect Asia and could spread elsewhere.

THE PANDEMIC AS A TRANSSTATE ISSUE

A word about terminology is necessary at this point. Although there is not complete consensus on a definition of a transstate issue, this one derived from Snow and Brown's *United States Foreign Policy,* will suffice: A transstate issue is a "problem caused by the actions of states or other actors that cannot be solved by the actions of individual states or other actors within individual states alone." The heart of this definition is its assertion of two common, interrelated characteristics of a classic transstate issue: Both its causation and its solution go beyond the ability of individual sovereign jurisdictions.

Not all the problems normally identified as transstate issues meet the criteria of this definition. Some environmental problems such as ozone depletion and the greenhouse effect do, but others, like human rights, do not. In the case of human rights, for instance, it is not physically impossible for individual states to enforce a uniform set of human rights standards; the problem is that some states choose not to do so, and the international community has to this point not been able to agree completely on appropriate standards and the means to enforce them. Problems that could be solved by individual states but are not can be referred to as *semi-transstate issues.*

There are also global problems that may rise to the severity of transstate issues but have not achieved that level of severity or notoriety in people's minds, depending on one's individual vantage point. Global overpopulation is recognized by many demographers and futurists as a grave future threat to the world, and it has engaged the efforts of many population planners and the like. Despite demographic projections of future doom, however, the results have not been so devastating to this point that they activate universal concern or action. Transstate issues in this category can be thought of as *potential transstate issues*.

Clearly, these distinctions form a hierarchy of international concerns. Potential transstate issues are at the bottom of the hierarchy (although by no means necessarily at the bottom of the list of international problems that the international system must consider), because they are less immediate in their effects than full-scale transstate issues. Likewise, semi-transstate issues are less worrisome than full-blown transstate issues because the problems are solvable if the international actors show the willingness to engage in the actions that would solve them.

Transstate issues, on the other hand, are the most intractable and difficult. Partly this is the case because, by definition, they require cooperative actions across sovereign state boundaries, which often generates friction and suspicion of intrusion on state prerogatives. At the same time, the solutions, where they are known, are often controversial. To cite an example from Chapter 13, how much reduction in greenhouse gas emissions is necessary to eliminate how much surface warming, and who will have to reduce how much? Where solutions to these issues are known, they are often quite expensive, and must compete for scarce resources with other domestic and international priorities for attention and funding. Where the effects of the problem are distant—either in time or who is affected—attention to the solutions may be disadvantaged in the competition for resources, and especially funds. Finally, when the transstate issue has a North–South, developed world–developing world overlay, as they often do, the heart of the debate often gets swept up in the ongoing differences regarding the "obligations" of the developed world more aggressively to address the developmental needs of the less developed countries.

How does the African AIDS pandemic rate in this scheme of concerns? Clearly, it is not a potential problem because, as noted in the introduction, millions of people have already died from the disease, millions are infected with HIV or AIDS and likely will die, and the fact and trend of infection will not abate without intervention. One can make a partial case, at least early on in the progression of the pandemic, that African AIDS has some of the characteristics of a semi-transstate disease, in that the efforts of states have either been inadequate to stem the problem before it reached such enormous proportions or, in some cases, in the physical denial that the problem existed (or even that it does exist). That may have been true earlier, but it is no longer the case. One of the major newer sources of HIV infection has been from African soldiers. Some soldiers sent into other African countries as peacekeepers have acquired the virus through sexual contact with infected natives, and then taken it home and transmitted it to their fellow countrymen. At the same time, already infected peacekeepers may spread the disease in countries where they serve through sexual contact with natives. Other than somehow enforcing abstinence or safe sex, it is not clear how the actions of individual states acting alone could stop that problem.

The pandemic thus has risen to the status of a full-scale transstate issue, with all the characteristics and problems associated with such an issue. Clearly, the divisions between states exacerbates the problem by making cross-boundary cooperative treatment programs impossible or ineffective. The motto of the World Health Organization (WHO), that "disease knows no frontiers," clearly applies to the pandemic; the response that solutions should be coterminous with the problem has not yet become the norm.

The other common characteristics apply as well. There is basic disagreement not only about causes of the pandemic but also the solutions. Within the scientific community, there is a small fringe that denies the relationship between HIV and AIDS and denies the disease kills anyone, a position endorsed by the president of one African country (South Africa) and vociferously denounced by virtually all of the global medical community. Solutions tend to center on the provision of cheap drugs to treat the disease or its symptoms, putting advocates into conflict with the pharmaceutical firms that produce HIV-AIDS drugs and activating debates over whether prevention or treatment is the best approach. The matter of treatment raises the question of cost, which most of the African states simply cannot come close to bearing and which can only be approached with either massive subsidizing of current drugs by the most developed states or the discovery of much cheaper alternatives. Major drug companies have offered substantial subsidization, but it is not clear this is adequate given the paucity of African health budgets. Finally, the issue also is tinged by the matter of developmental obligations: AIDS is arguably the single greatest barrier to African development today and, it is alleged, ultimately the most effective way to stem the behavior that creates the problem is through the economic development of the societies in which it is occurring.

DIMENSIONS OF THE PROBLEM

For most of the world, the severity of the problems facing African countries is almost inconceivable, and as long as the rampant spread of the disease is essentially isolated to the most marginalized continent of the globe, encouraging confronting and coming to terms with its effects will be difficult for most people. Yet, there is reason to do so on two counts that go beyond but by no means ignore the immediate horror.

One of these reasons is that the pandemic will almost certainly spread to other continents. There is, for instance, some evidence that AIDS is increasing in parts of Asia, where there are much larger populations that could be subject to infection but where the resources to deal with the problem are not much greater than they are in Africa. An AIDS pandemic in a country like China—where as many as a million cases have already been reported—could be catastrophic. The same is true of India. The other reason is that the way the AIDS pandemic is dealt with may provide a model—good or bad—of how the world might deal with similar problems in the future.

Directly connected to the immune deficiencies associated with AIDS has been the recurrence of some diseases (smallpox, for instance) that had virtually disappeared from the world but are returning. At the same time, there are other virulent diseases now isolated geographically that could also spread and become transstate problems. Prominent among these currently incurable diseases is Ebola, a highly contagious virus so far isolated to Africa that kills up to 90 percent of those who are infected by it in isolated outbreaks. In 2003 the SARS (sudden acute respiratory syndrome) outbreak raised great fears, surpassed by forebodings of the possible outbreak of avian flu among humans more recently. As we shall suggest in the conclusion, the ways in which the AIDS pandemic is treated may have value as a precedent for dealing with other potentially international pestilences such as avian flu and other diseases that may emerge in the future.

How the African AIDS transstate issue is handled, in other words, has both substantive and procedural importance for the future.

Origins and Parameters of the Pandemic

The AIDS virus was first identified in an African country, the then Belgian Congo, in 1959. Although public awareness of the disease in the developed world is generally associated with its outbreak in the United States in the 1980s and 1990s, the fact that the origins of the disease are African has helped mold the way Africans and the world view the disease. Currently, the most widely held explanation suggests that the disease first occurred in chimpanzees and was somehow transferred to humans, a point of some sensitivity among many Africans because of racist implications concerning the interactions between Africans and primates. In Africa, there is greater ignorance and denial of AIDS, and at least part of the reason for this denial is the imputation that AIDS is an "African disease."

Certainly the continent has suffered the bulk of the ravages of the pandemic, and there is no predictable end in sight. The raw statistics are staggering. According to UNAIDS—an umbrella group of UN agencies, the World Bank, and the WHO—42 million people worldwide had AIDS in 2003, and 30 million of them were African (about 70 percent of the total). Already, nearly 19 million people had died from AIDS, of whom 3.8 million were children under 15. In 1999, 4 million out of an estimated 5.4 million infected were African (about 74 percent), and 85 percent of the 2.8 million killed in 1999 by the disease were African. Approximately 13.2 million children have been orphaned by the disease; 12 million of them live in Africa (over 90 percent). Possibly most chillingly according to a CNN report, "The U.S. Census Board projects that AIDS deaths and the loss of future population from the deaths of women of childbearing age means that by 2010, sub-Saharan Africa will have 71 million fewer people than it would have otherwise." According to 2004 UNAIDS figures, in seven sub-Saharan African countries—Zambia, Zimbabwe, Swaziland, the Central African Republic, Lesotho, Mozambique, and Malawi—life expectancy for a newborn child is below 40 years. The overall AIDS infection rate on the continent is 8.6 percent (the worldwide average is 1.1 percent), with the highest rates in Swaziland (38.3%), Botswana (37.3%), and South Africa (25%). By contrast, 30 million people were estimated to have died in medieval Europe during the bubonic plague, thereby explaining the title of this case study. The population of Europe at the time was much smaller than the African population today, meaning a higher proportion of Europeans died of the plague, so the analogy between the two events is not perfect.

Why did this happen and why does it continue to happen? Some understanding of why the problem has reached the proportions that it has and of why it continues largely unchecked is necessary to understand the problem itself, its transstate nature, and how and whether there is an analogy between this tragedy and other similar transstate problems in the future.

There is not a general consensus on the reasons why the pandemic has reached the levels it has achieved, and thus any list will be subject to challenge and disagreement.

Having said that, we can identify at least six factors that have contributed to the current state of affairs. The reader is encouraged to look for others.

Ignorance and Denial. Part of the problem is ignorance of the disease and its consequences among many African citizens, and especially those who are undereducated and reside in the rural areas of the continent. In most countries (Uganda is a notable exception), governments have not mounted aggressive campaigns of citizen education about the dangers and consequences of HIV-AIDS and how personally to lessen those dangers. Originally, this absence itself was a form of denial of the severity of the problem, and it is currently made worse by limitations on government health budgets and the absence of treatments to give hope to those identified as infected.

Some of the results of ignorance and denial are macabre. In some parts of the continent, for instance, there is the belief that having sexual intercourse with a virgin will cure the disease in a male, thereby assuring a maximally high level of infection among young teenaged girls.

The most insidious form of denial comes from a small segment of the scientific community, which denies that the disease exists. The leading spokesman of this position is University of California at Berkeley molecular biologist Peter Duesberg, whose book *Inventing the AIDS Myth* argues there is no link between HIV and AIDS, and that the only reason the connection is maintained is because of the amount of research funding available to the scientific community to study the relationship. A variation of this theme is propounded by Ghanaian magazine publisher Baffour Ankomah, who maintains there is no such thing as AIDS and that the anti-AIDS campaign is nothing but a foreign plot to "destroy" Africa. In his magazine, *New African,* he has gone so far as to suggest, "What we call AIDS is actually U.S. biological warfare gone wrong." Among highly visible public figures, the most prominent skeptic of the existence and effects of the disease is South African president Thabo Mbeki.

Taboos on Discussion of the Pandemic. In a number of African countries, there is a strong reluctance to engage in open discussions of AIDS. Part of the reason for this reluctance can be found in social taboos about discussing sexuality and death. One result is that obituaries rarely refer to AIDS as the cause of death, preferring vague references to succumbing to a "long illness" or the like. This aversion to discussing sexual matters has also made things like "safe sex" programs promoting abstinence or contraception less effectiveness than they might otherwise have been.

In some cases, the reluctance to discuss the disease has more practical grounds. In a number of countries, public reportage of the pandemic is opposed on the grounds that publicizing it would discourage tourism, a principal source of foreign exchange for some states. Because they generally lack the resources to do anything about the pandemic anyway, many politicians are reluctant to discuss it, because their inability to treat sufferers makes them appear less effective as public servants. As evidence that ignoring the problem may appear to be a viable strategy to African leaders, the 11th International Conference of AIDS and STDs (Sexually Transmitted Diseases) in Africa, held in Lusaka, Zambia, in 1998, was not attended by a single African head of state.

Civil Wars. Particularly during the last decade, a number of African countries have been the victims of internal violence. In most cases (Liberia, Sierra Leone, parts of the Democratic Republic of Congo) these conflicts rarely rise to the level of organized conflict that a professional soldier would call war. Rather, they tend to involve attacks against the civilian population by more or less organized armed groups whose members are more likely to be referred to as "fighters" than as "soldiers." Often, the purpose of these activities is criminal. For instance, a basic motivation of the Revolutionary United Front (RUF) of Sierra Leone is to destabilize governance and thereby to facilitate their plundering of that country's diamond mines (so-called "blood diamonds").

In these circumstances, a major purpose of the "revolutionaries" is terrorizing and humiliating the target population (or portion of the general population), and an important tactic of that terror is often the systematic rape of females in the combat zones. Because many of the fighters are young teenagers, the result is increased infection rates among the young, a contributory factor in lowering life expectancy. There is also a chain effect, as young women are infected by HIV-positive fighters and then pass the disease along to other sexual partners. As noted earlier in discussing the transstate nature of the problem, when international peacekeepers are imported to quell the violence, they also sometimes contract the disease and take it back to their countries, or begin the cycle by infecting the natives they are charged with protecting. Finally, an important effect of these civil conflicts is to disrupt the provision of public services, including the primitive health care systems found in most African states, and to force the diversion of resources that might have otherwise been devoted to the pandemic to treating the more immediate and direct effects of the war effort.

Debt and Poverty. Even in countries not prone to violence, the existence of enormous poverty, often exacerbated by the widespread foreign debt under which many African countries labor makes matters worse. Poverty means the resources to try to treat the disease are unavailable, and this in turn has a multiplying effect. As Lawrence Altman explained in the *New York Times,* in July 2000, "while a virus causes AIDS, social conditions feed the epidemic. Patterns of behavior—fed by poverty, ignorance, and despair—have resulted in a disease so widespread that it has left millions of orphans and threatens to destroy much of Africa's economy and to wipe out a generation of young people."

A contributing factor to this dismal condition is the crushing levels of external debt that permeates many countries on the continent. As a result, scarce resources that might otherwise be devoted to education about HIV-AIDS, preventive programs such as the distribution of condoms, or treatment of victims are instead funneled into debt service (usually only paying off the *interest* on the accumulated debt, not reducing the principal). There are currently a number of African states that spend as much as four times the amount of money on debt service that they spend on their health systems as a whole, much less on the specific problem of HIV-AIDS.

Expense of Treatment. The extremely high death rate associated with the African AIDS pandemic is the result of the virtual absence of treatment options that are widely available in the West to prolong life and even to arrest the progress of HIV. The culprit, of course, is the cost of the treatments.

Slowing or arresting AIDS in patients in places like the United States, of course, is made possible through the administration of a combination of drugs known collectively as a "cocktail." The medicines in the cocktail are, however, quite expensive, with annual costs running at $10,000 per patient or more, as noted earlier. Using this lower figure, the Washington Office on Africa, an advocacy group for the continent, estimates that the cost of providing this kind of treatment for African AIDS patients would be roughly *$220 billion per year.* Given that the majority of African countries caught up in the pandemic are among the half of the world's population that subsists on an average income of $2 per capita per day (South Africa being the notable exception), the resources are simply not available even to begin reasonably modest programs of treatment. Instead, as already noted, about all the medical system can do is in effect perform triage on sufferers, sending them home to die rather than having them burden an already overly stressed health care system. Although newer and cheaper drug treatments are under development, pharmaceutical firms (as we shall see in a subsequent section) have shown some reluctance to bring these rapidly and widely to market in places like Africa while they are recovering the research costs by marketing other, more expensive AIDS medications through the high-priced cocktails, a situation that came to a head in 2001 and that caused embarrassed firms to lower prices.

Relative Powerlessness of Women.   One of the more notable aspects of the pandemic is that more women in Africa are infected with HIV-AIDS than men. The United Nations reported in late 1999 that, for the first time, infection rates for females exceeded that for males. As reported in the *New York Times,* 55 percent of infections occurred in women in that year. More dramatically, the UN report also stated that several studies completed in Africa indicate that African girls aged 15–19 are as much as five or six times as likely to be infected than their male counterparts.

The main reason for this phenomenon is the relatively dependent status of women in many traditional African societies. In many places, women have little control over reproductive decisions, and if a woman suggests the use of a condom, for instance, the result may be physical retribution. Despite international emphases on human and women's rights in recent years, translating that movement into sexual empowerment remains an uphill fight in numerous places where HIV-AIDS is rampant.

The list of factors contributing to the severity of the AIDS pandemic is not, as suggested earlier, intended to be exhaustive, and certain factors differ in emphasis from country to country and region to region. In a few countries like Uganda, the pandemic is actually abating, as a large government effort in sex education (centering on the use of condoms) has had the effect of lowering infection rates in important target groups in the population such as teenagers. Nonetheless, the problem remains monumental on the continent. Before looking at what is or might be done to stanch the pandemic, some discussion of its dimensions is in order.

Effects of the Pandemic

When the bubonic plague swept through Europe (and parts of Asia) during the middle 1300s, the "black death" (as it was known) claimed roughly one-quarter of the population as its victim. The epidemic finally ran its course, but because modern medicine had yet to come into existence, there was essentially nothing that could be done either to prevent infection nor to treat the disease when it occurred. Today, there are vaccines against the black death and antibiotics to treat anyone who might contract it. At the time, there was nothing but suffering and death.

The AIDS pandemic bears similarities to and differences from the great plague. Certainly the levels of human suffering are parallel; the social and economic fabric of affected African countries are being torn apart as surely as those medieval societies were destroyed. Now, as then, countless lives will be lost or cut tragically short.

There is also a significant difference. Through an aggressive program of biomedical research, there now exist treatments to deal with this disease that simply had no parallel during the Middle Ages. Very expensive treatments have been available to those who could afford them for a decade or so, and more affordable drugs are on the way. Although it is impossible to predict precisely when it will occur, research scientists believe a vaccination will soon be available with which to inoculate the uninfected. Both of these latter developments will hopefully bring the pandemic to an end. In the meantime, the suffering continues on a scale rivaling the great plague.

This is not the place to describe the structure of human suffering in any detail: Our focus on the AIDS pandemic is as a case in international action. However, we can mention illustrative effects that could recur in the future and that may have accompanied the bubonic plague during its course.

A notable attribute of AIDS is that it is, for many purposes, a young people's disease. Due to the nature of its transmission, it strikes particularly at people in their most sexually active stage of life, from early teens into their 20s and 30s. When there are no treatment options and the infected are just allowed to die, the result is a severe societal and demographic problem and imbalance that will take years, even generations, to correct.

A major consequence of the pandemic is that it is robbing the countries most affected of a future generation of leaders and productive workers. Attention has quite appropriately focused on indicators of the tragedy such as dramatic reductions in life expectancy that are the result of the fact that people are dying in their young adult years, not after leading full lives and then dying. In 1999, the American Foundation for AIDS Research noted that 80 percent of those succumbing to the disease worldwide are between ages 20 and 50, workers in their prime.

What happens when members of the current generation are dying in their 20s—who is supposed to assume leadership in their countries? Who will provide the working class that can contribute to the economic development of countries desperately in need of economic modernization? Where will the soldiers for the army come from? For that matter, who will parent the generation after that, when AIDS is hopefully a matter of history but its demographic consequences are not? And then there are the 12 million orphaned children. What will their psychological and developmental fate be? In the desperate rush to stanch the rampaging disease, many of these questions have only been asked, with the answers unknown or undiscovered.

We have no close parallels from which to devise answers. The black death killed a higher percentage of people than current estimates predict will die from AIDS, but the plague was presumably not demographically selective in the same way; the next generation of Europeans was diminished in numbers but presumably each age group was affected more or less equally. The enormous disruptions caused by forced displacement as the result of Africa's civil wars has affected large numbers, for instance, but the generational gap associated with the AIDS pandemic is not so obvious.

There is also the question of the broader health implications of the pandemic. As already noted, a major part of the classification of the pandemic as a transstate issue arises from its progression across national borders in ways that have to this point evaded control. At the same time, the immune deficiencies that AIDS creates also leaves the human body vulnerable to other diseases that are now occurring or recurring as public health problems—things like measles and smallpox, for instance. At a time when some diseases are developing resistance to treatment by antibiotics, the revival of old diseases or the emergence of new diseases (drug-resistant tuberculosis, strains of Ebola, for instance) present some chilling prospects for the future.

The AIDS pandemic in Africa has, by and large, been treated as an African problem, but the time may be running out on our ability to sustain that luxury. The disease is spreading geographically to parts of Asia, the continent on which over half of mankind resides. At the same time, the pandemic threatens to affect the rest of the world as well. Speaking in January 2000, Richard Holbrooke, then U.S. Ambassador to the United Nations, warned, "If we don't work with the Africans themselves to address these problems: we will have to deal with them later when they get more dangerous and more expensive." Looking directly at the economic consequences, World Bank President James Wolfensohn adds, "Many of us used to think of AIDS as a health issue. We were wrong. AIDS can no longer be confined to the health or social sector portfolios. AIDS is turning back the clock on development."

TRANSSTATE SOLUTIONS

As the discussion immediately above indicates, there is a growing recognition in the international community not only of the AIDS pandemic in Africa, but also an awareness that it is more than an African health problem. The result has been a modest international effort to try to come to grips with the problem. Although there is little evidence that the precedent being set in that effort may be important in how we will deal with future crises, that should be a matter of concern for us as well.

The 13th International AIDS Conference was held in July 2000 in Durban, South Africa (the 15th conference was held in Bangkok in 2004), to report on the state of the worldwide problem and efforts to control the disease. The location of the conference was of major symbolic importance on two counts. It was the first time that the meeting had been held in Africa, and it was held in South Africa, whose president, as noted earlier, has been one of the major politicians who are skeptics about the link between HIV and AIDS.

Beyond the recitation of the many horrors associated with the pandemic—including projections of population consequences in Africa—the conference focused on the progress that has been made in developing cheaper medicines to treat the disease. The conference noted that the progression of the AIDS pandemic was far enough along that the population will actually begin to drop in absolute terms in countries such as Botswana, South Africa, and Zimbabwe by 2003. At the same time, the 10,000 conferees were also presented with evidence that more affordable drug treatments that may reduce the rate of progression from HIV to full-blown AIDS are becoming available. The U.S. Centers for Disease Control (CDC), for instance, reported that an antibiotic marketed by Bristol Myers Squibb and Glaxo-Wellcome has been effective both in treating a form of pneumonia "indicates an HIV-infected person has developed AIDS" and can be administered to patients with therapeutic effects for about $60 a year. Even that reduced price is beyond the public health budgets of most African countries; nonetheless, it is an indication of progress. Likewise, drugs cheaper than AZT have been developed that prevent the transmission of HIV from infected mothers to their unborn children.

A similar entreaty was made at the United Nations in 2001. Known as UNGASS (UN General Assembly Special Session), it set deadlines for dealing with the disease: "universal access to treatment by 2010, a reversal of the epidemic by 2015," according to Kim. At a review conference in June 2006, known as UNGASS+5, U.N. Secretary-General Kofi Annan concluded somberly, "The epidemic that has inflicted the single greatest reversal in the history of human development . . . continues to outpace us."

The efforts reported at Durban are hopeful, but they are not the solution to what Dr. Roy M. Anderson of Oxford University described at the conference as "undoubtedly the most serious infectious threat in recorded human history." That is a very broad, serious statement, and one that you would think would produce a worldwide crash effort to contain. Although the research efforts to treat and eradicate AIDS are not inconsequential, neither are they of the monumental dimensions the disease would seem to merit. Why not?

The general experience with transstate issues suggests at least some partial answers to this question. Undoubtedly, they are inadequate to explain the phenomenon fully, and they are offered more to stimulate discussion than to foreclose investigating other solutions to the problem. To this end, three observations that have emerged from viewing transstate issues like the environment may be relevant to understanding international reaction to the AIDS pandemic.

The first is the *seriousness and immediacy of the problem.* In problems as diverse as dealing with carbon dioxide emissions and chlorofluorocarbons (CFCs), a major barrier to action is that the problem does not have an immediate injurious effect on those causing the problem and whose behavior will have to be amended to solve it. People who drive large sports utility vehicles (SUVs), for instance, might be chastened to change to more fuel-efficient and environmentally friendly forms of transportation if it somehow physically hurt when you drive the SUVs and gave physical pleasure when you drive 70-mile per gallon vehicles. Obviously, this does not happen, and advocates must rely on more abstract, less immediate arguments such as the effects of global warming on future generations.

The AIDS pandemic is the same way for most people outside Africa. One can read the kind of horrible tales and demographic consequences that have been detailed here, but they have no serious personal effects on the reader. One signature characteristic of

AIDS—as opposed to most other pandemics—reinforces this apparent lack of immediacy. Unlike the black death, the Spanish flu epidemic of 1918, and other widely publicized possibilities like avian flu, AIDS is a slow-acting disease. An outbreak of Ebola arises and kills its victims in days or weeks in large numbers; it has taken AIDS a human generation to produce its grisly toll. Moreover, unlike the quick reactions that helped contain SARS, AIDS has no "quick fix" solution. It will take decades to recover from AIDS once a cure or vaccine is found. Because dramatic action is impossible and the effects impersonal, there is a tendency to treat the AIDS pandemic as someone else's problem. When the Clinton administration publicly elevated the pandemic to the status of a threat to U.S. national security in 2000 (on the grounds that the demographic effects could destabilize African states and thus threaten U.S. interests in those states), hardly anyone outside the AIDS community took notice.

This leads to the second and related problem, the *lack of personalization* of the problem's effects on most people. The worldwide drug epidemic, which is arguably a form of transstate issue, offers an example. Drug enforcement officials maintain that their problem would be much easier if the immediate personal effects of drug use were negative; if, for instance, smoking marijuana caused respiratory congestion or ingesting cocaine caused sharp pain. Neither is the case, and so entreaties to avoid use fall on at least some deaf ears.

The problem with AIDS in Africa is in some ways similar. The impact of the pandemic is certainly affecting people on that continent, but the effects remain essentially isolated and concern is not personalized outside the continent. What this may suggest is that the only, or at least most effective, way to gain and focus global attention is for there to be concrete negative consequences of not solving the problem. The journalist Robert D. Kaplan (in *The Coming Anarchy*), for instance, argues that a good reason for the rest of the world to deal with the general deterioration of the quality of life in much of Africa is that eventually it will spill over into the rest of the world in the form of migration from that continent to the developed world. Similarly, as the immune deficiencies central to AIDS spawn the birth or rebirth of other diseases that could spread to other areas, the problems of the lack of seriousness and personalization may be overcome as well in developed societies suddenly vulnerable to those diseases.

The third problem is the *low prioritization of the problem,* especially in the area of international funding. As noted, Africa cannot afford to provide adequate funds itself even to attempt to control AIDS or its treatment, and thus help must come from elsewhere. In his 2003 State of the Union address, President George W. Bush appeared to adopt African AIDS as a personal cause, pledging $15 billion for AIDS treatment, but the pledge (the most dramatic symbol of which is PERFAR, the President's Emergency Plan for AIDS Relief) has languished among other priorities. The president asked for only $200 million for the Global Fund to administer the program for 2004 (the Congress appropriated $550 million), and the funds come with ideological strings: A third of the funds must be given to faith-based groups "which preach abstinence," according to a July 2004 BBC Online report. Moreover, the administration has resisted committing funds to purchasing WHO-approved generic AIDS drugs, insisting it will only pay for drugs currently under patent to pharmaceutical companies and thus much more expensive than the generics. According to Garrett, these requirements have led to considerable skepticism about the American effort.

The professional AIDS community knows what steps must be taken to gain control of the AIDS pandemic in Africa. The infection rate must be reduced through education about how AIDS is transmitted. Some countries, such as Uganda, have made major progress in "safe sex" education programs that have reduced infection rates, as already noted. Other countries, unfortunately, have not. In order to lessen the impact of AIDS infection, cheaper, more universally available treatments need to be made available, both to reduce suffering and to prolong useful life. Such treatments are available at great expense in the West; they are currently unavailable to almost all Africans. Ultimately, the pandemic can only be halted and the disease eradicated through the development of a preventive vaccine. AIDS research is reportedly not far from developing such a vaccine. Whether such a vaccine will be affordable and available where it is most needed is not yet certain.

It is easy to recite the steps necessary to cope with this catastrophic health problem, and what is frustrating is that it is a tragedy the effects of which can be ameliorated, if they cannot be eliminated. In that sense, the parallel between the AIDS pandemic and the black death of the Middle Ages does not hold. There simply was no possible way that the knowledge base of the thirteenth century could begin to cope with the plague, treat its victims, or find ways to eradicate the problem. AIDS can be, and eventually will be, eradicated. The question that will be asked in retrospect is why more resources were not made available more rapidly and massively to confront the problem. Why did it take so long?

CONCLUSION

The African AIDS case is fascinating for a number of reasons that include the dynamics of why it came about, what is being done about it, and how it can be viewed as a form of transstate issue. But the pandemic is more than a case in medical or international dynamics. In addition, there is the possibility that we may learn from the handling of the AIDS crisis how we should and should not deal with future health crises with international repercussions.

AIDS is neither the first nor will it be the last pandemic the modern world will face. At the end of World War I, that conflict's human toll was multiplied by the outbreak of the Spanish flu (so named because the first cases were reported in Spain) of 1918. A highly contagious, virulent strain , the virus attacked American soldiers being sent to Europe, and veterans brought it back to the United States. As Laurie Garrett chronicles, "President Wilson sent 43,000 soldiers to their deaths by forcing them aboard crowded ships to join in a war already won." In the end, Spanish flu killed 675,000 Americans out of a total U.S. population of 105 million at the time.

Contemporary examples abound. Ebola outbreaks have occurred periodically since the 1970s, killing up to 90 percent of those exposed to the disease but so far not spreading beyond isolated African settings where they occur—partially because the "victims die so quickly that they don't have a chance to spread infection very far," according to one study of the virus. In February 2003, the world became aware of SARS, when an outbreak that first occurred in China (in Foshan, Guangdong Province) became public. Although SARS was quickly contained (8,098 people worldwide were infected in 2003) and declared "eradicated" by the World Health Organization in 2005, it served as a warning as well.

Bird flu (technically H5N1 avian flu) has presented the most contemporary danger. Garrett provides the parameters of the possibilities: "If the relentlessly evolving virus becomes capable of human-to-human transmission, develops a power of contagion typical of human influenzas, and maintains its extraordinary virulence, humanity could face a pandemic unlike any other witnessed. Or nothing at all could happen." Currently, humans can only contract avian flu by contact with live (or uncooked) birds, and outside Asia, this has hardly happened. Moreover, the virus has not mutated (changed) so that it can be transmitted directly from infected people to other people.

But mutation could occur, and if it did, would we be any better equipped to deal with it than we have been with AIDS? The situations are not, of course, isomorphic: A mutation of avian flu would likely cause a sudden and very rapidly spreading epidemic more like the Spanish flu than AIDS. But there is also a similarity between AIDS and the avian flu. We knew about AIDS before it became the tragedy it is, and we failed to act decisively and concertedly to deal with it before it reached pandemic proportions. We also know about the potential devastation of avian flu. But how much guidance does the AIDS precedent provide: Avian flu could be a pandemic "unlike any other" or it could be "nothing at all." Did we once think the same way about AIDS?

There is the broader precedent that might be set. Will the AIDS pandemic provide the international community with a "wake-up call" regarding the consequences of not engaging the problem with all available resources earlier than it has? Will our retrospective on the devastation of Africa reveal that it might have been mitigated had we acted sooner and placed greater resources into finding vaccines and cures? Will our analysis provide some useful guidelines for dealing with present problems like Ebola or avian flu before they emerge as larger, more hideous disasters? Or, will we require a major Ebola outbreak in a European or North American location before we mount a major effort aimed at eradicating the problem?

And then there is the future. AIDS, SARS, Ebola, and the avian flu are unlikely to be the last major health problems with some or all the characteristics of a transstate issue. Will the experience to date inform the approaches the international community takes to the problem? It will be interesting to see.

Finally, there is a question that has only been addressed by indirection. Is the reason for the relative slowness and inattention to AIDS, and by extension, Asian-based diseases like SARS, the result of where the outbreaks have taken place? When AIDS was detected in the United States, action was initially less rapid than it might have been because it was equated, rightly or wrongly, with the gay community. When the disease reached significant numbers in the heterosexual, "straight" community, then efforts appeared to redouble. Is that the problem, in a geographic sense, with AIDS in Africa? It is a terrible moral indictment to suggest the treatment of great suffering depends on where one is from, but that may have been the case with this disaster.

1. What is a transstate issue? What are its characteristics? How well does the AIDS pandemic in Africa meet the criteria?

2. How did the AIDS pandemic come about? How has it progressed? What are its demographic consequences?

3. Part of the problem of AIDS in Africa arises from impediments for dealing with it on that continent. What are these? Are they similar or different from other transstate issue impediments? Can you think of other barriers to confronting the problem?

4. Think about the long-term effects of the pandemic on Africa. What will it take for Africa to recover from the effects (if they can)?

5. What international efforts have been undertaken to deal with the pandemic? Based on the experience of dealing with other transstate issues, what can one expect in the future? Have, for instance, the major pharmaceutical firms done a responsible job of responding to the pandemic?

6. Apply the experience of AIDS in Africa as a transstate issue to other current and potential health disasters like Ebola, SARS, and the avian flu. What can we learn from one experience to help with others?

READING/RESEARCH MATERIAL

"AIDS Orphans in Africa." *The Washington Office on Africa*, 2000 (http://www.woaafrica. org/Aorphans.htm)

"AIDS Pharmaceuticals and AIDS in Africa." *The Washington Office on Africa,* 2000 (http://www.woaafrcia.ord/Atrade.htm)

Christensen, John. "AIDS in Africa: Dying by the Numbers." *CNN.com,* November 8, 2000.

———. "Scarce Money, Few Drugs, Little Hope." *CNN.com,* November 8, 2000.

Duesberg, Peter. *Inventing the AIDS Myth,* New York: Regnery 1996.

"Ebola." (http://www.nyu.edu/education/mindsinmotion/ebola/htm.)

Garrett, Laurie. "The Lessons of HIV/AIDS." *Foreign Affairs* 84, 4 (July/August 2005), 51–64.

———. "The Next Pandemic?" *Foreign Affairs* 84, 4 (July/August 2005), 3–23.

"International AIDS Conference Offers Good News about Cheap Drug Treatments." *CNN.com,* July 11, 2000.

Kaplan, Robert D. *The Coming Anarchy: Shattering the Dreams of the Post Cold War.* New York: Random House, 2000.

Kim, Richard. "The People Versus AIDS." *The Nation* 283, 2 (July 10, 2006), 5–6.

Murphy, Claire. "Bush's Affair with Abstinence." *BBC Online,* July 12, 2004.

"Report: AIDS Pandemic Declared Threat to U.S. National Security." *CNN.com,* April 30, 2000.

Snow, Donald M. and Eugene Brown. *United States' Foreign Policy: Politics Beyond the Water's Edge* (2nd ed.). New York: Bedford/St. Martin's, 2000.

Wehrwein, Peter. "AIDS Leaves Africa's Economic Future in Doubt." *CNN.com,* November 8, 2000.

Wooten, James. "Africa's AIDS Tragedy: Monumental Health Crisis May Become Moral Catastrophe." *CNN.com,* November 8, 2000.

WEB SITES

Official Web site for United Nations Programme on AIDS/HIV
   UNAIDS at http://www.unaids.org

Lists of reports, fact sheets, U.S. government agencies and other online resources
   Global Issues: HIV/AIDS at http://usinfo.state.gov/topical/global/hiv

Regional AIDS updates and World Bank HIV/AIDS programs
   World AIDS Day at http://worldbank.org/worldaidsday

Official U.S. government programs, activities, and publications
   Office of National AIDS policy at http://www.whitehouse.gov/onap/aids.html

WebMD summary on avian flu
   http://www.webmd.com/hu/cold_and_flu/tp23639.asp

Understanding and Organizing a Post–September 11, 2001, World

THE CONTINUING CAMPAIGN AGAINST EVOLVING TERRORISM

PRÉCIS

The terrorist attacks of September 11, 2001, were a major trauma for the United States and the world at large, thrusting international religious terrorism onto center stage. It was a force that had been building for the better part of two decades but previously had not achieved the level of notoriety that the attacks evinced. Efforts to respond to the actions of Al Qaeda (the principal international terrorist group) have, in turn, caused the nature of the threat itself to change, a process of terrorism suppression and terrorist group adaptation that is likely to continue.

The purpose of this case is to investigate the nature of the terrorist problem, how it is changing, and what can be done about it. We begin by examining the dynamics of terrorism: What is it; what do terrorists seek to do; who are they; and what causes people to become terrorists? We then move to how terrorism has evolved as a problem since September 11 and what kinds of efforts we can mount against it. Based on this information and perspectives raised throughout the case, we conclude by suggesting some elements of a comprehensive terrorism suppression strategy.

The tragic terrorist attack by the Islamic terrorist group Al Qaeda against the World Trade Center towers and the Pentagon on September 11, 2001, was a seminal international and national event. Internationally, it signaled a new and frightening escalation of a problem that had troubled Europe and other parts of the world for a long time, and it produced an enormous outpouring of sympathy and support for the United States as the victim. Nationally, the attacks traumatized an American population suddenly aware of its vulnerability, even mortality, and spawned a major national priority to deal with this problem under the official sobriquet of the "global war on terrorism," or more compactly, GWOT.

The GWOT is now roughly six years old. It has had some successes, notably in capturing or otherwise suppressing elements of the old Al Qaeda network, to the point that Scott Atran suggested in 2005, "remnants of the mostly Egyptian hardcore around bin Laden have not managed a successful attack in three years," an observation that still holds. Others like Hoffman disagree: "not only is Al Qaeda alive and kicking, it is actively planning, supporting, and perhaps even directing attacks on a global canvas." Nonetheless the problem of terrorism has by no means diminished, much less abated. The apparently monolithic threat posed by Al Qaeda itself may be different than it was in 2001, but not the problem of terrorism itself: New permutations have arisen that are, if anything, more provocative and dangerous. Most share radical Islam as a foundation, but from Chechnya to Indonesia, new and different organizations have emerged as new challenges: International terrorism has become a hydra-headed beast, with Al Qaeda as its vital organ.

This case examines how the problem of international terrorism has evolved and is evolving and how to deal with it. In the process, we will describe aspects of the problem, including defining terrorism and describing how it works, looking at different ways to think about terrorism, how it has evolved since September 11, and how we deal with terrorism. This discussion is preface to the central purpose, which is thinking about how to devise a comprehensive strategy to combat the terrorist threat.

Before beginning our examination, three related observations are necessary to condition the comments that follow. First, although we speak of a GWOT, the use of the term "war" is unfortunate, deceiving, and distorting. As the term is usually used, war refers to armed conflict between combatants organized as states or states versus organized oppositions within states. War, in other words, is an action that pits people against other people, where the groups attack one another to impose their will on those other people. Terrorism, on the other hand, is a more intangible idea, one method by which people seek to accomplish goals. One cannot attack and subdue an idea. What one can do is to oppose and subdue people who act from ideas—we can make war on terrorist organizations like Al Qaeda (although its lack of a territorial base makes subduing it difficult); the best we can do with an idea is to discredit it.

The second observation flows from the first: The war analogy is further flawed because it implies that the opposition can be defeated—that the purpose of the war is to suppress and eliminate the opposition. Terrorism is an ancient practice that transcends efforts to suppress and defeat individual manifestations—defeating Al Qaeda or any other terrorist organization will not eliminate the phenomenon, just particular practitioners. There will always be terrorists somewhere, and the purpose of those opposed to terrorism is to *contain* the problem, not eliminate it.

Terrorism cannot ever be eliminated altogether; therefore, efforts to oppose it are exercises in *risk reduction,* not risk elimination. Risk, for our purposes, is the difference between threats to our interests and our capabilities (or resources) to counter, contain, or eliminate those threats. Although the level of terrorist threat ebbs and flows across time, it is essentially always potentially greater than the resources available to effectively thwart all manifestations of the threat. Terrorism, to paraphrase ex-German chancellor Helmut Schmidt, is a problem to be worked, not solved for once and for all. Any strategy or policy that is aimed at "smashing" or "defeating" terrorism is bound to fail.

WHAT IS TERRORISM?

The first step in coming to grips with terrorism is defining the term. It is an important consideration, because so many phenomena in the contemporary international arena are labeled terrorist. This makes a definition particularly important as a means to measure whether a particular movement, or act, is terrorist or not. Without a set of criteria to tell us what does and does not constitute terrorism, we are left disabled in trying to make a determination.

This is not a merely semantic exercise. Take, for instance, the current emphasis on Chechen separatists and their campaign, which the Russian government has called terrorist. Certainly, actions such as enlisting suicide terrorists to blow up two Russian airliners and the brutal siege of the school in Beslan in the Caucasus were hideous, brutal acts that comport with an understanding of terrorism, but is it correct to label the movement that commissioned and carried out the acts terrorist as a result? In context, when the Russian government of then-president Boris Yeltsin used the Russian army to attack Chechnya in 1995 to wipe out the secessionist movement there (among other things, leveling the capital of Grozny) and current president Vladimir Putin renewed the campaign in 1999, there were widespread international accusations the Russian government was terrorizing the Chechens and engaging in crimes against humanity (acts of state terrorism). So who is the terrorist here?

Having an agreed-on definition of terrorism would help answer this and similar questions, but unfortunately, such an agreement does not exist. Rather, there are virtually as many different definitions as there are people and organizations making the distinctions. There are also some commonalities that recur across definers and will allow us to adopt a definition for present purposes. A few arguably representative examples will aid in drawing distinctions.

The United States government offers the official definition in its 2003 *National Strategy for Combating Terrorism:* "premeditated, politically motivated violence perpetrated against noncombatant targets by subnational groups or clandestine agents." In *Attacking Terrorism,* coauthor Audrey Kurth Cronin says terrorism is distinguished by its political nature, its nonstate base, its targeting of innocent noncombatants, and the illegality of its acts. Jessica Stern, in *Terrorism in the Name of God,* defines terrorism as "an act or threat of violence against noncombatants with the objective of exacting revenge, intimidating, or otherwise influencing an audience." Alan Dershowitz (in *Why Terrorism Works*), offers no definition himself, but notes that definitions typically include reference to terrorist targets, perpetrators, and terrorist acts.

These definitions, and similar ones from others in the field, differ at the margins but have common cores. All of them share three common points of reference: terrorist acts (illegal, often hideous and atrocious), terrorist targets (usually innocent noncombatants), and terrorist purposes (political persuasion or influence). The only difference among them is whether they specify the nature of terrorists and their political base: the State Department, Cronin, and Dershowitz all identify terrorist organizations as nonstate-based actors. Cronin in particular emphasizes that "although states can terrorize, by definition they cannot be terrorists."

This brief discussion allows me to propose my own definition, which incorporates the three components of terrorist acts, targets, and purposes, but not the criterion of terrorist organizations as nonstate actors. Historically, states have been leading terrorists, either through the actions of government organizations like the secret police, or in creating, commissioning, or controlling the activities of terrorists. In the contemporary setting, almost all terrorist organizations are nonstate based, and this fact is at the heart of our difficulty in dealing with them. Defining terrorism as a nonstate-based activity, however, removes an important category of past (and conceivably future) activity from the definitional reach of terrorism. The nonstate basis is a characteristic of modern terrorism, not a defining element of terrorism per se.

For the rest of this case study, terrorism will be defined as "the commission of atrocious acts against a target population normally to gain compliance with some demands the terrorists insist upon." Terrorism thus consists of three related phenomena, each of which must be present in some manner for something to be considered an act of terrorism. The fourth element in other definitions, perpetrators of terrorism, is implicit in the three criteria. Discussing each helps enliven an understanding of what constitutes terrorism.

Terrorist Acts

The first part of the definition refers to *terrorist acts,* which are the visible manifestation of terrorism and the part of the phenomenon with which most people are most familiar. Several comments can be made about terrorist acts.

One comment is that terrorist acts are distinguished from other political expressions in that they are uniformly illegal. Terrorist acts are intended to upset the normalcy of life through destructive acts aimed at either injuring or killing people or destroying things. Regardless of the professed underlying motives of terrorists (normally couched in lofty political terms), the actions they commit—and especially their focus on noncombatants whose only "guilt" is being part of the targeted group—break laws and are subject to criminal prosecution. By raising the rhetoric of terrorist actions to acts of war (currently holy war or *jihad*), terrorists may seek to elevate what they do to a higher plane ("one man's terrorist is another man's freedom fighter"), but the simple fact remains that terrorist acts are criminal in nature.

The general purpose of terrorist acts is to frighten the target audience: Indeed, the word *terrorism* is derived from the Latin root *terrere*, which means "to frighten." The method of inducing fright is through the commission of random, unpredictable acts of violence that seek to induce such fear that those who witness the acts (or learn of them) will conclude that compliance with terrorist demands is preferable to living with the fear of being future victims themselves. Acts of terrorism are not particularly aimed at the actual victims themselves (who are normally randomly selected and whose fate does not "matter" to the terrorist) but at the audience who views the actions. As Brian Jenkins once put it, *"Terrorists want a lot of people watching and a lot of people listening, and not a lot of people dead."* (Emphasis in original.) The dynamic of inducing this fright is the disruption of the predictability and safety of life within society, one of whose principal functions is to make existence predictable and safe. Ultimately, a major purpose of terrorism may be to undermine this vital fiber of society.

Beyond frightening the target audience, individual terrorist acts are committed for a variety of reasons, not limited to the normally expressed political goals of particular terrorist organizations. Al Qaeda, for instance, says its most fundamental goal is the expulsion of the West (especially the United States) from the holy lands of Islam, and that its acts are intended to further that goal. But that is not the only motivation for particular actions.

Terrorists may also act for a variety of other reasons. Jenkins provides a list of six other, generally less lofty, purposes for terrorist actions. First, terrorist actions may be aimed at exacting special concessions, such as ransom, the release of prisoners (generally members of the terrorist group), or publicizing a message. Gaining the release of political prisoners was the stated reason that Hizbollah kidnapped Israeli soldiers in summer 2006, triggering the widespread violence there. Indonesia's Jemaah Islamiyah carried out its 2004 attack on the Australian embassy and promptly announced that it would perpetrate similar attacks if its leader, Abu Bakar Bashir, was not released from prison.

Second, terrorists may act to gain publicity for their causes. Before Palestinian terrorists kidnapped a series of airliners and then launched an attack on the Israeli compound at the Munich Olympics in the 1970s, hardly anyone outside the region had ever heard of the Palestinian cause; the terrorist actions got them that global awareness. The publicity may be intended to remind a world that has shifted its attention away from a particular group and its activities that it is still active and that it is still pursuing its goals. One apparent reason for the spate of Chechen violence in 2004 for which the late Chechen leader Shamil Basayev claimed credit was to remind the world that the Chechen movement to gain independence from Russia is still alive.

A third, and more fundamental, purpose of terrorist acts is to cause widespread disorder that demoralizes society and breaks down the social order in a country. This, of course, is a very ambitious purpose, and one that presumably can only be undertaken through a widespread campaign that includes a large number of terrorist acts, and it is the kind of objective most likely to be carried out by governments or semi-governmental actors. The suicide terror campaign by Hamas against Israeli civilians (and the Israeli counterattacks against Palestinians) could be an example of terrorism for this purpose.

A fourth, more tactical use of terrorism is to provoke overreaction by a government in the form of repressive action, reprisals, and overly brutal counter terrorism that may lead to the overthrow of the reactive government. This was a favorite tactic of the Viet Cong in the Vietnam War, and evoked the ironic analogy of building schools during the day (as a way to pacify the population) and then bombing those schools at night (because they became the source of Viet Cong actions after nightfall).

A fifth purpose of terror may be to enforce obedience and cooperation within a target population. Campaigns of terror directed by the governments of states against their own citizens often have this purpose, which is often assigned to a secret police or similar paramilitary organizations. The actions of the KGB in the Soviet Union, the Gestapo and other similar organization in Nazi Germany, and the infamous death squads in Argentina during the 1960s and 1970s are all examples of the use of government terror to intimidate and frighten their own population into submission. At a less formal governmental level, many actions of the Ku Klux Klan during the latter nineteenth and early twentieth centuries against Black Americans would qualify as well.

Jenkin's sixth purpose of terrorist action is punishment. Terrorists often argue that an action they take is aimed at a particular person or place because that person or institution is somehow guilty of a particular transgression and is thus being meted out appropriate punishment for what the terrorists consider a crime. Although the Israeli government would be appalled at the prospects of calling its rescinded counter terrorist campaign to bulldoze the homes of the families of suicide terrorists (or bombing the homes of dissident leaders) as acts of terror, from the vantage point of the Palestinian targets of the attacks, they certainly must seem so.

Stern adds a seventh motivation that is internal to the terrorist organization: morale. Like any other organization, and especially terrorist groups in which the "operatives" are generally young and not terribly mature, it may be necessary from time to time to carry out a terrorist attack simply to demonstrate to the membership the continuing potency of the group as a way to keep the membership focused and their morale high. As Stern puts it, "Attacks sometimes have more to do with rousing the troops than terrorizing the victims." Improving or maintaining morale may also have useful spin-off effects, such as helping in recruiting new members to the group or in raising funds to support the organization's activities.

A final comment about terrorist acts is whether, or to what degree, they are successful. The answer is rather clearly a mixed one that has to do with the scale of the actions and their intended results. In some cases, terrorism has been highly successful, but usually in relatively small ways when the terrorists' purposes were bounded and compliance with their demands was not overly odious. To cite one example, terrorist demands to release what they view as political prisoners (usually jailed members of their group) have, on occasion, been complied with, although some countries are more prone to comply than others. Likewise, the Iraqi resistance's campaign of kidnapping and threatening to execute foreign nationals if the countries involved did not leave Iraq has been somewhat successful and will almost certainly be duplicated in the future.

It is when terrorists make large demands and follow them up with sizable actions that they tend to be less successful. When terrorists come to pose a basic perceived threat (often because of the audacity of what they have done) to the target country, the reaction by the target may be, and usually is, increased resolve rather than compliance. The September 11, 2001, attacks, after all, did not result in a groundswell of sentiment for the United States to quit the Middle East (especially Saudi Arabia) as bin Laden and Al Qaeda demanded; rather, it stiffened the will of the country to resist. This poses something of a quandary to the terrorist: The more ambitious he becomes, the more likely he is to increase opposition to achievement of his goals. On the other hand, sizing terrorist acts downward to levels that will not increase resolve may result in positive, but less than satisfying, outcomes.

What this discussion of terrorist acts seeks to demonstrate is that, like virtually everything else about the subject, the acts that terrorists commit occur for a variety of reasons. Some of these are more purposive and "noble" than others, but it is not clear what may motivate a particular action. Moreover, different reasons may motivate different groups at different times and under different circumstances. Knowing that a terrorist attack has occurred, in other words, does not necessarily tell you why it has been committed.

Terrorist Targets

Akin to the military objectives in more conventional war, the targets of terrorists can be divided into two related categories. The first is people, and the objective is to kill, maim, or otherwise cause some members of the target population to suffer as an example for the rest of the population. The second category are physical targets, attacks against which are designed to disrupt and destroy societal capabilities and to demonstrate the vulnerability of the target society. The two categories are obviously related in that most physical targets worth attacking contain people who will be killed or injured in the process. As well, attacking either category demonstrates the inability of the target population to provide protection for its members and valued artifices, thus questioning the efficacy of resisting terrorist demands.

There are subtle differences and problems associated with concentrating on one category or another of target. Clearly, attacks directly intended to kill or injure people are the most personal and evoke the greatest emotion in the target population, including the will to resist and to seek vengeance. From the vantage point of the terrorist, the reason to attack people (beyond some simple blood lust) is to attack their will to resist the demands that terrorists make. Dennis Drew and I refer to this as *cost-tolerance,* the level of suffering one is willing to endure in the face of some undesirable situation. In the case of terrorist targeting, the terrorist seeks to exceed the target's cost-tolerance by making the target conclude that it is less painful (physically or mentally) to accede to the terrorist's demands than it is to continue to resist those demands. The terrorist seeks to exceed cost-tolerance by maximizing the level of fear and anxiety that the target experiences because of the effects (often hideous) of attacks on other members of the target group. The terrorist wants the target group to become so afraid of being the next victim that they cave in and accept the terrorist demands. If cost-tolerance is exceeded, the terrorist wins; if the target remains resolute, the terrorist does not succeed (which may not be the same thing as saying the terrorist loses).

Overcoming cost-tolerance is not an easy task, and it often fails. For one thing, terrorist organizations are generally small with limited resources, meaning that they usually lack the wherewithal to attack and kill a large enough portion of the target population to make members of that population become individually fearful enough to tip the scales (blowing up people on airplanes may be a partial exception). One of the great fears associated with terrorist groups obtaining and using weapons of mass destruction is that such a turn of events would change that calculus. For another thing, attacking and killing innocent members of a target group (at least innocent from the vantage point of the group) may (and usually does) infuriate its members and increase, rather than decrease, the will to resist. That was certainly the case during World War II in Germany, where constant aerial bombardment failed to destroy the German peoples' will to continue to resist.

Standing up to terrorist attacks on human targets is not always easy, as the example of hostage taking in Iraq early in the war shows. In that instance, officials were placed in an obvious quandary. When hostages are taken and their execution threatened if some demands are unmet, there is an obvious and understandable instinct to try to save the hostage(s), and in the absence of an ability to rescue them physically (which, in the Iraqi cases, was apparently impossible), the only means available is to accede to their demands (have cost-tolerance exceeded). Doing so, however, means the terrorists succeed and are likely to be emboldened do the same thing again, as was the case in Iraq when several countries pulled their workers out after their some of their nationals were kidnapped and threatened with execution. The Americans and British refused to accede in these demands and had a number of their citizens executed. In those cases, the terrorists did not prevail, but they also did not visibly lose, since (at this writing) none of them had been captured and brought to justice for their deeds.

When the targets are physical things rather than people per se, the problems and calculations change. When the target of terrorists is a whole society, the range of potential targets is virtually boundless. In attacking places, the terrorist seeks to deprive the target population of whatever pleasure or life-sustaining or -enhancing value the particular target may provide. The list of what we used to call *countervalue* targets when speaking of nuclear targeting (things people value, such as their lives and what makes those lives enjoyable) covers a very broad range of objects, from hydroelectric plants to athletic stadiums, from nuclear power generators to military facilities, from highways to research facilities, and so on. Compiling a list for any large community is a very sobering experience.

It is unreasonable to assume that the physical potential target list for any country can be made uniformly invulnerable. There are simply too many targets, and the means of protecting them are sufficiently discrete that there is little overlap in function (protecting a football stadium from bombers may or may not have much carryover in terms of protecting nuclear power plants from seizure). As a result, there will always be a gap between the potential threats and the ability to negate all those threats, and the consequence is a certain level of risk for which there are simply inadequate resources to cancel.

Terrorist Objectives

The final element in the definition of terrorism is the objectives, or reasons, for which terrorists do what they do. These objectives, of course, are directed against the target population and involve the commission of terrorist acts, so that the discussion of objectives cannot be entirely divorced from the other two elements of what constitutes terrorism.

For present purposes, our discussion of terrorist objectives will refer to the broader outcomes that terrorists seek (or say they seek) to accomplish. Objectives are the long-range reasons that terrorists wage campaigns of terrorism. In the short run, terrorists may engage in particular actions for a variety of reasons, as already noted (group morale or recruitment), for instance. What they seek ultimately to accomplish is the province of terrorist objectives.

It will be useful to make a distinction here among types of goals terrorists pursue. The major objectives of terrorists, their ultimate or strategic goals, refer to the long-term political objectives to which they aspire. For Al Qaeda, for instance, the removal of Americans from the Arabian Peninsula is a strategic goal; for Chechen separatists, independence from Russia is the ultimate objective. At the same time, terrorists also pursue interim, or tactical, goals, which generally involve the successful commission of terrorist acts against the target population. The purpose, in the case of tactical objectives, is to demonstrate continuing viability and potency, to remind the target of their presence and menace, and to erode resistance to their strategic goals.

Because most terrorist groups are ultimately political in their purposes, terrorist objectives are political as well. To paraphrase the Clausewitzian dictum that war is politics by other means, so too is terrorism politics by other, extreme, means. Likewise, the objectives that terrorists pursue are extreme, at least to the target population, if not to the terrorists themselves. Sometimes, terrorist objectives are widely known and clearly articulated, and at other times they are not. Ultimately, however, campaigns of terror gain their meaning in the pursuit of some goal or goals, and their success or failure is measured to the extent that those goals are achieved.

Terrorism is, of course, the method of the militarily weak and conceptually unacceptable. The extremely asymmetrical nature of terrorist actions arises from the fact that terrorists cannot compete with their targets by the accepted methods of the target society. Terrorists lack the military resources to engage in open warfare, at which they would be easily defeated, or in the forum of public discourse and decision, because their objectives are unacceptable, distasteful, or even bizarre to the target population. Thus, the terrorist can neither impose his purposes on the target, nor can he persuade the target to adopt whatever objectives he wants. These facts narrow his options.

The fact that terrorist objectives are politically objectionable to the target sets up the confrontation between the terrorists and the target. Normally, terrorist goals are stated in terms of changing policies (Palestinian statehood or the right to repatriation within Israel, for example) or laws (releasing classes of detained people) that the majority in the target state find unacceptable. Because the terrorists are in a minority, they cannot bring about the changes they demand by normal electoral or legislative means, and they are likely to be viewed as so basically lunatic and unrealistic by the target audience that it will not accord seriousness to the demands of those who make them. To the terrorists, of course, the demands make perfect sense, and they are frustrated and angered by the treatment their demands are given. The stage is thus set for confrontation.

Terrorists achieve their objectives by overcoming the cost-tolerance of the target population to resist. The campaign of terrorist threats and acts is intended to convince the target population that acceding to the terrorist demands is preferable to the continuing anxiety and fear of future terrorism.

The failure of terrorists to achieve strategic objectives is not the same thing as total failure, however. Successful terrorism of a large society by a small group of terrorists is a tall order, and one for which the terrorists (almost by definition) do not have the resources to achieve. At its zenith, after all, Al Qaeda consisted of probably fewer than 10,000 active members, who could hardly bring the United States to its knees. Terrorism is, after all, the "tactic of the weak," and there are real limitations on the extent of the danger such groups can physically pose.

Determining whether terrorists achieve their goals or fail is complicated by the contrast between the tactical and strategic levels of objectives, making the compilation of a "score card" difficult. Modern terrorists have rarely been successful at the strategic level of attaining long-range objectives. Al Qaeda has not forced the United States from the Arabian Peninsula (although the American presence is declining), Russia has not granted Chechnya independence, and Jemaah Aslamiyah has yet to achieve a sectarian Islamic state in Indonesia. At the same time, the terrorist record at achieving tactical objectives (carrying out terrorist attacks) is, if not perfect, not a total failure either. As long as terrorists continue to exist and to achieve some of their goals, they remain a force against the targets of their activities. Thus, the competition between terrorists and their targets over the accomplishment of terrorist objectives continues to exist within a kind of nether world where neither wins or loses decisively and thus both can claim some success: "We do not give in to terrorism," defined as resisting terrorist strategic objectives; versus "We succeed against the infidels," defined as the successful commission of acts of terrorism.

THINKING ABOUT TERRORISM: PERSPECTIVES AND CAUSES

For most of us, terrorism is such an alien phenomenon that we have difficulty conceptualizing exactly what it is and why people would engage in acts of terrorism, up to and including committing terrorist acts that include their own planned deaths (suicide). And yet, the historic and contemporary public records are strewn with enough instances of terrorism as to make confronting the conceptual "beast" necessary for understanding and coping with the reality around us.

Terrorism is too complex a phenomenon to capture entirely in this brief case study, but one can gain some insights into it by viewing it through two lenses. The first will be three perspectives that try to capture terrorism and its place in international politics. The second is to look at three of the explanations that are commonly put forward to answer the question, "Why is there terrorism?"

Three Perspectives

Where does terrorism fit into domestic and international politics? Is terrorism ever a legitimate enterprise, or is it always something outside the realm of legitimacy? Answers to these questions depend on one's perspective, as captured in a typecasting of terrorism as legitimate or illegitimate behavior. There are two polar opposite perspectives that are normally the basis for such a discussion: terrorism as crime and terrorism as war. To these two distinctions, we will add a third, which is terrorism as a specific kind of warfare, asymmetrical war.

The basic distinction serves two purposes. On the one hand, it speaks to the legitimacy of terrorism: A depiction of terrorism as crime clearly stamps it as illegal and thus illegitimate, whereas depicting it as war (of one sort or another) raises its status among actions of states and groups. The distinction also suggests the appropriate approach to dealing with terrorism either as a legal system or military problem.

The *terrorism as crime* perspective focuses on terrorist acts and their acceptability, with an emphasis on their illegality. All terrorist acts against people and things violate legal norms in all organized societies: It is against the law to murder people or to destroy property, after all, regardless of where and why one does so. If acts of terrorism are, at their core, criminal, then terrorists are little more than common criminals and should be treated as such. Terrorism thus becomes at heart a criminal problem, and terrorists are part of the criminal justice system subject to arrest, incarceration, trial, and, where appropriate, imprisonment or execution.

Terrorists simultaneously reject and accept this depiction. They reject the notion that what they do is criminal, because their acts—while technically illegal—are committed for higher political purposes, as discussed earlier. Terrorists kill people, but they do not murder them. Terrorists are not criminals, rather, they are warriors (in contemporary times, "holy" warriors). Thinking in this manner elevates the status of the terrorist from criminal to soldier, a far more exalted and acceptable position. At the same time, terrorists prefer for target societies to think of them as criminals in those situations in which they are captured and brought to justice (assuming the capturing society adheres to its own criminal procedures, which is not always the case). The reason is simple: At least in the West, criminal procedures are considerably more stringent in procedural and evidentiary senses than military law, affording the terrorist greater protections under the law and making their successful prosecution more difficult. Attempts in the United States to relax criminal safeguards regarding terrorists at places like Guantanamo Bay seek to change that status but have created legal controversies working their way through U.S. courts.

Terrorists prefer the second perspective, *terrorism as war*. This viewpoint emphasizes the political nature of terrorism and terrorist acts, adopting the Clausewitzian paraphrase that "terrorism is politics by other means." If one accepts the basic premise of this perspective, then terrorist acts are not crimes but acts of war, and as such are judged by the rules and laws of war rather than by criminal standards. The interactions between terrorist organizations and their targets are thus warlike, military affairs. Whereas outside situations of war killing is always illegal, within war it is permissible, at least within certain bounds regarding who and in what conditions killing is legal and acceptable.

The current global war on terrorism implicitly accepts this perspective, if not its implications. Within the GWOT, the term "war" is used rather loosely and almost allegorically rather than literally, and almost all apostles of the designation do not view terrorists as warriors but rather as wanton criminals to be brought to justice or killed. Within the antiterrorism campaign in Afghanistan, for instance, members (or alleged members) of Al Qaeda were not treated as prisoners of war, which would have afforded them certain legal rights under the Geneva Conventions on War, but instead under the legally vague designation of "detainees," who apparently do not possess Geneva Convention protections.

The problem of treating terrorism as crime or as war is that, in most cases, it is both. Terrorists do engage in criminal acts but they do so for reasons more normally associated with war. This suggests that there should be a third way of depicting terrorism, which we will call *terrorism as asymmetrical war*. As Chapter 10 suggested, asymmetrical warfare is different from the conventional forms of warfare that are covered by the traditional laws of war; indeed, a major characteristic of asymmetrical warfare is the rejection of traditional norms and rules as part of the attempt to level the playing field of conflict. The asymmetrical warrior does not distinguish between combatants and noncombatants, just as the terrorist considers all members of the target group as equally culpable and thus eligible for attack. Terrorism was depicted as one form of asymmetrical warfare in Chapter 10 because it is a tactic of a movement that cannot possibly compete under the acceptable rules of engagement.

Terrorism as asymmetrical war is a hybrid of the other two perspectives. The terrorists' rejection of accepted rules means they can treat their actions as acts of war while the target society rejects this contention and can continue to consider their actions as crimes against mankind. The status of asymmetrical warriors as warriors may be ambiguous within the rules of war, but leaving their actions within criminal jurisdiction satisfies the target society's depiction while affording captured terrorists the legal protections they seek. This perspective also allows terrorism to be depicted both as a criminal *and* a military problem, which it is, and thus to allow both law enforcement and military responses to terrorists. The only difficulty is in determining the appropriate mix of criminal justice and military responses generally and in specific situations.

Three Causes

What motivates individuals and groups to become terrorists and to engage in the often gruesome and dangerous acts that typify terrorism is also the source of considerable speculation and disagreement among experts and lay observers. Much of the difficulty in making such assessments derives from the absolute inability most of us have in imagining why anyone would become a terrorist and kill what, from our perspective, are innocent people. Whatever leads people to become terrorists is so alien to us that we cannot draw analogies from our own experiences or those arising in our society as we know it (which has, of course, produced its fair share of terrorists).

Three vantage points on what causes people and groups to adopt terrorism are often put forward, reflecting in some ways the disciplinary vantage points that various students of the phenomenon represent. Most of these explanations surfaced during the 1960s and 1970s, during the third or "New Left" wave of modern terrorism, according to David C. Rapaport (the first two were anarchism and anticolonialism; the fourth and present wave is religious). This is worth noting because the 1960s and 1970s tended to be more tolerant, of, even sympathetic to, politically aberrant movements than is true today. At any rate, terrorism is typified as primarily a societal, a psychological, or a political problem. The three explanations are neither mutually exclusive nor agreed on.

The *societal* argument is that it is social conditions that provide the breeding grounds for terrorism. Societies that consistently underachieve, fail to provide adequate material or spiritual advances or hope, and in which the citizens live in an unending and hopeless condition of deprivation provide a kind of intellectual and physical "swamp" in which terrorism "breeds" a ready supply of potential terrorism followers who are willing recruits for terrorist causes. These "failed societies" may even oppress specific groups that are even more prone to the appeals of terrorism recruiters. A variant of this argument also suggests it may be that some societies' values are better suited for producing terrorists than others. In the contemporary setting, for instance, some observers note that Islam has a more prominent, positive role for religious martyrdom than other religions, making the terrorist path and especially suicide terrorism more acceptable than it would be in other places.

If this argument is substantially correct, it leads to a potential solution to the terrorism problem: If the wretched conditions are removed and the society ceases to be a failed one, then the conditions that breed the terrorists may also be removed. This is the heart of the argument for "draining the swamp" as a way to combat terrorism. The tool for doing so is the infusion of (probably massive) amounts of developmental assistance to create the physical basis for greater prosperity and a sense of meaningful futures: People do not volunteer for potential self-immolation (such as suicide terrorist missions) if they have hope for the future. In the current debate, feeding resources into the Pakistani education system to create a peaceful alternative to the religious *madrassa* schools that teach anti-Americanism is a prime example of the application of the societal argument.

Critics point to a hole in this explanation of what creates terrorism. That argument is that many modern terrorists are not the product of societal deprivation. Sixteen of the nineteen September 11 terrorists, after all, were Saudi citizens, who could hardly be accused of coming from deprived backgrounds. Such an observation is obviously true but it does not completely negate the argument that inferior societal conditions produce terrorists. Rather, the observation conditions the argument by saying that *not all* terrorists come from societally deprived backgrounds. Most terrorist leaders, it appears, and some of their followers come from middle, even upper-class backgrounds (bin Laden, for instance), but a lot of their followers indeed emerge from the "swamp." As Atran points out, this is also true of suicide terrorists, "who are frequently middle-class, secularly well-educated, but often 'born-again' radical Islamists, including converts from Christianity."

The second explanation moves from the group to the individual. Rather than focusing on failed societies, the *psychological* argument shifts the emphasis from the failed society to failed peoples. The psychological argument is not entirely divorced from the societal argument, in that it basically contends that there are certain traits in people, certain psychological states, that make them more susceptible to the terrorist appeal and thus more willing to commit terrorist acts than is true in other individuals. Not everyone who possesses these traits becomes a terrorist (lots of people are frustrated, but do not react by blowing themselves up, for instance), however; there must be societal conditions that activate these tendencies.

Terrorist profiling is a clear example of the psychological explanation of terrorism. In many contemporary arguments, for instance, it has been observed that many of the individuals who perpetrate religious-based terrorism from Middle Eastern settings share several characteristics. Most terrorist followers (as opposed to the leaders who recruit, train, and direct them) tend to be teenaged boys with high school educations who do not have jobs at all or if they do, jobs that pay them so poorly that they have few prospects. They tend to be unmarried with few prospects of finding a wife (often because they cannot support them). They also tend to have low self-esteem intermixed with a high sense of helplessness and hopelessness about their futures. These perceptions lead to a high sense of humiliation, embarrassment, and impotence toward the future. Individuals with this kind of profile are believed to be especially vulnerable to recruitment by terrorist leaders who promise to restore their meaning and purpose and thus a sense of self-esteem. A particularly troubling recent trend has been the emergence of females with similar profiles in terrorist roles.

This profile is particularly disturbing, because the Middle East has a population "bulge" or, Benard describes it, a "youth overhang," that includes a large number of young people (50 percent under 19 years old) who meet the basic enabling characteristics described in the profile. Moreover, the societal conditions in most Middle Eastern states offer few prospects for reducing the conditions, notably of employment, that can turn the situation around. As long as life does not contain meaningful prospects that can prevent the triggering of psychological processes leading to terrorism, there will be fertile breeding grounds for new generations of terrorists. Benard describes it: "Membership in a clandestine terrorist cell, online linkages with glamourous dangerous individuals, the opportunity to belong to a feared and seemingly heroic movement complete with martyrs—all of this is inherently appealing to young people." It might be added that there are far fewer studies that suggest similar profiles for terrorist leaders, except that they come from higher socioeconomic situations.

The third explanation is *political,* that it is failed governments that produce the societal and psychological conditions in which terrorism emerges or that produce conditions in which terrorists emerge or are nurtured. Although it hardly exhausts the possibilities, state action can lead to terrorism in two ways. First, state oppression (indeed, including the use of terrorism *by* the government) may lead to political opposition that must be clandestine and resort to terrorism as their only means of survival (terrorism as the tool of the asymmetrical warrior). The Chechen resistance would certainly view itself in this manner. In other cases, the government may be so inept or ineffective that it provides a haven for terrorists to exist without being able to do anything about it. The ineffectiveness of the Pakistani government in being able to suppress remnants of Al Qaeda and other sympathetic groups in the mountainous areas bordering on Afghanistan is an example. In yet other cases, sympathetic governments may even provide refuge and sanctuary for terrorist organizations. The relationship between Afghanistan's Taliban regime of the 1990s and Al Qaeda is a frequently cited example.

As with the other explanations, the political model also suggests remedies. If it is bad governments that create, put up with, or consort with terrorists, then there are two ways to deal with the problem. One is to convince the government to abandon the terrorists, quit creating them, or capture/apprehend them, using either positive inducements (military or economic assistance) or threats of some form of sanctions to induce compliance. This has been the basic American strategy with Pakistan. If those efforts fail, a second option may be to replace those governments with more compliant regimes. That, of course, is at least part of the rationale for the American invasion of Iraq.

As noted, these explanations are not mutually exclusive. Failed governments have failed societal conditions as one of their causes and consequences, and it is failure at these levels that creates the triggering conditions for psychological forces that activate terrorists. It may be, as well, that these explanations are not comprehensive, but may be characteristic of the 1960s and 1970s variants of terrorism, which were, among other things, noticeably secular rather than religious. Strategies for dealing with the terrorism problem have to sort out the influences of various explanations and how well they apply to the current and evolving forms of terrorism.

EVOLVING TERRORISM SINCE SEPTEMBER 11

The events of September 11 understandably riveted national attention on a specific terrorist threat posed by Al Qaeda. The focus was natural given the audacity and shock value of the actual attacks and by the novelty of an organization such as Al Qaeda. To the extent that Americans had much of any previous understanding of terrorism, it was associated with more "classical" forms, such as highly politicized anti-colonialist movements like the Irish Republican Army (IRA); with state terrorism in the form of suppression by totalitarian regimes like Hitler's Germany or Stalin's Soviet Union; or with isolated anarchist assassinations or individual acts like the bombing of the Murrah Federal Building in Oklahoma City.

Understanding the nature of the current threat has been difficult for at least two reasons. First, the contemporary form of terrorism is very different from anything we have encountered before. It is nonstate-based terrorism that does not arise from specific political communities or jurisdictions but instead flows across national boundaries like oil slipping under doors. This makes it conceptually difficult to make it concrete and to counter it. It is also religious, showing signs of fanaticism that are present in all religious communities (including our own, historically) but are alien to our ability to conceptualize. Slaughter in the name of God goes beyond most of our intellectual frameworks. It is also fanatically anti-American and thus in sharp contrast to the general pro-Americanism that we at least believed dominated the end of the twentieth century. Additionally, it employs methods such as suicide terrorism that, if not historically unique, are deviant enough to go beyond most of our abilities to conjure.

Second, our understanding is made more difficult by the extremely changeable nature of contemporary terrorist opponents. The Al Qaeda of 2001 was hard enough for us to understand, but it has evolved greatly since then. Partly this is because international efforts since 2001 have been quite effective in dismantling the old Al Qaeda structure by capturing and killing many of its members. This success, however, has caused the threat to disperse and transform itself into forms that we find even less recognizable and thus more difficult to identify and attack. Thus, a discussion of organizational evolution is necessary to clarify the nature of the current terrorist threat.

Jessica Stern, in *Terrorism in the Name of God,* lays out the requirements for a successful terrorist organization. The effectiveness of a terrorist organization is dependent on two qualities: resiliency (the ability to withstand the loss of parts of its membership or workforce) and capacity (the ability to optimize the scale and impact of terrorist attacks). The larger the scale of operations that the terrorist organization can carry out without large losses to its members through capture or death, the more effective the organization is. Conversely, if an organization can only carry out small, relatively insignificant acts while having large portions of its membership captured or killed, it is less effective.

Resiliency and capacity are clearly related to one another. For a terrorist organization to carry out large operations such as the coordinated attacks on Spanish commuter trains in 2004, it must devise a sophisticated, coordinated plan involving a number of people or cells who must communicate with one another both to plan and to execute the attack. The Achilles' heel in terrorist activity is penetration of the organization by outsiders, and the key element is the interruption of communications that allows penetration into the organization and movement through the hierarchy to interfere with and destroy the organization and its ability to carry out attacks (in other words, to reduce its resiliency). The most effective way for the terrorist organization to avoid penetration is to minimize communications that can be intercepted, but doing this comes at the expense of the sophistication and extent of its actions (reduction in capacity).

The result is a dilemma that is changing the face of contemporary terrorist organizations. Historically, according to Stern and others, most terrorist organizations have followed an organizational form known as the *Commander-Cadre* (or *Hierarchical*) model. This form of organization is not dissimilar to the way complex organizations are structured everywhere: Executives (commanders) organize and plan activities (terrorist attacks) and pass instructions downward through the organization for implementation by employees (cadres). In order to try to maintain levels of secrecy that improve resiliency, terrorist organizations structure themselves so that any one level of the organization (cell) knows only of the cell directly above and below it.

Commander-cadre arrangements have the advantages of other large, complex organizations. They are able to coordinate activities maximizing capacity (the African embassy bombings, for instance); can organize recruitment and absorb, indoctrinate, and train recruits; and can carry out ancillary activities such as fund-raising, dealing with cooperative governments, and engaging in commerce and other forms of activity. The disadvantage of these organizations is that they may become more permeable by outside agencies because of their need to communicate among units. Modern electronics become a double-edged sword for the terrorist: Things like cell phones facilitate communications in executing attacks, but those communications can be intercepted, leading to resiliency-threatening penetration. In fact, electronic surveillance of terrorist communication has been extremely helpful in the pursuit of Al Qaeda to the point that the old organization of the 1990s, which basically followed the commander-cadre model, has been reduced in size "from about 4,000 members to a few hundred," according to Gunaratna in the Summer 2004 *Washington Quarterly*. Twenty-nine members of the Moroccan-dominated group that carried out the Madrid bombings were indicted by a Spanish court in April 2006.

The result of the campaign against Al Qaeda has been to cause it to adapt, to become what Stern refers to as the "protean enemy" that has "shown a surprising willingness to adapt its mission" and to alter its organizational form to make it more resilient. Al Qaeda is no longer a hierarchically organized entity that plans and carries out terrorist missions. Instead, it has adopted elements of the alternate form of terrorist organization, the *virtual network* or *leaderless resistance* model and has dispersed itself into a series of smaller, loosely affiliated terrorist organizations (Jemaah Islamiyah is a prime example) that draw inspiration from Al Qaeda. If it ever was a monolithic dragon, Al Qaeda has mutated into a hydra-headed monster.

The virtual network organizational model was apparently developed in the United States by the Aryan Nation hate group. Its problem was that its membership was constantly being penetrated and disrupted by law enforcement organizations like the FBI, which used extensive electronic surveillance (wiretapping) to uncover and suppress illegal Aryan Nation activity and to prosecute both the planners and executioners of its actions. The solution for Aryan Nation, recently adapted and adopted by international terrorist organizations like Al Qaeda, is the virtual network/leaderless resistance.

The core of this model is the reduction of direct communications between the leadership and its members. Rather than planning operations and instructing operatives to carry out plans, leaders instead exhort their followers to act through public pronouncements (for instance, through the use of Web sites). Leaders may issue general calls to action, but they have no direct communications with followers that can be intercepted or used as the basis for suppression or conspiracy indictments. The leader has no direct knowledge or control of individual terrorist acts, which he or she may inspire but not direct.

The "Army of God" movement in the United States is an example; its leaders condemn abortion doctors and suggest to followers that they should be suppressed, including by means of physical violence. The hope is that a devoted follower like Eric Rudolph (convicted of killing an off-duty policeman in an attack against a Birmingham, Alabama, abortion clinic in 2000 and for hate killings in Atlanta) will be inspired to carry out the mission. The advantage of this model is that it maximizes the resiliency of the organization and protects its leadership from capture or prosecution; its principal drawback is reduced capacity to order specific "desirable" actions (this is also a problem for law enforcement, as nobody but the individual inspired terrorist knows in advance what he or she plans to do).

With the success of terrorist suppression after September 11, Al Qaeda and its affiliates have apparently adopted some characteristics of a virtual network. Leaders like bin Laden continue to organize some operations in the traditional commander-cadre manner, but increasingly, bin Laden is seen as a virtual leader whose principal role is to make pronouncements that inspire the membership and that of affiliated organizations to continue the *jihad* that bin Laden has declared and continues to champion.

Part of this shift has taken the form of a dispersion of terrorist organizations. During the 1980s and 1990s, bin Laden and his associates trained literally thousands of religious terrorists who have formed movements of their own in their home countries. Levels of affiliation and control of these "franchises"—as they are sometimes known—vary considerably, but they do change the nature of the terrorism problem. Cutting off one "head" (capturing or killing bin Laden, for instance) would not decapitate the movement he leads, because other heads exist and doubtless other leaders would arise to replace and play the role of the fallen leader.

Hoffman argues contemporary Al Qaeda incorporates all these permutations. It has he says, four distinct dimensions: Al Qaeda Central (the remnants of the 9/11 organizations), Al Qaeda Affiliates and Associates (the spinoffs); Al Qaeda Locals (Virtual network cells); and the Al Qaeda Network ("homegrown Islamic radicals").

The nature of the terrorist threat is thus changing. It is becoming more diffuse as terrorist organizations become more adaptable organizationally and otherwise (become more "protean" in Stern's term). This means that the nature of trying to control or dismantle the problem of terrorism is becoming more complex as well.

DEALING WITH TERRORISM: THE GWOT

There is great rhetorical agreement in the United States and elsewhere that the threat posed by international terrorism—which currently means the threat posed by militant Islamic terrorist groups and most popularly associated with Al Qaeda—must and will be defeated: We are committed to "winning the global war on terrorism."

But what does that robust rhetoric mean? Is the GWOT really a war at all, or something else (in the immediate wake of September 11, French president Jacques Chirac suggested calling it a "campaign" to remove some of the military emphasis)? Is it really possible to make war, as we generally think of the term, against a method or idea, as opposed to some identifiable group of people? For that matter, how does one attack and defeat a nonstate-based enemy organization that has no territory or identified population base that can be subjected to military actions?

All of these are valid questions for which definitive, consensually agreed answers do not exist. Begin with the war analogy. It is frequently argued that it makes no sense to talk about war against an abstraction, and the idea of terrorism is the application of an idea. Can you "kill" an idea in some concrete or abstract manner? If so, how do you know you have accomplished the task? Where, quite literally, are the bodies or the surrendering enemies? Wars, at any level, are contests between members of different groups to assert control. People and their ideas are not the same thing.

The war analogy suffers even if one switches emphasis and says the GWOT is a war on global terrorists. Switching the emphasis at least has the virtue of making a war of people against other people (a conceptual improvement), but it still retains two problems in the current context.

First, warfare against terrorists is war against asymmetrical warriors, as noted in Chapter 10. That means the countries seeking to defeat terrorism are militarily superior in conventional terms and that terrorism is the means by which terrorists seek to create a situation in which they have a chance to succeed. The problem here lies in the criteria for success for those seeking to snuff out terrorists and for the terrorists themselves. For the United States (or any other country engaged in terrorism suppression), the criterion is very exacting: The war cannot be won until terrorists everywhere specified by the war (the globe as currently defined) have been defeated. Those seeking to suppress terrorists must crush their opponents; in a phrase, they can only "win by winning."

The situation is different for the terrorists. Terrorists know that they cannot win in the traditional sense of crushing their enemies (win by winning), but equally, they know their enemies cannot validly claim victory as long as the terrorists can continue to operate. Thus, terrorists (much like guerrillas) realize that their criterion for success is to avoid being defeated, and that the longer they remain a viable force, the more likely they are to becoming a sufficient irritant that their opponents conclude acquiescence to their demands is preferable to continuing the frustrating struggle against them. The terrorists, in other words, can "win by not losing," or, at a minimum, prevent their opponent from declaring victory by avoiding losing.

The problem of defeating terrorists is made more difficult by a second problem associated with modern asymmetrical warfare: Contemporary international terrorist organizations are nonstate actors. We know that most of the contemporary religious terrorists are Muslims who come from or have connections to parts of the Islamic Middle East. We also know that not all Muslims in the Middle East support the terrorists or what they do (although enough do to provide safe haven in which terrorists can hide), and that no state government has claimed association with major terrorist organizations since the overthrow of the Taliban in Afghanistan. To make matters worse, these nonstate actors generally imbed themselves within physical areas and among people sympathetic to them; they move around, including across international borders; and they rarely establish public physical symbols that can be identified with them (some Islamic charities that serve as fronts for terrorist activities such as recruitment and fund-raising are partial exceptions).

The problem this creates for a "war" on terrorists is finding and specifying targets that can be attacked and defeated. When Al Qaeda was openly running training camps in Afghanistan, this was not so much of a problem, and occasionally a military attack would be made on one of these facilities (for instance, cruise missile attacks on Al Qaeda training camps in 1998 in retaliation for the bombings of American embassies in Africa). Since the fall of the Taliban and the dispersal of Al Qaeda into greater nonstate anonymity, military actions directly against it or its associates have essentially ceased. The problem, quite literally, is that we do not know what to attack, and especially what we could attack that would move us measurably toward "victory." The most important military limitation is the inability to find and target the most vital parts of the terrorist existence—the so-called centers of gravity on which the terrorists rely for the continued viability. The result, according to Audrey Kurth Cronin, is "that it is virtually impossible to target the most vulnerable point in the organization." Moreover, even when a terrorist presence can be located and defined, attacking it is difficult to do and to explain. The Israeli attacks against Hizbollah targets in Lebanon in July 2006, for instance, had to be directed against urban targets in Beirut and other urban areas, with inevitable civilian casualties and the inconvenience and endangerment of tourists and other innocent visitors, including Americans.

Then there is the more specific problem of the ultimate nonstate-based opponent, Al Qaeda. In one sense, Al Qaeda remains the major focus because it remains the center of the (increasingly virtual network) movement, but as it has morphed into many smaller groups with varying degrees of affiliation, the problem of rounding up and punishing the entirety becomes even more difficult, especially in a military sense. Al Qaeda is now as much an inspiration for others as it is a concrete opponent.

In some sense, the GWOT requires a continuing Al Qaeda presence. As CIA official Paul R. Pillar explains, "the existence of a specific, recognized, hated terrorist enemy has helped the United States retain its focus. As long as Al Qaeda exists, even in its current, severely weakened form, it will serve that function." Were we to capture or kill bin Laden and his cohorts, we would destroy a terrorist focus, but we would not destroy terrorism; someone else would pick up the gauntlet. Al Qaeda and bin Laden help us keep our attention focused.

The continuing role of Al Qaeda is illustrated by a terrorist incident that occurred in October 7, 2004, at seaside resorts on Egyptian soil in the Sinai peninsula. Bombs tore apart a series of resort hotels where many of the occupants were Israelis celebrating the end of the Yom Kippur holiday. The immediate question was who was responsible, and within a day's time, Al Qaeda had been identified as the likely culprit. Although bin Laden has publicly condemned Israel for its suppression of the Palestinians, there are not publicly known instances of Al Qaeda attacks against Egyptian targets. So, was Al Qaeda really to blame directly (did, for instance, bin Laden order the attacks)? Or could the attacks have been carried out by an affiliate or franchise of Al Qaeda acting independently or simply deriving the inspiration to do so from bin Laden's general exhortations? For purposes of the GWOT, simply blaming Al Qaeda removed the need for such nuanced public judgments.

This introduction to dealing with terrorists is intended to convey that the problem is both physically and intellectually very difficult, and that any simple, sweeping antidotes to solving the problem of terrorism are likely both to be inadequate and to result in failure. That does not mean the task is hopeless or that things cannot be done to manage or mitigate the problem. In the paragraphs that follow, we will explore dealing with terrorism through three lenses: conventional methods of suppressing terrorism (what we can do), levels of effort (who can do it), and a focus on undercutting terrorist appeal (how can we make terrorism less attractive).

Suppressing Terrorists: Antiterrorism and Counter Terrorism

In conventional terrorism suppression circles, two methods for dealing with the terrorist problem are most often invoked: antiterrorism and counter terrorism. The two terms are sometimes used interchangeably, although each term refers to a distinct form of action with a specific purpose. Any program of terrorist suppression will necessarily contain elements of each of them, but failing to specify which is which generally or in specific applications only confuses the issue.

Antiterrorism refers to defensive efforts to reduce the vulnerability of targets to terrorist attacks and to lessen the effects of terrorist attacks that do occur. Antiterrorism efforts thus begin from the premise that some terrorist attacks will indeed occur, and that two forms of effort are necessary. First, antiterrorists seek to make it more difficult to mount terrorist attacks. Airport security to prevent potential terrorists from boarding airliners or the interception and detention of possible terrorists by border guards are examples. Second, antiterrorists try to mitigate the effects of terrorist attacks that do occur. An example might be blocking off streets in front of public buildings so that terrorists cannot get close enough to destroy them.

There are three related difficulties with conducting an effective antiterrorist campaign. One is that antiterrorism is necessarily reactive; terrorists choose where attacks will occur and against what kinds of targets, and antiterrorists must respond to the terrorist initiative. A second problem is the sheer variety and number of targets to be protected. As suggested earlier, the potential list of targets is almost infinite, and one purpose of attacks is randomness so that potential victims are always off guard and antiterrorists will have trouble anticipating where attacks may occur. The third problem is target substitution: If antiterrorist efforts are sufficiently successful that terrorists determine their likelihood of success against any particular target (or class of targets) is significantly diminished, they will simply go on to other, less well-defended targets. Given the variety of targets available, finding places and things that have not been protected is not impossible.

The other form of terrorist suppression is *counter terrorism,* offensive and military measures against terrorists or sponsoring agencies to prevent, deter, or respond to terrorist acts. As the definition suggests, counter terrorism consists of both preventive and retaliatory actions against terrorists. Preventive acts can include such things as penetration of terrorist cells and taking action—including apprehension and physical violence against terrorists—before they carry out their acts. Retaliation is more often military and paramilitary and includes attacks on terrorist camps or other facilities in response to terrorist attacks. The purposes of retaliation include both punishment, reducing terrorist capacity for future acts, and hopefully deterrence of future actions by instilling fear of the consequences.

Counter terrorism is inherently and intuitively attractive (which may be why there is a tendency to lump antiterrorist and other activities under the banner of counter terrorism). Preventive actions are proactive, taking the battle to the terrorists and punishing them in advance of creating harm. In its purest form, preventive counter terrorist actions reverse the tables in the relationship, effectively "terrorizing the terrorists." Pounding a terrorist facility as punishment from enduring a terrorist attack at least entails the satisfaction of knowing the enemy has suffered as well as the victim.

The problem with counter terrorism, like antiterrorism, is that it is insufficient on its own as a way to quell terrorism. Preventing terrorist actions requires a level of intelligence about the structures of terrorist organizations that is quite difficult to obtain, and it has been a central purpose of terrorist reorganization discussed above to increase that difficulty. If one does not know the terrorist organization in detail it is, for instance, difficult to penetrate, learn of its nefarious intentions, and interrupt those activities. The absence of a state base that can be attacked means it is more difficult to identify terrorist targets whose retaliatory destruction will cripple the organization, punish its members, or frighten it into ceasing future actions.

Ideally, antiterrorism and counter terrorism efforts act in tandem. Counter terrorists reduce the number and quality of possible attacks through preventive actions, making the task of antiterrorist efforts to ameliorate the effects of attacks that do succeed more manageable. Counter terrorists retaliation then can hopefully reduce the terrorists' capacity for future mayhem. In practice, however, these efforts sometimes come into operational conflict. The antiterrorist emphasis on lessening the effects of attacks may lead to publicizing the possibility of particular attacks as a way to alert citizens (the color-coded warning system, for instance), whereas counter terrorists prefer to keep operations as secret as possible to facilitate clandestine penetration and interruption. We will return to this problem in our conclusion.

International versus National Efforts

There has been considerable discussion since September 11 about the appropriate level at which to conduct operations aimed at suppressing this current wave of international terrorist activity. In the immediate aftermath of the attacks, there was an enormous international outpouring of sympathy for the United States and willingness to join a vigorous international effort to deal with terrorists around the globe. That resolve resulted in a good deal of international cooperation among law enforcement and intelligence agencies in various countries, much of which continues quietly to this day. The more visible manifestations of that internationalization have faded as the United States has "militarized" the terrorist suppression effort (the GWOT as primarily "war") and moved toward actions opposed by the major allies in the law enforcement and intelligence efforts through unilateral actions in places like Iraq.

The post–September 11 international effort has indeed experienced apparent successes in reducing the size and potency of Al Qaeda as it existed at the time. Within the United States, most of the visible activity on reforming the effort has been national. *The 9/11 Commission Report,* for instance, emphasized reform within the American government (principally in restructuring the intelligence community) as a way to respond to the evolving problem. One section in its recommendations chapter is titled "Unity of Effort Across the Foreign-Domestic Divide," but its primary function is to suggest improvements in America's ability to cooperate with foreign sources. Emphases on problems like border protection—port security, for instance—generally have a primarily national content.

Does the nature of the new threat suggest a greater inward or outward turning of efforts? Former CIA expert Paul Pillar suggests that the evolving nature of the threat reinforces the need for greater internationalization. As he describes it, "In a more decentralized network, individuals will go unnoticed not because data on analysts' screens are misinterpreted but because they will never appear on those screens in the first place." Much of the added data on the successors to Al Qaeda can only be collected in the countries where they operate, but Pillar sees two barriers to sustained international cooperation. On the one hand, "an underlying limitation on foreign willingness to cooperate with the United States is the skepticism among foreign publics and even elites that the most powerful nation on the planet needs to be preoccupied with small bands of radicals." This leads to a second misgiving, which is the perceived "ability to sustain the country's own determination to fight" the terrorist threat.

Other Aspects of the Problem

A final problem of the conceptual nature of the GWOT is that it does not capture the entirety of the problem that it has been asked to solve. The GWOT, as suggested, is really an effort aimed at suppressing terrorists, as are the forms of dealing with terrorists

Chapter Sixteen UNDERSTANDING AND ORGANIZING 299

discussed immediately above. Somehow capturing or killing all the existing terrorists does not, however, destroy *terrorism,* which is the underlying purpose of the entire enterprise. As long as individuals and groups choose terrorism as the means to realize their ideas, terrorism cannot be wholly eradicated; only its current manifestations can be contained.

This other part of any effort to suppress terrorism is intellectual, a war of ideas that has two basic parts. The first is the intellectual competition between terrorists and their enemies—the underlying reasons terrorists emerge, and the appeal they have among the populations that hide, nurture, sustain, and form the recruitment base for movements that employ terrorism as a method. In the current wave of religious terrorism, virulent anti-Americanism is the activator; the United States and the American way are portrayed as the major threat to Islam and the way of life that it promotes. As long as the United States (and the West generally) does not compete with this basic idea and assert and convince those in the Middle East that our ideas produce a superior existence *for them,* there will be an endless stream of recruits to the banner that no terrorist suppression efforts can even hope to overcome.

The second part of the intellectual battle is over the use of terrorism as the method of those whose ideas we oppose. Not only must we compete in the forum of ideas that can lead to terrorism, we must also deal with what causes people to become terrorists. Regardless of what the level of causation one begins at (societal, political, or psychological), one must persuade people that volunteering to be terrorists (in the most extreme case, agreeing to commit suicide to advance the terrorist cause) is not acceptable to them if we are to stanch the flow of recruits of terrorists intent on killing us. This problem, "draining the swamp" in which terrorists breed, is clearly a necessary part of any comprehensive strategy.

CONCLUSION: TOWARD A STRATEGY FOR TERRORISM

One thing has not changed since the terrorist attacks of September 11. The United States did not have a comprehensive, encompassing strategy for dealing with the risks associated with international terrorism then, and it does not truly have such a strategy today. The *National Strategy for Combating Terrorism* is the official public document on the subject, but it takes a basically narrow approach to the problem that emphasizes military and semi-military actions associated with antiterrorism and counterterrorism. It does not, however, link the suppression of terrorism to other parts of national policy such as energy policy, which seems odd, considering the primary link between the United States and the region results from American dependence on Middle Eastern petroleum. Clearly, manipulating that dependence and its consequences would appear to be an important strategic option.

The problem of coping with terrorism is twofold. First, it is a very complicated, complex problem of the kind with which political institutions are loathe to deal. Declaring a GWOT is a great deal simpler than dealing with the incredible complexities only broadly suggested in these pages. Individuals *within* governments can deal with these problems comprehensively, but large, cumbersome organizations with diverse purposes and agendas have a harder time. Second, the suppression of terrorism is not a conflict that can easily be won, if it can be "won" at all. Terrorism as an idea has been around for millennia, and it will likely continue to persist for a long time. The goal of terrorism strategy is to contain terrorism, to reduce the risks arising from it, not to exorcise it from national and international existence. That is not as high-flown a goal as obliterating terrorism, but it is more realistic.

What then are the goals and elements of a terrorism strategy? What we must do is raise questions, because there are no agreed-on answers (if there were and they worked, there would not be the problem there is). Thus, the purpose of this concluding section is to help the reader organize and articulate questions about how a comprehensive strategy toward terrorism might be fashioned, not to provide the definitive answers to those questions.

The first and obvious step in devising a strategy is deciding what its goal should be. It is clearly not enough to say the goal is to "win" the struggle; one must specify what winning means. In one of the televised debates during the 2004 presidential campaign, the principal candidates effectively—if inadvertently—framed this question. Democratic nominee John Kerry argued the only realistic goal was to contain the problem, to reduce it to the status of a nuisance rather than a central, encompassing fixation; he drew the analogy with containing prostitution and gambling. President George W. Bush replied fierily that Kerry was wrong and that the goal of the GWOT had to be to hunt down and destroy terrorism everywhere it existed; winning means eradicating terrorism.

Which of these goals should we adopt as the bedrock of strategy? Eradication of terrorism is clearly more emotionally attractive, but is it a realistic or attainable goal for policy and strategy? Terrorism has been a more or less permanent force for at least 2,000 years (many scholars date it back to the first century A.D. to groups like the Sicarii and the Zealots), and although its prominence has varied across time, it has never disappeared altogether. Similarly, terrorist movements, such as the current religiously based terrorism, come and go, but they seem always to be replaced by something else. In that case, is a strategy based in destroying terrorism (more properly, terrorists) bound to fail and frustrate those who pursue it? Or, is it more realistic (if less emotionally satisfying) to aim to minimize terrorism?

Then there is the question of how to implement the strategy. Clearly, any terrorism suppression strategy must begin with elements of both antiterrorism and counter terrorism, but in what balance? In the last section, it was noted that the two thrusts can be, and sometimes are, at odds with one another. An example shows this tension.

In August 2004, the American government announced it had seized computer diskettes from a suspected terrorist that contained blueprints for schools in New York City, New Jersey, the District of Columbia, and elsewhere. Coming on the heels of the school hostage taking and murders in Beslan, Russia, earlier that summer, homeland security officials extrapolated that the diskette might be evidence of a similar intent.

How should the situation have been handled? Through a quiet, behind-the-scenes counter terrorism effort in which the potential terrorists were not made aware the government had the diskette, but instead where counter terrorists observed, tried to penetrate, and then squelched any plans? Or through an antiterrorist approach that notified the public of the threat and urged them to take action that would make any attack less effective? The problem was that the two approaches contradicted one another. A counter terrorism approach meant the public would be uninformed, and if an attack occurred, would be unprepared to moderate the disaster. An antiterrorist approach meant any secrecy would be blown, making a counter terrorism effort much more difficult or impossible. In the real case, of course, the antiterrorists won, and the potential plot was widely publicized. Was that the right decision?

There is another structural concern in dealing with existing terrorists. How does one improve the effort to detect, penetrate, and frustrate terrorist activities? At the national level, for instance, the 9/11 Commission made some strong suggestions for reform and consolidation of governmental efforts, but all entail considerable change in how people go about their business. How much of the commission's efforts will or should be implemented? Further, how much of the effort should be internationalized? Should the United States remain largely independent of others in efforts ranging from counter terrorism and cooperation with United Nations or other international efforts? Or should the United States encourage greater cooperation across borders, even if it disagrees with some of those efforts?

There is the further question of what else is to be done. At least two concerns can be raised in this regard. Clearly, one way to eliminate or lessen the problem of terrorism is to discourage or lessen its appeal to potential terrorists: Fewer terrorists, by definition, would pose a smaller terrorism problem. Antiterrorism and counterterrorism efforts may influence the actions of current terrorists, but they apparently do little to discourage, and may actually encourage, the recruitment of future terrorists. Efforts to deal with suicide terrorists has rather clearly not discouraged others from signing up for that grisly mission, and the problem is growing. As Atran chronicles, "During 2000–2004, there were 472 suicide attacks in 22 countries killing more than 7,000 and wounding tens of thousands. . . . More suicide attacks occurred in 2004 than in any previous year, and 2005 has proven even more deadly, with attacks in Iraq alone averaging more than one a day." The intercommunal Sunni-Shia attacks in 2006 have only amplified this trend.

How does one make terrorism less attractive to potential recruits? One approach is to relieve the human conditions in which terrorism seems to prosper—to "drain the swamp" of terrorism-producing societal, psychological, and political conditions and thus make terrorism a less attractive alternative. Intuitively, such efforts appear to make sense, but they face objections. One is expense: Uplifting societies to the point that terrorism is unappealing to the citizens would require very large monetary and other resources (for instance, what would it cost to fund a Pakistani education system that would make the terrorist-producing *madrassa* system obsolete?). Are we willing to pay for such an effort? In addition, the results are uncertain: As many analysts point out, the 9/11 terrorists came from Saudi Arabia, not some wretched backwater "swamp," and all the developmental assistance in the world would not have changed these people. Moreover, Peter Bergen and Swati Pandrey question the effects of the attempt, arguing "madrassas generally cannot produce the skilled terrorists capable of committing or organizing attacks in Western countries."

A second possible thrust of strategy might be to make certain people less of a target of terrorists. Current Middle Eastern religious terrorism is fueled by a virulent anti-Americanism that we find intellectually ludicrous and incorrect. Should the United States be mounting a much more comprehensive campaign to convince people in the region that the Western model is superior to the worldview that fanatical religious spokespersons are propounding? If we think that the terrorists are trying to drag the people of the region a thousand years back in time to some imagined caliphate that is more nightmare than dream, why do we not say so more loudly and consistently?

Finally, there is the question of exposure. One reason for the underlying anti-Americanism in parts of the Middle East is the level of supposedly corrupting American physical presence in the region (this has been a particular obsession of bin Laden for some time). The obvious reason for that presence is Middle East oil, and without that need, the reason for American presence is reduced greatly or disappears altogether. If that is the case, should national energy policy not be an important element in terrorism strategy? As already suggested, some of the most vocal proponents of the GWOT in the United States simultaneously oppose higher fuel efficiency standards for vehicles (the so-called Corporate Average Fuel Efficiency—CAFÉ—standards). Oil revenue has clearly been linked to private support for terrorists in Saudi Arabia and elsewhere; is it not inconsistent to support strong terrorism suppression while one drives a large, gas-guzzling sports utility vehicle?

This discussion, of course, only explores the tip of the iceberg of what a comprehensive terrorism strategy would include. The problem to date, reflected in the artificial designation of the effort as a "war," has been to isolate terrorism and its suppression from other aspects of national and international concern. Terrorism, however, is a complex phenomenon that is part of a broader set of problems and international malaise. Until we start treating terrorism for what it is, our efforts are bound to languish.

STUDY/DISCUSSION QUESTIONS

1. Define terrorism. What are its common elements? How does the elaboration of the elements help us understand the nature of terrorism?

2. What do terrorist acts seek to accomplish? In what circumstances do they succeed or fail?

3. What kinds of targets do terrorists attack? What is cost-tolerance? How does it factor into resistance to terrorism and terrorist success?

4. Why do terrorists engage in terrorist activities? What do they seek to accomplish? Why do terrorists adopt asymmetrical means to achieve their objectives?

5. Three perspectives and causes of terrorism are discussed in the case. What are they? Do you find any of them more convincing than the rest?

6. How has international terrorism changed since 9/11, notably in terms of terrorist organization? What are the implications of these changes for dealing with terrorists?

7. Discuss the propriety of the "war" analogy when dealing with terrorism. Does it help or distort thinking about and countering the problem?

8. What are the three ways of dealing with terrorism discussed in the text? Describe each as an element in lessening or eliminating the problem of terrorism.

9. What are the elements of a comprehensive terrorism strategy discussed in the conclusion? Can you think of others?

10. The distinction between dealing with terrorism and terrorists is a recurring dichotomy in the text. What is this distinction? What are the implication for dealing with the problem from one perspective or the other?

READING/RESEARCH MATERIAL

Allison, Graham. *Nuclear Terrorism: The Ultimate Preventable Catastrophe*. New York: Times Books (Henry Holt and Company), 2004.

Art, Robert J., and Kenneth N. Waltz. *The Use of Force: Military Power and International Politics* (6th ed.). London: Rowm and Little field, 2003.

Atran, Scott. "Mishandling Suicide Terrorism." *Washington Quarterly* 27, 3 (Summer 2004), 67–90.

———. "The Moral Logic and Growth of Suicide Terrorism." *Washington Quarterly* 29, 2 (Spring 2006), 127–147.

Benard, Cheryl. "Toy Soldiers: The Youth Factor in the War on Terror." *Current History* 106, 696 (January 2007), 27–30.

Bergen, Peter, and Swati Pandrey. "The Madrassas Scapegoat." *Washington Quarterly* 29, 2 (Spring 2006), 117–125.

Burke, Jason. "Think Again, Al Qaeda." *Foreign Policy,* May/June 2004, 18–26.

Cronin, Audrey Kurth. "Sources of Contemporary Terrorism." In Cronin, Audrey Kurth, and James M. Ludes (eds). *Modern Terrorism: Elements of a Grand Strategy.* Washington, DC: Georgetown University Press, 2004.

Dershowitz, Alan M. *Why Terrorism Works: Understanding the Threat, Responding to the Challenge.* New Haven, CT: Yale University Press, 2002.

Gunaratna, Rohan. "The Post-Madrid Face of Al Qaeda." *Washington Quarterly* 27, 3 (Summer 2004), 91–100.

Hoffman, Bruce. "From the War on Terror to Global Insurgency." *Current History* 105, 695 (December 2006), 423–429.

Jenkins, Brian. "International Terrorism." In Robert J. Art and Kenneth N. Waltz (eds). *The Use of Force: Military Power and International Politics,* 77–84.

Krueger, Alan B., and David D. Laitin. "'Misunderestimating' Terrorism: The State Department's Big Mistake." *Foreign Affairs* 83, 5 (September/October 2004), 8–13.

Laqueur, Walter. "The Changing Face of Terror." In Art and Waltz, *The Use of Force.* 451–464.

McLean, Renwick. "29 Are Indicted in Connection with Attacks in Madrid." *New York Times* (online edition), April 12, 2006.

National Strategy for Combating Terrorism. Washington, DC: The White House, 2003.

Pillar, Paul D. "Counterterrorism after Al Qaeda." *Washington Quarterly* 27, 3 (Summer 2004), 101–113.

———. "Dealing with Terrorism." In Art and Waltz, *The Use of Force,* 469–476.

Rapaport, David C. "The Four Waves of Terrorism." In Cronin and Ludes, *Modern Terrorism.* 46–73.

The 9/11 Commission Report: Final Report of the National Commission on Terrorist Attacks Upon the United States (authorized ed.). New York: W.W. Norton, 2004.

Sloan, Stephen. *Beating International Terrorism: An Action Strategy for Preemption and Punishment.* Montgomery, AL: Air University Press, 2000.

Snow, Donald M. *September 11, 2001: The New Face of War?* New York: Longman, 2002.

———, and Dennis M. Drew. *From Lexington to Desert Storm and Beyond: War and Politics in the American Experience.* Armonk, NY: M. E. Sharpe, 2000.

Stern, Jessica. *Terrorism in the Name of God: Why Religious Militants Kill.* New York: ECCO, 2003.

———. "The Protean Enemy." *Foreign Affairs* 82, 4 (July/August 2003), 27–40.

Yew, Lee Kwan. "The United States, Iraq, and the War on Terror." *Foreign Affairs* 86, 1 (January/February 2007), 2–7.

WEB SITES

Official U.S. government Web sites dealing with terrorism

The Department of Homeland Security at http://www.Whitehouse.gov/homeland

The State Department at http://www.state.gov

Text of bin Laden "Epistles"

http://msanews.net/MSANEWS199610/19961012.3.html

Reports on Future Trends from Federal Research Division

http://www/loc.gov/rr/frd/terrorism.html

UN action against terrorism http://www/un/org/Docs/sc/committees/1373/

RAND Corporation on terrorism, homeland security

http://www.rand.org/research_areas/terrorism/

Terrorism Research Center at http://www.terrorism.com/

Index